BALTIMORE CEMETERIES

Volume 1:
Northern Area

Collected
by
Baltimore County
Historical Society

HERITAGE BOOKS
2012

HERITAGE BOOKS
AN IMPRINT OF HERITAGE BOOKS, INC.

Books, CDs, and more—Worldwide

For our listing of thousands of titles see our website at
www.HeritageBooks.com

Published 2012 by
HERITAGE BOOKS, INC.
Publishing Division
100 Railroad Ave. #104
Westminster, Maryland 21157

Copyright © 1985 Maryland Genealogical Society, Inc.

The Maryland Genealogical Society extends its thanks to the Baltimore County Historical Society for its permission to publish this volume, to Robert Barnes and the other dedicated people who did the work and who are listed in the heading for each cemetery, to John Winterbottom for editing and Helen Collison for retyping the material. We sincerely hope that this Volume 1 will be well received and to the extent that further volumes can be published of this outstanding genealogical effort.

All rights reserved. No part of this book may be reproduced or transmitted in any form or by any means, electronic or mechanical, including photocopying, recording or by any information storage and retrieval system without written permission from the author, except for the inclusion of brief quotations in a review.

International Standard Book Numbers
Paperbound: 978-1-58549-085-1
Clothbound: 978-0-7884-9185-6

INTRODUCTION - THE LITERATURE OF CEMETERIES

Genealogists have long been aware of the value of accurately transcribed tombstone inscriptions, and in Maryland have been fortunate enough to have had the benefits of the labors of a number of transcribers. In 1806 a Baltimore publisher brought out Memoirs of the Dead and the Tomb's Remembrancer which contained epitaphs from the cemeteries of Baltimore City at that time. A little over one hundred years later Helen W. Ridgely published Historic Graves of Maryland and the District of Columbia (1908; repr.; Baltimore, Gen. Pub. Col. 1967).

Throughout this century the local chapters of the Daughters of the American Revolution have copied all or parts of old cemeteries throughout the state. Copies of these transcriptions were sent to the DAR Library in Washington, D. C., and some transcriptions are at the Maryland Historical Society in Baltimore. Since many of these cemeteries have since been abondoned, overgrown, or destroyed by weathering and vandalism, these transcriptions may be the only record of information contained on the stones.

In the last two decades various local historical societies and genealogical societies have been active in copying these cemeteries. The Baltimore County Historical Society has now copied most of the cemeteries in the county, with the exception of the commercial cemeteries, which usually maintain their own records. The transcriptions of the Baltimore County Historical Society are to be found in their headquarters in the old county alms house, Cockeysville.

Perhaps the most recent development in the study and transcriptions of cemeteries is the scrutiny given them by professional historians. R. Kent Lancaster, professor of history at Goucher College has published "Green Mount: the Introduction of the Rural Cemetery into Baltimore" (Maryland Historical Magazine, v. 74, no. 1, March 1979, pp. 62-79), and "Old St. Paul's Cemetery, Baltimore" (Md. Hist. Magazine, v. 78, no. 2, Summer 1983, pp. 129-142).

This volume contains inscriptions from cemeteries in the northern part of the county and a few cemeteries in the central area. The inscriptions were copied over a period of years by volunteer members of the Cemetery Committee of the Baltimore County Historical Society, a committee which I had the pleasure of chairing for several years. It is to be hoped that the Maryland Genealogical Society and the Baltimore County Historical Society will continue to publish inscriptions for other parts of the county.

Robert Barnes

BALTIMORE COUNTY MARYLAND CEMETERIES

Table Of Contents

Page	
1	Alder-Bryan Family cemetery (Corbett Road)
1	Andrew White Burying Ground (Hereford area)
1	Hoffman Family cemetery Gunpowder
2	Oakland Methodist Church cemetery
3	Hereford Assembly of God Church cemetery
3	Merryman Family Burial Ground (Hereford)
4	Royston Family cemetery (Phoenix Road)
5	Jessup Family Burial Ground (Paper Mill Road)
6	Jacksonville First German Reformed Church cemetery
8	Fairview United Methodist Church cemetery
10	Marsh Family cemetery
11	Talbott Family cemetery
11	Price Family Lot (Cockeysville area)
12	Saters Baptist Church cemetery
29	Cockey Family cemetery (Padonia Road)
29	Old Gunpowder Meeting House cemetery
31	Mays Chapel cemetery
35	Ashland Presbyterian Church cemetery
37	Sherwood Protestant Episcopal Church cemetery (Cockeysville)
48	St. Josephs Church cemetery (Texas)
63	Bazil A.M.E. Church cemetery (Cockeysville)
65	Cemetery on Warren Road
65	Nisbet Family cemetery
65	Ridgely Family cemetery (Dulaney Springs Golf Course)
66	Stansbury-Bosley Family cemetery (Stella Maris)
67	Merryman Family cemetery (off Pot Spring Road)
68	Harryman Family cemetery (Pot Spring Road)
69	St. John the Evangelist R.C. cemetery (Carrol Manor Road)
69	Peerce Family cemetery (Dulaney Valley Road)
70	Long Green Mennonite cemetery
71	Wilson's M.E. Church cemetery (Long Green Road)
76	Long Green Valley Church cemetery
76	Waugh Chapel cemetery (Long Green Pike)
86	Worthington Family cemetery (Dogwood Road)
88	Cockey Family cemetery (Falls Road)
89	Hunt Family cemeteries (Hunt Church)
89	St. John Methodist Church cemetery (Bellona Ave.)
90	Whitaker Family Plot (Seminary Ave.)
91	Govane-Howard Family cemetery (Anneslie)
91	Providence United Methodist Church cemetery
94	Towson Family cemetery (Shealey Ave.)
95	Stansbury Family cemetery (Pleasant Plains Elementary School Ground
96	Salem E.U.B. Church cemetery (Falls Road)
98	Almony-Ayres Family cemetery (Garrett Road)
98	Whitaker Family Plot (Lincoln Ave.)
98	Hook Family cemetery (West of Jones Falls Expressway)
99	Rogers Family cemetery (Govans)
99	Dowdens Family cemetery (Ridge Road)

Table of Contents

100	Cockey Family cemeteries (Melindas Prospect)
100	Cockey Family cemetery (Brooklandwood)
101	Ridgely Family cemetery (Hampton Site)
102	St. John's Catholic Church cemetery (Long Green Pike)
124	Grace United Methodist Church cemetery (Falls and Ridge Roads)
134	Gitting Family cemetery (off Long Green Pike)
134	Fork Christian Church cemetery
136	Fork Methodist Church cemetery
149	Gorsuch Family cemetery (South of Cherry Hill Road)
149	Johnson Family cemetery (one mile north of Fork)
149	St. John's Episcopal Church cemetery (Bradshaw and Jerusalem Roads)
155	St. Paul's Lutheran Church cemetery (Jericho Road)
158	Salem Methodist Church cemetery (Frankville Road)

FAMILY CEMETERY NEAR CORBETT VILLAGE

Located 60 yards from Corbett Road, bearing 190 degrees from a culvert 2.0 miles from York Road.

Daniel Alder d. Aug. 25, 1899 in his 82nd year.*
Rachel A. Alder d. Sept. 19, 1890 in her 75th year.*
(S) Ann M. Bryan d. Nov. 30, 1908 in her 63rd year, beloved wife of Charles H. Bryan. (N) Charles H. Bryan d. May 31, 1905 in his 65th year, beloved husband of Ann M. Bryan.*

Copied 4/22/72 by D. Clemens

ANDREW SMITH BURIAL GROUND

Inscriptions copied October 11, 1947 by Harry Herbert Lee. The stones were located on "PRAGUE", farm owned in 1947 by Charles Chilcote, off Belfast-Yeoho Road, about 1 mile west of Priceville, up a rocky lane or drive (northward towards Buffalo Creek) opposite and east of junction of Belfast Road and Wheeler Lane, on the Hereford Quad.

Andrew Smith who departed this life, July 1st, 1811, aged 75 years.
Elizabeth Smith who departed this life, October 30th, 1815 in the 72nd year of her age.

Submitted, with three photos, by Harry H. Lee, San Diego, Calif.

GUNPOWDER BURYING GROUND
(Hoffman Family Cemetery)

This cemetery is on a hillside on the east side of Gunpowder Road, perhaps half a mile north of Mount Tabor Cemetery at Hoffmanville. It is not shown on any quad map, but is in the Lineboro Quadrangle. At the time it was visited, it was very much overgrown. All visible stones were copied on August 3, 1971 by Robert Barnes and Robert K. Headley, Jr.

William Hoffman, a native of Germany, d. 16 June 1811, age 71.
Susanna Hoffman, a native of Germany, d. 26 April, 1805, age 61 years.
Infant son of Daniel and Eliza Hilker.
Lydia, C. J., dau. of John and Rachel Kearney, d. 21 May 1865, age 3 years and 19 days.
James B., son of John and Rachel Kearney, d. 26 Feb. 1864, age 6 years, 6 mos. and 25 days.
Peter Hoffman, b. 1 Sept. 1770, d. 20 Aug. 1864, age 84 years, 11 mos., 20 days.
Lydia L., wife of Peter Hoffman, and dau. of Anthony and Salome Hinkle, d. 22 Nov. 1845, age 53 years, 9 mos., 22 days.
Susanna Michael, dau. of Peter and Lydia Hoffman, d. 30 Jan. 1840, age 22 years, 8 mos., 4 days.

Sarah Jane Michael, 8 March 1839--7 Oct. 1861.
John Michael, 3 July 1796--8 Sept., 186?
Elizabeth Beltz, 29 April 1779--30 Jan. 1861, age 71 years, 9 mos., 1 day.
Sweam, Charles G., son of Jacob and Joanna, 14 Jan. 1864-30 Jan. 1875, age 11 years and 16 days.
Sweam, Susan, dau. of Jacob and Joanna, d. 24 Oct. 1859, age 8 mos., and 29 days.
Christian Hoffman, 19 Sept. 1778-20 Feb. 1833.
Hannah Hoffman, 20 May 1786-5 Aug. 1847, age 61 years, 3 mos., 25 days.
Perry, William, son of Eli and Jane, d. 24 Jan. 1853, age 5 years, 2 mos., and 19 days.
Phoebe Ann, wife of Abraham Henry, d. 16 June 1885, age 38 years, 7 mos.
Susan E. Henry, 16 June 1871--11 April 1874.
Laura B., dau. of Phoebe Ann Henry, d. 24 April 1871, age 10 mos., 4 days.
Eliza M. Henry, dau. of Phoebe Ann, d. 10 Aug. 1885, age 11 mos., 27 days.
George F., son of Phoebe Ann Henry, d. 22 Feb. 1869, age 25 days.

OAKLAND METHODIST CHURCH
Oakland Road, 6th District, Baltimore County, Maryland
Copied April 14th, 1971 by Robert Barnes

McABEE, Jessie M.   McABEE, Annie-His wife/Aug. 11, 1867 - May 9, 1905
  Bertha May, dau, April 2, 1891 - Feb. 5, 1909.*
I.H.N. - Mazie Bertha, dau of Saml A. & Mary J. Sweeny, d. Feb. 27, 1891 aged 14 yrs., 7 mos. & 26 ds. *
Spurgeon H. Matthews - 1884-1921.
May Matthews - May 9, 1889 -
D. Nelson Sweeny, 1867 - 1936 - Ida R. Sweeny - 1865-1939 - Lillian A. Sweeny 1891-1895 - Cecil N. Sweeny - 1902-1926.
Lillian A., dau of D. N. & Ida R. Sweeny, d. April 1st or 4th 1895, aged 3 yrs., 10 mos. & 2 days.*
Ebaugh, Hikes E., b. June 12, 1864, d. Nov. 20, 1919 - Laura B. 1861 - 1943.*
Percy H., son of Hikes & Laura Ebaugh, d. Mar 19, 1902, aged 1 mo. & 28 days.*
Stella May Grogg, 1918-1963.
Lest. Grogg, 1956-1956.

HEREFORD ASSEMBLY OF GOD CEMETERY
Mt. Carmel Road near Evna
Hereford Quadrangle - 7th District
Copied April 14, 1971 by Robert W. Barnes

Chilcoat, Oliva J. - 1889-1937 - Lawrence E. 1891 -
Samuel C. Hackler, Feb. 23, 1939 - Mar 28, 1938.
Marvin R. Hackler, Dec. 6, 1907 - Aug. 11, 1951.
Shirley Hackler/Currier, Mar 16, 1939 - June 30, 1950
Infant, Sherry Lynn Currier, June 30, 1959.
Ruby Doris Heath, Sept. 25, 1940 - June 3, 1950.
Betty Jane Ooss, 1931-1941.

MERRYMAN FAMILY BURIAL GROUND
AT HEREFORD FARMS (DEEDED 1714)

The drive to the Merryman house is located .2 of a mile west of York Road on Piney Hill Road. The burial ground is 700 feet from the main house on a bearing of 10 degrees on top of a hill. The stone wall is 18" thick and 3'-4' high. The supports on either side of the iron gate are 2 ft. square and rise 18" above the wall.

Sarah Merryman, wife of John Merryman, departed this life on the 3rd day of March 1775 in the 67th year of her age.
John Merryman departed this life on the 13th day of August 1777 in the 74th year of his age.
(Two large sandstones - on in line with headstones 1, 2 & 7, the other 3 ft. straight East.)
Ann Merryman departed this life on the 8th day of March 1785, aged 4 months.
Harry G., son of H. N. & Mary G. Merryman d. Dec. 18, 1881, aged 20 yrs., and 1 mos., 29 days.
(Large base for headstone and large piece of sandstone.)

Clarissa, wife of N.R. Merryman, d. Nov. 5, 1877 in the 71st year of her age.
Nicholas R. Merryman departed this life, Jan. 21st, 1864 at Hereford, Balto. County, aged 76 years and 9 months.
John Merryman b. Nov. 3, 1775, d. June 21, 1851, aged 75 years, 7 mos., and 21 days.

This burial ground is in very poor condition. There are only two stones standing (Nos. 1 and 7 in Row 1) and it appears that there are some stones missing or buried. The ground is full of holes (woodchuck and perhaps, otherwise made) and abnormally uneven. There are many Locust trees and some blackberries but these are overshadowed by a large number of wild daffodils in bloom during this season.

In addition to the stones already listed, there runs a line of sandstones mounted in upright position 12 feet from the West Wall behind Row 1 grave locations 6, 3 and 2. They seem too far away to be footstones for Row 1. Two more stones are mounted behind the aforementioned stones in locations 6 and 3. These two stones lie 4 ft. west of the headstones of row 2 which has footstones as listed east of the headstones.   4/2/72 D. Clemens

ROYSTON FAMILY CEMETERY
Phoenix Quad

Most of the following inscriptions have been published in *Ridgely's Historic Graves*, pp. 137-138. The inscriptions were also copied more recently by Mrs. J. W. T. Armacost of the Baltimore County Historical Society. In this listing, the information from Ridgely is given, with additional or different information from Mrs. Armacost placed in parentheses. The cemetery does not appear to be shown on the quad map. Ridgely states that it is on land owned by the Royston family for many years, on the road running east (sic) from Phoenix factory to the York Turnpike, near the 14th milestone.

John Royston, d. 11 Sept. 1822, age 50 (66).
Ruth, wife of John Royston, d. 10 Feb. 1839 (16 Feb.), age 78 (79).
Thomas Royston, d. 6 Oct. (Dec.) 1823, age 36 (26) years, 5 mos., 11 days.
William Royston, d. 26 Aug. 1827, age 56 years.
Elizabeth, wife of William Royston, d. 26 Feb. 1870, age 69 years.
Georgie B., dau. of Wm. and E. Royston, d. 4 Aug. 1842.
John Royston, son of Wm. and E. Royston...M.L.R...S.G., 1834.
Wesley Royston, b. 15 Jan. 1804, d. 17 (19) Dec. 1892.*
Mary A., wife of Wesley Royston, d. 5 Jan. 1873, age 64 years.*
Emma, dau. of Wesley and Mary Royston, d. 24 May 1849, age 4 years.
Clara W., wife of Eli Matthews and dau. of Wesley and Mary A. Royston, d. 6 Aug. 1865, age 30 (31).*
Caleb Royston, d. 24 June (Jan.) 1860, age 62 (63) years.
Mary, wife of Caleb Royston, d. 5 June 1845, age 38.
Ariel Royston, d. 5 June 1824 (1858), age 24 (25).
Edmund S. Royston, d. 7 October 1859, age 24 (25) years.*
Sarah A., wife of William T. Royston, d. 2 Aug. 1894, age 76 years.
Mary Ellen, dau. of Wm. T. and S. Royston, d. 21 Aug. 1853.
Mary E. Royston, d. 17 Feb. 1871, age 27 years.*
Margaret E., beloved wife of George R. Royston, b. 16 Oct. 1834, d. 16 July 1879.

Mrs. Armacost also recorded in addition to the above:

Matthews, Willie Taylor, son of Eli and Clara, d. 19 July 1862, aged 5 months?.
Royston, Emma, dau. of W. and M., d. 26 May 1842, age 5.

JESSOP FAMILY BURIAL GROUND

The cemetery is located 1.1 miles west on Paper Mill Road from its "T" intersection with Phoenix Road. The burial ground is 195 feet due North of the road and has a large pine tree which has been struck by lightning in its center. It is surrounded by an iron fence approximately 4-1/2 to 5 feet high.

Copied by Mr. Clemens, who credits Dr. Hopkins, of "Ivanhoe" on Paper Mill Road with having given additional information.

A plan of the cemetery showing the location of the rows is on file at the Baltimore County Historical Society.

Charles Jessop who separated this life on the 2nd day of April 1828, in the 69th year of his age.
Mary Jessop, consort of Charles Jessop, Sr., who departed this life on the 29th day of July 1832 in the 65th year of her age.
David Jessop,b. 24th of March 1787, deceased 10th July 1788 (D.A.J.) (Son of Charles and Mary Jessop - Ridgely).
Elizabeth Jessop b. 28th Jan. 1793, d. (Sept. 20, 1794) (dau. of Charles and Mary Jessop - Ridgely).
Abraham Jessop b. 19th Dec. 1796, d. 30th of Sept. 1800. (Ridgely gives date of death as Dec. 19, 1800) (Son of Charles and Mary Jessop - Ridgely).
Jemima Jessop b. 12th Nov. 1807, departed this life 2nd Nov. 1822 (aged 15 years - Ridgely) (Dau. of Charles and Mary Jessop - Ridgely).
David Gorsuch Jessop b. 17th Nov. 1788 and departed this life on the 23rd May 1812. (Son of Charles and Mary Jessop - Ridgely).
Dr. Abraham Jessop who departed this life on the 17th date of Nov. 1825 in the 26th year of his age. (Born Dec. 1801, d. Nov. 17, 1827, son of Charles and Mary Jessop - Ridgely.)
No markers.
Harriet Ward, dau. of Charles Jessop of Wm. Sen. and Mary Jessop, b. Nov. 23, 1808. Became the lovely and devoted wife of William J. Ward Sept. 8th, 1831, d. Aug. 27th, 1839.*
Harriet Ward, babe of James P. and Arietta J. Bailey of Va., b. Oct. 25, 1857, d. at Glencoe, Aug. 10, 1858.
James, 2nd son of Jas.P. and Arietta J. (Ward) Bailey, b. June 5, 1861, d. Feb. 26, 1862.
Charles Jessop, son of Levi and Mary Merryman, who died Jan. 4, 1829 in the 3rd year of his age. (Ridgely gives date of death as June 4, 1829.)
James Jessop b. 26 Jan. 1799, d. 26 Jan. 1836.
Ann M. Jessop b. 17th April 1796, d. 5th July 1832. (Wife of James M. Jessop-Ridgely)
John Merryman b. 15th June 1828, d. 16th Sept. 1833.
Mary J. Merryman b. 20th Feb. 1833, d. 20th Dec. 1836.
Clara S. Merryman d. Aug. 4, 1858, aged 21 years. (Clara A., dau. of Levi and Mary Merryman - Ridgely)

Mary, relict of Levi Merryman and dau. of Charles Jessop, Sr., who departed this life Nov. 14, 1845 in the 50th year of her age. (Dau. of Charles and Mary Jessop, d. Nov. 14, 1854, aged 49 years - Ridgely)
Joseph Merryman d. Jan. 16th, 1866 in his 22nd year.* (Ridgely gives name as Joseph R., son of Levi and Mary Merryman.)
Gussie V. Merryman b. Feb. 14, 1845, d. March 15, 1871.*
Infant son of Levi and Mary Merryman.
Elizabeth A. Jessop b. Oct. 11th, 1881, d. Jan. 21, 1888. (Ridgely gives name as Elizabeth Ann, dau. of Charles and Mary Jessop, b. Oct. 11, 18<u>11</u>.)
Abraham, son of Mary B. and Dr. A. Jessop, d. Dec. 7, 1872, aged 45 years, 2 mos., and 22 days.*

The following names are listed in Ridgely's Historic Graves, pp. 135-137, as being buried in the Jessop lot - these stones have evidently disappeared:

Jemima Barry, aged 61, d. Aug. 31, 1830.
Charles, son of Charles and Mary Jessop, b. Dec. 18, 1790, d. July 19, 1882.
James, son of Charles and Mary Jessop, b. Jan. 26, 1799, d. Jan. 26, 1836.
George, son of Charles and Mary Jessop, b. July 6, 1803, d. April 3, 1887.
William, son of Charles and Mary Jessop, b. April 5, 1805, d. Jan. 23, 1866.
Joshua, son of Charles and Mary Jessop, aged 63 years, 2 mos., and 21 days, d. Aug. 25, 1869.
Cecelia, wife of Wm. Jessop, aged 39 years, d. June 4, 1840.
1st born of Wm. and Cecilia Jessop.
Mary, second wife of William Jessop, b. April 17, 1815, d. Jan. 27, 1883.
Our mother Ann C., wife of Joshua Jessop, aged 71 years, 10 mos., and 22 days, d. March 19, 1878.
Twins, children of Joshua and Ann C. Jessop, b. and d. March 4, 1843.
Jemima G. (Buck), wife of Charles Jessop, aged 39 years, d. April 24, 1833.
Jemima, dau. of Charles and Jemima Jessop, aged 34 years, d. June 1858.
Edward, son of Charles and Jemima Jessop, aged 40 years, 2 mos., and 29 days, d. July 28, 1884.
Mary G. (Buck), consort of Charles Jessop, aged 62 years, d. May 26, 1865.
Elizabeth, wife of George Jessop, and dau. of Joseph and Elizabeth Ashton, aged 35 years, d. May 5, 1854.
Emma, dau. of George and Elizabeth Jessop, b. April 23, 1854, d. Feb. 2, 1876.
Dr. Charles Ashton, son of George and Ellen Jessop (2nd wife), b. Nov. 14, 1859, d. Oct. 19, 1889.
Mother Cecilia P., wife of the late Charles W. Johnson, aged 52 years, 2 mos., 15 days, d. Oct. 22, 1892.
Amanda C., wife of Henry V. Marshall, b. April 5, 1835, d. Sept. 7, 1885.

JACKSONVILLE FIRST GERMAN REFORMED CHURCH CEMETERY
JACKSONVILLE, BALTIMORE COUNTY, MD.

The church, with cemetery behind it, is located on the Jarrettsville Pike, ¼ mile above Jacksonville, just south of the intersection with Southside Avenue.

The Church appears to be abandoned, and no sign hangs from the post on the front road. The corner stone of the church reads "First German Reformed Church 1888". The cemtery is laid out in long rows facing the road. Row 1 is nearest the church. All rows were copies left to right on May 22, 1971 by Robert W. Barnes.

George Spertzel b. July 10, 1824, d. Feb. 5, 1901. Anna Spertzel b. Oct. 20, 1827, d. Feb. 14, 1906.*
Adam Lintz b. Nov. 4, 1848, d. July 8, 1916.*
Barbara Lintz b. Aug. 25, 1848, d. Nov. 30, 1910.*
Benjamin F. Lintz 1857-1931. His wife, Jacobine 1850-1927.*
Father, Christian Lintz d. March 25, 1897, aged 81 years, 11 mos., and 28 days.
Mother, Catherina (Catharina) Lintz d. May 3, 1899, aged 77 years, 5 mos., and 18 days.*
Peter Lintz b. April 22, 1851, d. Aug. 16, 1914.
Father, John Zinkhan b. July 21, 1820, d. May 31, 1878. Mother, Elizabeth Zinkhan b. May 23, 1826, d. April 8, 1909.*
Zinkhan, Louis H., Sept. 3, 1892-July 22, 1940. Helen E. L., May 15, 1894-March 14, 1953.
Hannibal, Amelia, 1859-1895. Louis, 1854-1948. Lena, 1866-1950.
Theodore A. Hannibal, Sr., May 3, 1905-May 24, 1968.*
Zinkhan, Father, Conrad C. 1878-1944. Olive P. 1889-1961.
Troyer (head). Harry N. Troyer 1884-1943 (foot). B. Estella Troyer, 1884-1932 (foot).
B. Estella Engle Troyer 1884-1932.
Miriam G. Davis, April 25, 1913 - Sept. 1, 1963.
Graefe, Fred E., Jan. 27, 1877 - March 3, 1957. Magdalena, Aug. 8, 1878 - Feb. 13, 1956.
Lintz, George, b. Jan. 21, 1847, d. June 23, 1934. Hannah Jane, wife of George Lintz, b. June 2, 1858, d. March 12, 1902. Fredericka, wife of George Lintz, b. April 11, 1849, d. Jan. 28, 1931. Lizzie, wife of George Lintz, b. Nov. 8, 1847, d. Feb. 2, 1884.
Zinkhan, Mother, Catherina Marie, wife of Conrad Zinkhan, b. June 23, 1848, d. April 18, 1918. Father, Conrad Zinkhan, b. July 1, 1845, d. Sept. 6, 1939.*
Louis W., b. June 14, 1918, d. June 15, 1918. Charles, b. and d. June 13, 1919, children of Louis H. and Helena E. Zinkhan.
Zinkhan, Benjamin C. 1889-1965. Ruth Eva 1898-1960.
Benjamin C. Zinkhan, Jr., Maryland TEC 4 716 Engr. Co., World War II, Nov. 12, 1918 - Feb. 24, 1946.
Zur Erinnerung, Hans Christian Tanderur, b. 22ten Mai 1836 in Bau Schleswig-Holstein, d. 7th Jan. 1899 in Sunny Brook, Md.*
Sadler (head). Dora A. 1869-- (foot). Henry M. 1857--1928 (foot).
Lintz, Benjamin H. Feb. 24, 1873 - Nov. 18, 1926. Annie C. June 23, 1867 - April 13, 1845.
Esther Mildred, dau. of Benjamin & Annie Lintz, b. March 18, 1909, d. Jan. 29, 1917.*
Lintz, Charles E. Lintx, b. May 1, 1880, d. March 5, 1960. Clara Augusta, wife of Charles E. Lintz, b. Sept. 14, 1884, d. June 8, 1911.*
Zinkhan, Henry Zinkhan, Aug. 16, 1851 - March 1, 1917. Mary C. Zinkhan, his wife, July 22, 1850 - April 8, 1925.*
Zinkhan, Henry W., April 28, 1879 - July 12, 1930. His wife, Hattie May, April 18, 1885 - April 8, 1961.
Thompson, Shelben L., March 19, 1917 - September 10, 1963, Hattie M.
Cook, Margaret 1888-1957. Erwin 1923-1952. Fred 1886-1951.
John E. Ryan, May 2, 1919 - Sept. 16, 1956.
Ryan, Mary E., Nov. 15, 1891 - July 7, 1951. John R., Oct. 11, 1878 - June 23, 1946.
Lintz, Mary M. 1881-1956, Mother. I. Jacob 1876-1932, Father.
Father, John Zinkhan, d. May 7, 1918 aged 64 years. Mother, Margaret Fager, wife of John Zinkhan d. Nov. 1, 1916, aged 62 years.*
Ernest, son of John and Margaret Zinkhan, b. Oct. 20, 1888, d. Nov. 19, 1892.*
William Henry, son of John and Margaret Zinkhan, b. Aug. 17, 1880, d. May 7, 1882.
Zinkhan, Paul W. 1894-1968. Margaret L. 1896--

Cook, Benjamin E., May 26, 1889 - July 10, 1969. Martha M., April 23, 1897.
Zinkhan (head). Ruth Mackenzie 1912-1946.
Treut (head). George Treut 1854-1935 (foot). Sophia Pausch Treut 1862-1944 (foot).
Henry F. Fox 1858-1939.
Mary L. Fox 1868-1968
Garton (head). C. Lilburn 1887-1957 (foot).
Lins, Philip, Aug. 6, 1882 - Feb. 17, 1948. Estelle, Jan. 25, 1887 - Sept. 15, 1956.
Father, Mother, John C. Lins, July 21, 1840 - March 17, 1922. Margaretta Lins, Oct. 15, 1843 - Feb. 21, 1915.*
John George Lins, April 26, 1872 - Dec. 12, 1950.
Baker, Susie Z. 1890-1927. Charles C. 1893-- . Gladys M. 1907-1970.
Fried, Charles M. 1879-1938. Elizabeth K. 1880-1970.
Reter, Peter 1878-1920.
Father, Leonard Martin Lins, Sept. 18, 1866 - July 12, 1946.
Our son, Herman Christain Lins, April 19, 1894 - March 11, 1909.
Mother, Catherine Irene Lins, Feb. 26, 1877 - May 6, 1959.
Lydda Elverta 1901-1902.
Albert Henry Linx, May 6, 1877 - April 20, 1961.
Parsons, Mother, Catherine E. 1887-1954. Father, Wesley W. 1889-1970.
Hannibal, Lewis H., Oct. 22, 1882 - July 16, 1960. Anna M., Dec. 29, 1883 - Jan. 30, 1961.
Slade, Raymond C., Sr. 1907-1968. Martle V. 1911 - .
Lins, George M., June 25, 1900-- . Grace M., June 29, 1901--
Lins, Joseph, Nov. 2, 1874 - Dec. 28, 1939. Martha Z., July 3, 1877 - Jan. 7, 1960.
Father, Joseph Klein, b. April 22, 1833, d. Oct. 31, 1907 (illegible)
Mother, Anna, wife of Joseph Klein, b. Jan. 20, 1858, d. Jan. 5, 1930.
Frank Kniel, April 1, 1863, June 2, 1947.
Robert C. Jenkins, Feb. 7, 1893 - Nov. 20, 1963.

FAIRVIEW UNITED METHODIST CHURCH
Baltimore County, Md. - 10th District

Route 146 about 1 mile south of Jacksonville. Copied May 22, 1971 by Robert Barnes.

The tombstones are set in long rows facing the road. All rows were copied left to right, beginning with the row closest to the road.

Bryan, Charles Guy, Aug. 15, 1890 - April 8, 1964. Ella May, April 20, 1898--
Henry Lee Ruhl, 1897-1945.
Helen Ruhl Wood, 1903-1959.
Charles W. Hackett, Dec. 15, 1854 - March 22, 1944.
Margaret K., wife of Chas. W. Shelley, b. July 30, 1874, d. Oct. 4, 1901.*
Joseph L. Hackett, Nov. 30, 1827 - Oct. 28, 1920. Mary J. Hackett, Dec. 17, 1830 - Jan. 8, 1909.
Shelley, Joshua M., March 24, 1852 - May 9, 1933. Rebecca J., March 31, 1852 - July 5, 1941.
Skipper, Rex, 1883-1960. Bertha L., 1883-1962. L. Doris, 1912-1914.
Lena L. Bode, wife of Nicholas Bode, 1867-1940.
Wheeler, Herbert G., March 18, 1895 - Feb. 24, 1961. Edvena A., Jan. 16, 1897--
Raymond T. Wheeler, 1932-1942.

Lee N. Wheeler, 1929-1942.
Isennock, Mary Evalyn, wife of Maurice Isennock, July 9, 1899 - Oct. 4, 1925.
Sipes, Alvin F., July 26, 1886 - May 16, 1943. Blanche L., April 30, 1885--
Schurman, Helen S., Oct. 21, 1915 - Oct. 24, 1968. Paul F., Dec. 24, 1914--
Infant daughters of Paul F. and Helen S. Shurman, 1941-1941, 1947-1947.
King, W. Royston, 1886-1946. Ethel T., 1892--
Bange, George G. C., 1883-1954. Martha, 1875-1961.
Adeline Bange (footstone: no dates).
Bange, George G. C., Jr., 1917-1969.
In memory of William H., husband of Anna B. Curtis, b. Nov. 4, 1836, d. Jan. 14, 1929. (Footstone: "W.H.C.")*
Anna B., wife of Wm. H. Curtis, b. Feb. 22, 1848, d. April 23, 1902.*
Luretta, dau. of W. H. & Anna Curtis, d. Jan. 27, 1881, aged 8 mos.*
Marshall, Estella C., 1873--. C. Howard, 1871-1940.
Robertson, David Calvin, Sept. 5, 1875 - March 25, 1936. Mary Rhoda nee Shelley, May 12, 1879 - March 8, 1943.
Piersol (headstone).
John W. Piersol, Dec. 24, 1888 - Jan. 21, 1969.
Clara O. Piersol, April 2, 1881 - Feb. 16, 1959.
Florence E. Piersol, Aug. 9, 1898 - Feb. 5, 1963.
Clarence H. Piersol, Feb. 11, 1887 - Aug. 23, 1918 (Footstone: "C.H.P.").
H. Seymour Piersol, b. March 31, 1862, d. March 17, 1917. Etta Hood Piersol, b. June 24, 1870, d. Oct. 3, 1954 (Footstone: "H.S.P.").
Walter G., son of Seymour and Etta Piersol, May (22 or 27), 1901 - Oct. 18, 1913.
Lee, E. Rogers, 1882-1941. Bertha Haile, 1885--
Piersol, Edgar H., 1890--. Mary E., 1891-1952.
James H. Durham, b. April 10, 1852, d. Aug. 8, 1929.
Mary Virginia, wife of James Durham, b. March 26, 1852, d. Nov. 12, 1895.*
Laura E., 1891-1897. William, 1898-1899. (Note: These appear to be children of the following. RWB)
Horn, Adam, 1865-1934. Mary E., 1866--.
Grace, 1906-1906 (Note: Horn).
Pocock (Headstone), William E., 1863-1942 (foot). Lena S., 1866-1939 (foot).
Wm. H. Turnbaugh, Jan. 4, 1857 - Nov. 12, 1911. Virginia Turnbaugh, April 10, 1868 - May 8, 1932.
Elizabeth V., dau. of Albert & Emma Turnbaugh, Oct. (?), 1912 - Feb. 17, 1913.
Pocock (Headstone). John M., Feb. 3, 1850 - Oct. 25, 1926 (foot). Deette C., Aug. 22, 1860 - May 19, 1952 (foot). Ethel C. Rudigier, March 16, 1885 - Dec. 28, 1959 (foot). Clarence E., July 26, 1886 - Nov. 29, 1958 (foot).
Cox, William Henry, Oct. 4, 1876 - July 5, 1947. Naomi Grafton, Oct. 2, 1879--.
John Smith, b. Feb. 2, 1830, d. Sept. 22, 1911.
Maria, wife of John Smith, d. Jan. 28, 1899 in her 74th year.*
Ella F., dau. of John & Maria Smith, 1856-1935.
Richardson, Thomas, 1855-1930. Amanda E., 1859-1934.
Smith (headstone). John J., 1862-1935 (foot). Minnie S., 1877-1934 (foot). C. Herbert, 1899-1963 (foot). Mary R., 1900-- (foot).
Mary Kelsey, wife of Thomas L. Owens, Dec. 26, 1849 - March 20, 1913.
Thomas L. Owens, July 28, 1850 - Oct. 15, 1936.
Irving Wagner, son of T. L. & M. K. Owens, Dec. 7, 1888 - May 9, 1915.
Owens, Mabel E., April 26, 1878 - April 12, 1962. Helen M., July 12, 1882--.
Note: The following four names are on the same lot as the fifth entry. It would appear that their last name is Brown although it does not appear on the footstones.
John Ensor, March 24, 1855 - May 2, 1946 (foot).
Elizabeth Ray, June 25, 1862 - Dec. 1, 1942 (foot).

Guy Oswald, June 15, 1890 - Sept. 27, 1918 (foot).
Earl Leroy, March 31, 1907 - June 21, 1938 (foot).
Guy O. Brown, June 15, 1890 - Sept. 27, 1918. Killedin, France, 27 Sept. 1918 at
   the battle of Montfaucon, Guy O. Brown, Mechanic Co. E. 313th, U. S. Infantry.*
Isaac H. King, b. March 22, 1849, d. Jan. 9, 1933.
Miller, Harry C., March 19, 1894 - Nov. 7, 1968. Ella M., Nov. 15, 1898--.
Gallup (head). Bruce H., Oct. 24, 1887 - Oct. 10, 1956 (foot).
Kohler, Boyd S., 1904--. Alice D., 1915-1965.
Stambaugh, Hamilton, 1877-1953. Sarah Virginia, his wife, 1877--. Hamilton D.,
   1900-1901.*
Stambaugh, Elmer, 1889-1953. Naomi, 1886--.
Flemke, Fred D., 1887-1956. Mollie E., 1899--.
Stambaugh (head). Ed. Clay Stambaugh, March 1, 1911-- (foot). Anna A. Stambaugh,
   Sept. 19, 1914-- (foot).
Soth, Henry John, June 18, 1890--. Virginia, Sept. 2, 1895--.
New grave, unmarked as of May 22, 1971.
John George, 1839-1939.
Kate George, 1843-1910.
John H. Shermer, 1854-1925.
Kate E. Shermer, 1865-1929.
Smith, Father, Charles W., Aug. 22, 1852 - Jan. 13, 1905. Mother, Laura O.,
   April 30, 1858 - June 23, 1916. Sister, Edna A., June 2, 1896 - Jan. 13,
   1901. Brother, Vernon M., Sept. 15, 1881 - Aug. 20, 1886.
Joshua M. King, April 13, 1858 - Dec. 26, 1942. His wife, Isabella V. King,
   Jan. 2, 1855 - April 7, 1923.
Matilda A., dau. of J. M. & I. V. King, d. July 10, 1894, aged 6 mo & 25 days.
J. Goldie, dau. of J. M. & I. V. King, d. Jan. 3, 1897, aged 5 yrs. & 7 mos.
William I., son of J. M. & I. V. King, d. July 7, 1889, aged 23 days.
Josiah T., son of J. M. & I. V. King, d. July 22, 1892, aged 1 month.*
(Illegible)...d. _____19, 1844(?), aged 49 yrs., 10 months.
Nicholas Brooks (?), d. Dec. 19, 1844 (?), aged 16 months & 22 days. May E.
   Brooks, Dec. 20, 18__ (illegible).
E. C. Stambaugh, b. Feb. 25, 1836, d. Jan. 25, 1914.*
Marshall Stambaugh, Feb. 14, 1884 - Feb. 27, 1960.

MARSH FAMILY CEMETERY

The following inscriptions are copies from Ridgely's *Historic Graves*, p. 137.

The Marsh burying ground in the 10th district is located on the property owned
for many years by the family, about 1 mile from the bridge, on the turnpike
leading from Meredith's bridge to Sweet Air.

Joshua March, d. 5 Nov. 1825, in his 68th year.
Temperance, wife of Joshua Marsh, d. 29 April 1836, aged 80 years.
Stephen, son of Joshua and Temperance Marsh, d. 15 Sept. 1829, in the 43rd
   year of his age.
Nelson, son of Joshua and Temperance March, d. 20 Feb. 1826, in the 20th year
   of his age.
Dennis, son of Joshua and Temperance Marsh, b. 13 Aug. 1795, d. 15 Oct. 1831.
Elijah, son of Joshua and Temperance Marsh, b. 12 Oct. 1790, d. 11 April 1857.
Joshua, son of Joshua and Temperance Marsh, b. 8 July 1801, d. 11 Oct. 1875.
Beale Marsh, son of Joshua and Temperance, b. 13 Aug. 1803, d. 25 May 1880.
Amos Matthews, son of Mordecai, b. 17 April 1800, d. 26 June 1874.
Ellen Matthews, relict of Amos Matthews, and dau. of Joshua and Temperance
   Marsh, b. 17 Aug. 1799, d. 13 Jan. 1833.*

N.B. - The DAR Patriot Index Lists - Joshua Marsh, b. 22 May 1757, d. 5 Nov. 1825, m. Temperance Harryman, Capt., Md.

TALBOTT FAMILY CEMETERY

These inscriptions are found in Ridgely's *Historic Graves*, p. 128. The cemetery is on land formerly owned by the Talbott family, but in 1908 was owned by George Harryman. It lies in the northeast angle of the intersection of Overshot Road and the road running west from Meredith Bridge to the Warren Factory.

John Denmead (father of the late Adam Denmead, Sr.) d. (ca.) 1835.
George Ivory Willis (died ante 1840)
Frances Thwaites Willis, b. 18 Sept. 1763, d. 8 Feb. 1845.
Joshua F. C. Talbott, only son of Edward and Frances Thwaites Cockey Talbott, b. 9 June 1796, d. 24 Mar. 1869.
Eliza (Denmead), wife of Joshua F. C. Talbott, and sister of the late Adam Denmead, Sr., b. 2 April 1801, d. 12 March 1842.
Mary Frances, dau. of Joshua and Eliza Talbott, b. 24 Feb. 1824, d. 31 Dec. 1830.
Adam Denmead, son of Joshua and Eliza Talbott, b. 19 Nov. 1822, d. 4 Jan. 1831.
Eliza Jane, dau. of Joshua and Eliza Talbott, b. 23 Oct. 1830, d. 6 Jan. 1831.
Thwaites Charcilla, dau. of Joshua and Eliza Talbott, b. 24 May 1828, d. 8 Jan. 1831.
George Ivory Willis, son of Joshua and Eliza Talbott, b. 6 Nov. 1825, d. 9 Jan. 1831.
Elizabeth Slade, dau. of Joshua and Elizabeth Talbott, b. 22 July 1837, d. 7 Aug. 1838.
Susan Eliza, dau. of Joshua and Eliza Talbott, b. 3 March 1842, d. 1842.
Joshua F. C., son of Joshua and Eliza Talbott, b. 31 Jan. 1821, d. 26 Sept. 1885.
Edward Cockey, son of Joshua and Ann Eliza Talbott, b. 26 July 1851, d. 9 Aug. 1852.
Joshua F. C., son of Joshua and Ann Eliza Talbott, b. 10 Dec. 1849, d. 12 Aug. 1852.
Annie Florence, dau. of Joshua and Ann Eliza Talbott, b. 8 April 1860, d. 26 Aug. 1861.
Aquila Ridgely, son of Joshua and Ann Eliza Talbott, b. 10 May 1865, d. 24 May 1865.
Rebecca, dau. of Joshua and Ann Eliza Talbott, b. 8 July 1867, d. 4 March 1869.

PRICE FAMILY LOT
Cockeysville Quad

This burying ground is located in the angle of the intersection of Shawan and Beaver Dam Roads, about 8/10 mile west of the York Expressway. The cemetery contains several graves marked only with field stones. It appears that actual headstones began to be used about the time the Tyrie Monument Shop in Cockeysville began. At one time, a large brick house may have stood near the graveyard and the home of the present property owners, Mr. & Mrs. Edward Erler, Rt. 1, Box 13-A, Shawan Road, was originally one room and part of the slave quarters. Inscriptions were copies by Mrs. Erler.

Abraham H. Price, whose wife and two daughters are buried here, was born 1782 and died 8 April 1833, the son of Stephen and Elizabeth (Rowles) Price. On April 13, 1804, he married Martha (Elizabeth ?) Rose. (Genealogical notes by Robert W. Barnes.)

This graveyeard is shown on the map of the 8th district, in the 1877 Atlas of Baltimore County.

Wm. B. Lynch, son of Martha E. & Wm. Lynch, d. July 20, 1857 in the 17th year of his age. (Footstone - "Wm.B.L.")
Mary A. R. Price, dau. of Abraham H. & Martha Price, d. 15 Jan. 1864 in the 53rd year of her age. (Footstone-"M.A.R.P.")
Aseneth Wollet, d. Feb. 26, 1872 in the 85th year of her age.*
Jacob Barnhart, b. Nov. 26, 1792, d. June 4, 1855. (Footstone - "J.B.")
Martha Price, relict of Abraham H. Price, d. 3 July 1867 in the 85th year of her age. (Footstone - "M.P.")*
Elizabeth Rose, d. Aug. 29, 1867 in the 75th year of her age. (Footstone - "E.R.")*
Rebecca Constantia, wife of Abel E. W. James & dau. of Abraham H. and Martha Price who departed this life 19 Sept. 1855 in the 45th year of her age.*

SATER'S BAPTIST CHURCH
Falls Road, Eighth District, Baltimore County

Historical marker on Falls Road; Sater's Church, 1742, on land granted by the Fifth Lord Baltimore, Henry Sater, gentleman planter, founded this first church of Baptists in Maryland. To the congregation he deeded a plot and chapel. "Forever to the end of the world." Maryland Historical Society.

Bronze plaque on the front of the church: Sater's Church, 1742, pioneer of the Maryland Baptist denomination. Only eternity, interpreted by God can make known the moral, mental and spiritual work of the "Mother Church" of the Baptists in Maryland. Founded by Henry Sater 1690-1754. Resolute and inflexible, he carried his religion with him. Presented by Maryland State Society, Daughters of the American Colonists, 1962.

Inside the church, there are two plaques, one on either side of the door, and three marble plaques behind the pulpit.

Plaque inside the church, east of the door: Chestnut Ridge Church founded 1742, First Baptist Church in Maryland. "The progenitor of many other churches" --Watts renamed Sater's to honor Henry & Dorcas Towson Sater, donors of the land and original building. In gratitude for its years of service, this marker is given by Historical Committee, Baptist Convention of Maryland, June 13, 1965.

Plaque west of the door: In loving memory of John Thomas Burnham, Jr., b. March 16, 1926, killed in action March 3, 1945.

Marble plaques behind the pulpit, left to right, first plaque: In memory of Deacon Edward Rider, d. Nov. 25, 1866.*

Second plaque: In memoriam Augusta H. Laughlin, beloved wife of Rev. David Laughlin, b. June 26, 1859, d. Jan. 2, 1928.*

Third plaque: 1742-1893, in memory of Henry Sater, Founder of this Church and donor of the property.*

Marker on the organ: Presented to Sater's Baptist Church by Friends and members 1953. Dedicated to the glory of God and in loving memory of Rev. Hugh Pendleton McCormick and Anne Perry McCormick and others.

Two collection plates, each of which is inscribed: In memory of Susan B. Skipper, 1959.

An engraved plaque on one of two gateposts in the southeast corner of the churchyard: Presented to Sater Baptist Church by Anna Auld Bennett in memory of her mother, Catherine Ann Walker Auld, 1841-1919.

These inscriptions were copies in August and September 1971 and May 1972. Some of the older inscriptions were published in *Historic Graves of Maryland and the District of Columbia*, by Helen W. Ridgely, the Grafton Press, New York, 1908 (reprinted 1967, Baltimore, Genealogical Publishing Company), pages 121-23. These are identified by the word "Ridgely" following the inscription. Some parts of these inscriptions are underlined to indicate that they are not now readable and were provided by the book. All of the gravestones listed in the book were still in existence in 1971-1972 except the one for Morgeanna, dau. of John and Susanna Rennous.

The inscriptions were copied as accurately as possible. Errors in spelling, grammar, and punctuation were not corrected.

There are several four-sided shaft-type stones in the cemetery. Their inscriptions were copies in the following order: front, right side, left side, back. The front is the side that bears the main inscription, and the terms "right side" and "left side" refer to the viewer's right and left as he faces the front of the stone.

East of the church:
This and the following are altar tombs. They were repaired about 5 years ago.
Thomas Walker, b. Sept. 1742, d. 18 Oct. 1818, aged 76 years and 1 month. (Ridgely, p. 123). Bronze plaque on one of the sides: Daughters of the American Revolution, Revolutionary soldier, 1775-1783. Placed by Janet Montgomery Chapter, D.A.R.
Discretion Walker, relict of Thomas Walker, who departed this life, Dec. 7, 1823, aged 76 years. (Ridgely, p. 123)
Grave with uninscribed stones at head and foot.
Ann, wife of Phil. Towson who departed this life, June 5, 1809, aged 38 years, 10 mos. & 6 days. (Ridgely, p. 121)
Mary Merryman who departed this life, Feb. 24, 1809, aged 28 years, 1 mos. & 10 days. (Ridgely, p. 122)
Capt. John Cockey, who departed this life, Feb. 8, 1808, aged 84 years, 8 mos. & 24 days. (Ridgely, p. 121)
George Sater, who departed this life, Sept. 15, 1798, aged 28 years. (Ridgely, p. 121)
Grave with uninscribed stones at head and foot. Immediately in front of the headstone is:
Sater, 1917, A.H.L.
Henry Sater, who departed this life, March 8, 1788 in the 44th year of his age. (Ridgely, p. 121) This is an old stone.
Sater, 1917, A.H.L.
Sater, 1917, A.H.L.
Henry Sater, d. March 8, 1788, aged 44 years. (This appears to be the same person listed above, it is a comparatively recent stone.)
Henry Sater (Ridgely p. 121). (This is a very old, crude stone at the foot of the person above.

Father, Samuel Cockey, b. Oct. 18, 1792, d. July 12, 1859, aged 66 years, 8 mos. & 24 days. This grave has an iron fence around it.
Our little Babe, Charles D., son of Joseph D. & Annie Cockey, d. Jan. 1, 1886, aged 4 years and 5 mos.
Mother, Emily J., wife of Charles O. Cockey, Feb. 17, 1827 - Jan. 27, 1914.
Mother, Annie, wife of Jos. D. Cockey, Nov. 25, 1855 - Feb. 23, 1913.*
Anna E. Cockey, wife of Wilmer W. Elliott, d. June 12, 1925. This is at the head of a two-grave lot. The following stone is at the foot of one of the graves:
Joseph D. Cockey, 1851-1932.
Mercedes M. Cockey, d. Sept. 7, 1968.
Center stone: Colein. This is surrounded by two older stones and six footstones.
Father, John Colein, b. July 21, 1794, d. Nov. 25, 1882.*
Mother, Ann M., wife of John Colein, b. Aug. 12, 1801, d. March 29, 1881.*
Daughter, Jessie Mitchell, 1874-1936.
Daughter, Emma I, 1871-1940.
Father, John F., 1827-1901.
Mother, Sarah E., 1836-1917.
Daughter, Anne S., 1866-1962.
Sister, Katherine C. Eubank, 1877-1951.
Rachael, dau. of Greenbury & Ann Cook, d. March 31, 1853, aged 61 years.
Ann, wife of Greenbury Cook and dau. of Joseph & Rachael Baysman, d. Aug. 26, 1844, aged 39 years, 2 mos. and 24 days (Ridgely, p. 123).
Joseph Boswell, who departed this life, Aug. 15, 1813, aged 52 years. (Ridgely, p. 123) (Ridgely has his age as 32, but 52 seems to be correct.)
John Jones, who departed this life, April the 22nd in the year of our Lord 1814, aged 52 years. (Ridgely, p. 123)*
Grave with uninscribed stones at head and foot.
Sater, 1917, A.H.L.
Sater, 1917, A.H.L.
Grave with uninscribed stones at head and foot.
Grave with uninscribed stones at head and foot.
Elizabeth, wife of Robt. Jones, d. Aug. 12, 1847, aged 70 years.
George W., beloved son of Daniel M. & Sophia Doxzen, b. Feb. 22, 1874, d. Sept. 17, 1891.*
Sophia L. Doxzene (sic), wife of Daniel M. Doxzene, d. June 15, 1907.*
William D. H. Maglidt, son of Wm., Jr. & Martha Maglidt, b. July 11, 1905, d. April 9, 1906.*
Father, D. M. Doxzen, Aug. 24, 1840 - July 9, 1923.
Border stone: J. Frock.
John, beloved husband of Alice Frock, d. Feb. 15, 1888 in the 29th year of his age.*
(Odd Fellows emblem), Skelton Price, d. March 16, 1887 in the 73rd year of his age.
Father, Joshua Goodwin, b. April 1, 1840, d. Feb. 6, 1906.
M. Frances, wife of Joshua Goodwin, b. Dec. 28, 1848, d. Sept. 22, 1879.*
Infant son of Joseph & Celia (sic) Hedrick (No dates).
Charles C., son of Joseph & Cecelia Hedrick, d. July 7, 1885, aged 6 mos.*
Joseph Hedrick, beloved husband of Cecelia Hedrick, d. Aug. 13, 1894 in the 35th year of his age.*
Rev. John Moncure, 1880-1930.
(Masonic emblem), William F., son of Wm. H. & Annie McCann, d. Oct. 12, 1892, aged 20 years.*
John L. Fishpaw, b. April 12, 1830, d. Nov. 6, 1862.
William H., son of Geo. & Mary Harman, d. Oct. 29, 1889 in the 28th year of his age.*

George Harman, b. Feb. 1, 1834, d. Sept. 2, 1918. March C. Harman, b. Nov. 15, 1841, d. July 5, 1929.
Margaret, wife of William McCormick, d. Dec. 7, 1853, aged 44 years. A native of Ireland, but for the last 14 years a resident of Baltimore. (This is by itself in the northeast corner of the cemetery.)
Joshua, husband of Rachel Martin, d. Oct. 5, 1902, aged 70 years.*
Amor T., son of John A. & Jane M. Price, b. Nov. 25, 1861, d. Dec. 10, 1888.
Mother, Jane M. Price, b. Sept. 12, 1825, d. Sept. 16, 1896.
Husband, John A. Price, b. Oct. 11, 1827, d. April 25, 1861.
Jacob Ewen, who departed this life on the 26th March A.D. 1831 in the 68th year of his age.*
Husband, John E. Ewen, who departed this life, 17th of April 1857 in the 37th year of his age.*
Grave with finished stones at head and foot but no inscription.
Sister, Ann Hunter Scott, March 30, 1823 - Feb. 22, 1903.*
Sister, Lavinia Scott, d. May 1, 1889, aged 72 years, 10 mos. and 27 days.
Brother, Richard Scott, who departed this life, 12th of Nov. 1866, aged 55 years, 1 mo. & 23 days.
Sidney, wife of John Scott, b. July 13, 1793, d. July 3, 1857, aged 64 years, 1 mo. and 20 days.*
Henry P. Scott, b. Dec. 20, 1828, d. July 16, 1850 (Ridgely, p. 123).
John G., son of John & Mary J. Scott, d. March 29, 1856, aged 2 years & 3 days.
Richard A., son of John & Mary J. Scott, d. Aug. 16, 1860, aged 2 years, 4 mos. & 12 days.
Emma J., dau. of John & Mary J. Scott, d. Aug. 26, 1860, aged 10 mos. & 27 days.
Mary J. Scott, wife of John Scott, b. April 22, 1833, d. April 8, 1894, aged 60 years, 11 mos. & 16 days.
John Scott, husband of Mary J. Scott, b. Sept. 16, 1820, d. May 13, 1902.
Franklin, only son of Ignatius & Hannah M. Creager, d. April 8, 1857, aged 3 years, 9 mos. & 19 days.
Elizabeth Ann Burnham, Nov. 5, 1878 - Dec. 11, 1970.
Front: Elijah F., Sept. 6, 1839 - Oct. 19, 1920. Mary Lee, April 9, 1850-July 15, 1943.* At the base: Burnham, (Right side) J. Maurice, Feb. 15, 1876 - Sept. 4, 1895. (Left side) William A., May 22, 1877 - Oct. 21, 1955.
Grave with uninscribed stones at head and foot.
Caleb K. Rider, who departed this life Oct. 16, 1848, aged 18 years, 7 mos. & 11 days.
John Burnham who departed this life, 11th Oct. 1852 in the 55th year of his age.*
Elizabeth, beloved wife of the late John Burnham, d. 23 Aug. 1877, aged 77 years, 3 mos. & 11 days.* (Erected by her children.)
Francis Fishpaw, d. June 19, 1887 in the 72nd year of his age.
Harriet, wife of Jacob Wilson, d. Dec. 23, 18_2 (1872?), aged 82 years 6 mos.
Jacob Wilson (no dates).
Zachariah Burnham, May 5, 1824 - July 25, 1848.
Mother, Elizabeth, wife of Skelton Price, b. Oct. 22, 1819, d. July 13, 1901.*
Susannah Burnham, March 19, 1808 - March 15 - 1894.
Hare, Leonard A., 1885-1929, his wife, Ethel E., 1888-1955.
Sarah E. Hare, wife of David Hare, b. Dec. 20, 1864, d. Jan. 15, 1918.*
David, beloved husband of Clara P. Hare, Dec. 4, 1858 - Sept. 12, 1930.*
Arrementa Sullivan, who departed this life on the 11th of Sept. 1809, aged 39 years. (Ridgely, p. 122).*
John Burnham, May 19, 1806 - Oct. 19, 1820.
Samuel S. Burnham, who departed this life, Nov. 13, 1842, aged 23 years, 6 mos. & 8 days. (Ridgely, p. 122)*

Elizabeth, consort of Edward Burnham, who departed this life Feb. 9, 1843 in the 60th year of her age. (Ridgely, p. 123)*
Edward Burnham, who departed this life, 30th of March 1878, aged 100 years, 6 mos. & 18 days. (Ridgely, p. 123)*
Ann Burnham, April 2, 1817 - May 15, 1852.
Edward Burnham, March 28, 1810 - Aug. 11, 1897.
Samuel S., son of Absalom B. & Elizabeth Burnham, b. Oct. 4, 1843, d. Feb. 23, 1844.
Heir ruhet in Gott, Iohannes Meyer, gebohren den 22ten August 1790 und Gestorben den 22ten August 1812 Seines Alters 24 Jahr. In memory of Iohnmeyrs who was born the 22nd of August 1790 and d. the 22 of December 1812. (Ridgely, p. 122). The German gives the month of death as August and the English translation has December.)
Grave with an uninscribed stone.
Mary L. Cockey Swem, wife of George E. Swem, Jan. 14, 1902 - Jan. 11, 1956.
Cockey, Harriett C., May 3, 1874 - May 16, 1960.   Thomas O., Aug. 6, 1863 - April 17, 1941.
Johney, son of Thomas B. & Harriet (sic) E. Cockey, b. Dec. 27, 1879, d. May 3, 1889.
Thomas B. Cockey, beloved husband of Lizzie Cockey, d. Feb. 20, 1887 in the 59th year of his age.*
Mother, Amelia M. Cockey, d. April 14, 1867 in the 32nd year of her age.*
Edward Grice, departed this life Nov. 8, 1844, aged 53 years, 4 mos. and 28 days. (Ridgely, p. 121)*
Elder Geo. Grice, who departed this life, June 24, 1825, aged 65 years. (Ridgely, p. 121)*
Sarah Grice, consort of Elder George Grice who departed this life Jan. 4, 1836, aged 79 years. (Ridgely, p. 121)*
Susanna, consort of John A. Rennous, dau. of George and Sarah Grice, who departed this life, Sept. 19, 1842, aged 45 years, 10 mos. and 15 days. (Ridgely, p. 121). (Ridgely shows the surname as Rennons, but it is Rennous.)*
John A. Rennous, b. April 2, 1791, d. Oct. 19, 1861.*
Morgeanna, dau. of John and Susanna Rennous, who departed this life Oct. 20, 1849, aged 22 years, 4 mos. and 6 days. (Ridgely, p. 121) This stone is no longer in existence.*
Susie, youngest daughter of John & Susanna Rennous, d. Oct. 21, 1870.*
S. Ethel Price, b. Sept. 29, 1892, d. Dec. 25, 1929. Footstone: Ethel.
Price, John E., Dec. 7, 1852 - Jan. 11, 1930. His wife, Annie R. Leaf, March 17, 1853 - Dec. 4, 1921. Footstones: Father, Mother.
William S. Shade, husband of Mary E. Shade, b. Jan. 9, 1854, d. Dec. 15, 1908.
Joseph Hamilton, son of Thomas S. & Mary E. Brady, b. June 21, 1882, d. July 19, 1882.
On top of the stone: Alice S. Brady Cline, 1892-1918. (On front of the stone): Father, Thomas S. Brady, husband of Mary E. Brady, b. April 6, 1844, d. Sept. 18, 1912.*
Mother, Mary Elizabeth Brady, b. April 17, 1851, d. Jan. 1, 1939.
(Odd Fellows symbol), Greb, J. Winfield, Sept. 13, 1880 - Sept. 30, 1953. Rose Mae, May 24, 1873 - March 13, 1952.
(Odd Fellows emblem), Harry R. Greb, July 19, 1878 - Aug. 28, 1937.
(Odd Fellows emblem), John Greb, March 15, 1846 - Nov. 25, 1920. Annie R. Greb, Nov. 29, 1839 - March 3, 1932.
S. Edith Shock, 1860-1935.
William Shock, 1862-1902.
Harriet C. Shock, 1824-1908.
John B. Shock, 1812-1877.
John J. Chalk, beloved husband of Junie Chalk, d. Oct. 1, 1885 in the 32nd year of his age.

Averilla D. Chalk, b. Dec. 17, 1822, d. Sept. 14, 1898, aged 75 years, 8 mos., 28 days.
Father, James L. Chalk, beloved husband of Averilla Chalk, d. Feb. 12, 1885 in the 59th year of his age.
Father, Joseph M. Withers, d. Feb. 21, 1900, aged 80 years.*
Wife, Eudocia Withers, b. March 17, 1821, d. Feb. 17, 1875.
Richard G., b. Oct. 5, 1846, d. May 14, 1849. Mary C., b. Dec. 28, 1847, d. June 5, 1848, children of Joseph M. & Eudocia Withers.
Elizabeth A., b. Jan. 17, 1849, d. May 9, 1849. Isaac, b. Aug. 7, 1850, d. Aug. 8, 1850, children of Joseph M. _____,
M. Maggie, dau. of J. Wilson & R. Annie Brown, b. April 1, 1876, d. June 17, 1881.
Edward Loughridge, son of J. Wilson & Rachel A. Brown, Feb. 18, 1891 - Aug. 5, 1908.
J. Wilson Brown, April 24, 1838 - May 24, 1920. Rachel A. Brown, Nov. 22, 1846 - April 2, 1927.
Thomas B. Hutchison, Sr., 1872-1934.
Rolan L., son of R. C. & S. B. Bryon (sic), Jan. 8, 1915 - Jan. 9, 1915.
Jas. M. Bryan, husband of Caroline Bryan, d. Feb. 13, 1893 in his 81st year.*
Caroline, beloved wife of James M. Bryan, b. June 15, 1827, d. Dec. 11, 1885.*
The following 16 are enclosed in an iron fence. On the gate is a Masonic emblem and ...R, probably originally Oler.
Johnny Burnham, b. Jan. 14, 1822, d. May 1, 1915, aged 93 years, 3 mos. & 14 days.*
Sarah F. Oler, wife of J. Burnham, Feb. 12, 1821 - Oct. 22, 1896.*
Edward Oler, who departed this life Feb. 17, 1858, aged 43 years, 11 mos. & 27 days.*
George Grice, who departed this life, Aug. 8, 1843 in the 55th year of his age (Ridgely, p. 122) According to Ridgely, the following lines were on this stone, but they are not there now: Held up & cheered by Jesus' grace, he sweetly fell asleep. These lines are found on the gravestone of Edward Grice, who died in 1844.
Avarilla Grice, who departed this life, Sept. 24, 1841 in the 57th year of her age. (Ridgely, p. 122).
Sister, Mary Grice, b. 14 Feb. 1815, d. 3 June 1855 (Ridgely, p. 122).
Blair, husband, Joseph O., 1885-1946. (Blank space, probably for wife's name)
Calvin E. Oler, 1883-1932.
Elizabeth Oler, b. July 18, 1814, d. July 24, 1885.*
Mary A. Oler, b. 5 Oct. 1827 and departed this life 3 March 1880.*
Father, Jacob Oler, who departed this life 2 June 1868 in the 86th year of his age.*
Mother, Mary, consort of Jacob Oler, who departed this life, 26 July 1859, aged 66 years.*
Johnsey W., son of Geo. G. & Martha Oler, d. 29 Jan. 1863.
George G. Oler, b. 19 Jan. 1816, departed this life 20 Sept. 1875, aged 59 years, 8 mos. & 1 day.*
Martha O. Oler, consort of George G. Oler, b. Jan. 5, 1819, d. Aug. 25, 1889.*
Oler, Father, Edmund G., 1852-1937. Mother, Addie F., 1865-1938.
Netty, wife of John E. Merryman, b. March 1, 1815, d. Nov. 6, 1856, aged 41 years, 8 mos. & 6 days. (Ridgely, p. 122) Ridgely gives the date of birth as March 21, 1813, however, based on the age at death, March 1, 1815 seems correct. The year of birth on the stone looks like 1815 rather than 1813.
Iron Mattison, of Joseph, d. May 30, 1823 in the 85th year of his age. Footstone: A.M. (Ridgely, p. 122)
Charles E. Justus, b. April 11, 1850, d. April 2, 1889, aged 38 years, 11 mos. & 21 days.*

Clarence F., son of Chas. E. and the late Selena J. Justus, d. Oct. 16, 1886, aged 6 years, 6 mos. and 9 days.*
Selena J., beloved wife of Chas. E. Justus, dau. of the late Conrad and Elizabeth Scipp, d. June 11, 1886, aged 34 years and 16 days.*
Father, John Justice (sic), b. Jan. 22, 1822, d. Jan. 1, 1905.
Mother, Rebecca, beloved wife of John Justus and dau. of the late Wm. Wooden, d. March 11, 1887, aged 66 years and 4 days.*
Henrietta, wife of Levi Justus, d. Nov. 22, 1883 in her 38th year.*
Benrietta, d. Nov. 28, 1876, aged 5 years, 9 mos. and 25 days. Elizabeth, d. Nov. 29, 1876, aged 2 years, 9 mos. and 20 days, children of Levi and Henrietta Justus.*
Mamie E., wife of A. J. Wernsdorfer, 1879-1937.
George W., son of Samuel & Ollie E. Frock, d. Feb. 14, 1884, aged 8 years, 2 mos. and 4 days.*
Husband, Samuel Frock, b. May 26, 1845, d. July 30, 1883.*
Andrew J. Wernsdorfer, 1874-1940.
Abraham Brown, husband of Sarah Jane Brown, b. May 22, 1815, d. Nov. 22, 1890.*
Sarah Jane, wife of Abraham Brown, b. Aug. 27, 1816, d. Jan. 6, 1892.*
Willie, youngest son of Abraham & Sarah J. Brown, d. May 9, 1869, aged_____.
Sarah Jennet, dau. of Abraham and Sarah J. Brown, d. July 21, 1847, aged 1 year and 21 days.
Wife, Hattie A. Price, b. March 19, 1856, d. April 20, 1882.*
Husband, George W. Chalk, who departed this life 16 July 1872 in the 38th year of his age.*
Husband, Wm. H. H. Parks, b. Aug. 18, 1841, d. Feb. 15, 1879.*
Kate J., wife of Alpha M. Ruby, relict of William Parks, b. Aug. 27, 1844, d. Nov. 25, 1896, aged 52 years, 2 mos. & 28 days.
Maggie, wife of Elisha Parks, d. Feb. 25, 1891, aged 37 years, 9 mos. and 15 days.
Elisha J. Parks, who departed this life Dec. 24, 1878 in the 44th year of his age.*
Hester Wimsett, b. Feb. 27, 1813, d. March 17, 1876.
Rider, Howard Lodge, June 7, 1866 - Nov. 25, 1958. Cordelia Jones, Sept. 13, 1878 - July 18, 1942. Footstones: H.L.R. C.J.R.
Father, John G. Rider, b. Jan. 17, 1818, d. May 11, 1892.
Mother, Elizabeth Ann, wife of John G. Rider, b. Dec. 31, 1830, d. June 12, 1891.
George F., b. July 7, 1853, d. March 7, 1859. Katie F., b. Dec. 25, 1855, d. April 20, 1860. Edward F., b. Feb. 19, 1868, d. Aug. 26, 1869, children of George & Catherine Wenzel.
G. Willie Wenzel, b. Nov. 4, 1873, d. April 2, 1875.*
Daughter, Lillie A. Wenzel, b. Nov. 10, 1869, d. Sept. 4, 1876.*
John E. Frock, 1909-1939.
Frock, Laura E., 1880-1941. John S., 1878-1938.
Nellie Gray, dau. of George W. & Fannie Parsons, b. Dec. 24, 1870, d. Nov. 30, 1871, aged 11 mos. & 6 days.
Grace Elve, dau. of George W. & Fannie Parsons, b. May 9, 1878, d. Aug. 3, 1879, aged 1 year, 2 mos. & 24 days.
Catherine, wife of Stephen Musgrave (sic), d. May 15, 1883 in her 74th year.*
William S. Musgrove, b. Jan. 10, 1836, d. Mar. 9, 1922.
Mary Ann Musgrove, b. Oct. 7, 1838, d. Oct. 17, 1916.*
Clara Musgrove, wife of Richard T. Musgrove, b. Mar. 22, 1857, d. Apr. 18, 1923.*
Richard T. Musgrove, b. Jan. 10, 1849, d. Feb. 12, 1929.*
Father, Richard Stinehagen, b. May 27, 1811, d. Mar. 17, 1899.
Mary Ann, wife of Richard Stinhagen (sic), d. Feb. 23, 1885, aged 69 years, 4 mos. and 4 days.
Center stone: Wimsett (Five footstones:

Five footstones to Wimsett:
Maude I., 1882-1958.
Kate, 1849-1893.
Charles, 1845-1912.
H. Jeannette, 1883-1939.
Mary F., 1876-1948.
William Frock, husband of Sophia Frock, b. Mar. 23, 1817, d. Nov. 14, 1891.*
Sophia Frock, wife of William Frock, d. Sept. 14, 1886, aged 67 years, 9 mos. and 16 days.*
Joseph M. Frock, son of William & Sophia Frock, d. Oct. 18, 1868, aged 22 years, 5 mos. and 20 days.*
Benjamin Frock, Nov. 29, 1842 - Aug. 9, 1900.*
Edward Burnham, b. Aug. 13, 1841, d. Nov. 30, 1916, aged 75 years.
Hannah L., wife of Edward Burnham, d. April 5, 1903, aged 57 years.*
Temperance A. Burnham, b. Jan. 22, 1888, d. Feb. 25, 1900.
Rutha E., dau. of Edward & Hannah Burnham, d. April 4, 1879, aged 9 years & 11 mos.
Thomas Brady, son of Edward & Hannah Burnham, d. Oct. 25, 1885, aged 7 years and 10 mos.
Fannie P., wife of Alfred Callender and dau. of Edward & Hannah Burnham, b. June 13, 1867, d. Nov. 8, 1889.*
Estella May, dau. of Alfred and the late Fannie P. Callender, b. Nov. 14, 1887, d. Jan. 6, 1891.
Virginia P. Burnham, b. Aug. 14, 1880, d. Jan. 18, 1897.
John F. C. Burnham, b. March 20, 1871, d. Oct. 8, 1906, aged 36 years.
Ann R., wife of John S. Parks, b. June 19, 1851, d. March 31, 1881.*
Front: (Odd Fellows emblem). William, husband of Elizabeth Wooden, b. Sept. 3, 1829, d. Dec. 24, 1910. Right side: Wooden - Elizabeth, wife of William Wooden, b. Jan. 28, 1829, d. Jan. 6, 1914. Back: Susan, beloved wife of Peter Parks, b. Jan. 10, 1824, d. April 28, 1883.*
Carrie May, dau. of George H. & Ida Parks, d. July 8, 1872, aged 4 mos. and 15 days.
Merreyman (sic) Gittings, son of George H. & Ida Parks, d. June 23, 1876, aged 5 mos.
Elenorah, wife of William Parks, departed this life, Sept. 1, 1858 in the 30th year of her age.
Peter Parks, Jr., b. Jan. 10, 1803, d. Jan. 20, 1874, aged 71 years & 10 days.
Angeline Parks, b. June 9, 1808, d. June 17, 1897, age 89 years & 8 days.*
Eliza J., wife of J. T. Parks, Sept. 24, 1834 - Jan. 29, 1897.*
John T., husband of E. J. Parks, March 14, 1830 - June 30, 1909.*
Son, Albert Harris, d. 4 Nov. 1880, aged 24 years, 11 mos. & 21 days. Third son of Ephraim & Mary A. Harris.*
Emma, dau. of Ephraim & Mary Harris, b. Feb. 12, 1862, d. March 2, 1884, aged 22 years & 19 days.*
George T., son of Ephraim & Mary Harris, d. March 14, 1889, aged 23 years, 1 mos. and 21 days.*
(Fraternal emblem) Ephraim, son of Ephraim & Mary Harris, Nov. 16, 1857 - Nov. 1, 1892.*
Joseph, son of Ephraim & Mary Harris, April 2, 1850 - Dec. 20, 1898.*
Mary A., wife of Ephraim Harris, Nov. 22, 1826 - March 19, 1912. (Footstone - Mother)*
Ephraim Harris, Dec. 26, 1818 - Nov. 18, 1904. (Footstone - Father)*
Annie E. Flowers, 1881-1881. Willie P. Flowers, 1889-1892.
Herbert V. Flowers, 1893-1893. Florence V. Flowers, 1894-1895.
Flowers, Milford L. Flowers, 1852-1919. Kate E. Flowers, 1855-1922.
Frock, George F., 1856-1923. Helen G., his wife, 1860-1947.
Sophia C., wife of George F. Frock, d. Feb. 20, 1893, aged 36 years.*

George W. Frock, son of G. & S. Frock, b. March 17, 1884, d. July 6, 1884.
Greeley, John William 1889-1957. Elsie May, 1891-1971. William Emory, 1915-1916.
Betty Jane, 1922-1922.
Mary R., dau. of Wm. H. & Ellen L. Chenoweth, June 21, 1870 - July 15, 1943.
Katherine, wife of Wm. H. Chenoweth, b. Nov. 30, 1853, d. Dec. 18, 1903.*
Wm. H. Chenoweth, b. Oct. 16, 1840, d. Sept. 17, 1917.*
Ellen, wife of Wm. Chenoweth, b. June 25, 1844, d. Jan. 5, 1877, aged 32 years, 6 mos. and 11 days.*
Hampton, son of Wm. & Ellen Chenoweth, d. April 24, 1868, aged 19 days.
Bessie Gertrude, dau. of Wm. & Ellen Chenoweth, aged 10 mos.
Clarence Lane, son of Wm. & Ellen Chenoweth......
...perance R., dau. of Wm. & Ellen Chenoweth, aged 10 mos.
Eddy, son of Wm. & Ellen Chenoweth, aged 10 days.
Hattie Brown, dau. of Wm. & Ellen Chenoweth, aged 6 mos.
W. Frank Kelley, son of John G. & Mary J. Kelley, b. Feb. 29, 1860, d. Sept. 12, 1889, aged 29 years, 6 mos. & 14 days.*
Mary J. Kelley, 1825-1906.
Father, (2 fraternal emblems, the second of which is an Odd Fellows emblem) Samuel F. Cox, husband of Margaret A. Cox, Aug. 11, 1835 - July 29, 1902.*
Footstone: S.C.
Footstone: B.C.
Albert F. Cockey, b. Jan. 7, 1878, d. Oct. 31, 1911.
Mary A. Frock, wife of Samuel Frock, b. Aug. 23, 1818, d. Dec. 10, 1886.
Husband, Samuel Frock, who departed this life, March 12, 1873 in the 61 (64?) year of his age.
(Odd Fellows emblem) William Frock, who departed this life, Nov. 12, 1872 in the 30th year of his age.
Ellen Frock who departed this life, July 3, 1863 in the 22nd year of her age.
Mary, dau. of Samuel & Mary Frock, b. March 10, 1851, d. July 4, 1875.
Father, George Lane, b. Feb. 20, 1816, d. Dec. 18, 1875.*
Rebecca, wife of George Lane, b. July 24, 1815, d. July 22, 1866 in the 51st year of her age.*
Henry, son of Samuel and Mary Frock, d. Dec. 3, 1851, aged 14 years, 3 mos. and 24 days.
Father, Henry L., husband of Mary E. Stein, b. April 3, 1890, d. Aug. 30, 1955.*
Government marker: Stephen Franklin Frock, Maryland Pvt. 376, Casual Co. World War 1, Oct. 14, 1886 - June 16, 1957, PH.
Mother, Annie R. Swem, wife of Stephen F. Frock, b. April 1, 1864, d. April 28, 1942.*
Father, Stephen F. Frock, b. Feb. 28, 1863, d. Sept. 19, 1905.*
Mary E., wife of Ezekiel Ambrose, d. April 5, 1893, aged 74 years, 10 mos.*
Ezekiel, husband of Mary E. Ambrose, d. Oct. 19, 1879, aged 61 years, 1 mos.*
Headstone: Cross. One Footstone:
Mattie Cross, 1873-1936.
Mary E., wife of William T. Ambrose, who departed this life Nov. 2, 1877, aged 35 years, 7 mos.
Front: John R., husband of Mary E. Chenoweth, b. Oct. 8, 1845, d. Jan. 17, 1913. At bottom: Chenoweth. Left side: Mary E., wife of John R. Chenoweth, b. Sept. 21, 1846, d. Jan. 6, 1935.
Daniel S. Chenoweth, b. Aug. 19, 1854, d. July 6, 1921.
William Chenoweth, b. May 9, 1792, d. April 10, 1853, aged 60 years, 11 mos. & 1 day.
Amey Chenoweth, wife of Wm. Chenoweth, d. Sept. 26, 1896 in the 78th year of her age.
Hannah E. Uhler, dau. of John and Temperance Chenoweth, d. Aug. 24, 1856 in the 19th year of her age.

James Hisor, son of John & Temperance Chenoweth, d. Jan. 1, 1852 in the 9th year of his age.
John Chenoweth, b. Jan. 2, 1816, d. Feb. 14, 1875, aged 59 years, 1 mos. & 12 days.*
Temperance, wife of John Chenoweth, b. Dec. 9, 1817, d. April 4, 1895, aged 77 years, 3 mos. & 15 days.*
Absolom B. Chenoweth, b. June 6, 1851, d. April 29, 1875, aged 24 years.*
Skipper, William F., Sr., Aug. 13, 1901 - Oct. 9, 1960. Mary J.,Aug 21, 1908--.
Francis B. Skipper, Sept. 19, 1913 - July 23, 1961.*
Susan D. Skipper, Sept. 14, 1873 - Feb. 10, 1959.*
Stephen G. Skipper, Nov. 21, 1872 - March 24, 1963.*
George Washington, son of W. H. & R. A. Eckers, b. July 17, 1853, d. Dec. 10, 1872, aged 13 years, 5 mos. & 24 days.*
Rachel A., dau. of Thos. & B. Pocock, wife of W. H. Eckers, b. April 20, 1832, d. Jan. 10, 1873.
William H. Eckers, b. Sept. 19, 1822, d. June 8, 1893 in his 71st year.*
Left side: Charles E. Eckers, b. Jan. 25, 1866, d. Oct. 4, 1909. Right side: Eliza Ann Eckers, (no dates).*
Front: Raymond Hare, b. Feb. 6, 1894, d. Dec. 25, 1895. Right side: Mary E. Hare, b. Jan. 28, 1882, d. Feb. 13, 1882. Left side: Cathrine (sic) Hare, b. Nov. 19, 1884, d. Sept. 6, 1885.
John T., husband of Margaret Hare, b. July 14, 1853, d. April 5, 1901.
Mary A., wife of John T. Hare, b. July 12, 1859, d. May 27, 1880.
Annie M. Forwood, b. Nov. 15, 1870, d. Dec. 16, 1870.*
Father, Reuben T. Forwood, b. March 8, 1838, d. Sept. 2, 1876.*
Mother, Sidney P. Forwood, Oct. 21, 1832 - July 4, 1919.
Margueritte (sic) S. Trumen, wife of Clarence W. Burnham, Nov. 15, 1882 - June 15, 1927.*
Mary Bell and daus., Margaret Sophia, Selena (no dates).
David, husband of Martha A. Hare, b. Feb. 9, 1828, d. Jan. 25, 1892.*
Martha A. Hare, b. Dec. 20, 1832, d. June 5, 1912.*
David Hare, no dates.
Alvirte Wilson, b. April 6, 1854, d. Oct. 13, 1855.
Elizabeth E. Kenney, b. May 25, 1846, d. June 26, 1852.
A stone with no inscription.
A stone with no inscription.
Susan Emily Kenney, b. Jan. 17, 1809, d. _____.*
Staines, William H. Sr., July 9, 1894 - Sept. 22, 1958. Clara V., Nov. 13, 1898--.
Dorothy Louise, dau. of William H. and Clara V. Staines, b. June 13, 1924, d. Sept. 17, 1940.
J. Thomas Staines, b. Aug. 11, 1856, d. April 8, 1942.
Mary C., wife of J. Thomas Staines, b. May 6, 1861, d. Oct. 28, 1921.
Mother, Martha Ann Smith, b. May 23, 1829, d. Feb. 7, 1902.*
B. F. Smith, b. July 3, 1868, aged 2 years & 3 mos. (This and the next stone are joined at the base.)
Laura V. Smith, b. Oct. 5, 1871, aged 15 mos.
Husband, Thomas .. Smith...... .
William Jones, b. July 1, 1802, d. Dec. 23, 1888.
Mary A. Jones, b. Aug. 25, 1803, d. May 21, 1887.
Uninscribed stone.
Mother, Mary A. Wolf, b. Jan. 31, 1845, d. Feb. 4, 1884.*
Elizabeth A., dau. of John & Catharine Bowen, b. 20 Sept. and d. 13 Dec. 1865.
Samuel J. Bell, Nov. 25, 1840 - April 30, 1918.
Caroline W. Bell, April 17, 1850 - March 23, 1944.
Our Babes (no further inscription).

To my mother, Susan A. Smith, d. Nov. 10, 1886, aged 72 years.
Sophia Lyon, b. Jan. 12, 1809, d. Nov. 7, 1869.*
Charles W. Lyons, b. Nov. 27, 1867, d. Dec. 18, 1868. (This and the next stone are joined at the base.
John W. Lyons, b. July 15, 1869, d. Aug. 1, 1869.
Maggie S. Lyons, b. Aug. 6, 1872, d. Nov. 1, 1876. (This and the next stone are joined at the base.)
Lizzie M. Lyons, b. Dec. 14, 1870, d. Sept. 21, 1876.
Partially buried stone, no visible inscription.
Alice Lutz, b. Jan. 7, 1877, d. Nov. 20, 1883.*
George, son of Daniel W. & Mary B. Lutz, b. 15 Nov. 1878, d. 23 Feb. 1879.
Barbara A., wife of John G. Lutz, b. June 3, 1820, d. Nov. 15, 1883.*
John G. Lutz, husband of Barbara A. Lutz, b. Dec. 27, 1806, d. April 10, 1889.*
I + G.
H + G.
Husband, Peter Swem, d. May 5, 1880, aged 23 years, 11 mos. & 5 days.*
base of a stone.
Mary E. Green, dau. of J. W. & Elizabeth Green, d. Nov. 20, 1874, aged 17 years, 4 mos. & 1 day.
Joshua Lane,..... .
Center stone: Ince. Two footstones:
Mother, Kate, 1869-1945.
Father, Thomas 1859-1937.
Parks, Wilbert J., 1873 + 1939. Lottie A., 1875 + 1947.
Allen R. Zink, son of Conrad and Pauline E. Zink, Feb. 27, 1894 - Nov. 18, 1960.*
Sister, Edna L., dau. of C. & P. E. Zink, Jan. 15, 1884 - Oct. 30, 1918.*
Catharine E. Parks, b. July 21, 1897, d. Sept. 29, 1897.*
Mother, Margaret A. Arold, 1856-1898.
Our Babe, Willie, b. Feb. 12, 1893, d. Sept. 4, 1893, infant son of John W. & Ada Harman.*
Bessie P., infant daughter of John & Ada Harman, b. July 20, 1905, d. Feb. 19, 1906.*
Edward, infant son of John & Ada Harman, b. June 25, 1904, d. Oct. 20, 1904.*
Beauregard Harman, son of John & Ada Harman, b. Feb. 7, 1909, d. Sept. 26, 1909.*
Harman, Mother, Ada P., 1874-1955. Father, John W., 1864-1949.
Government stone: Lois Y. Weber, April 12, 1898 - May 19, 1952.
Shock, Sherman, Jan. 25, 1857 - Nov. 15, 1912. Rose W., Nov. 20, 1868 - Jan. 30, 1960.
Government stone: Willard K. Shock, Maryland, Pvt. Engineers, World War II, Aug. 17, 1906 - Oct. 15, 1944.
Julia A. Lutz, 1852-1930.
Alice E. Lutz, 1849-1926.
Annie W. Lutz, 1855-1926.
Center stone: Robinson. Four footstones:
James E. Robinson, Oct. 17, 1872 - May 31, 1943, husband of Sadie Cowling Robinson.
Sadie Cowling Robinson, Nov. 17, 1878 - June 22, 1964, wife of James E. Robinson.
Elizabeth C. Robinson, July 7, 1907 - Jan. 12, 1926, dau. of James E. and Sadie Cowling Robinson.
Oswald C. Robinson, Dec. 13, 1902 - Dec. 24, 1964. Ida Louise Robinson, his wife, July 17, 1913--.
Shock, dau. Zella E., 1928-1929. Husband, Oliver M., 1893-1962. Wife, Mary C., 1899--.
Betty Lee Shock, 1929-1931.
Carol Lynn Shock, 1943-1946.
Larua B. Shock, 1901-1960.

Jones, Laura V., 1865-1932. William E. B., 1859-1934.
Engle, Henry Scarff, 1886-1932.
Holliday, (blank space—probably for wife's name) I.O.O.F., Robert 1868-1949.
Rae E. Wildner, March 27, 189_ - July 29, 1938.
F. Joseph Wildner, Feb. 24, 1888 - Dec. 4, 1962.
Government stone: Edward D. Karns, III, Maryland, 1st Sgt. 1884 Combat Engrs., World War II, Sept. 7, 1920 - Aug. 23, 1955.
Paul S. LeFaivre, Dec. 19, 1905 - Feb. 8, 1970.
Center stone: Brannock. No footstones.
(An emblem that reads: Chaplain, Vol. Fire Co., Md., Minter (Masonic emblem) Rev. James W., Feb. 22, 1891 - Jan. 18, 1968 (Eastern Star emblem) Rosa L., Sept. 29, 1891--.
Derbin Parks, b. Aug. 12, 1868, d. June 4, 1924.*
John P. D. Parks, b. May 3, 1837 - d. Aug. 11, 1918.*
Catharine A. Parks, wife of J. P. D. Parks, b. May 10, 1840, d. Aug. 19, 1897.*
William M., son of Thomas & Mary Cowling, b. Jan. 31, 1871, d. Jan. 3, 1895.
Mary Ince, wife of Edward Cowling, b. Feb. 23, 1848, d. Jan. 8, 1917.
Edward Cowling, b. Feb. 25, 1850, d. Feb. 5, 1900.
Katie Florence, dau. of Conrad & Pauline E. Zink, b. Aug. 13, 1895, d. Sept. 5, 1895.*
Pauline E., wife of Conrad Zink, b. July 4, 1855, d. Aug. 3, 1898.*
Conrad, husband of Pauline E. Zink, b. Jan. 15, 1856, d. Oct. 24, 1904.*
Sister, E. Irene Jarrett, dau. of C. & P. E. Zink, May 17, 1882 - July 30, 1915.*
Brother, Walter C., son of C. & P. E. Zink, Oct. 15, 1885 - Oct. 24, 1918.*
Center stone: McNeave. Two footstones.
Joseph S., 1868-1938.
Appolonia A., 1871-1933
Smith, George A., Aug. 19, 1860 - Dec. 31, 1956. Ella R., Sept. 1, 1862 - Dec. 10, 1941.
Sister, Margaret F., dau. of Andrew & Mary J. Fisher, b. Jan. 16, 1874, d. Oct. 18, 1896.*
Eliza Fisher, March 26, 1868 - June 3, 1954.
Mother, Mary J. Fisher, wife of Andrew Fisher, May 22, 1834 - Aug. 18, 1911.*
(Odd Fellows emblem) Andrew, husband of M. J. Fisher, Oct. 22, 1828 - Feb. 24, 1905.
Elisha G. O., dau. (sic) of Malcolm A. & Maggie M. Fishpaw, b. Aug. 6, 1896, d. Feb. 28, 1897.*
Virginia & Johnnie, infant children of Malcolm A. & Maggie M. Fishpaw, (no dates).
Fishpaw, Maggie Mary, March 25, 1876 - Nov. 15, 1950. Malcolm A., May 10, 1873 - May 24, 1950.
Thomas F., husband of Elizabeth F. Smith, d. Feb. 28, 1897, aged 42 years.*
Catherine M. Dey, b. Nov. 28, 1896, d. Oct. 14, 1918, wife of Pearce B. Dey.
Devese, Samual (sic) A., 1867-1935. Alberta, 1864-1951.
Front: Sarah J. Fishpaugh, wife of Robert Fishpaugh, b. July 24, 1837, d. Oct. 15, 1905. Right side: Cora L. Fishpaugh, b. Jan. 31, 1886, d. July 11, 1919. Left side: Robert Fishpaugh, husband of Sarah J. Fishpaugh, b. Jan. 20, 1830, d. Dec. 13, 1906.
Howard E., son of J. F. & Laura Bell, d. July 25, 1892, aged 1 year, 2 mos. and 2 days.*
James West, born in Gloucester Co., Va., Oct. 13, 1910, d. April 3, 1928, C.H.W.
Grave with uninscribed stones at head and foot; seems to be a child's grave.
Uninscribed stone.

Center stone: Clusman. One footstone.
Wife, Mildred J., 1905-1935.
Laura V. Bell, 1866-1958.
Bell, Wm. Wheeler, 1919--. Lossie Mae, 1918--.
Bell, Maggie A., 1894-1966. William W., 1888-1956.
John Oliver, son of Jacob & Margaret Keller, d. March 18, 1862, aged 18 years, 11 mos. & 25 days.*
Jacob Keller, 1842-1931. His wife, Margaret H. Keller, 1831-1910.
Margret (sic) R., dau. of Washington & Mary Chenoweth, b. April 28, 1903, d. Sept. 27, 1903.*
James G., son of M. J. and S. E. Armacost, d. Aug. 25, 1900, aged 9 years and 9 mos.
Melchior J., husband of Sarah E. Armacost, July 30, 1842 - July 25, 1915.
Sarah Elizabeth, wife of M? J? Armacost, Dec. 25, 1845 - June 28, 1928.
Edgar J., son of M. J. & S. E. Armacost, May 18, 1885 - June 25, 1930.
Center stone: Pearce. Two footstones.
George C., Oct. 20, 1876 - Oct. 23, 1942.
Blanche C., Dec. 14, 1879 - Feb. 23, 1958.
George William, infant son of George C. & Blanche Pearce, b. Oct. 15, 1898, d. Nov. 3, 1898.
Joseph Earle, infant son of George C. & Blanche Pearce, b. June 7, 1901, d. Nov. 5, 1901.
Mary C., dau. of George C. & Blanche Pearce, b. April 30, 1910, d. July 28, 1910.
Flossie Fishpaugh, d. June 27, 1902, aged 8 mos., 19 days, infant child of Ella and Adolphus Fishpaugh.*
Adolphus, infant son of Mary E. & A. Fishpaw (sic), b. Dec. 21, 1903, d. Dec. 28, 1903.
Earnest (sic) L. Fishpaugh, son of Adolphus & Mary E. Fishpaugh, d. July 3, 1908, aged 9 years, 9 mos. and 10 days.
Mary Ellen, wife of Adolphus Fishpaugh, b. June 20, 1868, d. Jan. 6, 1918.*
Mother, Hattie Staines, d. 1902. Ethel Staines, 1921-1922.
Father, Harry Staines, d. 1902.
Staines, Ethel C., July 25, 1916--. Nancy M., Aug. 2, 1938--. Christian A., Dec. 24, 1892 - May 4, 1965. Margaretta L., June 30, 1895 - Feb. 15, 1960.
Center stone: Bell. Five footstones.
Chas. H. Bell, 1848-1925.
Fannie A. Bell, 1847-1927.
Husband, M. Neal Goodman, 1918-1965.
Father, William C., 1881-1941.
Husband, John Klueber, 1886-1957.
Kate R. Ports, d. May 29, 1923, aged 73 years.*
James D. Wadsworth, June 14, 1920 - Aug. 13, 1969.
Husband, John E. Bassler, 1891-1967.
Center stone: Shock. Two footstones.
Minnie C., 1898-1937.
Eli K., 1886-1960.
Hipple, Donald E., 1908--. Eleanor H., 1908-1967.
Joseph Richard, son of Joseph R. & Martha E. Brown, b. July 28, 1889, d. March 1, 1897.
Mother, Martha E. Brown, Dec. 8, 1866 - July 25, 1916.
Mother, A. Elizabeth Keiffer, Dec. 11, 1826 - Jan. 12, 1899. (This and the following stone are joined at the base.)*
Father, Daniel B. Keiffer, May 1, 1825 - Aug. 17, 1901. Elsie C. Justice, Jan. 5, 1910 - Jan. 13, 1912.
Justice, Adelia K., May 2, 1871 - Feb. 12, 1944. John S., Nov. 22, 1868 - Dec. 24, 1959.

Oliver R. Ritter, husband of Julia A. Ritter, Feb. 28, 1832 - Nov. 7, 1899.*
Mary Estella, dau. of L. M. & A. E. Armacost, b. Oct. 30, 1913, d. Dec. 18, 1913.
Armacost, Annie E., May 14, 1893---. Leo M., Feb. 1, 1886 - July 26, 1960.
Mother, Edith I. Smith, 1865-1938.
Granddaughter, Margaret L. Islaub, 1920-1956.
Harmon, John M., 1898-1932. Edna P., 1923-1923. Charles F., 1928-1928.
Versie C., 1901-1933. Emma M., 1898-1928. (At the bottom) - Sumrell.
Bassler, John W., 1857-1947. Lena F., 1866-1935.
Triplett, L. Frances, 1899-1967. George C., 1894-1963.
William H., 1870-1938. Kate, 1880-1968. (At the bottom) - Ayre.
Joshua O. Ritter, Dec. 13, 1872 - Sept. 17, 1961. Sister, Sarah E. Ritter, June 22, 1887---.
The following is a new section, west of a driveway. The next six graves comprise a lot that extends back three rows; these graves were said to have been moved here from a farm.
Thomas J. German, Aug. 17, 1864 - Dec. 11, 1932.*
Josephine German, Jan. 18, 1858 - Jan. 13, 1939.*
Charles E. M., son of Thomas J. & J. German, b. July 22, 1887, d. Nov. 14, 1905.*
Lillian (sic) M. German Donovan, Nov. 10, 1892 - Sept. 1, 1931.*
Front: Mary A., wife of David M. German, b. May 30, 1830, d. March 14, 1916.
Right side: David M. German, b. Jan. 1, 1832, d. Feb. 13, 1907. Left side: Mollie E. German, b. Feb. 10, 1862, d. June 21, 1906.*
Webster T. German, husband of Eva Donovan German, 1899-1955.
Continuation of first row west of driveway:
Front: (Masonic emblem) George L., b. Nov. 2, 1862, d. March 12, 1929. Mollie J., b. Dec. 9, 1869, d. May 23, 1944. (at the bottom): Bishop, Right side: Edgar A., b. Feb. 17, 1891, d. April 24, 1970. Christine A., b. Sep-. 24, 1897---. Left side: Pauline H., b. Aug. 17, 1898, d. Jan. 29, 1906. George A., b. May 2, 1929, d. Feb. 28, 1957.
Nettie G. Miller, June 30, 1896 - July 25, 1968.
Government stone: Charles E. Miller, Maryland, PFC Co. G 111 Infantry, World War I PH, April 23, 1896 - Nov. 13, 1966.
Howard N. Maglidt, son of William & Elmira Maglidt, b. Dec. 10, 1876, d. Sept. 17, 1907.*
Mother, Catherine M. Herminau, 1913-1943.
Center stone: Burnham. Two footstones.
Thomas C., 1871-1932.*
Mollie L., 1866-1962.*
Shock, George H., Sept. 23, 1849 - Sept. 11, 1913. Rebecca V., May 5, 1861 - Jan. 24, 1948.
Arthur W. Shock, June 7, 1896 - Jan. 23, 1967.
Harriet A., dau. of H. E. & M. A. Crue, b. Sept. 15, 1913, d. Oct. 4, 1916.*
Mother, Mary A., wife of Harry E. Crue, April 27, 1879 - March 25, 1919.*
Father, Harry E., husband of Mary A. Crue, Dec. 8, 1862 - March 9, 1934.*
Wheatley, Benjamin F., July (no day given) 1869 - May 25, 1919. Amanda V., Dec. 1, 1871 - Dec. 2, 1917. Margaret A., April 18, 1903 - April 20, 1968.
Bell, Charles H., March 22, 1880 - June 3, 1954. Annie B., April 16, 1888 (no date of death).*
Chas. Howard, Jr., son of Chas. H. & Annie M. Bell, b. June 28, 1908, d. May 12, 1923.*
Burnham, Harry R., 1882-1955. Mary E., 1893-1954. Paul H., 1929-1944. Melvin R., 1923---.
Front: (Masonic emblem) Conrad Ditzel, March 6, 1878 - Dec. 1, 1919. Right side: Julia Gill Ditzel, July 18, 1880 - Feb. 23, 1955.*
Center stone: Chenoweth. Three footstones.
Father, Edgar A. P., 1873 (masonic emblem) 1938.
Mother, Mary A., 1875-1956.
Edward J. Yagel, 1899-1949, husband of Lillian Chenoweth Yagel.

Center stone: Byrd. Two footstones.
Thomas B. Byrd, 1884-1942.
Edith Cowling Byrd, 1889-1960.
Center stone: Riley-McMahon. Two footstones.
John J. Riley, 1876-1944.
C. Herbert McMahon, 1909-1957.
Keller, E. Jackson, Jan. 6, 1869 - July 23, 1956. Ida Merrick, Dec. 1, 1873 - Jan. 13, 1964.
Harry Franklin Marsh. (This is a crude stone.)
Husband, Frederick Marsh, 1888-1952.
Mary E. Disney, b. March 20, 1852, d. July 31, 1910. Mamie V. Disney, b. May 6, 1880, d. Nov. 20, 1904.
Sadie C. Ambrose, b. April 12, 1857, d. Feb. 2, 1944.
Center stone: Zink. Three footstones.
Cora Marie, 1883-1939.
Daughter, Edna V. (Dotty), wife of Harry O. Link, d. Aug. 22, 1963.
William M., 1880-1954.
David G. Hisley, d. July 15, 1971. Elsie Zink Hisley, d. Oct. 11, 1968. (In 1971, there was a different stone here which read: Daughter, Elsie E. Zink, wife of David G. Hisley, d. Oct. 11, 1968.)
C. A. Williams, June 4, 1870 - July 15, 1932.*
Sophia S. Williams, 1868-1935.*
Elenora Criss, June 2, 1891 - August 13, 1933.*
Raymond D. Surratt, 1942-1971.
Anna Julia Surratt, 1906-1957.
Hamilton, Father, William M., 1880-1955. Mother, Anna J., 1882-1968.
Russell F. Talbott, 1912 (Masonic Emblem) 1969. Myrtle C. Talbott, 1908---.
McKann, (Masonic emblem) Howard, March 15, 1903---. Sophia M., Nov. 27, 1894 - March 7, 1971.
William G. Bigley, Sr., 1898-1955.
Mother, Margaret A. Matthews, 1870-1944. Husband, William H. Lake, 1885-1952. Wife, Frances M. Lake, 1890---.
Musgrove, G. Mowbray, Sept. 30, 1889 - Sept. 16, 1966. Orella M., Dec. 17, 1890---.
Harman, Alice E., 1876-1966. Charles E., 1873-1944.
Headstone: Burnham, Helen R., 1905-1944. (Space, probably for husband's name) One footstone:
Helen R. Burnham, April 6, 1905 - May 20, 1944. (Note: same name as headstone)
Burnham, son, Sgt. John T. Burnham, Jr., 78th Div. 309th Inf., March 16, 1926- March 3, 1945, killed in action in Germany.
Burnham, Ruth A., 1902---. John T., 1896-1960.
Smith, James W., 1888-1963 (space, probably for wife's name). May R., 1917-1920.
William D., 1914-1925.
Bell, Catherine A., 1894-1964. John F., Sr., 1865-1941.
Brewer, Edwin G., 1868-1951. Matilda M., 1874-1959.
Carrie R., wife of Tolly E. Brown, Nov. 27, 1885 - Jan. 31, 1921.*
Joseh A., husband of Nettie V. Brown, March 9, 1906 - May 26, 1954.
Tolly Brown, 1879-1961. (This is a crude stone.)
Albertha (sic), wife of Tolly E. Brown, Oct. 10, 1891 - March 5, 1967.
Center stone: Shock. Two footstones.
E. Mildred, April 1, 1916 - March 9, 1922.
Edna M., Dec. 9, 1891 - July 13, 1969.
Lewis, Francis J., 1891-1968. Edith A., 1894-1950.*
Young, Arthur G., 1910-1945. Anna M., 1905-1961.
IHS, Clarke, George Arthur, Minister, Nov. 10, 1887 - Oct. 20, 1965. Annie Letitia, wife, Feb. 20, 1894---.

Watts, Rev. Joseth T. Watts, D.D., March 19, 1874 - Feb. 7, 1957. Neva Hawkins Watts, July 9, 1877 - May 28, 1950.*
Sipe, Samuel A, 1885-1956. Maude E., 1897-1948. Lewis Burnham, 1930-1965.
Justice, Levi C., July 27, 1881 - Dec. 20, 1951. Rachel L., Sept. 5, 1886 - Dec. 22, 1966.
Bond, Edna G., 1889---. Charles S., 1886-1965.
Mother, Carrie M. Bond, 1866-1963.
William J. Eckers, July 1, 1861 - May 11, 1918. Catherine R. Eckers, March 9, 1867 - Nov. 26, 1933.
George W. Eckers, Jan. 10, 1888 - May 27, 1959.
Amanda Jane Burns, March 4, 1882 - May 2, 1967.
Border stone: Dobson. No other stones.
Dedal, Florence M., March 20, 1897 - March 23, 1949. George A., Nov. 15, 1888-June 15, 1955. Dau., Elizabeth A., March 6, 1920 - March 21, 1961.
William O. Stran, 1872-1921.
Jean H. Stran, 1874-1966.
David E. Taylor, 1903-1941.
Stran, Claude F., 1905-1968. Grace L., 1908-1956.
Son, Lawrence W. Stran, 1932-1942.
Carvilla Bryan Smith, 1896-1950.
Ditzel, Daniel J. Ditzel, March 8, 1912---. Grace M., his wife, July 20, 1912---. Daniel J., Jr., their son, Aug. 14, 1936 - Aug. 19, 1951.
Day, John L., 1898-1971. Gladys M., 1902---.
Gemmill, Frank R., 1885-1954. (Space, probably for wife's name.)
Burnham, Albert W., May 3, 1886 - June 6, 1967. Margaret Ann nee Wust, Jan. 20, 1880 - April 28, 1952.
Clements, Edward Joseph, 1893-1952. (Space, probably for wife's name.)
Laslett, John P., 1892-1971. Anna C., 1897---.
Crue, Edward, Nov. 12, 1867 - Jan. 13, 1943. Queen L., Jan. 3, 1869 - Oct. 5, 1958.
Smith, Mattie E., 1885-1956. John W., 1884-1967.
Bowen, Goldie N., 1910-1952. William M., 1897---.
McCullough, Ruth E., 1911---. Thomas N., 1908-1951.
Center Stone: Shock. Three footstones in front, two behind.
Michael L., Oct. 22, 1924 - March 5, 1943.
Arthur J., May 13, 1914 - Jan. 15, 1947.
Anna M., May 29, 1920 - Jan. 15, 1947.
Charles E., March 8, 1890 - May 25, 1971.
Helena A., Sept. 27, 1890 - May 24, 1947.
Edwards, Sarah M., July 31, 1863 - Oct. 19, 1945. William O., Aug. 20, 1866 - Oct. 22, 1956.
Edwards, William R. C., Aug. 4, 1902 - Aug. 12, 1957. Elva L., Nov. 17, 1903---.
Albert C. Jones, Nov. 4, 1899 - Nov. 14, 1945.
Richards, Vernon A., 1894-1965. Manila H., 1898-1947.
Center Stone: Hare. One footstone.
Son, David A., 1950-1950.
Standiford, Charles W., 1892-1965. Emma M., 1891---.
Field, Father, George Samuel, 1880-1965. Mother, Mary Ellen, (No dates). Dau., Mary Irene, (No dates).
Center stone with two surnames: McMahon-Bryan. Four footstones.
Bessie Cowling McMahon, 1883---.
Harry McMahon, 1882-1968.
Isabel Cowling Bryan, 1893-1956.
Guy A. Bryan, 1866-1956.
George L. Burnham, March 20, 1875 - April 6, 1969.*
Charles E. Burnham, Sept. 8, 1885 - Oct. 8, 1971.*
Father, Joseph Pedone, Sr., 1887-1957.

These five stones were moved from the Cockey family cemetery, east of Falls Road near Green Spring Valley Road. See Ridgely, pages 141-142.
Stephen Cockey, 1835-1920.
Charles O. Cockey, b. April 6, 1830, d. Nov. 24, 1896. (Ridgely, p. 142) According to Ridgely, there was a line after the name which read: Son of John and Mary Cockey, however, it isn't on this stone.
Mary, wife of John Cockey, b. Aug. 13, 1792, d. Oct. 13, 1846. (Ridgely, p. 142).
John Cockey, b. Nov. 5, 1788, d. May 4, 1873. (Ridgely, p. 142).
John Cockey, son of Thomas and Prudence Cockey, b. Dec. 20, 1758, d. Oct. 22, 1824, aged 65 years, 10 mos. and 2 days. (Ridgely, p. 141).
Vaughn, Elwood W., 1914---. Delphine E., 1921-1956.
Mother, Martha A. Ison, 1879-1961.
McCaffrey, John Thomas, Oct. 11, 1887 - Jan. 7, 1958.
Gilbert, (No names or dates).
Robert Marshall Staines, husband of Catherine Lee Staines, June 3, 1931 - May 6, 1960.
Giles, Elmer F. Jacobs, 1918. Son, 1969. Nettie M. Jacobs, 1883. Mother, 1961.
Leonard Mathews Levering, son of Edwin Walker & Mary Gould Levering, May 22, 1886 - Feb. 21, 1966. His wife, Mary Donnell Tilghman, dau. of Charles Henry and Elizabeth Donnell Tilghman, Feb. 15, 1892---.
Gill, George A., May 23, 1876 - March 26, 1969. Margaret M., Dec. 7, 1884 - May 17, 1970.
Husband, Raymond R. Butler, 1899-1960, Veteran World War I. Wife, Viola V. Butler, 1892---.*
Shock, (Space, probably for a husband's name). Esther Ince, 1894-1968.
Shields, Dr. Thomas, July 26, 1887 - Nov. 17, 1964. Marcia E. B., (No dates).
Cline, Harvey E., July 11, 1915 - Dec. 16, 1960. Viola G., June 13, 1913---.
Government marker: Walter S. Crue, Maryland, PFC Btry D, 110 Field Arty, World War I, March 23, 1894 - July 13, 1967.
(Masonic emblem). Russell, William E., Oct. 25, 1885 - Dec. 17, 1967. Bessie M., Dec. 8, 1882 - Aug. 12, 1966.
John T. Bennett "Jack", Jan. 29, 1914 - July 7, 1962.
Rowles, Rev. James R., Sr., Jan. 17, 1893---. Mattie Grace, March 7, 1893 - Dec. 10, 1961 (at the bottom) Pastor of Saters Baptist Church 1951-1959.
Ober, Husband, George W., 1918---. Wife, Margaret L., 1917-1972.
Gray, Russell P., 1927---. Hope A., 1926-1962.*
Thompson, Leonard A., Nov. 4, 1887 - Dec. 19, 1962. Norman A. Hare, Jr., Oct. 21, 1960 - June 9, 1963.
Norman, Anthony Hare, Jr., infant son of Sheila and Norman Hare.
Jacobs, Charles R., Sr., 1912-1964. Viola M., 1914---.
Mother, Martha A. Doxzen, 1890-1963. Dau., Cecelia H. Lane, 1909---.
Smith, Lewis N., Sr., Aug. 25, 1897---. Rose H., April 2, 1902 - Dec. 9, 1966.
Center stone: Ensor. No footstones.
Pearce, husband, M. Kenneth, Nov. 13, 1909 - Dec. 29, 1969. Wife, Mildred M., June 22, 1907---.*
Litchfield, Father, Burnice P., June 7, 1915 - Jan. 21, 1969. (Space, probably for wife's name.)*
Virginia C. Beall, Nov. 17, 1928 - April 3, 1970.
Hall, (Space, probably for husband's name). Mildred E., 1923-1967.
Kerchner, George H., 1891-1959. Adele M., 1886---.
Sibley, R. Lewis, (No dates). Anna M., 1969-(No other date, probably the date of death.)
Kennedy, Melvin J., Aug. 23, 1897 (no date of death). Hilda Ellard, Nov. 16, 1898 - May 12, 1971.
Center stone: Newsom. One footstone.

Francis Ward Newsom, Poet-Author-Teacher, 1895-1970.
Following were moved from Greenmount Cemetery:
Center stone: Levering. Three footstones.*
Joshua Levering, III, son of Ernest D. & Grace Wade, July 14, 1909 - Feb. 15, 1921.
Ernest D. Levering, son of Joshua & Martha Keyser, Sept. 26, 1882 - June 21, 1938.
Ernest D. Levering, Jr., son of Ernest D. & Grace Wade, Aug. 31, 1910 - Aug. 30, 1922.
The following stone is no longer in existence. It was recorded on page 43 of "Henry Sater, 1690-1754", by Isaac Walker Maclay, 1897. This is a typed manuscript in the Maryland Historical Society. The above source mentions on page 26 that the large marble tombs for Thomas and Discretion Walker were erected by their descendants, the Leverings of Baltimore. Discretion Walker was a daughter of Henry Sater.
Charles Gorsuch, d. April 1806 in the 91st year of his age.

COCKEY FAMILY CEMETERY

Located on hill on North side of Padonia Road, between Baltimore-Harrisburg Expressway and York Road. Not shown on quadrangle map. Copied Aug. 8, 1971 by Robert Barnes.

Nicholson Lux Cockey, son of Thomas Deye Cockey of Thomas and Sarah Stuart Lux Cockey, b. Aug. 17, 1839, d. Feb. 11, 1883. Erected by his fond brother, Colegate. (Footstone - N.L.C.)
Sarah Stuart Cockey, wife of Thomas Deye Cockey of Thomas, dau. of Darby and Mary Nicholson Lux, b. Sept. 13, 1807, d. June 8, 1874. Erected to the memory of his mother by her son Colegate. (Footstone - S.S.C.)
Rachel R. Cockey, d. Nov. 5, 1887 in the 73rd year of her age.
Mary S. E. Cockey, dau. of Joshua and Elizabeth Cockey, b. 26 May 1817(?), d. 18 June ____(?)8.
Wm. F. Cockey, son of Joshua F. and Elizabeth Cockey, b. April 20, 1822, d. April 26, 1822.
Elizabeth, consort of the late Joshua F. Cockey who died 11 Feb. 1834 in the 56th year of her age.*
Joshua F. Cockey, who departed this transitory life on the 9th day of October in the year of our Lord 1821 in the 57th year of his age.
Harriet N., wife of Thomas D. Cockey, who died July the 1st, 1841, in the 30th year of her age.*
Ann L. Cock___, b. 22nd of ___. 1840, d. on 20 June _____, aged 9 mos. and 29 days.
A.L.C., 1841.
Note: Many scattered fragments remain.

OLD GUNPOWDER MEETING HOUSE

Located on Beaver Dam Road, east side, north of Beaver Dam Swimming Club, Cockeysville Quadrant. Begin in the Southwest corner of churchyard.

Oliver Matthews, b. 11th Mo. 28th 1724, d. 1st Mo. 17th 1824 (Head marker-O.M.).
Elizabeth Scott, aged 87 years, 3 mos. 11 days, d. 8th Mo. 20th 1832 (Head marker-E.S.).
Thomas Scott, d. 2nd Mo. 8th 1832, aged 81 years, 7 mos. 1 day (Head marker-T.S.).

Unmarked stone.
Inscribed on top "I I P 18 II" (?).
Unmarked or illegible stone.
East of Meeting House.
Chilcoat, Lewis Griffith Chilcoat, Feb. 28, 1861 - Jan. 12, 1936. His wife, Elizabeth Bosley Wheeler, Sept. 20, 1865 - April 17, 1935. (Headstones L.G.C., E.B.W.C.).
Marion Josephine, dau. of George and Josephine Chilcoat, b. 11th Mo. 10th 1860, d. 3rd Mo. 18th 1949. (Headstone M.J.C.).*
Edward Eugene, husband of Anna P. Chilcoat, b. Oct. 2, 1855, d. July 20, 1924. (Head - E.E.C.).*
Anna P. Chilcoat, wife of Edward Eugene Chilcoat, b. 1850, d. Dec. 23, 1927.*
Our Father, James B. Wainwright, d. Aug. 17, 1876 in the 64th year of his age. (Head - J.B.W.).
Amanda, wife of James B. Wainwright, d. on the 11th of 1st Mo. 1836 (?), aged 35 years, 2 mos. and 9 days.
Ella Rebecca, dau. of George and Josephine Chilcoat, b. 5th Mo. 11th 1858, d. 4th Mo. 11th 1926. (Head - E.R.C.).*
Mary Matilda, dau. of George and Josephone Chilcoat, b. 1st Mo. 21st 1857, d. 5th Mo. 21st 1925. (Head - M.M.C.).*
(Top) Father.
(Front) George Chilcoat, b. 4th Mo. 12th 1827, d. 9th Mo. 17th 1914. (Head - G.C.).
(Top) Mother.
(Front) Elizabeth Josephine, wife of Geo. Chilcoat of G., b. 11th Mo. 7th 1831, d. 3rd Mo. 12th 1904. (Head - E.J.C.).*
Geo. Chilcoat, Sr., d. 2nd Mo. 12th 1876, aged 82 years. (Head - G.C.).
Matilda, wife of Geo. Chilcoat, Sr., d. 12th Mo. 6th 1875, aged 84 years. (Head - M.C.).
Leah Ann, wife of John Loats (?), d. Aug. 20, 1844, aged 21 years, 25 days.
Oscar P., son of John & Leah A. Loats (?), b. Nov. 29, 1843, d. June 28, 1844.
Father, Robert Mortland, b. Sept. 23rd, 1770, d. April 14th, 1838. (R.M. - foot).*
Ellen M. Griffith, b. Nov. 27, 1826, d. March 29, 1895. (Head - E.M.G.).
Abram Griffith, b. 2, d. 5, mo. 1829, d. 8, d. 9, mo. 1898.
Edward G. Wheeler, 1856-1927. Wheeler (Head - Father).
Anna L. Griffith, wife of Isaac K. Griffith, b. Sept. 14, 1864, d. Aug. 6, 1930.
Griffith, R. Adele, 1872-19__. Isaac K., 1862-1936.
Maggie P., dau. of Edwin & Penelope Griffith, d. 8th Jan. 1876 in her 16th year (M.P.G. - head).
Edwin Griffith, b. 20th of 12th Mo. 1826, d. 1st of 4th Mo. 1896.
Penelope Parks, wife of Edwin Griffith, b. 31st day 7th Mo. 1830, d. 13th day 12th Mo. 1909. (Head - P.P.G.).
Elizabeth M., dau. of Edwin & Penelope Griffith, b. 9th day 9th Mo 1854, d. 22nd day 2 Mo. 1901.
William D. Griffith, husband of Emma Given, b. 26th day 8th Mo. 1856, d. 27th day 1st Mo. 1929 (W.D.G.).
Emma Given Griffith, wife of William D. Griffith, b. 22nd day 6th Mo. 1855, d. 22nd day 3rd Mo. 1939 (E.G.G.).
Roberta Griffith, b. 26th day 1st Mo. 1891, d. 3rd day 7th Mo. 1967 (R.G.-head).
Thos. T. Griffith, b. 10th of the 5th Mo. 1825, d. 3rd of the 4th Mo. 1897 (T.T.G. - foot).
John M. Griffith, b. tenth month 5th 1837, d. tenth month 4th 1914 (J.M.G.-Foot).
R. Julia Griffith, b. first month 9th 1840, d. sixth month 11th 1918 (R.J.G.-foot).
(Front) Bertha E. G. Greenwell, April 25, 1869 - May 20, 1938. Somerset Spencer Greenwell, Jan. 15, 1862 - June 9, 1948.

(Rear)   To my beloved wife, her beloved husband. (Footers - B.E.G.G. and
S.S.G.).*
Thomas T. Griffith, b. 26 of 10 mo. 1788, d. 15 of 8 mo. 1871 (head - T.T.G.).
Rachel M. Griffith, b. 29th 11th mo. 1795, d. 8th 4th mo. 1888 (R.M.G. - head).
Martha E. Gent, d. 3 mo. 31st 1889, aged 68 years.
Wm. Gent, May 18, 1823, d. May 1, 1901, aged 80 years (W.G.).
Rachel Philena Gent, wife of J. Griffith Gent, d. Jan. 1, 1917, aged 59 years.
(R.P.G. - head).
J. Griffith Gent, d. April 18, 1917, aged 64 years (J.G.G.).
Note: North of the meeting house there are some rough unmarked stones that
probably designate burials of early days of cemetery.

MAYS CHAPEL

Mays Chapel Methodist Church is located at Jenifer and Mays Chapel Roads in the Eighth District of Baltimore County. The old church is on the southeast corner. It is a wooden building painted white. It and the cemetery are enclosed by a white wooden fence. The new church is on the northeast corner. Its cornerstone reads "Mays, M. E. Church, 1902". The cemetery is behind the church. Copied in May 1972 by William Hollifield, III.

THE OLD CHURCH

Mama, Margaret C., wife of W. A. Eppley, b. Aug 6, 1863, d. Dec. 27, 1897.
(At the base of the stone - W. G. Brooks, Philopolis - the stonecutter.)*
Father, Joshua L. Mays, d. April 10, 1888, aged 59 years, 2 mos. and 14 days.
(At base of the stone - Birehall, the stonecutter.)*
Dorcas J., wife of Joshua L. Mayes, d. June 8, 1877, aged 43 years, 5 mos. and 2 days. (At base of stone - Birchall, Glen Rock.)*
Joshua L., son of Joshua L. & Dorcas J. Mayes, d. Oct. 1, 1876, aged 6 days.*
William R., son of Joshua L. & Dorcas J.Mayes, d. Jan. 26, 1875, aged 6 years, 2 mos. & 6 days.*
Joshua R., son of J. L. & D. J. Mayes, b. Dec. 23, 1860, d. Dec. 29, 1862.
Dorcas Mayes, d. Jan. 6, 1886, aged 79 years.*
Jeremiah Mayes, d. Nov. 4, 1886, aged 84 years. (At base of stone - Birchall, Glen Rock, Pa.)*
Achsah, wife of Jeremiah Mayes, d. Feb. 22, 1883, aged 83 years. (At base of the stone - Birchall.)*
Elizabeth, wife of Thomas Burns, d. Oct. 4, 1889 in the ____year of her age.
(At the base of the stone - Taylor, Jarrettsville.)
Thomas Burns, Sr., b. Oct. 29, 1789, d. Sept. 23, 1873.
Eliza Jane, dau. of John & Eliza Thomas, aged 23 years and 2 mos.*
Henry Eigus, d. Dec. 14, 1884, aged 55 years.*
Husband, Charles Phillips, d. Nov. 16, 1894, aged 33 years.*
__n W. F. Tracey, d. July 28, 1899, aged 22 years, son of Wm. & Elizabeth Tracey. (Footstone - J.W.F.T.)
Frances L., dau. of Roebuck & Elizabh Russell, b. 3rd Dec. 1862, d. 6th March 1866.
Our Mother, Elizabeth Russell who departed this life April 26, 1884, aged 68 years.
Our Father, Roebuck Russell who departed this life, Oct. 24, 1882, aged 66 years.
Katie L., dau. of John H. & Maggie Warner, d. May 14, 1890, aged 2 years, 7 mos.
William F. Duering, husband of Elizabeth Duering, d. March 16, 1909, aged 23 years.

Mary A. Duering, b. June 2, 1834, d. Sept. 11, 1901, aged 67 years.*
George T. Duering, b. Feb. 20, 1859, d. March 8, 1889. William A. Duering, June 17, 1875 - Sept. 6, 1892.*
Our Father, Robert F. Price, b. 14th Nov. 1807, d. 26th May 1866.
Baby, 1889-1889.
Father, Frederick, husband of Susanah Greaser, Dec. 22, 1836 - Oct. 2, 1885.*
Sister, Sarah A., dau. of Susanah and the late Frederick Greaser, Jan. 1, 1868 - April 20, 1884.*
Sylvester Greaser, d. Dec. 18, 1878 in the 77th year of his age.*
Annie B. Greaser, d. July 14, 1887, aged 82 years.*
Father, Jacob Greaser, 1832-1900.
Mother, Matilda Greaser, 1839-1919.
Mother, Lydia E. Osborne, 1864-1906.
William R. Greaser, d. April 1, 1891, aged 23 years.*
Mary Olevia, dau. of Jacob & Matilda Greaser, d. Aug. 6, 1863, aged 11 mos., and 12 days.*
Bertha Greaser Cross, Dec. 1873 - June 1901.

THE NEW CHURCH

Parks, John F., Sept. 2, 1868 - June 26, 1916. Martha Parks Bagley, May 11, 1878 - Dec. 28, 1945.
James Glen Miller, Feb. 19, 1945 - Dec. 25, 1950.
Spencer, Melvin E., Jan. 4, 1910 - April 9, 1959. (Space, probably for wife's name).
William Cockey, son of Thomas B. & Harriet E. Cockey, b. May 30, 1882, d. June 7, 1904, aged 22 years.*
Greaser, John E., Dec. 11, 1870 - Feb. 19, 1959. Elisha G., Aug. 25, 1878 - Feb. 10, 1953. (There is space for a third name.) On other side of this stone: Greaser, J. Robert, March 27, 1900 - April 23, 1959. Stephen E., Jan. 31, 1905 - May 16, 1922. Theodore E., Nov. 9, 1902 - Dec. 10, 1902.
Poe, George C., 1865-1942. His wife, Emma J., 1873-1949. Footstones: Mother, Father.
Government marker with a cross at the top: William H. Poe, Maryland, Sgt. 320 Field Arty, 82 Div., World War I, Oct. 8, 1889 - Sept. 8, 1951.
Mahlon M. Poe, Feb. 2, 1904 - Aug. 17, 1960.
Raymond Burns, May 15, 1891 - Sept. 29, 1951.*
Parks, Charles, d. 1904. Eudoica, d. 1932.
Government marker with a cross at the top: William P. Parks, Maryland PFC, 313 Infantry 79 Div., World War I, June 6, 1887 - Aug. 28, 1949.
Parks, Alverta Frances, Feb. 22, 1879 - May 10, 1927. Howard, Sept. 8, 1876 - Feb. 4, 1942.
Freeland, William R., 1887-1958. Vera M., 1886 (No date of death).
Parks, Howard E., Jan. 11, 1903 - March 23, 1966. Ruth R., Sept. 15, 1907---.
Bayne, John Earl, 1900-1955. Frances E., 1914---.
Headstone: Poe. One footstone.
Ethel E., Aug. 21, 1888 - Nov. 11, 1960.
Charles G. Parks, 1897-1946.
Mother, Mamie C. Parks, wife of Michael H. Haviland, April 18, 1892 - May 14, 1954.
Father, Michael H. Haviland, husband of Mamie C. Parks, Jan. 31, 1892 - Dec. 6, 1964.
Parks, Durbin D., July 5, 1904 - July 11, 1950. Hazel M., Aug. 22, 1906---.
Crout, Clinton W., May 17, 1885 - April 18, 1957. Gertrude I., Aug. 4, 1896---.
Bennett Francis, son of Edward & Annie Parks, b. Feb. 25, 1910, d. July 12, 1912. By his parents.*

Mother, Anna May, wife of John E. Parks, Aug. 12, 1884 - June 20, 1927. By her husband and children.*
Father, John E. Parks, Nov. 21, 1875 - Sept. 10, 1945.
Father, Albert S. Bagley, b. March 10, 1844, d. Feb. 4, 1913.*
Mother, Mary Elizabeth, wife of Albert S. Bagley, b. Feb. 12, 1852, d. Sept. 5, 1926.*
Bagley, Eugene M., Feb. 16, 1879 - Jan. 6, 1958, Father. Mary R., Nov. 5, 1874- Feb. 8, 1945, Mother.
Front: Hezekiah Musgrove, b. Feb. 8, 1851, d. Feb. 16, 1915. Rebecca Musgrove, b. Feb. 10, 1856, d. Sept. 27, 1925.
South side of this stone: Virginia M. Musgrove, b. Feb. 13, 1916, d. Aug. 21, 1919.
North side of this stone: Harry C. Musgrove, b. Aug. 18, 1884, d. Dec. 1, 1957.
This stone is in the center of a lot, next eight are footstones. Five are on the west side of the lot and three are on the east side.
H.M.
R.M.
Laura V. Musgrove, July 4, 1886 - Oct. 25, 1969.
H.C.M.
T.P.H.
V.M.M.
William Lloyd Musgrove, Aug. 5, 1906 - Feb. 18, 1964.
Sara C. Downey, Oct. 18, 1911 - Dec. 28, 1967.
Irene, wife of Chas. E. Parks, b. Jan. 16, 1869, d. Feb. 17, 1922.*
John F. Coffey, May 4, 1909, Sept. 8, 1966.
William F. Coffey, Feb. 23, 1912 - April 19, 1971.
James I. Wetherell, b. Dec. 10, 1841, d. April 23, 1913, aged 72 years.
Harold L., husband of Elizabeth J. Greaser, July 18, 1902 - March 21, 1927.*
Isiah J. Kenney, Nov. 7, 1871 - Jan. 6, 1915.
Greaser, Edgar E., Aug. 2, 1876 - Nov. 21, 1966. Elizabeth V., Oct. 4, 1877 - Dec. 25, 1960.
William H. Myers, Jan. 13, 1877 - April 2, 1930.
Bessie M. Myers, Dec. 15, 1879 - Sept. 14, 1948.
Thomas E., son of Wm. H. & Bessie M. Myers, June 11, 1905 - Nov. 6, 1917.*
Bennett F. Myers, March 15, 1908 - April 13, 1920.
Samuel Doll, d. Feb. 15, 1934.
Evelyn G. Parks, 1921-1950.
Carolyn C. Parks, Sept. 9, 1918 - Dec. 3, 1958.
Anna L. Parks, 1915-1946.
Mott G. Parks, husband of Lois M. Parks, June 28, 1914 - Dec. 5, 1958.
Parks, Matilda L., 1891-1954. A. G. Mott, 1886-1950.
Headstone: Musgrove. One footstone.
Pinkney W., March 15, 1908 - Sept. 28, 1971.
Florence S. Rapp, Feb. 8, 1879 - April 24, 1965.
Harry Bender Rapp, Sept. 26, 1875 - Feb. 4, 1943.
Parks, Julia A. July 12, 1905 - Aug. 6, 1956. John E., Dec. 31, 1900---.
Joseph M. Staton, June 29, 1907 - Nov. 4, 1964. (Footstone: Dad)
Parks, Lloyd L. "Butts", 1921-1969. Flossie E., 1921---.
Bagley, Mother, Mary V., 1910-1967. Paul T., 1936---. Nancy C., 1940---.
Thomas, John B., 1886---. Eva P., 1890-1957.
Lucas, Laverne, Aug. 14, 1919---. Edward, Feb. 15, 1910 - June 2, 1964. Patricia, Sept. 10, 1940 - April 6, 1958.
Dawson, Granville, Sept. 29, 1908 - April 29, 1961. Margaret E., Sept. 22, 1917 - Feb. 26, 1959.
Reber, Harold W., July 25, 1905 - Jan. 9, 1963. Esther M., Dec. 20, 1912---.
Parks, Allen Owens, June 3, 1907 - Sept. 22, 1964. Evelyn M., Jan. 14, 1911---.

Schaefer, Walter G., July 31, 1884 - Jan. 28, 1964.   Bazie A., Aug. 28, 1887-
Jan. 29, 1960.
Schaefer, Margaret Hazel, May 27, 1910 - May 31, 1966. Walter E., May 29,
1911---.
Jackson, Dorothy D., July 21, 1911 - July 11, 1960. James C., July 21, 1908---.
Baby, Marian Ellen Beardsley, Oct. 22, 1957 - Dec. 9, 1957.
Frank K. G. Peters, March 21, 1880 - April 25, 1963.
Nona F. Peters, June 28, 1894 - May 13, 1968.
Ayers, John W., May 4, 1901---. Wadie E., Dec. 26, 1902 - Nov. 11, 1964.
Wagner, L. Sterling, Jan. 19, 1894---. Florence M., June 22, 1892---.
On the back of this stone is the surname Shock.
Frank M. Fisher, 1886-1961.
Grace G. Fisher, 1897-1970.
Headstone with Fisher on the front and Burrier on the back. One footstone.
Olivia P. Fisher, April 18, 1898 - Aug. 24, 1966.
Headstone: Stanley-Spicer - In loving memory. One Footstone.
Virginia Dare, 1929-1964.
Headstone: Harrison. One Footstone.
James Joshua Harrison, June 10, 1908 - April 13, 1971.
Ruhl, Frances M., April 29, 1909 - Dec. 9, 1957. Preston, Dec. 23, 1902---.
Headstone: Kelley-Mays, Joshua Talbott Kelley, Oct. 14, 1888 - July 28, 1971.
Hanna- Frances Kelley, Oct. 18, 1913---. On the back of this stone is the
surname Bell. Two footstones.
Martha E. Mays, Mother of H. Frances Kelley, 1875-1967.
Government marker with a cross at the top: Joshua T. Kelley, Maryland PFC,
313 Inf. 79 Div., World War I PH, Oct. 14, 1888 - July 28, 1971.
Bacon, Qalvin E., Aug. 30, 1925---. Virginia Mae, June 13, 1927 - Feb. 2, 1971.
Headstone: Merryman. One footstone.
Dora M. Merryman, June 15, 1889 - Sept. 2, 1958.
Daughter, Pamela Lynne Luttrell "Tinkerbell", Jan. ___, 1960 - Dec. 28, 1969.*
Ethel Fisher Vogt, Oct. 13, 1897 - Dec. 23, 1960.
Guy Naylor, Sept. 3, 1923 - Dec. 23, 1965.
Juanita C. Broach, 1922-1969.
Cofiell, Alverta Frances, Oct. 12, 1909 - July 3, 1960. William M., May 25,
1902---.
Bubert, Howard Matheson, Dec. 5, 1922 - Jan. 8, 1971. Footstone.
Government marker with a cross at the top: Howard M. Bubert, Jr., Maryland,
1st Lieut., U. S. Army, World War II, Dec. 5, 1922 - Jan. 8, 1971.
Joseph F. Chenowith, Dec. 26, 1924 - Sept. 8, 1971.
Frank P. Dunlap, Oct. 16, 1902 - May 27, 1967.
Theodore Zachary Turney, son of Septhen and Carolyn, Sept. 2, 1964 - Oct. 12,
1969.
Edwin Harvey Tillery, Nov. 28, 1910 - July 12, 1971.
Mother, Bertha V. Hatten, June 26, 1892 - May 12, 1970.
Government marker with a cross at the top: Harry J. McDowell, Pvt., 1303
Service Unit, World War II, Feb. 17, 1922 - Nov. 9, 1970.
Walter Morgan Morris, Nov. 9, 1915 - Oct. 7, 1971.
Weissman, Charles, 1895-1966.
Harrington, (blank space, probably for wife's name) Earle, Nov. 24, 1899 -
Nov. 18, 1960.
Mother, Elizabeth K. Minton, March 5, 1916 - May 15, 1955.
Charles W. Deitz, 1923-1969.

ASHLAND PRESBYTERIAN CHURCH CEMETERY

Located on Paper Mill Road, north side of road east of York Road. Cockeysville Quadrant. Church founded 1874. Cemetery begins at road, west of the church, and swings in an arc around to the north side of the church.

(From West to east)
Beach, father, Clifton E., June 12, 1902 - Dec. 29, 1960. Mother, Dorothy M., July 16, 1908 - Jan. 29, 1957.
Mary R. Kelly, dau. of E. F. and Elizabeth Kelly, b. Dec. 19, 1869, d. Nov. 12, 1870 (M.R.K. - foot).
(Front - south) Husband, Elisha F. Kelley, b. April 19, 1840, d. June 21, 1886.
(Left - West) Jane Denmead, b. Nov. 22, 1868, d. Nov. 23, 1868. Mary Ridgely, b. Dec. 19, 1869, d. Nov. 12, 1870, children of Elisha F. & Elizabeth S. C. Kelley.*
Richardson (Monument - both sides).
James P. Richardson, Maryland, RD 3 U. S. Navy, June 3, 1935 - Sept. 25, 1957.
Lawrence Everett, son of William & Charcilla Parks, d. May 18, 1866, aged 1 year and 2 mos. (G.F.P. - foot).
Maggie Owens, dau. of William & Charcilla Parks, d. July 16, 1875, aged 4 years, 6 mos. and 13 days (M.O.P.).
Seymour Gowan, son of William & Charcilla Parks, d. July 5, 1875, aged 2 years, 3 mos. and 3 days.
(Top) Mother.
Sarah Grafton, d. Sept. 8, 1926, aged 85 years. (S.G.)*
Sadie, b. May 4, 1894, d. July 28, 1903, dau. of Ephraim and Hannah J. Harding.*
Mary E., b. Aug. 18, 1892, d. Feb. 13, 1893, dau. of Ephraim & Hannah J. Harding (M.E.H. - foot).
(Monument to rear) Harding, William J., Sept. 8, 1897 - June 23, 1967.
Ephraim M., April 3, 1866 - June 4, 1948, Hannah J., July 30, 1872 - July 15, 1939.
(Top) Parks.
(Front) John Parks, d. July 5, 1917, aged 76 years. (J.P. - foot).*
(Top) Parks.
(Front) Sarah, wife of John Parks, b. May 16, 1838, d. May 25, 1895. (S.P. - head).*
Margaret, wife of John Parks, d. Aug. 10, 1889 in her 83rd year. (M.P.)*
John Parks, Sr., b. June 5, 1796, d. Feb. 9, 1878 (J.P. - foot).
Our Mother, Elizabeth H. Deal, May 22, 1859 - July 17, 1915.*
Elmer B., son of John E. & Kate Hilgerman, b. July 11, 1880, d. Sept. 23, 1881 (E.B.H. - foot).
Sheeler (monument - both sides).
Father, Bradley T. Sheeler, June 5, 1854 - Nov. 25, 1932.
Mother, Mary E. Sheeler, Nov. 11, 1860 - Feb. 21, 1924.
(Row to north) Son, Jacob K. Sheeler, Dec. 10, 1878 - Dec. 20, 1942.
Wife, Mary E. Sheeler, Dec. 19, 1880 - May 31, 1946.
Husband, Charles E. Sheeler, March 13, 1875 - Jan. 31, 1954.
(Backs to above 6 graves)
Thomas B. Herrington, b. Nov. 15, 1838, d. Feb. 15, 1918. Mary E. Herrington, b. June 5, 1829, d. Feb. 21, 1897.
Elvira D., wife of Benjamin Bennett, b. March 15, 1816, d. May 5, 1888. (E.D.P. - foot) By her daughter, Mary A. Bennett.*
North of Thomas B. Herrington. Elvira J., wife of J. W. Bennett, b. March 3, 1844, d. April 30, 1885. (E.J.B. - foot)*
(Monument - South) Kurtz.
(North) Thacker.
Sherman L., 1878-1935.

May C., 1880-1926.
G. McCullough Thacker, 1914-1964.
(Front & South) Harriet Leutz, b. Nov. 20, 1820, d. March 17, 1908, Kurtz.
(Left-West) Catharine Kurtz, Nov. 25, 1851 - June 11, 1938. William F. Kurtz, Dec. 24, 1880 - June 23, 1969.
Thomas Kurtz, d. Aug. 29, 1895, aged 53 years, 8 mos. and 3 days.*
(Also individual markers: H.L., C.K., T.K.)
(East) Kone.
(North) Harry W. Kone, b. Aug. 29, 1866, d. March 21, 1901. Sarah E., wife of Harry W. Kone, b. March 31, 1867.
Amanda J. Kone, 1844-1926. William H. Kone, 1842-1929.
(Individual markers, S.E.K., H.W.K.).
Our brother, Daniel Webster, son of Daniel W. & Mary E. Chipman, d. March 22, 1933.
Robert Hollenshade, 1868-1926. His wife, Julia H. Hollenshade, 1880-1958.
(Foot markers - J.H.H., R.H.)
(This brings us to the rear of church, where the cemetery becomes wider.)
John W. Frankenfield, d. May 17, 1930, aged 86 years (J.W.F. - foot).
Elizabeth F. Frankenfield, d. April 4, 1910, aged 63 years (E.F.F. - foot).
Shipley (Monument)*
Emory C., Sr., Jan. 25, 1869 - May 14, 1953.
Sarah S., March 10, 1872 - Sept. 9, 1966.
Mary Jane, June 6, 1900 - May 3, 1907, dau. of Emory C. & Sarah Shipley.
(Three lines illegible verse.)
Lloyd M., July 10, 1899 - July 25, 1968.
(Begin an enclosure).
(South) Harry F. Thuma, b. Feb. 12, 1871, d. Aug. 25, 1893.*
(West) Jeremigh A. Thuma, b. Jun 7, 1848, d. Nov. 17, 1899.
(North) Laura E. Thuma, b. Feb. 14, 1850, d. Aug. 8, 1929. Mary E. Thuma, April 3, 1882 - Oct. 27, 1955.
(East) Lulu A. Thuma, b. April 29, 1886, d. Feb. 21, 1900. James E., b. Aug. 5, 1874, d. Oct. 27, 1876. T. C. Blair, b. Nov. 26, 1883, d. July 6, 1884. G. M., b. Oct. 20, 1878, d. Sept. 7, 1887.
M.E.P.T.
Mother, L.E.T.
Father, J.A.T.
M.F.T.
L.A.T.
Richard R. Thumas, Dec. 3, 1890 - Jan. 28, 1961
(End of Thuma enclosure).
Thomas T. Thuma, b. Dec. 21, 1870, d. Nov. 15, 1902. Nannie C. Rippeon, d. April 6, 1941 (foot - T.T.T. - N.C.R.).
Riley
Halbert (Monument).
Naomi E., 1850 - 1929.
(Row behind Halbert Monument)
Sarah Burnett Halbert, b. March 13, 1828, d. July 9, 1906.*
William Halbert, b. June 23, 1828, d. Feb. 2, 1900.
Kate L., dau. of William & Sarah R. Halbert, b. May 8, 1863, d. Aug. 25, 1886.*
W. Montroville, son of William & Sarah R. Halbert, b. Nov. 23, 1860, d. Aug. 15, 1885 (W.M.H. - foot).
Corbett D. Nelson, April 4, 1893 - May 13, 1961.
Michael Keith Uhler, son of Richard A. and Marlene Y. Uhler, July 1, 1863 - Jan. 22, 1964.
Aquilla Bareham, Aug. 19, 1886 - Sept. 10, 1962.
Howard Sheeler, Sept. 12, 1868 - March 6, 1927.
(Top) Brother

(Front) James Edwards, Jan. 22, 1856 - Feb. 10, 1914 (J.E. - foot).
George Greig Fraser, b. April 12, 1870, d. Oct. 17, 1913 (G.G.F. - foot).
Bessie Kone Dornin, 1876-1939.
A. Lardner Dornin, 1880-1920.
Ambrose, James Thomas, 1862-1938. His wife, Sallie J., 1868-1942.
Lu Ambrose Fay, 1891-1924.
Lucretia E. Ambrose, 1839-1909.
(Behind the above grave) Cora Coale, wife of Thomas J. Casey, 1894-1921 (C.C.C.-foot).
(Row back at woods)
The Rev. Dr. E. D. Newberry, late pastor of the Ashland Presbyterian Church, d. March 7, 1911, aged 84 years.*
Unmarked fieldstone.
Sarah, dau. of William & Amanda Smith, b. Dec. 21, 1877, d. July 3, 1878, aged 6 mos., 12 days. (S.S. - foot).*

SHERWOOD PROTESTANT EPISCOPAL CHURCH
COCKEYSVILLE, MD.

Sherwood Episcopal Church was founded 1835. It is east of York Road, south of Sherwood Road in the town of Cockeysville. Cockeysville Quadrant. Cemetery begins east of driveway and bounding on Sherwood Road. Rows are recorded north to south, from west of the church to the east of the church and up the slope.

(Begin enclosed plot)
Isabella McK. Merryman, b. Sept. 22, 1896, d. Sept. 27, 1896 (I.McK.M. - foot).
James McKenney Merryman, b. Oct. 21, 1867, d. Aug. 27, 1917.
Isabella Brown Merryman, b. June 1, 1872, d. Jan. 20, 1924.
(End of plot)
John Merryman Franklin, Jr., April 10, 1925 - Oct. 26, 1946.
(Front) Tyrie.
(Rear) The G. Walter Tyrie Family.
G. Walter Tyrie, Jan. 20, 1889 - Sept. 11, 1970.
Elwood H. Banister, June 12, 1886 - Dec. 20, 1946.
Yingling (Monument)
Mary G., 1915-1940 (To left of above).
Donald W. Merryman, Oct. 12, 1931 - March 5, 1957.
O. T. S. (Pointed corner marker).
Nellie Z. Minnick, Feb. 21, 1887 (Still living).
O. L. Minnick, May 30, 1885 - Nov. 2, 1951.
Minnick (Monument)
Lee Zink Minnick, Dec. 27, 1918 - Feb. 6, 1919.
Dorothy Tenant Love, wife of Albert Louis Thomas, Aug. 5, 1890 - March 22, 1968.
Janet Mitchell Love, Dec. 7, 1909 - March 8, 1952.
Dorothy Horner, dau. of Joshua Horner, Jr., and wife of Harry Adair Love, b. March 22, 1882, d. Oct. 17, 1967.
Harry Adair Love, Feb. 3, 1878 - July 4, 1912.
Ida May Goldberg, Jan. 13, 1932 - March 26, 1965.
Viola E. Goldberg, Jan 14, 1897 - Feb. 26, 1966.
Laura J. Lynch, July 26, 1856 - Feb. 25, 1935.
Benjamin Robert Benson, Jr., M.D., d. Sept. 22, 1936.
Caroline Sumner Bartleson, d. Aug. 17, 1937.
Hibberd E. Bartleson, 1852-1923.
Eichler, Eliza A., Feb. 24, 1872 - Feb. 11, 1959. Lawrence C., June 19, 1876-July 7, 1950.

Fanny Holland, b. May 13, 1846, d. Aug. 7, 1854, children of Thomas & Fanny P.
Love (front).
(Rear) Johanna, b. Jan. 14, 1853, d. Aug. 7, 1854.
(Left) John Thomas, b. March 3, 1844, d. Nov. 15, 1852.
(Right) Bessie, b. Aug. 3, 1857, d. June 8, 1859.
Capt. Thomas Love, b. Aug. 27, 1803, d. April 13, 1885.
Fanny Priscilla, dau. of George G. Presbury and wife of Thomas Love, b. Sept. 18, 1817, d. Feb. 4, 1877.
IHS, Eleanor Bond Love, wife of Albert T. Love, d. April 15, 1904, aged 55 years.
Albert Thomas Love, July 23, 1848, Jan. 18, 1910.
Thomas Love, M.D., b. March 25, 1753, d. March 1, 1821. His wife, Martha Worthington, b. April 9, 1775, d. Jan. 23, 1846.
Vachel Worthington, b on 8th of Eb. 1769, d. at Loveton the 22nd of Oct. 1832.*
Berry, J. Mauduit Berry, 1879-1941. John Hay Berry, 1946-1946. Helen L. Berry, 1881-1960.
Ann Ridgely Hartman, March 1, 1909 - July 27, 1938 (A.R.H. - foot).
Minnick, Dorothy B., 1916-1945. Millard A., 1911-1964.
(Continuation of Yinglings) Mary E., 1883----.
Charles E., 1876-1937.
Wilmer A., 1903-1929.
(Front) Fauntleroy, Margaret Galloway, Sept. 25, 1863 - Aug. 16, 1960.
(Rear) Francis Chalk, d. Nov. 18, 1943. Sarah E. Eichler, April 3, 1911 - Dec. 20, 1919.
Bolton Jackson Love, Aug. 18, 1879 - March 6, 1962.
Frances Louisa Love, 1881-1944.
A. Gallatin Love, July 27, 1888 - May 14, 1958.
(On Cross) John Adolphus Pindell, b. Dec. 20, 1884, d. May 14, 1916.
(On base) Lewin Hutcheson, wife of John Adolphus Pindell, b. Dec. 1, 1892, d. July 30, 1958.
(Rear) IHS, John A. Pindell, Jr., son of John A. & Lewin H. Pindell, b. May 26, 1916, d. Dec. 9, 1938. (Individual markers L.H.P., J.A.P., J.A.P., Jr.)
Robert Dunlop Wight, son of William H. & Agnes Dunlop Wight, 1876-1950.
Phillip Russell, Sept. 23, 1921 - March 3, 1925.
Helen M. Kone, Nov. 14, 1923 - May 9, 1952.
Frank J. Mungovan, Oct. 8, 1900 - Jan. 3, 1955.
(Stones now reverse orientation)
Ella Frances Scott, wife of William H. Bosley, Jr., Feb. 6, 1870 - April 5, 1957.
William H. Bosley, Jr., son of Wm. H. and Mary Cockey Bosley, April 24, 1878 - May 30, 1956.
Galloway, Aquilla C., 1871-1939. Alice W.,(Blank).
B. J. Franklin.
Bettie Austen, dau. of W. Harry & Virginia S. Jessop, Jan. 19, 1920 - Dec. 12, 1930.
W. Harry Jessop, April 1, 1890 - Dec. 21, 1962.
Dorothy Crowther, Feb. 28, 1894 - June 19, 1968.*
(Stones face either way)
William J. Bray, March 15, 1879 - July 6, 1950, friend of Susan, Sally and Stephen Redd, and Bobby Schenk.
James W. Hampton, Feb. 29, 1862 - July 4, 1946.
Bythenia C., dau. of William H. & Nancy Butler, d. Nov. 24, 1920, aged 65 years (B.C.B. - foot).
Staines, John C., 1873-1933. His wife, Margaret A., 1870-1929.*
George Jessop, Jr., March 11, 1887 - Dec. 29, 1944.
George Jessop, Sept. 3, 1847 - July 16, 1923 (G.J. - foot).
Bettie B. Jessop, July 1851 - May 1918 (B.B.J. - foot).
John Bosley Jessop, Oct. 12, 1885 - Dec. 18, 1960. Norton Merryman Jessop, Aug. 29, 1889 - Dec. 19, 1959 (Foot - N.M.J. - J.B.J.).

Woodall, Casper G., 1854-1934. Mary G., 1868-1947. (C.G.W.-M.G.W.)
G. Hilbinger (Footstone).
(Front) George Hilbinger, Dec. 31, 1854 - March 22, 1940. Ella A. Hilbinger, May 6, 1869 - July 14, 1952.
(Right) Margaret Hilbinger, wife of Ernest Chell, Dec. 2, 1903 - May 30, 1932.
(Rear) Wiley K. Hilbinger, Dec. 12, 1900. Anna G. Hilbinger, Aug. 12, 1907 - Oct. 16, 1963.
Booth.
John Albert Booth, husband of Fannie Thwaites Talbott, June 12, 1860 - June 6, 1940. His wife, Fannie Thwaites Talbott, Dec. 6, 1861 - June 24, 1943 (Foot - J.A.B., F.T.T.B.).
William Crawford Crowther, b. Sept. 10, 1882, d. Jan. 10, 1902.*
Eliza Jewell Crowther, wife of William B. Crowther, Nov. 4, 1859 - May 29, 1939 (E.J.C. foot).*
William Bosley Crowther, July 23, 1857 - July 16, 1920 (W.B.C. - foot).*
Hanna, J. Leland Hanna, July 1, 1850 - Jan. 8, 1931. Miriam E. Hanna, Dec. 20, 1859 - April 24, 1947 (Front).
(Rear) Hanna, Andrew J. Hanna, d. March 12, 1938.
(Front) Zink.
(Rear) B. C. Zink.
Mary Katherine, Nov. 26, 1924 - Feb. 10, 1926.
Frances B. Zink, Dec. 22, 1920 - Dec. 12, 1969.
Benjamin C. Zink, March 17, 1886 - Feb. 15, 1957.
Berdie P. Zink, Aug. 18, 1890 - July 9, 1862.
Henry Hess Zink, Aug. 31, 1896 - April 27, 1952.
Francis Bosley Crowther, July 3, 1874 - July 21, 1950. Eliza Leisenring Crowther, Nov. 16, 1877 - April 11, 1960.
Philip F. Zink, 1900-1956.
Kenney, Barbara S., 1863-1944. George B., 1861-1933.
T. Kenney.
Griffin, Father, Herbert Foster Griffin, 1866-1949. Mother, Sallie Bosley Talbott, 1867-1942.
Hess (Central monument surrounded by SHANK burials).
Harry H. Shank, d. May 23, 1940.
Theodore B. Shank, d. Jan. 8, 1943.
A. Margaretha Shank, d. Oct. 23, 1959.
(In row to rear) Henry Hess, April 4, 1842 - Oct. 29, 1915.
Elizabeth Hess, Oct. 9, 1841 - Jan. 30, 1919.
Rosa May Hess, d. May 16, 1927.
Mary B. Hess, Feb. 15, 1873 - Dec. 6, 1966. (End of Hess plot).
Robert E. Malone, d. July 29, 1944.
(Rear) Frantz.
(Front) A. Margaret, Jan. 3, 1866 - March 5, 1959. Thomas E., Nov. 11, 1861 - June 3, 1937. Frantz.
Clark, Adeline, Oct. 1, 1853 - Feb. 2, 1932. Robert, Aug. 16, 1846 - May 3, 1929.
Zink, Lilly H., 1879-1916. Leopold, 1865-1942.
Sophia S. Talbott, dau. of Joshua F. C. & Ann Eliza Talbott, April 27, 1857 - Aug. 2, 1915. (S.S.T. - to east).
Eliza Talbott, dau. of Joshua F.C. and Ann Eliza Talbott, Jan. 10, 1847 - Aug. 8, 1925 (E.T. - to east).
Anne C. Zink, Aug. 25, 1864 - Feb. 7, 1949.
John J. Zink, Sept. 15, 1861 - Nov. 8, 1917.
Howard C. Krout, Feb. 7, 1870 - Jan. 17, 1944. Annie Amelia Krout, Aug. 4, 1870 - Jan. 27, 1960.
Anna E. Evans, April 15, 1917 - July 28, 1964.
Edna C. Evans, Dec. 8, 1884 - Oct. 30, 1966.
Cockran, Ellen B., Nov. 22, 1861 - March 26, 1949.

George W. Evans, Jr., April 4, 1878 - July 8, 1935.
Cockran, Montgomery B., May 17, 1861 - Nov. 3, 1929.
J. Fred C. Talbott, July 29, 1843 - Oct. 5, 1918. Laura Beall Talbott, Oct. 8,
   1841 - Feb. 15, 1913. (Also Talbott on rear)
(Front) Edward G. Talbott, 1819-1851. T. Ellen Talbott, 1815-1906. Eliza M.
   Strahan, 1841-1864. Rebecca B. Glass, 1844-1875.
(Left) Sallie B. Talbott, 1846---. Grafton M. B. Talbott, 1848-1852. Joshia
   M. Talbott, 1849---.
Mary E. Bosley, 1851-1903. Grafton B. Strahan, 1864-1864.
(The "W. H. Wight" enclosure)
James Montell Wight, 1850-1905.
Mary Susan Griffith, widow of Nicholas R. Griffith of Montgomery Co., Md., b.
   March 7, 1825, d. June 20, 1899. Griffith (J. Tyrie, stonecutter's sig. on
   left).
John J. Wight, 1821-1900. His wife, Amelia A. Hyatt, 1826, 1901. Wight.
William H. Wight, 1847-1927. Agnes A. Dunlop Wight, 1855-1919.
Comfort M. W. Morrison, dau. of Judge Joshua F. Cockey, 1830-1904. (Foot -
   C.M.W.M.).
Comfort M. W. Offutt, 1868-1916.
Offutt (Massive cross monument).
N. Edward Offutt, Jr., 1902-1970.
Hoffman (Monument).
Lewis N. Zink, Nov. 3, 1872 - May 2, 1925.
Emma Z. Hoffman, April 6, 1874 - Jan. 31, 1922.
Charles C. Hoffman, March 12, 1871 - Feb. 28, 1945 (end group).
(Front) Marten Anzel, b. July 29, 1834, d. Oct. 25, 1905. Emma Anzel, 1852-
   1931.*
(Right) Christian Hoffman, b. Sept. 2, 1823, d. July 1911 (?). Wilhelmina
   Hoffman, b. Nov. 11, 1831, d. Dec. 21, 1878(?).
(Masonic symbol) John Tyrie, Oct. 3, 1860 - Aug. 19, 1944. Mary Jane Stubbs,
   wife of John Tyrie, Sept. 3, 1862 - March 14, 1936. Mabel Tyrie, dau. of
   John and Mary Jane Tyrie, March 16, 1891 - March 1, 1892.
Richard P. Clark, March 14, 1801 - Feb. 11, 1864, aged 68 years. Mary Clark,
   July 3, 1808 - April 1, 1892, aged 84 years. Clark.
Ella B. Clark, wife of George Zink, May 30, 1852 - Sept. 1, 1898.
George Zink, May 23, 1854 - March 27, 1925.
Hottes, Luella B., Aug. 15, 1900 - July 15, 1968.
(Front) A. Anderson.
(Right) (Odd Fellows Symbol) George Lucas Anderson, b. Jan. 2, 1819, d. Jan.
   17, 1896.*
(Rear) Ruth Ann, wife of George Lucas Anderson, b. Sept. 25, 1825, d. April
   16, 1899 (G.L.A. - foot).*
Charlotte D. Galloway, 1853-1923 (C.D.G. - foot).
Penelope S. Armstrong, 1864-1923. (P.S.A. - foot).
Roscoe G. Cross, Jr., Aug. 9, 1921 - May 17, 1937.
Maggie L. Cross, b. Sept. 16, 1959.*
Mark William T., b. Oct. 6, 1829, d. March 2, 1921. Elizabeth, b. Oct. 16,
   1834, d. April 16, 1909.
May Clark Zink, Sept. 13, 1871 - Oct. 25, 1904. Nellie Zink, March 18, 1903-
   Dec. 2, 1903.
Georgia B. Eckhart, Aug. 5, 1882 - Nov. 2, 1969.
Ruth A. Angel, 1894-1963.
CROSS (Monument)
Roscoe, Z. G. Cross, M.D., June 11, 1882 - Oct. 13, 1952.
William L. Boyce, April 21, 1907 - Sept. 10, 1955.
Maria M. Buckley, b. Dec. 20, 1832, d. June 2, 1915.
Emanuel Buckley, d. aged 68 years, 3 mos. and 24 days.*

Geo. Fowble, b. 1864, d. 1908. Wilhelmina A. Fowble, b. 1847, d. 1915.
Francis Ehret, b. 1877, d. 1898 (W.F., F.F., G.F.).
(West) William H. H. Loftus, b. June 25, 1875, d. March 27, 1917.
(North) James L. Halliwell, Nov. 26, 1884 - Dec. 22, 1964. His wife, Grace O.
Knapp, June 4, 1886 - June 10, 1962.
(East) John Knapp, b. Feb. 23, 1855, d. Nov. 4, 1930. Silinda Knapp, b. Jan.
1, 1858, d. June 1, 1934. Stella E. Knapp, b. Aug. 14, 1888, d. July 30,
1889. John Knapp, 1821-1894. Helwig Knapp, 1846-1893.
(This is the end of front portion of cemetery; resume at rear of church.)
Sadler, John Thomas, Feb. 27, 1905 - Oct. 28, 1966.
Louis McLane Merryman, Jr., Oct. 23, 1920 - Sept. 24, 1953.
Emily McLane Merryman, June 2, 1864 - March 5, 1950.
E. Gittings Merryman, Feb. 19, 1858 - April 8, 1913.
Josephine Brodix Merryman, Nov. 6, 1894 - Nov. 3, 1953.
Louis McLane Merryman, Jan. 5, 1890 - Oct. 19, 1960.
(Cockey Plot)
(North) Elizabeth Stansbury, b. May 26, 1853, d. Oct. 29, 1930.
(South) Stephen P. Hilbinger, b. Oct. 19, 1829, d. April 13, 1917. Margaret
Hilbinger, b. March 24, 1821, d. May 30, 1897. Albert G. Loftus, 1885-1888.
Edith I. Loftus, 1889-1905.
(East) Rupert J. Stansbury, b. May 26, 1850, d. Dec. 16, 1913. Susan P. Loftus,
1900-1911. Helen Lautenbach, 1890-1929.
Ella, wife of Graham Barker, dau. of George Jessop, Sr., d. March 25, 1882,*
Elizabeth Jessop, 1815-1854 (E.J. on rear).
George Jessop, Sr., b. July 6, 1803, d. April 3, 1887.
Ellen Ashton, wife of George Jessop, b. Oct. 24, 1821, d. May 6, 1906.
Nettie Jessop, wife of Pietro Palagano, b. May 8, 1862, d. June 1, 1886
(Sweitzer, Glen Rock, Pa., signature of carver).
Pietro Palagano, b. March 1, 1857, d. Oct. 28, 1942. Elizabeth A. Jessop, wife
of Pietro Palagano, b. May 11, 1859, d. Feb. 12, 1936.
William Holz Hall, b. Feb. 15, 1885, d. March 10, 1967. His wife, Marie A.
Palagano, b. March 15, 1894, d. Feb. 15, 1959.*
(Partially fenced enclosure):
Charles H. Black, Lieut. Commander U.S.N., b. March 28, 1844, d. Jan. 20,
1891.*
Elizabeth Merryman, wife of Charles H. Black and dau. of the late John Merryman,
d. at Hayfields, March 16, 1895, aged 45 years, 7 mos and 20 days. John
Merryman, son of Charles H. and Elizabeth Merryman Black, b. July 13, 1882,
d. Nov. 23, 1883.
E. G. M., Jr., March 16, 1898 - July 9, 1966.
John Merryman of Hayfields, b. Aug. 9, 1824, d. Nov. 15, 1881 - Merryman.
Ann Louisa Gittings, wife of John Merryman, d. at Hayfields, Feb. 15, 1897,
aged 71 years, 6 mos. and 23 days.*
Ann Gott, dau. of John and Ann Louisa Merryman, b. Aug. 3, 1845, d. April 19,
1917.*
William D. Merryman, fifth son of John & Ann Louisa Merryman of Hayfields, b.
Oct. 29, 1859, d. April 14, 1915. (W.D.M.-head)
John Merryman, second son of John Merryman of Hayfields and Ann Louisa, his
wife, d. Nov. 3, 1885, aged 31 years, 1 mo. and 29 days.
(Row of headstones: C.H.B., E.M.B., J.M.B., J.M. of H., A.L.M., W.D.M. & J.M.)
(Second row of enclosure)
J. Merryman Black, Oct. 2, 1885 - Feb. 23, 1955. (J.M.B.-head)
Nicholas Bosley Merryman of Hayfields, b. Feb. 19, 1852, d. Feb. 24, 1921.*
Wilmington N. McCleskey, wife of N. Bosley Merryman, b. Oct. 24, 1852, d. Oct.
26, 1923.* (W.N.M.-head)
John Merryman, April 22, 1884 - May 13, 1945. (J.M.-head)

41

Sally Love Merryman, wife of John Merryman, Nov. 3, 1884 - May 18, 1957.
(S.L.M.-head)
(A vault) N. M. Boxley
Louisa G. Merryman Nussear, Dec. 14, 1937.
Roger Brooke Taney, son of John & Ann Louisa Merryman, b. Dec. 5, 1864, d. July 5, 1865. (R.B.T.M.-head)
(Next to vault) Charles T. Kemp, Jr., Dec. 30, 1894 - Aug. 8, 1965. (C.T.K.-head)
Louisa Gittings, infant dau. of N. Bosley & Willie N. Merryman, d. Jan. 21, 1882. (L.G.M.-head)
George McCleskey, son of N. B. & W. N. Merryman, b. April 5, 1892, d. Sept. 26, 1892.* (G.M.M.-head)
(End of Merryman plot - begin Cockey plot)
Cockey (Monument)
Our son, Albert Cockey, who departed this life, June 27, 1893, aged 21 years.* (A.C.-head)
Joshua Frederick Cockey, b. Aug. 26, 1807, d. July 14, 1920. Sarah Jane,wife of Joshua F. Cockey, d. Sept. 1, 1895.* (S.J.C. and J.F.C. - head markers)
Bennett B. Cockey, May 21, 1901 - April 4, 1960.
Joshua F. Cockey, 5th son of Joshua F. and Nannie T. Cockey, husband of Ruth E. Cockey, April 10, 1895 - Feb. 19, 1959. (Headstone) Joshua F. Cockey, 5th, Pvt. 1st Class 313 Inf., U.S.A., decorated by U. S. and French Governments World War I.
Joshua F. Cockey, Jr., 1870-1919.
(Front) Father, Adam D. Talbott, b. Feb. 3, 1833, d. Feb. 26, 1897. Mother, Mary Ann Talbott, b. March 20, 1833, d. Oct. 27, 1895. Talbott.
(Left) Colgate A., wife of Thos. W. Offutt, b. April 2, 1865, d. Oct. 2, 1896. (A.D.T., M.A.T. at foot)
Parents, Adam D. & Mary Ann Talbott in memory of beloved dau. Fannie, b. Jan. 25, 1863, d. Feb. 15, 1889.* (F.T.-head)
Worthington, only son of Adam D. and Mary Ann Talbot(sic) who died suddenly Dec. 13, 1871 in the 16th year of his age.*
(Plot with iron fence)
Oswald Tilghman Shreve, husband of Ann Lux Buchanan and eldest son of Rosalie Tilghman and Thomas Jefferson Shreve, b. at Oxford, Talbot Co., Oct. 30, 1866, d. at Ruxton, Baltimore Co., Aug. 22, 1927.* (O.T.S.-head)
Ann Lux Buchanan, wife of Oswald Tilghman Shreve and dau. of Henrietta Gittings and James Hollis Buchanan, b. Aug. 3, 1865 at Mt. Vernon Place, Baltimore, the home of her Grandfather, Lambert Gittings, d. Sept. 13, 1949, Roland Park, Baltimore. (A.L.B.S.-head)
David Perin Buchanan, b. Feb. 23, 1837, d. Oct. 9, 1853, son of Charles Adams Buchanan and Ann Lus (sic), his wife.* (D.P.B.-head)
Ann Lux Buchanan, b. March 4, 1803, d. Dec. 18, 1883, dau. of Col. Thomas Deye Cockey and Ann Lux, his wife and wife of Charles Adams Buchanan.* (A.L.B.-head)
Charles Adams Buchanan, son of William, son of Dr. George Buchanan (Primus) of Druid Hill, son of Nungo Buchanan and Anna Barclay, his wife of Hiltoun and Auchentorlie, Scotland, b. on the third day of the tenth month, 1808 and departed this life on the twenty-fourth day of April, 1891.* (C.A.B.)
James Hollis Buchanan, son of Charles Adams Buchanan and Ann Lux, his wife, b. at Homeland, Baltimore Co., June 12, 1834, d. in Baltimore, May 23, 1911. (J.H.B.-head)
Dr. Charles Ashton, son of George & Ellen Jessop, b. Nov. 14, 1859, d. Oct. 19, 1889. (C.A.J.-head)
Emma Jessop, b. April 23, 1851, d. Feb. 2, 1876.
Smith, dau. Dorothy Crue, 1919-1948. Father, David John 1891-1959.
(Rear) Benson
(Front) Benson, Jeannette K., 1879-1965. Carroll P., 1879-1954.

Husband, Harry E. Crue, Jan. 14, 1947 - July 15, 1969.
Olevia Ann, dau. to Jacob & Mary Malehorn, d. April 24, 1841.*
(Rear) Zink
(Front) Margaret M., April 4, 1889. John H., Oct. 17, 1889 - Dec. 10, 1952.
Jane, wife of the Rev. Ira A. Easter, d. 18 May 1840, aged 44 years.
(East) Rev. Ira A. Easter, Paster of Sherwood Chapel, d. the 16th of Jan. 1840, aged 46 years.*
(Rear) Ricketts
(Front) Ricketts, Mary Zink, May 13, 1884 - July 26, 1957. Walter E., Oct. 7, 1883 - Nov. 23, 1960.
Maggie, only dau. of Rev. Cyrus & Emily Waters, d. Aug. 7, 1859, aged 5 years, 3 mos. & 8 days.*
Charles F. Meyers, Jan. 26, 1893 - Dec. 23, 1960.
Josiah Mason, son of Joshua A. L. and Penelope H. Bosley, d. Sept. 6, 1848, aged 2 years, 10 mos., 23 days.
George Keys, d. Feb. 3, 1891, aged 76 years, 9 mos. & 25 days.*
(Right) Ann R., wife of George Keys, d. Sept. 11, 1851, aged 29 years, 10 mos., and 6 days.
(Left-South) Mary J., wife of Geo. Keys, d. Sept. 7, 1906, aged 92 years, 2 mos, & 1 day.
Jane M. Pindell, March 15, 1873 - July 26, 1958.
Rev. Adolphus Thomas Pindell, 1840-1918, St. Johns, Kingsville, Trinity, Long Green 1866-1876, Sherwood Church, 1876-1916. Jane Hall Yellott Pindell, March 23, 1843 - May 12, 1924.*
Laura M. Pindell, Aug. 25, 1878 - March 24, 1958.
Thomas N. Pindell, Aug. 20, 1869 - Nov. 21, 1932.
Hettie Noble Pindell, Jan. 20, 1876 - Jan. 22, 1916.
David Sterrett Pindell, March 6, 1875 - June 2, 1955.
William Johnson, second son of Doctor and Anna J. Buck, d. Nov. 19, 1846, aged 1 year.
Dr. John S. Buck, d. July 2, 1847, aged 44 years.
Elizabeth Crowther Case, d. 1939, her husband,Howard Brown Case, lost in the Titanic, April 15, 1912, aged 47 years.
John Crowther, b. Aug. 24, 1831, d. Dec. 11, 1918.
Fannie, wife of John Crowther, b. Nov. 24, 1834, d. July 26, 1874. (Ind. Markers E.C.C., J.C., F.C.)
David Buchanan Merryman, May 9, 1856 - March 11, 1900. His wife, Bessie Montague Merryman, Aug. 19, 1864 - Nov. 28, 1964.
Arthur Yellott Pindell, son of the Rev. Adolphus T. and Jand H. Pindell of Cockeysville, June 23, 1882 - April 17, 1961. (A.Y.P.)
Daisy Warner Cockey, wife of Arthur Yellott Pindell and dau. of Joshua H. & Annie R. Cockey of My Lady's Manor, Dec. 14, 1881 - Feb. 24, 1955. (D.W.C.P.)
Herbert Bickford, Oct. 17, 1871 - Sept. 10, 1951.
Joshua Marsh, son of Amon & Rebecca Bosley, b. April 4, 1814, d. March 10, 1871.
Penellope H. Bosley, consort of Joshua M. Bosley, b. April 15, 1825, d. June 7, 1859, aged 34 years, 1 mo., and 22 days.
Rebecca B. Carrick, dau. of Penelope Merryman & Joshua Marsh Bosley, b. Jan. 27, 1859, d. July 9, 1931. (R.B.C.-foot)
Ann Louise, dau. of Penelope Merryman & Joshua Marsh Bosley, b. July 15, 1849, d. Feb. 27, 1934. (A.L.B.-foot)
Thomas L., son of T. L. & F. E. Worthington, d. July 30, 1872, aged 3 mos. (T.L.W.-foot)
Catherine Campbell, formerly of Philadelphia, but late of this County, d. March 31, 1853, aged 76 years. (McBride & Shaw, Balto, signature of stonemason) (C.C.-foot)
Gist T., son of Petter E. and Elizabeth R. Cockey, b. May 6, 1846, d. Feb. 9, 1849. (G.T.C.-foot)

Belinda Elizabeth Cockey, b. Oct. 9, 1825, d. April 5, 1849. (B.E.C.-foot)
Peter F. Cockey, b. at Cockeysville, Oct. 21, 1812, d. Aug. 15, 1906.
 (P.F.C., E.R.C.)
Charlotte D. Owings, d. April 6, 1857, aged 83 years.
(North) John C. Owings, Jr., d. April 25, 1813, aged 28 years.
(East) Cassandra D. Van Pradelles, lost at sea in 1815, aged 40 years.
(South) Colegate D. Owings, d. March 1, 1828, aged 78 years.
(West) Fanny T. D. Taylor, d. June 23, 1870, aged 81 years.
John C. Owings, Sr., d. Feb. 3, 1810, aged 74 years.
Fanny T. D. Taylor, b. Jan. 9, 1789, d. June 23, 1870.* (F.T.D.T.-on urn at head)
(Bosley Enclosure)
(Central Monument) (Front) Eleanor C. Thompson, d. Dec. 26, 1931, dau. of Rachel
 Cole and John Bosley of Wm. & Mollie Bosley, d. Feb. 6, 1943, dau. of Rachel
 Cole and John Bosley of Wm. Bosley.
(North) Rachel H. Bosley, b. Nov. 6, 1825, d. April 3, 1909.
(South) John Bosley of Wm., b. July 2, 1822, d. Dec. 22, 1885.
(Rear) Richard W. Bosley, b. Dec. 3, 1860, d. Feb. 27, 1910.
(Large individual stones marked R.H.B., J.B., E.C.T., R.W.B., and M.B.)
Lewis C. Bosley, b. Sept. 4, 1858, d. Jan. 4, 1876.*
Price (Central Monument)
John Owings Price, 1815-1880.
Ann Price, 1818-1902.
Colgate Owings Price, 1848-1934.
Charlotte Owings Price, 1852-1921.
Mary Bisnell Price, 1854-1923.
Frederick Risdon Price, 1853-1916.
Maria Price Webster, 1859-1952.
Lee Webster, 1860-1890.
Mary Eliza Price, 1831-1901.
Martha Green---
Frederick W. Wright, 1851-1915. Sarah Bruen, wife of Frederick W. Wright,
 Sept. 1, 1854 - April 23, 1951.
Kathleen Wright, 1882-1966.
N. Bosley Merryman, 1886-1939. Mary Wright, wife of Nicholas Bosley Merryman,
 Dec. 19, 1888 - June 30, 1962.
Richard W. Wright, son of N. Bosley and Mary W. Merryman, Nov. 20, 1918 - Oct.
 12, 1938.
Annie R. Parlett, Nov. 23, 1850 - April 1, 1941.
Sophia Belle Cockey, b. July 5, 1850, d. Oct. 30, 1944. (S.B.C.-foot)
Ella Gist Cockey, b. March 29, 1862, d. Oct. 30, 1944. (E.G.C.-foot)
Sara L. Gilmore Cockey, b. April 29, 1857, d. Oct. 16, 1929. (S.L.G.C.-foot)
Gist T. Cockey, b. at Cockeysville, Dec. 25, 1819, d. Nov. 16, 1896. (G.T.C.
 at foot)
Jemima, wife of John H. Merryman, d. Dec. 16, 1862, aged 30 years and 24 days.
Father, Wm. Duncan, b. July 8, 1799, d. April 8, 1878, aged 78 years and 9
 mos.*
Ellen, wife of William Duncan, b. 5th March 1804, d. 8th March 1873.*
William Duncan, Jr., who departed this life, Sept. 25, 1853 in the 19th year
 of his age.*
Fannie E. Duncan, b. Feb. 24, 1871, d. Aug. 25, 1871.*
Nettie V., dau. of J. R. & S. B. Parks, b. Oct. 17, 1870, d. Sept., 1871.
 (N.V.P.-head)
John R. Parks, b. March 1, 1841, d. March 13, 1906.
Alline & Willie, infant children of Aquila & Mary E. Galloway.
Arthur Cecil, son of Aquila & M. E. Galloway, b. 12 April, and died 11 Aug.,
 1878.

Mary Elizabeth, wife of Aquila Galloway, b. 20th Oct. 1833, d. 10 Aug. 1905.
Aquila Galloway, b. 28th April 1826, d. 25th Sept. 1879.
Rebecca Coale Parks, wife of Joseph Parks, b. Sept. 2, 1803, d. Jan. 9, 1894.
Joseph Parks, b. Feb. 16, 1801, d. April 4, 1873. (J.P.-foot)
Abram Johnson Jessop, son of William & Mary Jessop, b. July 7, 1856, d. May 20, 1925.
Mary Cecelia Jessop, dau. of William and Mary Jessop, b. Jan. 14, 1844, d. Dec. 3, 1938.
Jessop (A Cross)
William Henry Jessop, son of William & Mary Jessop, b. May 27, 1848, d. Jan. 28, 1907.
Sarah Olivia Jessop, dau. of William & Mary Jessop, b. Feb. 11, 1845, d. June 2, 1918, aged 73 years.
Ada Austin, dau. of William & Mary Jessop, Oct. 9, 1852 - March 31, 1934.
(Accompanies cross)
Boyce (Monument)
Edward Gillet Boyce, Nov. 9, 1911 - June 6, 1958.
Elva M. Green, child of Henry A. Green d. Nov. 4, 1886, aged 9 years. William A. Green, d. March 10, 1887, aged 5 weeks. (E.M.G. & W.A.G.)
Kendre Riley, son of John H. & Jemima Merryman, b. Feb. 29, 1856, d. Nov. 31(?), 1860 (lying flat).
William Talbott (?) son of John H. and Jemima Merryman, b. Jan. 19, 1854, d. April 15, 1854.
(Book Shaped) Ella, d. Feb. 2, 1874, aged 2 years.*
Rev. Jackson L. Duncan, 1848-1918. Effie Lee Duncan, 1862-1933. C. Lillian Duncan, 1887-1942.* (J.L.D., G.L.C., #.L.D.)
Elisha Parks, b. Feb. 9, 1799, d. Aug. 20, 1871. (E.P.)
Mary Parks, wife of Elisha Parks, b. July 9, 1812, d. Sept. 10, 1904. (M.P.-head)
Mary Jane Parks, b. March 12, 1846, d. Feb. 13, 1926. (M.J.P.-head)
George N., son of S. E. and M. E. Parks, b. Jan. 13, 1873, d. Feb. 8, 1873.
Johnie Gray, beloved child of S. E. & M. E. Parks, b. April 10, 1877, d. Feb. 5, 1878.*
Charles Daniel, son of S. E. and Martha E. Parks, b. Feb. 27, 1875, d. April 27, 1880.*
Joseph Lee, eldest child of S. E. and Martha E. Parks, b. Jan. 23, 1862, d. March 24, 1879.*
(Griffith plot - central marker)
(Front) Dr. Edward J. Griffith, b. Oct. 23, 1829, d. Sept. 25, 1864. Eleanor Griffith Cole, 1831-1914. Abram Cole of A., 1832-1900 Griffith.
(Left-North) Theodora, wife of Dr. Tjos. K. Galloway and dau. of the late Dr. E. J. and Eleanor Griffith, b. Jan. 7, 1860, d. May 28, 1881. Edna C., dau. of Dr. Thos. E. and Theodora Galloway, b. April 2, 1881, d. July 28, 1881.
(Right-South) George C. Hendrickson, 1856-1906.
(Individual markers, E.G.C., Dr.E.J.G., A.C., E.C.C., E.G.C., T.C., E.G.C.)
(Rear) Harris
(Front) George Edward Harris, June 1, 1937 - Jan. 31, 1961.
Aunt, Rebecca, wife of Benjamin Jones, d. Feb. 7, 1885, aged 72 years.*
Elijah M., son of Amon & Rebecca Bosley, b. Nov. 12, 1830, d. July 13, 1869.
Sarah Bosley, b. Jan. 1, 1818, d. June 24, 1850.
Rebecca, wife of Amon Bosley, b. Jan. 4, 1789, d. Sept. 23, 1853 in the 64th year of her age.*
Amon Bosley, b. Feb. 27, 1779, d. Aug. 25, 1858, aged 59 years and 5 mos., and 27 days.*
James _____ Bosley, b. Sept. 29, 1821, d. Dec. 20, 1830, aged 9 years, 2 mos., and 2 days.*
Herman Froescher (sic), b. July 29, 1855, d. July 26, 1863.
Paulina, wife of George Froesher (sic), d. June 12, 1869 in her 43rd year.

Mary, wife of Wm. C. Gent, who departed this life June 19, 1865 in the 78th year of her age.
William C. Gent, d. Dec. 28, 1870 in the 84th year of his age.
Alfred Jackson, son of William Cole & Mary Gorsuch Gent, b. Jan. 16, 1828, d. Dec. 10, 1905.
Mary Elizabeth, wife of Alfred Jackson Gent, dau. of Zana Hutchins & John Bacon Holmes, b. May 11, 1841, d. Jan. 21, 1908.
Rachel, wife of John Burton, Sr., b. Nov. 22, 1810, departed this life March 18, 1883. (R.B.-foot)
John Burton, Sr., b. April 19, 1806, d. Dec. 26, 1889. (J.B.-foot)
(North) Samuel W. Burton, b. Sept. 13, 1847, d. April 12, 1917.
(South) Sarah J. Burton, b. March 12, 1852, d. Jan. 8, 1928.
Ellen Burton, departed this life April 11, 1920, aged 89 years.
Ray B. Lynch, 1881-1926.
(Front-west) Mary, wife of Wm. Jessop, b. April 17, 1815, d. Jan. 22, 1883.
(Left-North)*
(Right-South)*
William Jessop, Sr., b. April 5, 1800, d. Jan. 23, 1866.*
(Pyramid-West) Cecilia, wife of William Jessop, d. 4th of June 1840 in the 40th year of her age.*
(South) Jemima Barry, wife of Lavallin Barry.
(East) Infant Children of William & Cecilia Jessop, their first born, Annette, Mary Cecilia, George Morrison.
Jessop (Monument)
Ruby B. Jessop, May 13, 1873 - Feb. 5, 1947.
Clinton Jessop, Aug. 5, 1858 - Feb. 18, 1927 (American Legion metal marker).
H. Francies LeBrun, Sept. 21, 1908 - Jan. 29, 1958.
Father, Joseph Kelly, b. Nov. 2, 1798, d. Feb. 8, 1881.
Ann Kelley, wife of Joseph Kelley, b. March 16, 1806, d. Jan. 14, 1872.*
(A.K.-foot)
Father, William B. Coe, b. March 14, 1809, d. March 14, 1892.* (By his sons, James P. and Joshua C. Coe)
Carrie C., wife of Joshua C. Coe and mother of Harry W. Coe, d. Oct. 5, 1890 in the 45th year of her age.*
Harry W., only son of J. C. & Carrie C. Coe, d. July 5, 1889 in the 19th year of his age.*
(Front-East) Ellen Talbott Cockey, March 21, 1848 - Sept. 14, 1919. Francis Colegate Cockey, June 11, 1875 - Dec. 11, 1919.
(Right-North) (Odd Fellows Symbol) Thomas Clayton Cockey, son of the late Thomas D. & Ella T. Cockey, b. Dec. 5, 1877, d. Oct. 31, 1905.
(Left-South) Thomas Deye Cockey, husband of Ella T. Cockey, b. _eb. 27, 1837, d. May 28, 1892. (Markers T.C.C., E.T.C., T.D.C.)
Annie Laurie, dau. of Alfred J. & Mary E. Gent.
Grayson H. Gent, son of Alfred J. & Mary E. Gent, Sept. 17, 1856 - March 26, 1922.
(Rear) Love
(Front) Irma Crowther, Sept. 7, 1907 - May 14, 1970, dau. of W. Guy Crowther, wife of John T. Love, Jr. (I.C.L.-foot)
Love, Baylis R., 1913----. George, 1904----.
Charles Duer, son of Dr. W. G. & R. N. McGreary, b. Nov. 8, 1863, d. July 4, 1864.
Belle, dau. of J. S. & M. B. Wood, b. March 22, 1859, d. Nov. 10, 1865.*
Charles Duer, 1790-1873. Martha E. Moores, Dec. 16, 1835 - Nov. 26, 1904.
Elizabeth Ann, wife of Charles Duer, b. July 10, 1803, d. April 8, 1862. (E.A.D.)
Martha, b. (rest illegible).

Mary C. Henry, wife of John H. Henry, b. Oct. 3, 1830 - ___ 3, 1861. (Rest illegible - 4 lines)*
(Stone missing)
G. Charles E. R. Goodwin, b. 1823, d. 1899, Goodwin (C.E.R.C.-head)
Mary, infant dau. of W. S. and Bettie J. Cowley, b. Jan. 6, 1885, d. Jan. 30, 1885. Alice, b. June 13, 1895, d. Sept. 14, 1896.
Cowley (Monument)
Mother, Bettie J. Cowley, Aug. 28, 1850 - Sept. 22, 1923.
Father, William S. Cowley, May 15, 1851 - Nov. 5, 1921.
Clinton W. Cowley, Nov. 1, 1890 - Nov. 6, 1948.
Edwin Bond Cowley, May 18, 1887 - Aug. 21, 1967.
Natalie H. Cowley, May 28, 1889 - Dec. 2, 1952.
Thomas D. Cowley, Feb. 26, 1892 - Jan. 17, 1963.
Poe, Carrie E., 1906---. Ervin G., 1903---.
Poe, Ervin G., 1870-1945. Maude E., 1870-1937. Leo C., 1910-1918.
James Smith Moores, July 17, 1835 - March 16, 1907.
Grandmother, Ann Stinchcomb, relict of Victor Stinchcomb, d. Jan. 30, 1850 in the 77th year of her age.
Father, Beale C. Stinchcomb, d. 27th April 1861 in the 70th year of his age.
Mary Ann, wife of Hugh Witmer, d. March 2, 1848, aged 32 years 4 (rest sunken).
Hugh Witmer, d. Sept. 3, 1849, aged 43 years and 9 mos.
Margaret Ann Peirsol, who departed this life Oct. 27, 1848, aged 25 years, 2 mos. and 28 days. (M.A.P.-foot)
Thomas Peirsol, d. Oct. 18, 1853 (stone fallen and covered with turf).
Alice Moores, Oct. 31, 1959(?) - Sept. 18, 1950. Bettie Gathwright, Oct. 25, 1863 - April 7, 1945.
Mary Ross, d. 8 Sept. 1860, aged about 80 years.
Margaret Goslen, a native of Virginia, d. at the residence of Mrs. E. Webster, Balto. Co., 17 Jan. 1861, aged about 75 years.
Thomas John Tongue, Jan. 29, 1954 - Sept. 23, 1967.
Berry (Monument)
George Mauduit Berry, Sept. 4, 1907 - Aug. 22, 1968.
Charles L. Jessop, d. June 7, 1887 aged 53 years.*
Mary Stewart, wife of Charles L. Jessop, b. Sept. 20, 1833, d. Jan. 20, 1917.
Barry J. Emerson, Aug. 20, 1863 - June 12, 1920.
Loftus (Monument)
Mother, Annie C., 1860-1937.
Father, James W., 1859-1934.
(Crowther Plot)
Irma Megraw Crowther, b. Oct. 23, 1878, d. Jan. 23, 1966.
Walter Guy Crowther, b. Sept. 5, 1868, d. April 20, 1944.
Granville Hamilton Swope, II, husband of Irma Crowther Swope, March 17, 1908 - July 31, 1935.
Leonard Isaac Davis, b. Sept. 17, 1896, d. June 20, 1970. (L.I.D.)
Mary Valliant Crowther, b. Oct. 19, 1911, d. Oct. 16, 1970, mother of Mary Crowther Lauritzen and Collins M. Crowther, Jr.
Collins, Megraw Crowther, b. July 11, 1909, d. May 19, 1965.
Rebecca, wife of Leonard Anderson, who departed this life Sept. 1, 1841, in the 60th year of her age.
Zephaniah Poteet, April 8, 1834 - May 12, 1917.
Frederick R. Proctor, April 21, 1877 - April 2, 1953.
The Rev. R. J. Gunkel, Nov. 30, 1891 - Aug. 22, 1953.
Robert A. Reitz, Jan. 21, 1893 - Jan. 18, 1964.
Virginia B. Reitz, Jan. 30, 1895 - Oct. 6, 1970.
Cockey, William T., 1899---. Rebecca C., 1896---.
Jesse Poteet, d. Jan. 1848, aged 36 years.
John Jackson, d. June 21, 1848, aged 48 years.
(Masonic symbol) Jacob Carroll, b. Nov. 2, 1848, d. April 9, 1899, aged 50 years, 5 mos., and 7 days.*

Carolyn Hinman McCay Ames, Nov. 30, 1895 - Nov. 14, 1964.
Andrew, eldest son of James and Hanna McBride, who died June 21, 1847, aged 7 years, 7 mos., and 6 days.
Futts Marshall, b. Aug. 12, 1802, d. June 14, 1849.
Mother, Jeannett Marshall, relict of Futts Marshall and dau. of the late Hugh and Agnes Jamison, b. March 17, 1807, d. Feb. 13, 1884.*
Margaret J. Marshall, 1833-1919.
Lorba Butler, dau. of H. W. & A. Butler, d. May 14, 1850, aged 5 mos. and 14 days.
John Butler, who departed this life Aug. 23, 1850, aged 57 years.
Elizabeth, relict of John Butler, who departed this life, Feb. 17, 1870, aged 72 years.
Mother, Sarah, wife of Philip Russell, b. Dec. 30, 1839, d. Nov. 7, 1887.*
Father, Philip, husband of Sarah Russell, d. June 4, 1896.*
Russell (Monument)
Floyd F. Russell, Jan. 6, 1906 - July 18, 1966.
Josiah Gill Skipper, d. Sept. 14, 1881, aged 21 years.
Rosalie Winslow, b. Aug. 12, 1892, d. Oct. 24, 1892.
Alice Annie, dau. of John T. and Charlotte Riley, d. Aug. 29, 1871, aged 2 years, 7 mos., and 9 days.
Nettie V. Kirk, infant dau. of J. T. & Charlotte A. Riley, b. Sept. 26, 1871, d. July 11, 1872.*
Effie Black, d. 12 Sept. 1895, aged 13 mos.
Henry Storey, b. Jan. 7, 1854, d. Nov. 25, 1894.
Hier ruhen in Gott, Bruno Binder, Geb. 29, Juli 1889, Gest. 1 August 1889, und Theo. Wm. Binder, Geb. 14 Mai 1893, Gest. 8 Januar 1894.
Ann L. Bassler, b. July 25, 1890, d. Feb. 14, 1891.
James Wm., youngest son of Jacob & Caroline Bassler, b. March 5, 1871, d. Aug. 31, 1887. (W.B.-head)
Mother, Caroline Bassler, 1827-1915.
Father, Jacob Bassler, 1828-1903.
Rose, d. June 30, 1892, aged 48 years (no last name, head marker "R").

An account of the Sherwood Episcopal Church is found in Scharf, *History of Baltimore City and Baltimore County*, p. 879. Date of building, 1835.

ST. JOSEPH'S CEMETERY, TEXAS, MD.

St. Joseph's R. C. Church, Church Lane, Texas, Md., Cockeysville Quadrant. South of Church Lane and south of Church and school buildings. Listing begins at S.E. corner in newer portion of cemetery. Read south to north, move from east to west.

(Between tree line and unpaved path)
Marble, Mother, Mary E., Oct. 11, 1856 - Aug. 26, 1944. Son, James O., July 1, 1884 - Oct. 15, 1942.
Douglas, Richard, 1898-1968. Madeline, 1896---.
Spera, Rocco, 1884-1959. Mamie M., 1889-1965.
DeLucia, Michael, 1895-1957. Rose Mary, 1895-1957.
Walker (Monument)
Clement T. W., July 10, 1900, May 10, 1955.
Roger Lee Snyder, March 18, 1948 - Sept. 24, 1966.
Calvert, husband, James W., 1895-1964. Wife, Josephine C., 1907---.
Ella Rafferty.

Caslin, John L., 1887-1954. Ethel E., 1896-19___.
Elaine Caslin Burns, July 24, 1924 - April 4, 1971.
James Michael Caslin, Maryland, Sgt. U.S. Marine Corps Res., June 29, 1891 - Nov. 26, 1955.
Hauptman, Mary G., 1878-1969. Albert L., 1887-1945.
Ball, Lillian A., Sept. 1, 1883 - July 3, 1945. Ernest E., Oct. 10, 1883 - May 14, 1945.
Walter D. Hoffman, July 25, 1891 - Feb. 14, 1944.
Miller, Elizabeth T., May 25, 1885 - Sept. 20, 1951. Joseph C., Jan. 9, 1876 - March 7, 1963.
Mary M. Murray, April 22, 1882 - April 23, 1957.
Catherine Murray, May 14, 1891 - Jan. 3, 1945.
James Murray, Oct. 12, 1880, March 21, 1943.
Shea (Monument)
Husband, Henry P. Lindemon, July 21, 1889 - March 23, 1921.
John T. Shea and family.
Caslin (Monument)
Anna V. Caslin, Oct. 4, 1918 - May 11, 1961.
Steltz, Little Flower, Pray for us. Myers Brothers, Guaranteed Memorials, Hanover, Pa.
Cofiell, Jo Ann Lee, April 20, 1952 - June 17, 1952. Pauline E., Dec. 6, 1926---.
Morris K., Nov. 8, 1924 - July 17, 1963.
McGarity, Bernard J.---. Kathryn W., 1916-1969.
Mother, Mabel Moll Reid Morgan, May 15, 1906 - Jan. 1, 1950.
Shoul, W. Russell, 1906-1953. Clarice M., 1907---.
Regina (Shoul), March 3, 1929 - Dec. 4, 1934.
In the service of his country, J. Elmiran Chilcoat, Oct. 7, 1923 - Sept. 7, 1944.
Shoul, William F., 1882-1947. Elsie M., 1882-1968.
Mary Dorothy, dau. of Wm. T. and Mary C. Scally, b. Oct. 24, 1921, d. Oct. 7, 1932.*
Merryman, Nellie E., Sept. 13, 1904---. William E., April 28, 1899 - May 8, 1962.
James Lester, son of Charles A. & Maria Snyder, July 11, 1952 - April 18, 1954.
Charles A. Snyder, husband of Maria Paradisi, April 8, 1927 - June 1, 1968.*
(Council, Jr. OUAM - Masonic symbol 6")
Etrusco Paradisi, N 2.8-1923 - M. 9.23-1962.*
Barrett, Helen B., Dec. 26, 1915 - Aug. 20, 1964. James F., Sept. 16, 1911---.
Susie, dau. of John & Mattie Zsenyuch, May 15, 1918 - June 26, 1921.
George, son of John & Mattie Zsenyuch, Sept. 10, 1920 - April 3, 1921.
Howard, son of Wm. A. & Henrietta Walker, b. Nov. 15, 1901, d. July 20, 1916.*
Raftury
James W. Shea Family.
(Enclosure) Kennedy/Tully.
John Kennedy Family (On flat railing)
Fogle
Fogle - Little Flower, pray for us.
W. Walter, 1889-1940.
Frances M., April 9, 1861 - June 28, 1940.
Mary Ellen, Jan. 31, 1867 - March 5, 1956. (End of Fogle plot).
(West) Canova, Father, Vito, May 26, 1907 - Oct. 8, 1959. Mother, Margaret M., May 10, 1919 - Dec. 29, 1945.
(East) Canova, parents, Anthony, June 13, 1872 - May 20, 1941. Christina P., May 14, 1882 - Sept. 28, 1941. Son, Charles J., Oct. 18, 1905 - Aug. 23, 1948.
(East of Canova Monument)
Father, Anthony.
Mother, Christina.
Charles.

James V. Canova, Aug. 23, 1943 - Sept. 19, 1969.
(West of Canova Monument)
Margaret.
Vito.
James V. Canova, Jr., son of James V. and Gladys M. Canova - Nov. 7, 1963 - May 30, 1964.
Lynn M. Canova, dau. of James V. and Gladys M. Canova, Feb. 9, 1969 - Aug. 16, 1969.
(End of Plot).
Williams, Arthur LeRoy, May 31, 1901 - Feb. 2, 1952. Josephine G., June 17, 1905----.
Price, Lottie G., 1885-1950. George W., 1875-1952.
Leech.
(Two blank markers).
Elizabeth Houck Leech, Jan. 9-1889 - Nov. 2, 1958.
Maurice E. Leech, Jan. 1, 1886 - Oct. 8, 1945.
Deal, Josephine A., 1884-1930. Benjamin F., 1881-1960.
Benjamin H., son of Benjamin F. & Josephine Deal, Sept. 1, 1914 - Jan. 26, 1930.* (R.H.D.-foot)
Rudd, son, Charles A., Dec. 11, 1919 - Nov. 22, 1920. Mother, Pauline M., June 29, 1895----. Father, Charles L., Dec. 6, 1889 - Sept. 24, 1967.
Fendlay, 1908-James B.-1934. 1878-Hannah T.-1947. 1875-Harry E.-1961.
Kelly (Flat monument)
George T. Kelly, Nov. 10, 1904 - Feb. 4, 1962.
(Enclosure)
Cherbonnier (On Railing)
Lucie Cherbonnier Flanigan, 1889-1939.
1858-1928 (On base of missing stone).
Lucie Boisliniere Cherbonnier.
Louis C. Cherbonnier, March 6, 1890 - Aug. 23, 1913.* (L.C.C-foot)
(End of Enclosure)
Canavan (No individual stones)
Noppenberger (Flat monument)
Mother, Catherine E. Noppenberger, d. Jan. 12, 1940, age 69.
Father, Charles B. Noppenberger, d. Oct. 7, 1909, age 42.
Ditschler, Wilbur G., 1897-1964.
Logan (Monument)
(East of monument) M. Ellen Logan, May 27, 1884 - May 16, 1957.
(West of monument) Mary Catherine, wife of Thomas F. Logan nee Hartigan, 1874-1910.
Thomas F. Logan, Dec. 7, 1873 - Dec. 14, 1952.
Jas. T. Shea (Flat monument).
Rafferty (Flat monument - west of Shea plot)
Welsh (Flat monument in gate)
Ann, wife of Michael J. Welsh, d. Feb. 23, 1898, aged 54 years, native of Ballybrachen Co., Roscommon, Ireland.*
Maguire (Flat monument in gate)
Cecelia Armstrong Anderson, d. May 15, 1947.
Lamar, Charles W., 1850-1911. Ella F., 1863-1929.
Connell.*
Leach, Elizabeth M., June 14, 1892 - Dec. 25, 1959. Walter E., Oct. 22, 1891 - March 17, 1960.
Vernon C. Sanders, Feb. 18, 1914 - Dec. 4, 1959.
Wife, Irene McDonough Spicer, Sept. 4, 1901 - Aug. 6, 1969.
Niemczyk, Father, Henry, 1915----. Mother, Lillian, 1920 - 1959.
Mother, Katherine T. McDonough, Aug. 22, 1874 - June 7, 1959.
Reilly (Monument-both sides)
(East of monument) Mary T. Reilly, April 12, 1882 - July 17, 1966.

Joseph M. Reilly, April 30, 1880 - Oct. 27, 1945.
Farley, Michael, 1884-1948. Patrick, 1893-1952. James E., 1886-1954.
(East) Patrick E. Farley, Sept. 21, 1893 - Jan. 11, 1952.
(West) Dent, husband, Benjamin B., Jr., 1926-1955. Mother, Margaret C., 1898-1943.*
(East) Chambers, Charles A., Jan. 4, 1962. John L., March 26, 1952.*
(East of above) Charles A. Chambers, Jan. 4, 1962.*
John L. Chambers, March 26, 1952.*
Benjamin B. Dent, Jr., Nov. 16, 1926 - Feb. 7, 1955.*
Margaret C. Dent, May 13, 1898 - Aug. 14, 1943, Mother. (End of Plot)
Son, Otto L. Marsh, May 19, 1906.
Father, Andrew J. Marsh, March 6, 1872 - April 18, 1944.
Mother, Lillian A. Marsh, Sept. 16, 1883 - Jan. 16, 1935.
Nieberding (Monument)
Mother, Margaret, 1884-1945.
Father, Anthony, 1883-1938.
Son, Raymond, 1909-1931.
Noppenberger (Monument)
Father, George J., 1858 - 1951.
Mother, Elizabeth T., d. May 13, 1929.
Kane (Flat Monument)
Joseph (apparently in line with Kane)
"Mert", Milton R. Roberts, son of Francis A. and Catherine E. Roberts, Jan. 22, 1945 - March 10, 1964.
William Earl Snyder, husband of Catherine E. Stroh, Feb. 22, 1901 - Nov. 5, 1929.
Mother, Mary L. Stroh, b. Sept. 29, 1885, d. Feb. 2, 1918.*
Caslin, Patrick J., 1885-1962. Edna H., 1891---.
Francis Robert, son of Patrick J. & Edna Caslin, June 6, 1915 - Sept. 12, 1916.
Grimm, William F., 1896---. Sara C., 1898---.
Caslin, Mary, 1883-1926. Michael, 1855-1931. Catherine, 1863-1939.
John B. Ensor, July 25, 1869 - Sept. 25, 1946. His wife, Mary E. Ensor, March 13, 1874 - Aug. 1, 1959.
John B. Ensor, July 25, 1869 - Sept. 25, 1946.
Edward A. Sparks, b. Dec. 1, 1836, d. Feb. 14, 1905. Elizabeth A., his wife, b. April 14, 1840, d. Feb. 19, 1914.*
George Lawrence Sparks, Dec. 24, 1869 - April 11, 1944.
Egan (Flat Monument)
Plot with "O" at each corner.
O'Conor-Dalton (Flat Monument with plot)
O'Conor (Flat Monument)
(Central Monument) John E. O'Conor, Feb. 23, 1863 - Dec. 19, 1887. Mary A. O'Conor, d. Feb. 8, 1949. Ella L. O'Conor, d. Nov. 23, 1949.
Catherine O'Conor, d. Jan. 27, 1932. Thomas J. O'Conor, d. July 16, 1935.
James O'Conor, d. Nov. 24, 1911. Sara O'Conor, Dec. 24, 1839 - Jan. 31, 1903.
(East of Monument) Mother.
Father.
Ormond (Flat Monument with gate).
John Regan, b. in County Mayo, Ireland, d. Nov. 11, 1891 in his 56th year.*
Sallie Regan, d. March 17, 1895 in her 19th year.
Mary E. Hoffman, dau. of John and Mary Regan, d. Jan. 27, 1901 in her 36th year.
Katherine Regan, d. March 9, 1902 in her 16th year.
Moore.
Margaret Landrigan Moore, a native of Ballybrood County, Limerick, Ireland.*
Cath. Hanly Doyle (Flat Monument).
Ensor (Flat Monument).
Wilmer C. Ensor, M.C., Oct. 11, 1879 - Oct. 4, 1969.
Mary Virginia Stromberg, wife of Dr. Wilmer C. Ensor, May 3, 1881 - Aug. 11, 1955.
John Wayson, Feb. 22, 1907 - Aug. 21, 1917.

Joseph Clifton, June 8, 1918 - Aug. 8, 1939.
Rafferty (Flat Monument)
Covahey, John T., June 4, 1890 - June 7, 1960. Mary L., June 29, 1900---.
Robert Reed Person, Jr., 1951-1959.
Somerville, Margaret Adelaide, 1866-1950.
James P. Powers, Sept. 28, 1878 - Dec. 15, 1949. Jennie H. Powers, Feb. 18, 1884 - Jan. 30, 1932.
Kennedy (Flat Monument)
Kearns, Frank C., March 13, 1898 - Oct. 14, 1944. Mary V., June 12, 1907---.
O'Conor (Flat Monument)
Gagliano, Rosa M., June 12, 1901---. Samuel J., Nov. 1, 1885 - April 11, 1963.*
Rosario Gagliano, b. June 1, 1842, d. March 4, 1924. His wife, Domenica, b. June 30, 1840, d. Dec. 19, 1926.
(Front-East) John P. Noppenberger, husband of Catherine E. Noppenberger, b. April 18, 1866, d. Dec. 30, 1912.* (J.P.N.-head).
(Left-South) A(?), Annie C. Noppenberger, June 2, 1898 - June 9, 1968. (C.E.N.-foot)
(Right-North) PX, Catherine E. Noppenberger, wife of John P. Noppenberger, b. March 24, 1874, d. Jan. 11, 1963.
(Rear-West) N. Gault & Son, Balto., Md.
(nearest to unpaved path)
Van Horn, Carl R., 1919-1964.
Somerville, John Howard, Jan. 9, 1901 - June 11, 1964. Ruth M., June 1, 1903---.
Meredith, Alice Wells, Oct. 21, 1908 - March 15, 1962.
Peters, Husband, J. George, 1894-1964. Wife, Marie K., 1908---.
Tyrie (Monument, both sides).
Robert Tyrie, Sept. 30, 1892 - May 23, 1949.
Ford (Monument, both sides).
Christopher J., Oct. 23, 1887 - Feb. 23, 1966.
James L., June 20, 1889 - March 2, 1951.
Mother, Mary Agnes, March 8, 1864 - Nov. 8, 1952.
Father, Nicholas Rogan, March 3, 1858 - Feb. 3, 1940. (End of Ford Plot).
Gagliano.*
Gagliano-Bosley.*
Mother, Josephine Gagliano, 1890-1946.
Father, Joseph Gagliano, 1881-1934.
Mother, Mary Gagliano Bosley, 1916-1956. (end of plot).
Fanny Combs Gough, b. July 4, 1860, d. April 8, 1948.*
Virginia Combs Bond, b. Dec. 25, 1865, d. Nov. 3, 1931.*
Wm. Grayson Bond, b. Sept. 9, 1865, d. May 22, 1931.*
Hyland, Martin W., 1859-1942. Katherine B., 1858-1937. Catherine D., 1894-1933.
Shaneybrook (Flat Monument)
Wm. George, son of Wm. & Anna Shaneybrook, Oct. 22, 1925 - March 27, 1928.
J. Frank Lupo, Dec. 23, 1884 - Jan. 3, 1969.
Angelo Lupo, June 21, 1853 - June 6, 1927.
Anne Regan, wife of Angelo Lupo, April 11, 1859 - Dec. 23, 1926.
Haviland, Mary C., Jan. 11, 1868 - Nov. 7, 1924. Hary P., Dec. 23, 1866 - April 16, 1935.
Guyton.
Mary White, d. Feb. 21, 1913. Patrick J. Lynch, d. March 6, 1913.
Charles E. Guyton, Mary E., Beloved wife of Charles E. Guyton, d. June 28, 1928. (Foot markers M.E.G., M.W., ..., P.J.L.)
McGraw/Barrett (Monument)
John F. Moore, beloved husband of Margaret Moore, b. Feb. 16, 1850, d. April 15, 1908. (J.F.M.-foot)
Magee (Flat monument with gate)

Bussey (Monument).
Bennett F. Bussey, M.D., Oct. 8, 1863 - July 26, 1933.
Katherine M. Bussey, Jan. 6, 1892 - April 12, 1949.
Rev. P. Lenaghan, Pastor of St. Joseph's Church, Texas, Md., Jan., 1875-March 4, 1896, b. in Crossmaglen Co., Armaugh, Ireland, Sept. 22, 1814, d. March 4, 1896.*
Rev. Patrick Lenaghan, b. March 9, 1857, d. May 28, 1906. Pastor of St. Bernard's Church, Baltimore, Md.*
Erected Dec. 21, 1896, dedicated May 2, 1897 by Rev. P. H. Lenaghan and members of the congregation of St. Joseph's Church, Texas, to the loving memory of Rev. P. B. Lenaghan, ordained June 22, 1849 by the Most. Rev. Samuel Eccleston, A.B. of Baltimore.
Rev. John H. Lenaghan, b. April 1, 1902, Clarnagh, Crossmaglen County, Armagh, Ireland, ordained a priest May 20, 1928 for Concordia Diocese now Salina, Kansas, d. Sept. 9, 1954 at Salina, Kansas, buried Sept. 16, 1954.
Cockey-Bussey (Flat Monument)
Clement J. Bussey, 1913-1962.
(Tall Memorial Shaft) Rev. Richard C. Campbell, 1858-1914, ordained Oct. 28, 1889, Pastor of St. Joseph Church, 1896-1914.
Rev. R. C. C., Mary Louise, dau. of Bernard and Ann Campbell.
Theresa G. Scally, Sept. 12, 1885 - June 18, 1951.
Patrick H. Scally, March 1, 1877 - Dec. 9, 1949.
Alicia C. Scally, March 12, 1924 - Oct. 7, 1959.
Plot marked by corner marker G.J.S.
Keough (East)
Leonard (West)
Louise Woodworth, 1867-1943.
Thomas Keough, 1868-1944.
Henry Keough, 1873-1938.
Annie K. Leonard, 1877-1949.
Donnelly (Monument)
Mary A., Feb. 2, 1888 - Feb. 21, 1963.
John I., June 11, 1886 - Sept. 1, 1938.
Murray (Monument - both sides)
Lawrence F., July 31, 1916 - Dec. 25, 1937.
Thomas M., April 16, 1909 - Nov. 8, 1969.
Rose H., March 17, 1883 - Sept. 22, 1960.
Thomas P., Oct. 12, 1873 - Jan. 31, 1936.
Plot with "D" corner markers.
Annie T. McGinnis, 1871-1937.*
John J. McGinnis, 1856-1918.*
Ella Price Warren, Aug. 6, 1890 - May 13, 1932.
Price, George F. Price, Feb. 26, 1856 - Jan. 11, 1944. Rosie B. Price, Nov. 30, 1862 - May 23, 1937.
James R. Price, Maryland, Sgt. Co. B, 115 Infantry, World War I PH, Dec. 31, 1895 - Sept. 24, 1956.
Clara, James Mulcahy (Foot - C.M./J.M./1859-1913).
Peter (Doesn't match any other stones nearby).
Luke A. Kelly, 1845-1910. Anna M. Kelly, 1854-1935. (Kelly on flat marker).
Joseph J. Kelly, 1880-1951.
John Kenney, 1859-1889. Catherine D. Kenney, his wife, 1867-1923. Second wife of Francis McDevitt, 1852-1937.
Catherine C. D. Kenney
Sarah, aged 9 years. Clair Isabell, aged 11 years, children of John & Catherine D. Kenney.
George I. Kennedy, Maryland, HS Sup. Co., 110 Field Arty, World War I, April 23, 1894 - Feb. 16, 1969.
John J. Kennedy, Maryland Horseshoer, Sup. Co. 110 FA, World War I, June 24, 1889 - Aug., 1965.

Father, Wm. Henry Hoffman, April 9, 1862 - Jan. 18, 1935.
Mother, Catherine T. Hoffman, June 25, 1864 - June 13, 1902.
O'Hara (Flat Monument).
McDonnell (Flat Monument and gate).
William T. Connor, 1887-1956.
Margaret B. Connor, 1862-1948.
Ella N. Connor, 1856-1934.
Mary M. Connor, 1882-1960.
M. F. Connor (Flat Monument).
Father.
Mother.
Margaret Connor, widow of Patrick Connor, d. Dec. 13, 1906, aged 86 years.*
    (Foot-M.C.).
Arnold (Monument).
Charles F., June 26, 1886 - March 4, 1950.
Margaret Jennings Clark, Oct. 15, 1874 - June 17, 1960.
H. Stanislaus Clark, March 30, 1869 - Aug. 31, 1942.
M. Varina Clark, May 4, 1867 - Jan. 29, 1947.
Shea, Julia F., July 9, 1890 - Jan. 22, 1963. John A., June 18, 1889 - Oct. 8, 1962.
Josephine A. Shea, dau. of John & Mary Shea, July 21, 1868 - Nov. 6, 1943.
Daniel J. Shea Family (Flat Monument).
Joseph L. Brennan, March 28, 1926 - Oct. 18, 1938.
Reilly (Monument - lost in arbor vitae).
J. Harry Reilly, April 29, 1880 - Sept. 2, 1939.
Regan (Monument - both sides).
Thomas E. Regan, Oct. 27, 1900 - Aug. 31, 1959.
Francis J. Regan, Aug. 26, 1891 - Dec. 13, 1966.
John Regan, June 16, 1867 - Nov. 11, 1943.
Thomas C. Regan, Nov. 24, 1862 - June 17, 1945.
Annie L. Regan, March 10, 1886 - Aug. 10, 1936.
Dorethea A. Regan, Nov. 24, 1879 - April 15, 1937.
Kennedy, Martin, 1858-1929. Mary Ann, 1870-1942. Clara K. Graham, 1891-1918.
Michael Flynn, 1828-1917, Father. Mary Flynn, 1840-1923, Mother.
Michael Welsh, Nov. 1, 1850 - March 24, 1922. Winifred Welsh, April 8, 1856 - March 7, 1937. (Foot markers M.W. and W.W.).
Thomas Lanahan, d. Aug. 24, 1913. Ellen C. Lanahan, d. Aug. 6, 1933.*
Cavaney.
Quinn.
M. Thomas, Father, 1832-1919. Ellen, Mother, 1842-1935, b. County Mayo, Ireland, MacNicholas.
Elizabeth, 1877-1931. Anna DeSales Connor, 1881-1918. Richard Paul, 1889-1933.
Our beloved son, John Joseph MacNicholas, May 16, 1869 - Dec. 22, 1904.*
Sister Mary Bernad, C.S.V.P., 1871-1956, St. Vincint's, Birmingham, Ala.. James P. B., 1878-1955, Holy Sepulchre, Omaha, Nebraska.
Elizabeth, 1877-1931.
Father.
Anna DeSales Connor, nee MacNicholas, 1881-1918.
John.
Mother.
Richard P., 1889-1933.
Edward Powers, b. Sept. 29, 1847, d. Aug. 20, 1926. Catherine Brown Powers, b. Sept. 21, 1856, d. Oct. 6, 1913.
Thomas Powers, b. Oct. 30, 1845, d. Oct. 21, 1904. Edward A. Powers, d. June 7, 1950.
Martin V. Sherrer, 1894-1954. Margaret L. Sherrer, 1883-1953.
Edward Livingston Powers, b. Jan. 18, 1918, d. Jan. 21, 1918.
(Foot markers: E.A.P., E.P., C.B.C., T.P.).
John Leo Livingstone, d. Nov. 18, 1888. Mary Forien Livingston, d. June 29, 1898

Ialeen J. Forien, d. Aug. 31, 1933. (Also foot markers M.L.S., M.V.S.).
Thomas Murphy, d. April 7, 1877, aged 52 years. A native of the County Mayo, Ireland. Also his beloved wife, Eleanor Gordon, d. Jan. 17, 1903, aged 70 years. A native of the County Roscommon, Ireland.*
John T. Murphy, d. Sept. 29, 1896, aged 37 years. Martin W. Murphy, d. March 9, 1890, aged 28 years. Beloved sons of Thomas and Eleanor Murphy.*
Mary A. Murphy, d. Aug. 10, 1902, aged 32 years, beloved dau. of Thomas and Eleanor Murphy. B. Ellen Murphy, Feb. 2, 1872 - April 4, 1954, beloved wife of Owen H. Harrison.
Nevin (Monument - both sides).
Father, Leander S., 1865-1941.
Mother, Mary A., 1867-1939.
Sean Joseph Nevin, Aug. 2, 1962 - Dec. 31, 1963.
Lawrence P. Covahey, May 19, 1908 - Nov. 2, 1967.
Covahey, Mother, Mary E., 1868-1948. Father, Thomas J., 1857-1924.
Chambers (Flat monument with gate).
Kearns.
Covahey, Mary K., March 6, 1893 - Sept. 21, 1967. James M., July 24, 1892---.
Mary, beloved wife of William McDermott, d. July 17, 1902, aged 67 years. A native of the County Galway, Ireland.*
John J. Carr, 1892-1960. Mary E. Carr, 1895-1966.
Mary E. McDermott, b. March 23, 1855, d. Nov. 17, 1889. Frank J. McDermott, b. Dec. 16, 1867, d. Feb. 10, 1898.*
John J. Carr, 1892-1960. Mary E. Carr, 1895-1966.
Carney, Michael T., April 5, 1864 - March 11, 1907. Ella T., April 25, 1865 - May 1, 1939. Thomas J., Oct. 23, 1899 - July 9, 1939. William T., Oct. 12, 1894 - Feb. 25, 1964.
Kane (Flat Monument).
McLhinney, Catherine G., 1914---. Frank J., 1913-1966.
Mary Doyle Bussey, Aug. 9, 1914 - April 17, 1964.
McGlannan, Alexius, III, April 30, 1902 - Dec. 18, 1967. His wife, Jane Clark, June 7, 1905 ---.
Henry A. Doran, June 19, 1902 - Feb. 15, 1965.
Natalie H. Doran, March 1, 1900.
Daughter, Lillian Marie Brown, 1910-1971.
Costa, Mother, Maria Concetta, Dec. 8, 1875 - Aug. 12, 1951. Father, Joseph Dominico, Sept. 27, 1871 - July 24, 1952.
O. Eugene Beck, Nov. 8, 1890 - Nov. 19, 1953. Michael J. Sullivan, April 13, 1875 - April 11, 1954.*
Mother, Mary Catherine nee Sullivan, wife of O. Eugene Beck, May 13, 1888 - Aug. 10, 1939.*
Kloss, Mary Theresa Dooling, Mother, Jan. 3, 1872 - Jan. 31, 1940,b. in Roscommon, Ireland, wife of Frederick W. Kloss, Feb. 13, 1868 - Sept. 2, 1942.
Saverd (Flat Monument).
William Kilmurray, Maryland, Pvt. 1 CL. 115 Inf. 29 Div., Sept. 10, 1919.
Charles William Hicks, Nov. 10, 1902 - March 7, 1967.* (Foot-C.W.H.)
Agnes V. Dement, July 23, 1897 - Sept. 2, 1965.
Mary Elizabeth Cary, Oct. 28, 1884 - July 22, 1965.
Frank, Mary B., 1900-1941. Norman R., 1894---.
McDermott (Monument - both sides).
Edward P. McDermott, 1866-1957. Julia Q. McDermott, 1864-1953.
Luke F., Dec. 28, 1907 - Sept. 3, 1937.
L. Carroll Markland, June 24, 1896 - Sept. 29, 1968.
Helen L. Markland, Feb. 16, 1901 ---.
Noppenberger (Monument)
John L., Sr., Nov. 9, 1889 - Dec. 30, 1962.
Mary C., Aug. 20, 1902 - Nov. 6, 1966.

Belvin (Flat Monument)
James E. Barron, March 25, 1874 - May 5, 1935. (J.E.B. - foot).
Mary A., beloved wife of Marcus W. Funkhouser, dau. of Patrick J. & Bridget
Murray, d. Nov. 12, 1903, aged 32 years, 2 mos., 23 days.*
John T., beloved son of Patrick J. & Bridget Murray, d. Jan. 20, 1900, aged 29
years and 7 mos.*
Beloved Father & Mother, Patrick J. Murray, d. Feb. 27, 1925. Bridget A.
Murray, d. March 5, 1965.*
Preble, John Edward, beloved son of M. C. & E. T. Preble, Oct. 29, 1902 - Oct.
28, 1923.* (Foot-brother).
S. E. Shepperd Harris, Dec. 31, 1869 - April 21, 1935.
Halligan, Thomas, 1853-1922. His wife, Bridget Phelan, 1849-1905.*
Elizabeth, beloved wife of John McDonough, b. Sept. 22, 1854, d. Nov. 30, 1901.
John, beloved husband of Elizabeth McDonough, d. Dec. 11, 1919, aged 67 years.
Kilroy (Flat monument with gate)
Catherine T., beloved wife of John Kilroy, d. Oct. 3, 1901, aged 37 years and
10 mos.*
John C., son of John & Ellen T. Kilkenny, d. May 11, 1901, aged 23 years and
4 mos.*
Eleanor E., d. June 4, 1959. Edmond F., d. Aug. 11, 1959. Dorothy V., d.
April 15, 1961. Rt. Rev. J. Lawrence, d. Sept. 15, 1964.
John, d. Feb. 24, 1931. His wife, Ellen Hanley, d. Dec. 1, 1911. Joseph P.,
d. May 12, 1904. Bernard I., d. Dec. 22, 1919. Mary L., d. July 1, 1924
Kilkenny.
Katherine A., dau. of John & Ellen T. Kilkenny, d. Oct. 17, 1898, aged 16 years
and 5 mos.*
Jeremiah O'Brien, Dec. 1, 1872 - March 4, 1929.
Nora Kenny, wife of Clarence Wyatt, 1900-1921. (Foot - N.K.W.).
John F., son of John P. & Lona Kenny, 1902-1910. John P., husband of Lona
Kenny, 1860-1907. (J.P.K. - J.F.K.)
Kenny (Flat monument).
Erected by Hannorah Kenny to the memory of her beloved husvand, Patrick W. Kenny,
who departed this life, Aug. 19, 1869, aged 47 years. A native of the parish
of Killy Kings Co., Ireland.* (P.W.K.-foot)
Lindsay (Flat monument with gate).
Fitzgerald (Flat monument with gate).
Edward, beloved husband of Johanna Fitzgerald. A native of Co. Limerick,
Ireland, d. Oct. 27 (?), 1893, aged 64 years. G. Sillery, 36 Harford Ave.,
Fitzgerald.
Sophie E. Beale, Aug. 5, 1918 - March 9, 1965.
Son, Raymond B. Airey, 1904-1970.
Mother, Margaret Airey Kelleher, 1877-1969, b. in Beaver Dam, Md.
Rest in Peace. (Foot)
Buck-Jim-Ray. (Foot)
Waldenberger (Monument).
Mary A. McKittrick, 1881-1957, sister of Alice J. Waldenberger.
Noppenberger (Monument).
Alice J., 1879-1945.
Louis, 1874-1934.
Frank E. Baker, April 25, 1909 - May 15, 1966.
Emma L. Baker, Nov. 13, 1912---.
Elizabeth Marie Baker, Aug. 25, 1930 - Oct. 7, 1930.*
Tracey, son, John W., Father, Eugene A., Mother, Mary A., son, Eugene A.
Feeney.
John Eagan, d. Dec. 24, 1892, aged 46 years. Mary Eagan, d. March 3, 1920,
aged 64 years.*
B.Leane, b. 1845, d. 1905, wife of Thomas Brady, native of Drinana P. of Elphin
Co., Rosscommon, Ireland.*

Thomas Brady, b. 1843 in the Parish of Elphin County, Roscommon, Ireland, d.
  June 24, 1908, age 65 years.
McKnight (Flat Monument).
Son, George J., 1883-1953. Daughter, Margaret I., 1888-1966. Noppenberger.
J.C.N.
Father, James C., 1858-1900. Mother, Margaret A., 1857-1944. Noppenberger.
John Moore, beloved son of Cornelius and Mary Moore, b. Jan. 5, 1859, d. Aug.
  22, 1891.*
Andrew C. Campbell, Jan. 28, 1884 - Sept. 26, 1949.
Gregory C. Daughton, May 24, 1947 - March 14, 1952.*
Eugene Albert, son of George and Mary Waters, March 7, 1938 - Dec. 8, 1956.
Robert Waters, Maryland Sp4, Co. A. 5 Inf. 25 Inf. Div., Vietnam PH, Feb. 27,
  1944 - Sept. 23, 1966.
Hall, Greval S., Aug. 15, 1863 - June 24, 1926. Annie A., March 15, 1864 -
  Sept. 26, 1942. Lillian H. Morrison, 1898-1925. M. Ethel Martin, 1883-1967.
  Joseph M. Hall, 1890-1937. Gertrude Hall, 1892-1966.
Matthew Francis Reilly, July 28, 1915 - March 7, 1955. (W.F.R.-foot)
Matthew Francis Reilly, Jan. 22, 1888 - Aug. 29, 1932. (W.F.R.-foot)
Elizabeth C. Gladfelter, beloved wife of John H. Gladfelter, Feb. 10, 1894 -
  Nov. 29, 1960.
Mary E. Gill, 1871-1951.
J. H. Gill, 1868-1928.
Father, Wm. E. Tracey, 1889-1953.
Connell, Patrick Henry Connell, Oct. 31, 1869 - Jan. 4, 1927. Mary McDonnell,
  his beloved wife, Dec. 23, 1874 - Dec. 16, 1933.
Fuller, Thomas R., July 23, 1902 - May 16, 1943.* (Seems to be with Preble
  plot.)
Preble, Elmer T., 1872-1926. His wife, Mary C. Halligan, 1876-1939.*
Margaret E., wife of Frank E. Farley, b. March 25, 1858, d. June 30, 1909.*
Frank E., husband of Margaret E. Farley, 1855-1911.*
Husband, Thomas G. Farley, July 8, 1883 - March 4, 1927.
McEvoy, Patrick J., Jan. 16, 1872 - April 15, 1908. Catherine A., Oct. 15,
  1876 - Nov. 16, 1962.
Kupisch, Catherine M., Jan. 6, 1907. John P., March 21, 1905 - Feb. 23, 19__(?).
George Richard Kupisch, July 13, 1948 - Dec. 28, 1962.
A. Bahn (Flat Monument).
Cotter (Flat Monument).
A. Max (Flat Monument).
Unidentified Plot.
M. Duke (Flat Monument).
Unidentified Plot.
John McNicolas, b. in the parish of Bohola County Mayo, Ireland, d. Jan. 2,
  1881, aged 59 years.* (J.McN. - foot)
Unidentified mound in McNicholas enclosure.
(Two or more presumed plots)
Matthew Feeney, a native of the county Galway, Ireland, d. Aug. 13, 1877, age
  55 years.*
(Presumed plots)
Thomas, 1830-1893. His wife, Ann, 1833-1907. Carney (Corner post also marked
  Thomas Carney.)
John Banahan, beloved husband of Bridget Banahan, d. April 16, 1887, aged 65
  years. Bridget Banahan, beloved wife of John Banahan, d. Dec. 19, 1868,
  aged 40 years.* (J.B./B.B.)
Keough (Monument)
Andrew, 1857-1911.
Ellen, 1834-1919.
Patrick, 1832-1907.
(Five or more presumed plots)

57

Mary Holmes, wife of John Holmes, a native of the parish of Dunmore County Galway, Ireland, who departed this life 10 May 1862, aged 30 years.* (M.H.-foot)
Karl P. Ward, b. March 8, 1914, d. Oct. 15, 1915. Warren J. Ward, b. Jan. 17, 1923, d. April 26, 1923.
John T. Ward, b. March 18, 1870, d. Feb. 10, 1888.* (J.T.W.-foot)
Thomas Ward, d. July 15, 1899, aged 64 years.* (T.W.)
Charles F. Ward, Feb. 12, 1879 - Sept. 2, 1926.
(At least two plots)
Mary Halligan, d. May 2, 1899.*
Bridget Powers, d. Jan. 18, 1886.*
Unidentified Plot.
Husband, Charles O'Hara, a native of Co. Antrim, Ireland, d. June 29, 1884, aged 54 years.*
(Stump of marker)
(Two to three plots)
Conroy (Flat Marker)
(Unidentified Plot)
(Plot with pointed corner posts)
M. J. Collins, b. March 1, 1857 (?), d. Aug. 27, 1881.*
Kohlhoff, Herman A., 1889-1968. Mary T., 1894----.
(Plot formerly railed with iron bars; Martin Lavin on corner post)
(Two to three unidentified plots)
Husband, William Fitzgerald, d. July 12, 1878 in the 62nd year of his age. A native of the Parish of Allydorny, County Kerry, Ireland. (W.F. foot).
Patrick Fitzgerald, native of the Parish of Dedagh, County Kerry, Ireland, d. Sept. 15, 1894, aged 67 years.*
(Stump)
Father (Goes with Fitz-Gerald)
(Plot with J. M. on corner post)
John, beloved husband of Ann Durkin, d. March 2, 1883, aged 60 years. A native of Parish Draum, County Mayo, Ireland.* (Signature, C.E. Ehman, Balto.) (J.D.-foot)
(Plot with cornerstones)
Agnes Ann, beloved dau. of Patrick & Mary Fitzpatrick, b. Jan. 4, 1874, d. Dec. 20, 1891.*
(Plot with corner posts)
August Primus, d. June 14, 1897, aged 60 years.*
Mary Primus, d. Jan. 1, 1891, aged 40 years.*
(Corner post marked P.F.)
P. T. Kelly, d. Sept. 26, 1888, aged 19 years, 3 mos. and 12 days.* (signature, Meads & Bro, Md. Line) (P.T.K.-foot)
Bridget McGowan, beloved wife of Thomas McNicholas. A native of the parish of Straid County Mayo, Ireland, d. Jan. 14, 1901, aged 32 years.* (B.McN-foot)
Michael Joseph, son of James T. & Katie A. Byrnes, b. Dec. 4, 1885, d. Dec. 17, 1932.* (M.J.B.)
John P., beloved son of James T. & the late Katie A. Byrnes, b. Oct. 6, 1879, d. Oct. 16, 1907.* (J.P.B.-foot)
Katie A. Byrnes, who departed this life Dec. 29, 1887 in the 38th year of her age.* (K.A.B.-foot)
Jos. Noppenberger, Aug. 27, 1826 - Sept. 3, 1893. M. C. Noppenberger, Feb. 2, 1834 - Oct. 25, 1906. (Signature, Gault & Son, Balto) (Foot-Father - Mother)
Catherine, Conrad, John (Noppenberger) (C.N. - foot)
Hier rube in Gott, Andread Noppenberger, Geboren, Den 16 Marz 1856, Gestorben, Den 7 Dez 1883.*
(Enclosed plot with Barron on flat monument)
Patrick J. Fitzgerald, d. Oct. 8, 1883 at White Hall, Balto. Co., Md., aged 33 years.* Erected by his mother, Margaret J. Fitzgerald.

John D. Fitzgerald, a native of Dromtrasna O'Brine, Parish of Abbeyfeale
County, Limerick, Ireland, d. March 14, 1878, aged 53 years, 8 mos. and 20
days.* (Signature, Birchall, Glen Rock)
Patrick Fitzgerald, by his beloved wife, Margaret who departed this life, Feb.
12, 1868. A native of the Parish, Abyfale County Limerick, Ireland, in his
38th year.* (P.F.-foot)
Gibbons, Fahey (Walled enclosure)
John Melvin, d. Aug. 20, 1879, aged 62 years.*
Seeburger (Flat Monument)
Husband, Patrick Mannion, born in County Mayo, Ireland, d. in Baltimore County,
Maryland, Dec. 6, 1867, aged 54 years.* (P.M.)
Mary, wife of Patrick Mannion, b. in County Mayo, Ireland, d. May 27, 1892,
aged 80 years.*
James, son of Patrick and Mary Mannion, d. Jan. 4, 1913, aged 65 years.
(Plot with J.M. on corner posts)
Frank E. Rodgers, Maryland PFC, Co K, 313 Infantry, World War I, Sept. 15, 1893-
Aug. 20, 1959(?).
John Rogers, a native of the Parish of Ballabroughan, County of Roscommon,
Ireland, d. Dec. 28, 1879, age 52 years.* Erected by his wife, Bridget
Rogers.* (J.R.-foot, uprooted).
Margaret Ann Rogers, a native of the parish of Drum County of May, Ireland,
d. Dec. 1, 1871, age 37 years.* Erected by Peter Rogers.(M.A.R.-foot)
Michael C. Walsh (Flat Monument)
Bridget Walsh, wife of Michael C. Walsh, d. July 7, 1866. A native of County
Mayo, Ireland.* (B.W.-foot)
John Lindsay, beloved husband of Catherine Lindsay, a native of Cross Molona,
County Mayo, Ireland, d. Dec. 24, 1891, aged 62 years.* (J.L.-foot).
Mary, widow of the late Martin Connor, d. Jan. 24, 1889, aged 65 years. A
native of County Roscommon, Ireland. Erected by her daughter. (Foot-Mother)
Brennan (Flat Monument)
Dooling.
Annie, d. April 6, 1911, beloved wife of William Dooling, d. April 21, 1931.
(Foot-Mother-Father)
John Dooling, b. in Roscommon, Ireland, d. March 13, 1883, age 10 years.
(Foot-J.D.)
Catherine Dooling, wife of Irvin Schario, 1881-1926.* (C.D.S.-foot)
Bridget, wife of Patrick Wynn, d. Aug. 15, 1872. Also their dau. Mary, d. Oct.
30, 1874.* (M.W.-foot)
Kane (Flat Monument)
John Elwood, d. Aug. 12, 1878 in the 52nd year of his age. A native of Curras-
lira Parish, Bally Broughan County, Roscommon, Ireland.
(Corner Posts marked J.P.)
Kling, John J., 1834-1902. Mary 1836-1900.*
George C. Noppenberger, b. May 23, 1854, d. Nov. 14, 1899.
Margaret Noppenberger, b. 1823, d. 1903, aged 80 years.
Conrad Noppenberger, d. Nov. 16, 1888, aged 64 years, 6 mos. & 27 days.
Daniel Donnelly departed this life Feb. 5, 1888, aged 48 years. A native of
Clonfree, Strokestown, Roscommon Co., Ireland. Agrandson of the late
Captain Owen McDermott of 31st Regiment of foot.* (D.D.-foot).
Hanly, Mary Hanly Lundy, 1854-1929. Catherine Hanly, 1863-1942. (Foot markers
C.H., M.H.L.)
Our parents, James Hanly, beloved husband of Margaret Hanly, d. March 13, 1891
in the 73rd year of his age. A native of the Parish of Kilbride Co. Ros-
common, Ireland. Margaret Hanly, beloved wife of James Hanly, d. March 16,
1891 in the 71st year of her age. A native of the Parish of Kilbride Co.,
Roscommon, Ireland.*
E. Concannon, 1845-1888. M. Concannon, 1848-1917.
T. Conway (Flat monument with gate posts)

Bridget Hagerty, a native of Crossmolina, County Mayo, Ireland, d. July 26, 1880, aged 60 years by her son, Michael. (B.H.-foot)
Catherine Hartigan Barry, a native of Mt. Larens, Limerick County, Ireland, d. Feb. 25, 1908, aged 87 years.* (C.H.B.-foot)
James Barry, d. April 5, 1876, aged 55 years, 6 mos. and 27 days. A native of the parrish of Ballabricken, Friars Town, County Limerick, Ireland.* (J.B.-foot)
Mary Ann Barry, March 17, 1856 - March 29, 1936.
Catherine Lindsay, d. June 7, 1865, age 75 years.
Thomas & Ann Smith, Kane & Family.
Susan, beloved wife of Peter Mannion, d. April 2, 1891, aged 75 years.*
Monahan, John, Mary K., Mary C., Ann C. (Also Flat monument - Monahan) (Cornerpost of C. Dougherty plot)
Burns (Flat monument)
Wife, Bridget Welsh, wife of John Welsh, a native of Tuam, County Galway, Ireland, d. Jan. 22, 1896, aged 71 years.* (B.W.)
Father, John Welsh, beloved husband of Bridget Welsh, a native of Tuam County Galway, Ireland, d. April 19, 1900, aged 75 years.* (J.W.)
Husband, Patrick Martin, a native of Tuam, County Galway, Ireland, d. Dec. 2, 1894, aged 55 years.* (P.M.-foot)
Patrick J., son of Patrick & Mary Martin, d. Oct. 27, 1899, aged 28 years and 8 mos.*
Mary Martin, wife of Patrick Martin, b. 1840, d. 1923.*
Charles L., son of Patrick & Mary Martin, b. Aug. 7, 1880, d. March 23, 1907.
Bessie, dau. of Patrick & Mary Martin, b. Feb. 14, 1875, d. Nov. 2, 1909.
Hessian (Monument - both sides)
Mary M., 1899-1913.
John W., 1861-1943.
Ella A., 1866-1949.
Hier ruhet in Gott, Margtha Rothenhoefer, Geb. den 18 Juli 1885, Gest den 12 Aug. 1887.
Mary E. Shade, Feb. 8, 1854 - Dec. 5, 1935.
Mother, Mary Kay, d. Aug. 13, 1911. (Rest, if any, sunken)
James, son of James & Mary E. Hines, d. Feb. 26, 1893, aged 6 years, 3 mos. and 15 days.
James Hines, Jr., beloved husband of Mary E. Hines, d. Aug. 9, 1886 in the 42nd year of his age.* (J.H.Jr.-foot)
Space
Nora Flynn, d. June 19, 1882, aged 2 years, 4 mos.
T. Keating (Flat monument)
Gerardo Smith, June 15, 1913 - June 29, 1970.
Mary, beloved wife of John Barry, departed this life, Aug. 6, 1886 in the 40th year of her age. A native of the parish of Ballybrouthan, County Roscommon, Ireland.*
(Several plots)
Edward Nestor, d. Feb. 27, 1887, aged 62 years. Katherine Nestor, d. Aug. 2, 1889, aged 67 years. John Nestor, d. Nov. 22, 1896, aged 50 years.* (J.N., K.N., E.N.)
John, beloved husband of Elizabeth Connor, d. Jan. 15, 1864, aged 65 years. A native of Parish Kilbride, County Roscommon, Ireland.* (J.C.-foot)
Mary, dau. of Luke & Bridget Logan, d. Jan. 6, 1869, aged 13 mos. & 26 days.*
J. Bryne (Flat Monument)
(Plot with "K" corner posts)
Spera, Veto Anthony, Sept. 21, 1913 - Dec. 4, 1937. Augusta M. Spera, wife of Stanley M. Kennedy, Oct. 17, 1921 - Dec. 4, 1937, killed in accident near Hereford, Md.
James J. Kelley (Flat monument)
Kelley, Delia, d. Aug. 31, 1916, aged 50 years.*

Naughton-Quinn (Flat Monument)
Leo Boylston Smith, d. July 4, 1918.
Thomas J. Naughton, d. Feb. 22, 1891.
Annie M. Naughton, d. Dec. 29, 1921.
Joseph L. Naughton, Jan. 11, 1888 - April 20, 1956.
Bessie B. Naughton, d. Oct. 14, 1960.
F.O.B. (Lying flat)
James Hines, Sr., departed this life, Nov. 16, 1887, aged 72 years, a native of Kilkenny, Ireland (rest sunken).
Thomas P. Keating, Aug. 13, 1890 - March 12, 1967.
Elsie H. Keating, May 22, 1893 - (blank)
John H. Keating, d. June 22, 1897 and his beloved wife, Mary A. Keating, d. Sept. 30, 1904.* (J.H.K., M.A.K.-foot)
C. Fitzgerald (Large walled plot)
Tully (Large walled plot)
Thomas Murray, a native of the Parish of Tuam (rest sunken).
Michael Murray, a native of the Parish Tuam, County Galway, Ireland, d. March 19, 1880 in his 77th year. Thomas, son of Michael and Margaret Murray, d. in his 5th year.* (M.M.-foot)
John T. Costello, b. Dec. 22, 1865, d. Jan. 19, 1867, aged 1 year and 28 days.
E. Byrne (flat monument)
(Plot once enclosed by rails)
(Plot marked by corner posts)
Owens, b. in County Roscommon, Ireland. Father, John, Feb. 2, 1817 - Aug. 8, 1901. Mother, Catherine Elwood, March 20, 1818 - Feb. 8, 1902.
John Malone, a native of the parish Mulloch County Clare, Ireland, d. July 20, 1866, aged 17 years. Erected by his beloved wife.*
Hester Sterrett, b. Sept. 21, 1849, d. July 2, 1913.
Many spaces.
O. Hanley (Flat monument in railed enclosure)
Owen Hanley, his wife, Catherine Toomey Hanley, dau. Elizabeth Hanley.
(Plot with pointed corner markers)
Patrick Croghan, d. July 21, 1879, aged 46 years. A native of County Roscommon, Ireland. Bridget, wife of Patrick Croghan, d. April 24, 1881, aged 38 years, a native of County Roscommon, Ireland.*
Iron fenced enclosure with foot marker M.O'H. Martin O'Hara, a native of the County Roscommon, Ireland, d. Feb. 26, 1877 in the 55th year of his age.*
John Welsh, who departed this life, April 11, 1876 in the 37th year of his age. A native of the Parish of Straid County Mayo, Ireland.*
Plot with pointed corner markers, iron rails missing.
Scally (flat monument)
Annie, beloved wife of Patrick Scally, b. May 17, 1850, d. March 4, 1906. Patrick Scally, b. Jan. 1, 1839, d. July 15, 1921.* (A.S.-foot)
(Much space)
(plot with corner markers)
(space)
Lawrence Cummings, a native of the county of Roscommon, Ireland, d. Nov. 5, 1878 in the 63rd year of his age.*
Son, Dr. John Cummings, d. March 16, 1887 in the 35th year of his age. Only son of the late Lawrence and Catherine Cummings. Mary Cummings Harlow, d. Aug. 12, 1805 in the 22nd year of her age.*
John Ellwood, son of Michael & Margaret Ellwood, who departed this life on the 19th of Dec. 1848, aged 15 mos. and 26 days.
Erected by Francis McAleer to the memory of his Mother, Margaret, consort of Henry McAlleer, who departed this life 18 July 1863, aged 80 years, a native of the parish and (rest sunken) (foot-M.McA.)
Owen Monaghan, b. in the parish of Killukin, County of Roscommon, Ireland, d. in Texas, Baltimore County, Aug. 17, 1872, aged 62 years.* (O.M.-foot)

Patrick Monaghan, beloved son of Owen and Mary Monaghan, native of County
  Roscommon, Parish of Killuckin, Ireland, d. June 2, 1863, aged 25 years.*
  (P.M.-foot)
Michael Hines, b. 1814, d. 1879, aged 65 years.* (M.H.)
Erected by Daniel Burk to the memory of his son, William of the County of Water-
  ford, Parish of Piltown, Ireland, d. Nov. 27, 1862, (?) years and 14 days.
  (W.B.-foot)
In memory of John and Mary Shea.
(Head and footstones, but unmarked)
James Loftus, b. Jan. 6, 1838, d. Feb. 27, 1899, age 61 years.
John J. Driver, 1883-1943.*
(Plot with "A.Driver" on corner post)
Michael Croghen, husband, who departed this life, July 22, 1884 in the 44th year
  of his age. A native of County Roscommon, Ireland.* (M.C.)
Patrick Croghan of Beechwood parish of Kilteven, County Roscommon, Ireland, d.
  Aug. 27, 1887 in the 87th year of his age. Erected by his dau., Anna Croghan.*
  (P.C.-foot)
Erected by her husband to Julia, beloved wife of Thomas Lenihan, b. in the parish
  of Duringree, County Cork, Ireland, d. Nov. 1, 1875, aged 29 years.*
M. Kelly (Flat monument)
Kelly (Monument)
(Several plots with corner markers)
John O'Hara, a native of County Roscommon, Ireland, d. April 8, 1881, aged 45 years.
  His wife, Annie, d. Feb. 18, 1901.*
Mary A., d. Jan. 28, 1888, aged 19 years. Ellen, d. Sept. 12, 1880, aged 5 years,
  children of John and Annie O'Hara.
Catherine A., d. Jan. 8, 1924.
Margaret T. Kelly, d. Feb. 23, 1944.
Michael, husband of Mary J. Farley, d. Aug. 16, 1905, aged 75 years.* (M.F.-foot)
Mary Jane, beloved wife of Michael Farley, a native of County Cavan, Ireland,
  d. May 27, 1890, aged 67 years.* (M.J.F.-foot)
(Corner post marked P. McNeeve)
Stone fallen on face, J.D. at foot.
Our father, Michael Duggan, d. Nov. 14, 1882 in the 67th year of his age, a
  native of the County Kerry, Ireland.* (M.D.-foot)
(Plot with pointed corner posts)
Hugh O'Connor (Flat Monument)
Peter McGann, a native of Parish Ogula, County Roscommon, Ireland, d. May 12,
  1893, aged 68 years.* Erected by his sister E. Leech McGann.
Catherine McGann, a native of the parish of Ogula, County Roscommon, Ireland,
  d. Feb. 6, 1867, aged 36 years. Also her sister, Ann McGann, a native of
  said parish and county, d. July 1, 1871, aged 17 years.* (C.McG., A.McG.-foot)
M. Horan (Flat monument)
W. Michael Watson, Sept. 27, 1839 - March 4, 1910. Albert A. Watson, 1867-1869.
  Sarah E. Watson, 1869-1870. (S.E.W.-foot)
Albert A., son of Michael & Celinda E. Watson, d. Aug. 22, 1869, aged 1 year,
  8 mos and 18 days.*
Sarah E., dau. of Michael and Celinda E. Watson, d. Oct. 1, 1870, aged 11 mos.
  and 23 days.*
Mary Toolan, beloved wife of Edward Toolan, d. June 21, 1872, aged 35 years.
  A native of county Roscommon, Ireland. Edward Toolan, b. April 3, 1836, d.
  April 9, 1905. Erected by her husband, Edward Toolan.* (Foot-M.T., E.T.)
J. Keating (Flat Monument)
Mother, Mary A. McKeon, 1858-1931.
Father, Bernard McKeon, 1855-1928.
(Recent burial - no marks on stone)
Our mother, Mary, wife of Thomas Stanton, b. in Co. Mayo, Ireland, 1820, d.
  March 11, 1892.*

Our father, Thomas Stanton, b. in County Mayo, Ireland, 1814, d. July 30, 1897(?).*
(Plot with "B" corner posts)
Our baby, John F. Patterson, Feb. 17, 1965 - Feb. 19, 1965.*
Meinschein, George J., Nov. 3, 1895 - Jan. 11, 1964. Mary A., March 3, 1897---.
Mother, Florence L. Higgins, 1891-1967.
(Plot with "P.B." corner markers)
(Unidentified, marked plot)
Croghan (Monument with P.C. corner posts)
(Iron Cross) P.H./R.I.P. (P.H.-foot)
Hoffman, Casper Hoffman, 1825-1897. Theresa Hoffman, 1829-1904.
G.C.H. - corner posts
Husband, Charles Edward Gibbons, d. Oct. 6, 1893 in the 34th year of his age.*
(Plot with corner posts)
McConnall (Walled enclosure)
Mary McDonnell, beloved wife of Thos. McDonnell, departed this life Aug. 15, 1883, aged 56 years. Also my beloved son, Francis P. McDonnell, aged 20 years.*
Kate, beloved dau. of Robert & Ellen Colbert, d. July 23, 1883, aged 22 years.*
(K.C.-foot)
Thomas James Higgins, May 5, 1960 - May 31, 1964, son of James J. and Eileen M. Higgins.
Michelle Louise and Marie Patricia Lauzon, April 25, 1962.
Ralph Marks, 1876-1958.
Stella O'Hearn McLaughlin, Nov. 23, 1883 - June 23, 1958.*
William D. Beale, son of James J. and Maryann Beale, Dec. 12, 1942 - April 26, 1968.
Mother, Laura Smith, Jan. 13, 1888 - Dec. 28, 1963.
Rafferty, Maurice J., 1917-1970. Genevieve B., 1931---.
William S. Hughes, b. Dec. 18, 1860, d. April 19, 1873. (rest, if any, sunken)
Katherine Gleason, 1856-1946.
Thomas Gleason, a native of the County Limerick, Ireland, b. in the year 1810, d. Aug. 6, 1874.*
Margaret, wife of Thomas Gleason, d. Sept. 6, 1904, aged 75 years. A native of County Cork. (rest if any, sunken)
John T., son of Timothy & Mary Feehely, d. Nov. 22, 1893, aged 36 years.
Timothy Feehely, d. April 3, 1878, aged 52 years. Mary, wife of Timothy Feehley, d. Oct. 21, 1887, aged 54 years.*

Copied by J. McGrain, August-October, 1971.

BAZIL A.M.E. CHURCH
320 Sherwood Road
Cockeysville, MD

Located on north side of road, west of Powers Avenue and east of Church on the Cockeysville Quadrant.

JLF
John L. Foote, 1050-1920.
E. Alberta Foote, Dec. 20, 1866 - Aug. 22, 1943.
Mary Jane Smith, 1847-1924.
John L. Foote, Jr., Feb. 19, 1896 - Oct. 24, 1957.
Leona G. Foote, March 5, 1900 - March 11, 1968.
Unmarked plot.

Lizzie Marshall d. in the year of our Lord, Nov. 6, 1938.
W.
S. A. Frazier, b. 1838, d. 1895.
Foote (large marker, name on both sides)
Elizabeth Ann Foote, b. Jan. 19, 1818, d. Dec. 1897.
E. J.
J. L. F. (corner)
J. Cornelius Foote, June 3, 1869 - Nov. 18, 1969.
Daisy Wilson Foote, Aug. 15, 1889 - Oct. 5, 1958.
J. L. F. (corner)
Eliza Jane, widow of J. Randolph Johnson, b. Jan. 15, 1841, d. Nov. 2, 1913.
Johnson (rest sunken)
Ellswirth Winder, Feb. 5, 1916 - July 3, 1942.
Metal marker and azalea plant
W. ?. and W. S.
Marion E. Smith, b. Jan. 10, 1886, d. Sept. 1906 (M.E.S. - foot).
William H. Smith, b. 1865, d. Jan. 5, 1907 (W.H.S. - foot).
Payne, Anne L. Smith, Jan. 16, 1868 - Jan. 3, 1934.
S. (corner)
Adaline Martina A. Johnson, Aug. 3, 1936 - June 24, 1940.
Edith Alverdia Johnson, Dec. 28, 1915 - March 16, 1940.
Rosalba Barbara Johnson, July 4, 1925 - Feb. 20, 1927.
Alfred Johnson, husband of Margaret Johnson, 1841-1920.
Edith Victoria Johnson, June 19, 1884 - July 17, 1938.
George Henry Johnson, Aug. 31, 1882 - Sept. 1, 1960.
Black metal marker
Clarence Edward Swann, Maryland Corp. 154 Depot Brig., March 2, 1941. (rest, if any sunken.)
Mother, Rachel E. Smith, 1860-1940.
Charles W., husband of Carrie M. Larks, b. April 29, 1870, d. May 10, 1927.
Leroy Robert Harrison Winder, son of Alice Winder, b. Oct. 29, 1916, d. April 7, 1918.
Tucker (Monument, both sides)
Joseph F. Tucker, March 27, 1866 - March 17, 1941.
Rufus A. Tucker, Dec. 29, 1929 - Aug. 17, 1944.
Joseph Levi Tucker, June 20, 1866 - Jan. 10, 1955.
Husband and father, Melvin R. Tucker, Oct. 19, 1900 - Feb. 2, 1951.
Wilson (monument)
Husband, Henry, Sr., 1865-1946.
Wife, Nancy Wilson, 1867-1947.
Wooden cross.
Wooden cross.
Wooden cross.
Roebuck (with "R" corner marker).
Four to five unmarked mounds
Georgianna Randalph, Dec. 16, 1881 - June 22, 1948.
Lee T. Davenport, 1903-1964.
Florence Lillie May, wife of Jacob Cole, dau. of Harvey & Lillie May Wright, d. May 26, 1943.
William A. Wright, Dec. 24, 1926 - March 5, 1950.
Henry Wright, May 10, 1895 - May 28, 1954.
Lillie L. Wright, wife of Henry wright, March 10, 1896 - Feb. 22, 1965.
Davenport, William Oscar, Sept. 26, 1890 - July 16, 1956. Mary Louise, Feb. 22, 1898---
William H. Jackson, Dec. 24, 1912 - May 16, 1956.

NISBET FAMILY CEMETERY

Located at foot of hill from "Home for the Aged" (new building used by Baltimore County Genealogical Society) in the N. E. corner of the Cockeysville Quadrant. Copies April, 1971 by John McGrain.

Alexander Nisbet, b. at Montrose, Scotland, came to the United States 1784, d. Nov. 22, 1857. For nearly 40 years one of the Judges of the Baltimore City Court, President of the St. Andrews Society 26 years.*

Departed this life, Aug. 30, 1864, Mary C. Nisbet, wife of Alexander Nisbet and dau. of the late John C. Owings.*

Charles, Thomas and John Nisbet, infant sons of Alexander and Mary Nisbet. John Owings Nisbet, b. Sept. 9, 1819, d. Feb. 1, 1825. Charles Nisbet, b. May 21, 1810, d. Dec. 13, 1813. Thomas Deye Nisbet, b. Sept. 21, 1811, d. July 23, 1812.*

Note: Mr. McGrain's notes cover two pages and include a map showing the location of the cemetery.

CEMETERY ON WARREN ROAD
Towson Quad

This cemetery is on the property of Mr. & Mrs. Ted Lissauer, 805 Warren Road, Cockeysville. It may have been on the property of a now vanished Baptist Church. The inscriptions were copied Nov. 6, 1971 by Robert Barnes.

Elder Thomas Poteet, Pastor of the Warren and Saters Particular Baptist Churches who departed this life March 6, 1843 in the 53rd year of his age.*
Susan, wife of Thomas Poteet, b. Dec. 24, 1798, d. Feb. 18, 1869.*
Flat stone with same information as the two names above. "Erected by their son, Z. Poteet."
Ann, consort of Abram Owen, d. Aug. 8, 1846, aged 30 years. Foot A.O.
Casander Daniels, d. Aug. 2, 1827, aged 55 years.*

RIDGELY FAMILY CEMETERY

Located on grounds of Dulaney Springs Golf Course; copied Aug. 1, 1971 by Robert W. Barnes, Sr. and Robert W. Barnes, Jr.

Martha Taylor, colored, d. Oct. 1, 1916, aged 70 years. A servant in the family 31 years.
Georgianna Poteet.
Neville Rush Ridgely, husband of Margaret Bates Ridgely, son of Benjamin Talbott Ridgely and Elizabeth Talbott Ridgely, Nov. 27, 1883 - July 14, 1956.
Joshua Talbott, son of Dr. Aquila T. and Mary F. Ridgely, b. Aug. 13, 1873, d. Oct. 16, 1934.*
Aquila Wilmott, son of Dr. Aquila T. and Mary F. Ridgely, b. Sept. 1, 1871, d. Feb. 26, 1903.
Greenberry, Ridgely, 1849.
Charles Washington, son of Charles W. and Mary (?) Ridgely, b. Aug. 30, 1845, d. Sept. ?, 1845.*

Mrs. Harriett Ridgely, b. April 18, 1792, d. April 10, 1872.*
Sarah Talbot Ridgely, b. Dec. 17, 1819, d. May 10, 1867.*
Susie D., wife of Joshua Ridgely, b. Sept. 11, 1859, d. Feb. 3, 1887.*
Ridgely, Benjamin Talbott, Oct. 4, 1856 - Dec. 13, 1840. His wife, Elizabeth C. Talbott, Aug. 23, 1855 - Jan. 18, 1942.
Infant son of B. T. & E. C. Ridgely, b. and d. March 31, 1889.
Stones, 1, 2, 3, 4, 5 - weathered stumps of rocks.
Mary Edwards.
Edward Talbott, b. July 15, 1723, d. Aug. 29, 1797 and Temperance, his wife, b. Sept. 13, 1720, d. Jan. 4, 1813. Footstone: Revolutionary Patriot.
Joshua Talbott, b. May 26, 1775, d. Jan. 14, 1803.
Ann, dau. of V. & M. Talbott, b. Feb. 11, 1804, d. July 19, 1805.
Benjamin Talbott, b. Feb. 11, 1750, d. Jan. 5, 1816.* Footstone - Revolutionary Soldier.
Sarah, consort of Banjamin Talbott, b. Sept. 27, 1749, d. Jan. 8, 1815.*
James Henry, son of G. & H. Ridgely, b. Nov. 16, 1817, d. Aug. 19, 1819.
Infant son of G. & H. Ridgely, b. and d. 1822.
Infant dau. of G. & H. Ridgely, b. and d. 1830.
Mary Frances, wife of Dr. Aquila T. Ridgely, b. Jan. 22, 1836, d. Jan. 5, 1911.*
Dr. Aquila T. Ridgely, b. May 4, 1827, d. Nov. 15, 1892.*
Catherine, relict of Joshua Talbott, who departed this life Nov. 1, 1853 in the 76th year of her age.*
Aquila Talbot, b. Feb. 15, 1781, d. Feb. 24, 1865.*
Eleanor Talbott, b. Jan. 25, 1786, d. April 6, 1871.
Sarah M. Talbott, b. Oct. 28, 1788, d. July 24, 187?.*
Stones - 1, 2, 3 and 4 - weathered stumps.
Rebecca Talbott, 1783-1787.
Temperance Talbott, 1782-1793.
Penelope D. C. Talbott, 1798.
Edward Talbott, 1764-1801.
Thomas Talbott, son of John and Mary Talbott, who departed this life June 27, 180?, aged ? years and 5 ? (below ground)
Elizabeth, wife of Vincent Talbott, d. May 12, 1822.
Vincent Talbott, b. Oct. 15, 1752, d. Dec. 26, 1819.
John Talbott, 1773-1824.
Vincent Talbott, who departed this life, Feb. 5, 1832, aged 55 years, 3 mos., 21 days.*
Mary, consort of Vincent Talbott, who died March 13, 1840?, aged 56 years, 5 mos. and 11 days.*
Illegible
Alice Duncan Ridgely, dau. of Herbert and Alice Ridgely, b. Feb. 12, 1912, d. Dec. 3, 1916.*
Ichabod? Talbott, son of J. and Eliza? Talbott, 1853-1932.
Clara Merryman Todd, 1847-1930.
George Vincent Todd, 1834-1927.
Mary Catherine Todd, 1838-1901.
Miss .... Talbott, who died ....(illegible).
Mary (Slade) Talbott, 1775-1853.
Dr. Benjamin C. Ridgely, b. Jan. 20, 1824, d. Feb. 2, 1917.
Mary Catherine Ridgely, b. Sept. 1, 1835, d. Jan. 17, 1919.

STANSBURY-BOSLEY FAMILY CEMETERY
TOWSON QUAD

Located on the grounds of Stella Maris, on the Dulaney Valley Road. It was copied Nov. 6, 1971 by Robert W. Barnes.

Elizabeth, consort of William Bosley, b. April 12, 1785, d. Sept. 25, 1850.*
Footstone E.B.
William Bosley of W. who was born on the 13th day of Feb. 1774 and d. March 25, 1837. For many years a respectable merchant of the city of Baltimore. Footstone W.B.
William Stansbury, who departed this life on the 23rd day of June, 1818, in the 70th year of his age.
Hannah, wife of Thomas Stansbury, who departed this life on the 11th? of Sept. 1800, in the 85th year of her age. Footstone H.S.
Thomas Stansbury, who departed this life on the 15th of June, 179?, in the 88th year of his age. Footstone T.S.
Luke? Stansbury, b. Dec. ?, d. ? 1787 or 1797.
Too weathered to read.
D'd (David?) Andrew, d. 1808.
Walter T., son of William and Elizabeth Bosley, b. June 21, 1818, d. Oct. 8, 1884.*
Mary Jane Bosley, who departed this life on the 19th day of February, 1831, aged 20 years and 15 days. Footstone M.J.B.
Ellen Bosley, b. 28 May 1813, d. 23 July 1814. Footstone E.B.
Mary Jane Bosley, b. 28 June 1809, d. Aug. 3, 1810.
Walter Bosley, aged ? months who departed this life Feb. 29, 1804.
..ohn (John?) Campbell, departed this life, June 23, 1805, aged...
Margaret Campbell, departed this ..., Sept. 25, ..., aged...
William Welch, d. March 25, 1805 (1903?), aged 35 years.

Numerous other stumps of rocks remain but cannot be read.

MERRYMAN FAMILY CEMETERY

Off dirt road which leads east from end of Pot Spring Road towards Loch Raven Reservoir on Quadrange Map - Aug. 8, 1971 - Robert Barnes.

Henry C. Merryman, son of Micajah Merryman, Jr. and Clarisse Merryman, Dec. 27, 1838 - Sept. 19, 1934.*
Eleanor C. Merryman, Dec. 20, 1834 - July 16, 1905.*
Laura Virginia Merryman, Oct. 20, 1870 - Jan. 23, 1952.*
Harry Lee Merryman, Feb. 9, 1867 - Jan. 4, 1945.*
S. Howard Merryman, Dec. 9, 1868 - March 17, 1940.*
George M. Merryman, Feb. 9, 1863 - Dec. 12, 1899.*
Rev. Charles G. Merryman, 1860-1894.*
George H. Merryman, Sept. 8, 1831 - March 30, 1922.*
Mary G. Merryman, May 25, 1830 - June 14, 1924.*
Obelisk - erected by the family of Micajah Merryman, Jr., 1855. Micajah Merryman, son of Micajah and Mary Merryman, d. 29 April 1854, aged 66 years. Clarissa Merryman, wife of Micajah Merryman, Jr. d. 15 April 1879, aged 80 years. George Merryman, d. 10 Aug. 1829, aged 6 mos. and 14 days. Mary, d. 26 Sept. 1830, aged 2 mos. and 17 days, children of Micajah and Clara Merryman. Henry C. Merryman, Dec. 27, 1838 - Sept. 19, 1934. George H. Merryman, son of Micajah and Clarissa Merryman, b. Sept. 8, 1831, d. March 30, 1922. Mary Gorsuch, wife of George H. Merryman, b. May 25, 1830, d. June 14, 1924. Micajah, son of G. H. and M. G. Merryman, b. Dec. 31, 1860, d. Jan. 5, 1961. Andrew Lowndes, son of G. H. & M. G. Merryman, b. Dec. 11, 1864, d. 19 Jan. 1868. Charles Gorsuch Merryman d. July 3, 1894 in his 34th year. George M. Merryman, d. Dec. 12, 1899 in his 37th year. Laura Virginia M., dau. of George H. and Mary Gorsuch Merryman, Oct. 20, 1870 - Jan. 23, 1952.
Micajah Merryman, d. 7 June 1842, aged 92 years. Mary Ensor, his wife, d. June 1788, aged 35 years. Sarah, dau. of Micajah and M. E. Merryman d. Sept.

1804, aged 23 years. Moses Merryman, M.D., son of M. & M. E. Merryman d.
19 Nov. 1819, age 36 years. Eleanor, dau. of M. & Mary E. M. d. 26 Sept.
1832, age 47 years. Mary M. Todd, wife of Benj. Bucknell and dau. of Micajah
and Mary Ensor Merryman, d. 2 Jan. 1829, age 42 years. Eleanor, dau. of
George and Mary M. Todd, d. 7 June 1835, aged 30 years.
Laura Virginia, dau. of Micajah and Clara Merryman, b. July 9, 1841, d. Oct. 3,
1870. Dr. Moses W. Merryman, Jr., son of Micajah and Clarissa Merryman, b.
Feb. 15, 1827, d. Jan. 25, 1904. Eleanor C. Merryman, b. Dec. 20, 1834, d.
July 16, 1905. S. Howard Merryman, son of Geo. H. & Mary Gorsuch Merryman,
Dec. 9, 1868 - March 17, 1940. Harry Lee Merryman, son of George H. and Mary
Grosuch Merryman, Feb. 9, 1867 - Jan. 4, 1945.
Hannah Lemmon departed this life Aug. 31, 1840, aged 88 years.*
Mary Myers Morris d. April 15, 1903, aged 70 years.
Footstone with "Revolutionary Soldier" marker DAR M.M.

HARRYMAN FAMILY CEMETERY
TOWSON QUAD

This cemetery is located on property owned by the Clap family, at the end of
Pot Spring Road, north of Bosley Road, in the Towson Quad. The cemtery is
shown on the Quad map. Ridgely's *Historic Graves*, pp. 132-133, describes
the cemetery as being on the tract "Cumberland" on the northwest side of the
Overshot Road, half a mile north of the point where this is intersected by the
road running from the Warren Road to Meredith's Bridge.

The inscriptions were copied Nov. 6, 1971 by Robert Barnes. Names and dates in
parentheses in this list are supplied from Ridgely. The cemetery is rectangular in shape, with a gate in the eastern end. The first row is farthest from
the gate. Stones were copies left to right.

Sarah Harryman, d. in Nov. 1790 (1799).
(George) Harryman, d. Dec. 1794.
George Harryman, b. (10) April (1768), d. (27 Nov. 1854) in the 87th year of
his age.
Rachel Harryman, who d. the 21st of June 1837 in the 76th year of her age.
Grace Lindley, wife of Chauncey Brooks Harryman, June 11, 1905 - Nov. 29, 1928.
Ann Plat, d. in the year 1808.
George Harryman, son of John Gorsuch and Sarah Hood Harryman, b. June 27, 1870,
d. Jan. 25, 1950.*
Elizabeth Barnes Brooks, wife of George Harryman, Aug. 8, 1873 - Feb. 25, 1846.*
John Gorsuch of Thomas, who departed this life, July 1, 1833 in the 64th year
of his age.
Sarah Gorsuch, who departed this life Dec. 2, 1851 in the 81st (85th?) year of her
age.
Harriett, wife of John Harryman, departed this life July the (3rd, 1841), aged
49 (40) years.
John Harryman, son of George and Rachel Bond Harryman, b. Nov. 6, 1788, d. Aug.
27, 1854, aged 66 years. (Foot - J.H.)
George, son of John and Harriet Gorsuch Harryman, b. April 18, 1833, d. April
7, 1920. (Foot-G.H.)
John Gorsuch Harryman, b. Jan. 16, 1838, d. May 27, 1893. (Foot J.G.H.)
Sarah Eleanor Hood, wife of John Gorsuch Harryman, b. Sept. 10, 1845, d. Aug.
8, 1893. (Foot S.E.H.)

Chauncey B. Harryman, b. Dec. 3, 1873, d. July 12, 1923. (Foot C.B.H.)
Henry P. Brooks, second son of Chauncey and Marilla P. Brooks. (On footstone,
H.P.B., b. Nov. 13, 1825, d. Sept. 26, 1874.)
Rachael, only dau. of John and Harriet Harryman and wife of Henry Brooks.
On footstone: R.H.B., b. Aug. 15, 1827, d. Dec. 9, 1892.
Marilla Phelps, eldest dau. of Rachael Harryman and Henry Phelps Brooks, June
11, 1851 - April 5, 1915. Foot: M.P.B.
Eleanor Merryman, sixth dau. of Rachel Harryman and Henry P. Brooks, 1861-
1918. Foot: E.M.B.
Katherine Gaylord, second dau. of Rachael Harryman and Henry Pehlps Brooks,
July 9, 1852 - Oct. 30, 1939. Foot: K.C.B.
Rachel Harryman, 1827, only dau. of John and Harriett Gorsuch Harryman, wife
of Henry Pehlps Brooks, 1825. Erected 1918 by her children. George and
Keturah Harryman, George and Sarah Harryman, d. 1794, George and Rachel
Bond Harryman, b. 1768, John and Harriet Gorsuch Harryman, b. 1788.

SAINT JOHN THE EVANGELIST R.C. CEMETERY

Located on the west side of Carroll Manor Road, 10th District. Abandoned.
Site of the wooden church burned in 1855, after which a new site at Long
Green was established.

Sophia, widow of William Hubert, d. July 15, 1890, 89 years of age.
William Hubert, d. June 9, 1882, aged 78 years, 2 mos., 28 days.
John Medary, father, b. Dec. 2, 1810, d. Dec. 13, 1878, aged 68 years, 11 days.
Henry Parker, son of John and Eve Clark, Aug. 14, 1825 - July 22, 1827.
Elizabeth, dau. of Tho. and Elizabeth Galloway, who departed this life May 6,
1829, aged 11 mos., 19 days.
Thomas, son of Tho. and Elizabeth was born Nov. 11, 1829 and d. March 29,
1831, aged 1 year, 4 mos. and 18 days.
(Note: This is presumably a Galloway stone.)

Information supplied by Mr. Clarence V. Joerndt of Bel Air, who wasn't sure
whether months were spelled or abbreviated. Letter to J. McGrain, Dec. 10,
1970.

PEERCE CEMETERY

Located on Dulaney Valley Road, one-half mile N.E. of the intersection with
Loch Raven Road, on a hill almost under the transmission lines. The sign
post near entrance reads - Old Peerce Cemetery/Dulaney Valley 1797-1897.

Aunt, Susan Smith, b. June 10, 1789, d. Aug. 4, 1862.*
Mother, Louise, wife of Wm. F. Peerce, b. Aug. 13, 1800, d. Nov. 4, 1865.*
George Peerce, b. Oct. 31, 1840, d. Oct. 11, 1894.*
Brother, Henry Peerce, b. Sept. 10, 1838, d. Aug. 15, 1844 (or 1840).*
David B. Ferguson, b. Jan. 1, 1784, d. Dec. 29, 1863.*
Mary, consort (?) of David E. Ferguson who was born July 25, 1785? and departed
this life, Aug. 10, 1835, aged 50 years and 16 days.
Thomas Dewitt, son of Tho's and Emma Peerce, b. Aug. 17, 1895, d. July 26,
1896.
Edward Dewitt, son of Tho's and Emma Peerce, b. Sept. 16, 1896, d. Aug. 5,
1897.

James Peerce who departed this life, Aug. 1797, aged 2 years and 6 mos.
Edward Peerce who departed this life, April 27, 1823 (or 1825), aged 68 years.
Anna, consort of Edward Peerce, b. Nov. 17, 1771, departed this life Jan. 1, 1831, aged 59 years and 46 days.
Eliz., consort of Wm. Ferguson, Sr., who departed this life Sept. 1, 1830, aged 84 years.
Eliza Ferguson, consort of Rev. Levi Ferguson, b. July 15, 1788, d. Sept. 27, 1870.*
Levi Ferguson, Sr., b. March 4, 1777, d. Feb. 4, 1833, aged 66 years (sic) and 11 mos.
Large center monument reads - William F. Peerce/Meads/Md. Line. Louisa Peerce.
Copied in August 1971 by Bob Zahner.

LONG GREEN MENNONITE CEMETERY - 1849

Kane's Road - enclosed in a whitewashed stone wall. Completed on August 14, 1971 by Robert Barnes.

Anna Waltz, b. Jan. 29, 1854, d. Feb. 1, 1854.
Magdalena Waltz, b. March 29, 1856, d. April 4, 1857.
Christian Waltz, b. Aug. 26, 1843, d. Jan. 14, 1863.
Jacob Waltz, b. Aug. 5, 1845, d. Jan. 11, 1866.
Rebecca Ritter, b. Jan. 30, 1879?, d. ?, 188?.
George Ritter, b. May ?, 1872?, d. D ?, 188?.
Menno S. Miller, d. May 31, 1898, aged 28 years, 5 mos., 19 days.
Silas Walters, husband of Mary E. Walters, d. Aug. 21, 1911, aged 58 years.*
Joseph Schnider, 1855-1937.
Annie E. Schnider, 1881-1955.
Mary M. Schnider, 1883-1953.
Footstone: I.T. or I.F.
Amanda Kennel, b. Sept. 25, 1868, d. March ?, 1871, age 3 years, 5 mos., 25 days.
Joseph Kennel, b. Jan. 6, 1858, d. Oct. 23, 1858, aged 9 mos., 17 days.
Adam Kennel, b. March 15, 1852, d. Jan. ?, ?, age 9 mos., ? days.
Rebecca Mast, b. Nov. ?, 182?, d. ?, 186?.
Daniel Mast, b. June 9, 186/, d. July 16, 18?, aged 10 or 19 years.
Jacob K. Mast, b. May 31, 1823, d. May 9, 1893, aged 69 years, 11 mos., 9 days.
Frances Meuhauser, wife of Jacob K. Mast, b. Oct. 6, 1835, d. April 26, 1911, aged 75 years, 6 mos., 20 days.
Mother, Elizabeth Neuhauser, dau. of John and Elizabeth Mast, b. July 25, 1835, d. Oct. 1, 1903, ated 68 years, 2 mos. and 9 days.*
Father, Christian Neuhauser, b. Jan. 5, 1830, d. March 18, 1905, aged 75 years, 2 mos. 13 days.*
Christian Neuhauser, son of Christian and Elizabeth, b. April 4, 1856, d. Feb. 10, 1928.*
Uncle, Samuel Neuhauser, son of Christian and Elizabeth, b. July 21, 1862, d. April 27, 1935.*
Elizabeth Zook, wife of Daniel K. Mast, d. March 22, 1905, aged 82 years, 7 mos.*
Daniel K. Mast, b. April 15, 1821, d. April 19, 1891, aged 70 years and 4 days.
Lydia, wife of Peter Nafzinger, 1838-1919, aged 86 years, 5 mos. and 15 days.*
Peter Nafzinger, d. Jan. 18, 1908, aged 81 years, 10 mos. and 12 days.*
Mary, wife of John Kennel, b. July ?, 1827, d. March ?, 1899?
John Kennel, b. ?, 182?, d. ?, 187?

Father, in memory of Christian M. Neuhauser, husband of Cora E. Neuhauser,
b. July 1, 1860, d. June 8, 1916.*
Mother, Cora E. Neuhauser, wife of Christian M. Neuhauser, b. Dec. 25, 1859,
d. July 28, 1924.*
Mast, Henry Z., 1844-1927.   Barbara B., 1858-1919.
Elizabeth Mast, b. March ?, 1798, d. ?, 1881.
John Mast, b. Feb. ?, 1795, d. Oct. ? 2, 18?3, aged ?
Lida Mast, d. May 24, 1864, aged 4 years, 4 mos., and 26 days.*
Samuel Mast, b. March 11, 1830, d. Jan. 12, 1862, aged 32 years and ? mos.
Mast, b. Oct. ?, 18.., d. ....., aged 2 years, 5 mos., and 11 days.
Bessie D., dau. of C. & M. J. Mast, d. Aug. 16, 1888, aged 8 mos. and 7 days.*
Corel H., child of C. & M. J. Mast, d. July 17, 1889, aged 4 mos. and 13 days.
Stump of rock.
Christian Mast, b. Jan. 11, 1856, d. Aug. 2, 1930.
David, son of Isaac and Mary Hertzler, b. Sept. 28, 1860, d. Aug. 13, 1865, 4
years, 10 mos., and 15 days.
Amy, dau. of Joseph and Nancy J. Hertzler, d. July 26, 1893, ated 7 mos. and
10 days.*
Yoder, Footstones - Elizabeth A., 1873-1930.
                    Sarah Rebecca, Dec. 17, 1852 - Dec. 8, 1920.
                    Rev. Lewis, April 18, 1846 - June 16, 1893.
Jacob Hertzler, b._____, d._____.
Baby Nafzinger
Baby Nafzinger.
Baby Nafzinger.
Baby Nafzinger.
Frances, dau. of Moses and Martha Yoder, d. April ___, 1888, aged 9 years, 7
mos., 26 days.
Martha, wife of Moses Yoder, d. Nov. 28, 1883?, aged 46 years, 1 mo, ? days.
Moses Yoder, d. Jan. 31, 1880, aged 40 years, 1 mo. and 28 days.
Frances, consort of Bishop Solomon Yoder, d. Aug. 20, 1868?, aged 65 years,
5 mos. and 3 days.
Bishop Solomon Yoder, d. Feb. 22, 1880, age 70 years, 3 mos., and 6 days.
John Yoder, d. July 28, 186?, aged 26? years, 8? mos., 21? days.
Helene Mast.
Walter Mast.
Baby Nafzinger.
Annie P. Nafzinger, 1865-1902.
Elizabeth Warfel, wife of David Warfel, b. June 4, 1826, d. June 7, 1905,
aged 79 years and 3 days.
David Warfel, d. May 25, 1885, aged 34 years, 5 mos., and 5 days.*
Anna Miller, b. Dec. 180?, d. Feb. 13, 1878, age 72 years, 2 mos., and 12 days.
Moses Miller, b. April 5, 1793?, d. July 6, 1871 (or 4), aged 77 years, 3 mos.,
and 1 day.
John Miller, d. May 15, 1907, age 75 years and 3 days.
Christian Kennel, b. March ___, 1825.
Ellen A., wife of James A. Hopkins, d. March 7, 1908, aged 67 years.
James W. Hopkins, 1844-1914.
Husband, Joseph Miller, b. Nov. 27, 1841, d. Sept. 6, 1928.*
Wife, Rebecca Miller, b. Aug. 24, 1836, d. March 14, 1919.*
    Footstones: J.M. and R.M.
Ebert M. Warfel, b. April 26, 1852, d. Aug. 1, 1880.

WILSONS M.E. CHURCH

Located on south side of Long Green Road, east of Manor Road, Towson Quad.

The cornerstone of the existing church reads "Wilsons M.E. Church, 1892."
The 1877 atlas shows "M.E. Ch." Rows run north to south, copied moving from
east to west.

Infant dau. of Theodore and C. Bernice Fornwalt, b. and d. April 5, 1913.
Fornwalt, Theodore, 1876-1968. C. Bernice 1881-1970. Peter, 1836-1909. Lydia, 1840-1929.
Reinhardt (mon.)
Dau. Edith F., 1898-1968.
Son, John F., 1892-1959.
Mother, Emily A. F., 1870-1952.
Father, Charles E., 1871-1938.
Elizabeth B. Gorsuch, nee Grau, b. Sept. 15, 1852, d. May 13, 1926, 73 years, 8 mos., 29 days.
Anna Mary, dau. of John and Elizabeth Barbara Grau, b. October 28, 1849, d. April 16, 1873.* (Foot A.M.G.)
John Grau, b. Feb. 28, 1816, d. Nov. 23, 1898. Eliz. B. Grau, b. Jan. 4, 1822, d. June 28, 1905.* (Footstone - Mother, Father)
Son, C. E. Reinhard, Jr., 1896-1896.
Son, Aaron D. Francis, 1867-1869.
Louisa, wife of Alexander Francis, d. Dec. 8, 1886, aged 52 years.* (Foot L.F.)
Alexander Francis, b. March 2, 1824, d. Oct. 14, 1904. (Foot A.F.)
Maud, dau.of Rev. J. S. and Sarah Perry, d. June 9, 1874, 3 mos., and 11 days.* (Foot M.P.)
George Wesley, son of George R. and Barbara Hunt, b. Jan. 2, 1855, d. Aug. 28, 1863. (Foot G.W.H.)
William Thomas, son of George R. and Barbara Hunt, b. Oct. 22, 1851, d. April 8, 1864. (Foot W.T.H.)
Wiley St. Clair, son of George R. and Barbara Hunt, b. May 13, 1840, d. June 5, 1865. (Foot W.St. C.H.)
Elmer Dorsey, youngest son of William and Caroline Gorsuch, 1872-1896.*
Catharine Grace, dau. of Sidney and Elizabeth Smith, b. Feb. 9, 1865, d. March 20, 1867.
Companion to above - eroded.
Francis, son of Sidney and Elizabeth Smith, b. Nov. 24, 186_, d. Dec. 28, 1863.*
_____ Morgan, son of Sidney and Elizabeth Smith, b. Nov. 1, 186_, d. Nov. 20, 1863.*
Sidney Smith, b. July 4, 1831, d. Oct. 20, 1869.*
Elizabeth Morgan Smith, wife of Sidney Smith, July 9, 1834 - May 28, 1904.
Seth Smith, June 30, 1800 - Oct. 26, 1860. Grace, his wife, June 25, 1797 - May 9, 1859.
Mary Margaret Smith, Sept. 9, 1837 - Aug. 18, 1898. Asa B. Smith, Sept. 17, 1830 - May 23, 1904.
Seth Smith, June 25, 1828 - July 3, 1896. Catharine A., his wife, June 2, 1837- Feb. 26, 1896.
Sidney Smith, July 4, 1834 - Oct. 20, 1869. (Foot S.S., Sr., A.S.S., M.M.S.)
Joseph Divers, b. Jan. 23, 1798, d. March 18, 1852. (Illeg. verse)
Adele B. Gorsuch, Nov. 8, 1889 - Dec. 1, 1968.
Klapp, Elroy C. 1891-1958. Edith L., 1890-1971.
Lillie B. Phillips, 1872-1948.
John W. Phillips, 1862-1937.
J. Maurice Phillips, 1894-1930.
Dagmar B. Phillips, 1901-1953.
Frank E. Phillips, 1901-1953.
Blanshard (mon.)
Laura V., 1848-1918.
Charles K., 1844-1903.

Lillian and Annie, children of Charles K. and Laura V. Blanshard. (Foot A.B., L.B.)
Cursey, William H. Cursey, b. Aug. 30, 1879, d. Nov. 2, 1955. Minnie W. Cursey, b. Aug. 7, 1880, d. July 25, 1942.* (Husband, wife - footstone)
Charles W. Cursey, b. June 26, 1882, d. Aug. 3, 1882.*
Mother, Caroline Francis, wife of William Gorsuch, and dau. of George R. and Rebecca Hunt, d. July 14, 1901 in her 53rd year.* (C.F.G.)
Father, William Gorsuch, husband of the late Caroline Francis Gorsuch, d. July 12, 1926, in his 93rd year.*
Fales, Laura G. E., 1864-1935. (rest blank)
Fales, James H., 1836-1907. Ellen E., 1844-1898.
Seth Smith, son of Seth and Grace Smith, b. in Norwalk, Conn., June 25, 1828, d. July 3, 1896.
Catharine Ann, wife of Seth Smith and dau. of Hiram H. and Catharine A. Hoyt, b. in Norwalk, Conn., June 2, 1837, d. Feb. 26, 1896. (Foot S.A.S.)
Infant dau. of Seth and Catharine A. Smith.
Dau. of Job and Sarah Smith.
Mother, Sarah Ann Morgan, wife of Job Smith, b. Feb. 19, 1840, d. Jan. 28, 1897, and her infant children.
Brother, John Reider Morgan, Nov. 28, 1841 - Dec. 18, 1863.
Alberta Louisa, dau. of John and Sarah H. Halbert (?), d. July 2, 1863.
Hannah E., wife of Geo. S. Tyson, b. Aug. 20, 1845, d. July 18, 1903.* (H.E.T.-foot)
Mother, Josephine S., wife of George S. Mumma, b. Oct., 1861, d. April 27, 1912.* Mumma (J.S.M.
Son, Carvall Joseph, son of George W. and Josephine S. Mumma, b. Aug. 4, 1885, d. Sept. 12, 1905.* (C.J.M.)
Son, Emory Yellott, son of George W. and Josephine Mumma, b. Dec. 26, 1889, d. Nov. 14, 1903.* (E.Y.M.)
Baby, Joseph Raaman, son of J. W. & L. R. Phillips, b. Feb. 9, 1895, d. July 6, 1895.*
Baby, Luke Arthur, son of J. W. & L. R. Phillips, b. Jan. 1, 1897, d. Aug. 20, 1899.*
Helen M. Slade, April 16, 1889 - April 7, 1971.
Mabel G. Slade, dau. of Elisha and Kate G. Slade, b. March 5, 1893, d. July 5, 1894.* (M.G.S.)
Slade, Elisha, Jan. 15, 1857 - Jan. 12, 1924. His wife, Catherine G., June 30, 1866 - Jan. 10, 1951. (E.S. - C.G.S.)
Harvey B. Slade, 1888-1960.
Mother, Hannah G. Slade, b. Jan. 12, 1821, d. Aug. 2, 1899.
Father, James D. Slade, b. May 3, 1820, d. March 10, 1891.
Cursey, Charles H. Cursey, b. July 4, 1852, d. June 9, 1924. Sarah J., his wife, b. July 28, 1848, d. July 2, 1904.*
Rebecca, wife of George R. Hunt, d. April 11, 1891, aged 73 years, 2 mos. and 5 days.*
George R. Hunt, husband of Rebecca Hunt, d. Sept. 18, 1886, aged 68 years, 10 days.* R.H., G.R.H. - foots)
Fales (flat monument)
Smith, Seth Seymour, son of Seth and Catharine A. Smith, 1872-1952.
Smith, Lottie Alberta, dau. of Isaiah S. and Eliza R. Watkins, 1872-1943.
Smith, Burton Watkins, 1905-1933. Seymour Hoyt, age 8 days.
Lizzie G., wife of Peter Fornwalt, d. Aug. 4, 1869, aged 28 years, 9 mos. and 20 days.
Horst (mon.)
William H. Horst, Jan. 26, 1907 - Jan. 1, 1959.
Thomas W., Sept. 23, 1882 - Feb. 15, 1970.
Caroline, April 5, 1885 - Jan. 28, 1967.

McKelvey, Glen W., Sr., 1901-1972. M. Elizabeth, 1904---
Yoder (mon.)
Anna M., March 30, 1883.
C. Emory, Aug. 30, 1883 - June 12, 1952.
Bowers (mon.)
Dau., Mary Ellen, 1879-1956.
Dau., I. Mae, 1890-____.
Mother, Anna E., 1849-1932.
Father, Bernard, 1845-1921.
Brother, Harry, 1884-1939.
Husband, Wm. Riefner, 1888-____.
Myrtle G., wife of Wm. Riefner, 1893-1971.
Ethel, wife of Thomas, 1885-1944.
Yoder, Solomon Moses, 1875-1905. Lida Francies, 1880-1954.
John H. Shertzer, Nov. 12, 1831 - March 8, 1928. Anna, his wife, March 29, 1920.*
Father, Charles W. Taylor, d. March 18, 1890, in the 29th year of his age.*
David Barnhart, 1818-1894. His wife, Sarah Barnhart, 1825-1882.
Sarah S. Barnhart, dau., 1857-1924.
Mary Mumma, b. Nov. 5, 1850 (?), d. April 18, 1870.
Enos Mumma, b. April 18, 1818, d. May 17, 1882.
Susannah Mumma, b. May 3, 1823, d. March 30, 1890.
(M.M., S.M.,E.M.-foot)
Harry G. Tuchton, son of John and Sallie Tuchton, Dec. 9, 1875 - May 19, 1914.
Infant son of L. Morris and Anna M. Yoder, Aug. 14, 1919.
John William, son of L. Morris and Anna M. Yoder, May 2, 1921 - Dec. 10, 1921.
Yoder, L. Morris, 1891-____. Anna M., 1892-1937.
Harrison, Marion James, Jan. 25, 1930 - Nov. 29, 1963.
Mother, Annie G. Francis Atkins, 1883-1967.*
Father, A. Micajah Francis, 1873-1911.* (foot - husband)
Baby, E. Louise, dau. of A. M. & A. G. Francis, June 2, 1909, aged 2 mos.(E.L.F.)
James Doyle, b. Jan. 9, 1875, d. Oct. 22, 1899.
Hugh Doyle, b. July 1, 1835, d. Feb. 5, 1908. Mary E. Doyle, b. Sept. 4, 1848, d. June 22, 1891. (Foot - J.D., M.E.D., H.D.)
Johnson, Charles B., b. July 1, 1845, d. May 8, 1931, veteran of the Grand Army of the Republic. Susan A., b. Aug. 28, 1848, d. Jan. 17, 1923.
John P. Schmidt, 1893-1942.
Laura C. Mengenhardt, b. Jan. 6, 1878, d. Oct. 25, 1910.
Andrew D. Johnson, b. Sept. 10, 1890, d. March 29, 1910.
Charles A., son of C. B. & S. A. Johnson, b. Dec. 7, 1869, d. Sept. 7, 1891.
Bertha M., dau. of George and Sarah W. Leaman, d. April 9, 1890, aged 5 years, 5 mos., and 11 days.
Father, Harry W. Strayer, April 4, 1887 - July 5, 1956. Dau. Nellie A. Strayer, April 5, 1910.
Lulu May Klein, July 16, 1889 - Oct. 12, 1951.
John W. Strayer, 1907-1930.
Clara Lindsey, 1898-1967 (metal marker)
John Henry Mullenberg, Jan. 7, 1877 - Dec. 29, 1942. Wife, Sarah E., Nov. 17, 1872 - March 28, 1903. Son, Walter E., Feb. 18, 1902 - Aug. 17, 1919. Wife, L. Virginia, June 21, 1870 - June 30, 1968. Dau. Clara May, Sept. 26, 1898 - June 18, 1967.
Neal (monument)
Margaret Neal, 1842-1923.
Alfred W. Neal, 1844-1907.
Laura J. Neal, 1877-1905.
Leroy McD. Neal, 1879-1897.

E. Walton, 1902-____. Ruth A., 1908-____. Meyers.
Isennock & Meyers (flat monument)
Enos Meyers, 1875-1929. Rachel B., his wife, 1875-1925. (R.B.M., E.M. foot)
Father, S. Columbus, Aug. 5, 1844 - Aug. 17, 1920. Mother, Amanda, Feb. 17, 1844 - Sept. 13, 1922. Allen.
Son, George L. Allen, son of S. C. and A. Allen and husband of Gertrude N. Allen, d. July 26, 1906, aged 26 years, 1 mo., and 2 days.*
Mary E. Strayer, 1908-1909.
Eicholtz, Arnold J., 1901-1957. March C., 1901-____.
E. Father, John W. Eicholtz, d. April 29, 1917, aged 63 years.*
E. Elizabeth Eicholtz, Feb. 5, 1858 - July 26, 1959.
William Henry, son of John and Elizabeth Eicholtz, d. Sept. 14, 1897, aged 18 years, 2 mos., and 15 days.*
Kate Curran, mother of Myrtle German, Jan. 9, 1866 - Aug. 20, 1937.*
Mother, Eliza, wife of Henry Isennock, b. April 15, 1847, d. June 29, 1911.*
Father, Henry Isennock, b. Jan. 28, 1842, d. Nov. 2, 1927.* (E.I.)
Mast, Daniel K., May 31, 1869 - Dec. 31, 1943. Sarah L., Nov. 14, 1871 - Nov. 8, 1940.
McInturff, Edmond W., Nov. 24, 1896 - May 15, 1956. Mary, Dec. 2, 1909 - Jan. 20, 1969.
Son, Daniel Earl, son of David K. and Sadie L. Mast, d. Nov. 19, 1906, aged 7 years, 2 mos., and 2 days.*
Mumma, Susie Hilgartner, b. Oct. 9, 1867, d. March 28, 1905.*
James L. Eicholtz, Dec. 10, 1897 - March 2, 1966.
Ady, Benjamin W., 1888-1937. Florence C., 1899-1965 (marked with Am. flag).
Sallie R. Eicholtz, June 30, 1845 - July 19, 1931.
Husband, Conrad Eicholtz, d. Dec. 30, 1900, aged 37 years, 3 mos., and 15 days.*
Lone foot marker.
Mumma, C. Donald, 1872-1954. Mary L., 1894-1956.
John D., 1884-1965. Ida J., 1883-1955. Barnhart.
Baby, Mildred Lenora, dau. of Hayes and Frances Mast Barnhart, b. June 19, 1916, d. July 19, 1917.*
Jacobs, John R., 1901-1940. Laura V., blank.
Joseph T. Barnhart, son of William H. and Effie C. Barnhart, 1887-1966.
Barnhart, William H., 1855-1912. His wife, Effie C. Barnhart, 1862-1929.* (Foot E.C.B., W.H.B.)
Mother, Fianna, wife of Joseph Meyers, d. March 15, 1918, aged 73 years and 10 days.*
Joseph E., June 16, 1878, April 17, 1924.
Father, Joseph, Nov. 11, 1840 - July 2, 1920.
Meyers (foots - J.E.M., F.M., J.M.)
Fishpaw, William H., Nov. 24, 1883 - March 10, 1968. Edith I., July 15, 1887- Feb. 1972.
John Klein, husband of Lulu May Klein, May 17, 1885 - Dec. 8, 1861.
Lunger, Lloyd C., 1886-1954. Marie B., blank.
Barnhart, Henry E., 1899-1969. Viola B., 1906-1973.
Three unmarked footstones.
Sarah Jane E_____, b. 1859, d. March 15, 1894, aged 36 years.
blank footstone.
Laura Kendrick Muzzy, April 1, 1873 - Jan. 4, 1958.
Susanne Guyton, 1873-1935.
Charles E. Guyton, d. May 6, 1924, age 78 years. His wife, Katherine.
Husband and Wife, George G. Guyton, 1883-19__. Margaret, his wife, 1894-1917.*
James Thomas, Jr., Aug. 24, 1939 - Oct. 13, 1943.
O'Bannon (Monument)
Copied 23 November 1973 by J. McGrain.

LONG GREEN VALLEY CHURCH

West side of Long Green Road, below junction with Kanes Road. Copied Aug. 14, 1971 by Robert Barnes.

Otto L. Leutner, Feb. 16, 1834 - July 15, 1921. Amelia H. Leutner, Jan. 20, 1850 - Sept. 15, 1886.
Infant dau. of Edward and Anna Loomis, b. and d. 3rd mo., 27th, 1914.
Anna Virginia, dau. of Edward and Anna Loomis, b. 3rd mo. 15th, 1917, d. 8th mo., 26th, 1917, aged 5 mos. and 10 days.
Tresse E., dau. of Edward and Anna Loomis, b. ___, 1907, d. ___ 2, 1909.
Mildred M. Loomis, Dec. 31, 1919.
Edward R. Loomis, March 3, 1905 - May 18, 1963.
Dayhoff, Ida N., 1884-1919. Karl O., 188?-19__.
Prigel, (Foot) Edith M., Feb. 12, 1898. Sylvester J., Aug. 18, 1898 - May 2, 1958.
Joseph S.Southard, May 11, 1852 - May 12, 1921.
Baby Breidenaugh.
Loomis, James E., 1880-1965. Anne E., 1879-1953.
Robert C. Currens, Jr., Dec. 13, 1943 - March 21, 1944.
John Emery Currens, 1880-1921.
Ella Shue Currens, 1882-1957.
Clayton S. Currens, 1910-1948.
John T. Dayhoof, b. Nov. 5, 1842, d. Sept. 26, 1912, age 69 years, 10 mos. and 21 days.* (Foot J.T.D.)
Catherine M., wife of John T. Dayhoof, b. Dec. 1, 1853 - Oct. 7, 1929.* (Foot C.M.D.)
Paul C. Prigel, son of J. M. & Wilhelmina Prigel, b. Jan. 20, 1905, d. March 15, 1905.*
Prigel, Wilhelmina E., Aug. 23, 1879 - Feb. 14, 1932. John M., Jan. 21, 1873 - Oct. 5, 1960.
William E. Liddle, Sept. 3, 1872 - Aug. 5, 1948.
Bertha M. Liddle, July 4, 1879 - April 10, 1964.
James F. Lubey, Oct. 25, 1897 - Dec. 8, 1966.
Beamer, Robert L., 1876-1957. Lila A., 1892--.
Currens, Lottie G., March 27, 1911 - Nov. 25, 1968. R. Chester, Jan. 10, 1903 ---
Martha E. Reed, 1926-1928.
Barr, Joseph Earl, Feb. 1, 1921 - Feb. 1, 1967. Opal Marie, Feb. 10, 1928 ---
Reed, John P., 1890-1954. Flora I., 1893---.
Brenda J. Currens, March 19, 1940 - March 20, 1940.
Skipper, Paul, Feb. 2, 1905 - Oct. 30, 1952.

WAUGH CHAPEL CEMETERY
White Marsh Quad

This cemetery is located on Long Green Pike, near Harford Road, between Greenwood and Glen Arm, Maryland. It was copies by Ronald D. Standiford in 1971.

Mary Fox, d. May 1, 1877 in her 77th year.
John Fox, d. June 3, 1872 in his 78th year.
Howard Burton, 1874-1928.

Amanda M., wife of John W. Booze, b. Feb. 22, 1865, d. May 14, 1900.*
Thomas Burton, 1838-1914.
Burton, his wife, Sarah E. Hammond, 1840-1873.
Burton, his wife, Amanda V. Hammond, 1852-1922.
Burton, Thomas, 1883-1885.
Burton, W. Hammond, 1888-1890.
Burton, C. Raymond, 1894-1898, sons of Thomas and Amanda V. Burton.
Thomas Francis, June 18, 1787 - June 5, 1832.
Priscilla Francis, July 13, 1792 - Aug. 29, 1885.
Coe, Elizabeth Coe, 1812-1901.
Grace Francis, 1877-1877.
Standiford, Eleanor A., 1870-1959.
Standiford, C. Albert, 1869-1949.
Francis, Richard C., July 3, 1827 - Aug. 13, 1929.
Francis, his wife, Eleanor, Sept. 7, 1832 - Jan. 18, 1914.
Francis, R. Louis Francis, 1856-1890.
Francis, Francis M. Francis, 1875-1969.
Nunnally, Burton L., Maryland, M. Sgt. 2 Major Port. TC, World War II, Korea, Sept. 9, 1906 - Dec. 31, 1959.
Foard, Daniel R., Nov., 1884 - Jan. 1954.
Foard, R. Wesley, 1847-1901.
Foard, Sarah E., 1851-1903.
Foard, Nannie E., 1882-1902.
Francis, B. S. Francis
Francis, Susie, infant dau. of Robert and Maria Francis, b. Nov. 19, 1899, d. Aug. 7, 1900, aged 8 mos., and 22 days.
Munroe, Mother, Julia May, wife of Robert Eli Munroe, d. Aug. 11, 1911, aged 34 years, 2 mos., and 29 days.*
Munroe, Robert LeRoy, only child of Robert Eli and Mary Holley Munroe, b. Jan. 19, 1898, d. April 4, 1903.*
Munroe, Robert Eli, husband of Julia May Munroe, Oct. 31, 1873 - June 20, 1950.
Burton, Anna J., 1886-1969.
Burton, Herbert L., 1887-1965.
Breidenbaugh, Elizabeth A., 1881-1968.
Breidenbaugh, William P., 1878-1956.
Knox, our baby, Deborah Ann Knox, April 24, 1953.
Foard, Benjamin Ford, son of Robert and Cassandra Foard, d. April 28, 1908, aged 84 years, 6 mos. and 3 days.*
Foard, Mary A., wife of Benjamin Ford, d. July 3, 1869 in the 43rd year of her age.*
Foard, Elizabeth A., wife of Benjamin Foard, d. July 11, 1881 in the 49th year of her age.*
Munroe, Robert H. Munroe, husband of Ella C. Munroe, d. March 3, 1891 in the 45th year of her age.*
Munroe, Ella C. Munroe, Nov. 14, 1851 - Dec. 2, 1930, aged 79 years.
Grover, William J. Grover, b. July 4, 1829, d. Jan. 25, 1893.*
Grover, Jacob McC. Grover, son of William and Ann Grover, b. Oct. 1, 1825, d. Dec. 9, 1888.
Willingham, Charles C. Willingham, b. Feb. 5, 1847, d. Dec. 31, 1886.*
Willingham, our Mother, Ann J., relict of Wm. G. Willingham, d. March 4, 1882, aged 74 years and 7 days.*
Willingham, Martha P., dau. of Wm. C. and S. C. Willingham, b. Feb. 7, 1883, d. July 15, 1892.*
Grover, our sister, Martha E. Grover, d. July 31, 1890, aged 17 years.*
Grover, James W. Grover, d. Jan. 29, 1883, aged 55 years, 11 mos. and 23 days.*
Grover, Mary Louisa, wife of James W. Grover, b. May 2, 1843, d. March 31, 1881.*

Tarbert, Andrew Tarbert, b. March 21, 1816, d. April 3, 1882.*
Tarbert, Agnes R., wife of Andrew Tarbert, b. Dec. 15, 1809, d. Nov. 30, 1879.*
Tarbert, Sallie R., dau.of the late Andrew and Agnes R. Tarbert, b. April 24, 1842, d. Sept. 22, 1885.*
Tarbert, Rebecca Tarbert, b. Feb. 22, 1844, d. Aug. 14, 1891.*
Reese, Father, Edward Reese, d. March 10, 1891, aged (underground).
Reese, Mary A., wife of Edward Reese, d. May 31, 1888.
Archer, Jack Archer.
Hetrick, Harold S. Hetrick, 1884-1951.
Zealor, Florence E. Zealor, 1903-1939.
Zealor, James C., 1897-1954.
Pearce, our son, E. Frank, son of the late Greenbury A. and Martha J. Pearce, b. Aug. 5, 1870, d. July 28, 1919.* By his mother.
Pearce, Martha Jane, beloved wife of Greenbury A. Pearce, d. April 5, 1927, aged 79 years.*
Pearce, husband, Greenbury A. Pearce, d. March 9, 1915, aged 74 years. A member of Capt. Snow's Battery B, 1st Md. Lt. Artillery.*
Pearce, Arthur, son of G. A. & M. J. Pearce, b. Feb. 13, 1883, d. July 26, 1892.*
Woolf, Brother, James Woolf, b. March 31, 1812, d. April 5, 1888, aged 76 years and 4 days.
Neuhauser, husband, John M. Neuhauser, 1854-1902.*
Neuhauser, Mary Ellen, wife of John M. Neuhauser, 1863-1941.*
Neuhauser, Carl S., son of John M. & Mary E. Neuhauser, d. May 1, 1905, aged 8 years.*
Sims, Parents, Thomas Sims, 1852-1926.
Sims, his wife, Cordelia, 1857-1921.
Simms, James E., 1881-1936.
Simms, Mother, Mary J., 1864-1945.
Simms, Father, Andrew J., 1859-1929.
Billingslea, Jacob A. Billingslea, 1854-1928.*
Billingsley, Jesse Billingsley, March 12, 1849 - March 17, 1925.
Billingsley, Mother, Mary C., wife of Jesse Billingsley, d. May 30, 1907, aged 55 years, 2 mos., and 28 days.*
Billingsley, our son, Thomas Edgar, son of Jesse and Mary C. Billingsley, d. May 25, 1902, aged 19 years, 5 mos., and 23 days.*
Dance, Leta Shearman Dance, Jan. 28, 1894 - Nov. 15, 1951.
Dance, Carrie Old Dance, April 10, 1881 - Dec. 31, 1961.
Mackenzie, Son, James D., 1883-1913.
Mackenzie, Father, Andrew M., 1846-1918.
Mackenzie, Mother, Jesse A., 1861-1932.
Mackenzie, Father, Wilheim, 1879-1921.
Mackenzie, Mother, Margaret J., 1887-1949.
Billingsley, Father, J. Raymond, 1888-1969.
Billingsley, Mother, Emma L., 1890---.
Billingsley, Son, J. Raymond, Jr., 1922---.
Roberts, Lambert Roberts, Nov. 4, 1890, aged 55 years.*
Roberts, Mother, Elizabeth J. Roberts, wife of Lambert Roberts, b. Aug. 2, 1832, d. March 27, 1906.*
Billingsley, Wife, Liela R., wife of William C. Billingsley, d. Sept. 26, 1913, aged 45 years, 6 mos. and 6 days.*
Roberts, Tillie Virginia, dau. of Lambert and Elizabeth Roberts, b. June 23, 1862, d. Dec. 3, 1872, aged 10 years, 5 mos., and 10 days.*
Roberts, Lizzie, dau. of Lambert and Elizabeth Roberts, b. Feb. 21, 1873, d. March 7, 1873, aged 11 days. (verse illegible)
Hamp, Wife, Blanche I., May 13, 1896 - Oct. 10, 1939.
Hackel, Olive, dau. of F. M. & O. P. Hackel, Nov. 15, 1905 - March 20, 1906.

Grover, J. Wilbur, July 21, 1869 - Feb. 27, 1932.
Grover, Hazel Marie, dau. of J. Wilbur and W'mina Grover, d. Sept. 2, 1898, aged 5 mos., and 16 days.*
Evans, Ellsworth, son of C. H. & A. M. Evans, b. Nov. 29, 1893, d. July 23, 1894, aged 8 months.
Burton, Edna L. Lips.
Burton, Lawrence H., husband of Edna L. Lips and son of Thomas W. and Emily Bull Burton, Feb. 26, 1876 - Dec. 25, 1947.
Burton, Baby, Hillen Lee, son of Thomas W. and Emily H. Burton, d. July 27, 1838, aged 4 months, 24 days. (Verse illegible)
Burton, Mother, Emily Hillen, wife of Thomas W. Burton, b. Dec. 29, 1850, d. Nov. 9, 1901.*
Burton, Thomas W., husband of Emily H. Burton, b. June 29, 1846, d. Aug. 10, 1923.*
Parlett, Lydia May, wife of the late William Parlett, dau. of Thomas W. and Emily H. Burton, b. April 26, 1871, d. Feb. 14, 1932.
Mary C. Fox, 1883-1957.
J. Lawrence Fox, 1879-1947.
Mother, Martha E. Fox, 1849-1933.
Father, William O. Fox, 1841-1903.
William H. Fox, 1883-1959.
Burton, Husband, Charles C., Oct. 23, 1920—.
Burton, Wife, Naomi W., July 7, 1921 - Sept. 18, 1968.
Burton, Caleb C., Sept. 22, 1863 - Dec. 9, 1948.
Burton, Ruth A., Nov. 28, 1862 - Nov. 7, 1922.
Faust, Claude S., 1882-1966.
Faust, Rhoda, 1882-1965.
Burton, Wife, Almira E., wife of George L. Burton, d. March 21, 1908, aged 41 years, 10 mos., 9 days.*
Counsel, Jacob D. Counsel, b. July 11, 1824, d. Jan. 21, 1909.
Counsel, Priscilla, wife of Jacob D. Counsel, d. March 21, 1897, aged 75 years and 1 month. (Verse illegible)
Ehlers, Husband, Henry Ehlers, d. July 21, 1905, in the 76th year of his age.
Ehlers, Wife, Mary Ann, wife of Henry Ehlers, d. Feb. 27, 1914.
Stover, Jacob Stover, b. Sept. 8, 1797, d. Aug. 25, 1868, in the 71st year of his age.*
Stover, Eleanor, wife of Jacob Stover, b. June 24, 1802, d. July 29, 1885.*
Chenworth, Mary Frances, dau. of John T. and Mary E. Chenworth, b. Aug. 16, 1863, d. Aug. 8, 1873.
Chenworth, Father, JohnT. Chenworth, 1836-1919.
Chenworth, Mother, Mary E. Chenworth, 1829-1919.
Isaac German, 1865-1935.
His wife, Nellie R. German, 1866-1940.
Shearman, Harry G., 1868-1952.
Shearman, Ada B., 1873-1954.
Shearman, our baby, Erma Jessie, dau. of Harry and Ada Shearman, b. Jan. 21, 1893, d. March 3, 1893.
Shearman, Father, Washington Shearman, son of Jacob and Mary Shearman, d. May 13, 1907, in the 71st year of his age.*
George Fox, b. Feb. 4, 1826, d. Aug. 2, 1898.*
Adeline, wife of George Fox, b. April 10, 1841, d. Oct. 22, 1905.*
Sister, Mary A. Fox, dau. of George and Adeline Fox, b. Jan. 9, 1869, d. Feb. 15, 1917.*
J. Howard Fox, b. Oct. 31, 1884, d. Feb. 3, 1917.
Tarbert, Father, John R., husband of Carrie L. Tarbert, b. June 3, 1840, d. Jan. 13, 1900.*
Tarbert, Mother, Carrie L., wife of John R. Tarbert, b. Feb. 2, 1845, d. April 24, 1912.*

Tarbert, Mamie, dau. of John and Carrie Tarbert, d. July 10, 1882, aged 6 years.*
Simms, Wife, Virginia, 1864-1947.
Simms, Baby, John Thomas, 1908.
Simms, Husband, Thomas E., 1872-1950.
Shanklin, William T., 1883-1947.
Green, Ferdinand Green, d. Aug. 22, 1894, aged 82 years, 11 mos., and 10 days.
Mumma, John F., 1869-1946.
Mumma, Louise E., 1860-1964.
Holland, Mabel, 1887—.
Holland, Emma J., infant dau. of Bernie and Mabel Holland, b. and d. May 9, 1917.
Creamer, Emma M., 1853-1891.
Creamer, John, 1853-1930.
Creamer, Ida L., 1857-1927.
Francies, Mary F., dau. of Charles & Martha Francies, b. Nov. 3, 1869, d. Dec. 6, 1871.
Francies, Maria Frances, dau. of Thomas and Priscilla Francies, d. Oct. 7, 1903, aged 89 years and 10 mos. (Verse illegible)
LeBrun, Mother, infant of Harry and Emma J. LeBrun, d. March 6, 1902, aged 12 days.
Isennock, J. Wesley, 1873-1937.
Isennock, Minnie F., 1878-1969.
Francies, Charles Albert, youngest son of Charles and Martha Francies, b. Oct. 29, 1885, d. March 18, 1905.*
Francies, Martha A. Francies, wife of Charles Francies, b. June 28, 1842, d. July 9, 1942.
Francies, Father, Charles Francies, husband of Martha A. Francies, b. Oct. 8, 1832, d. Feb. 19, 1892.*
Francies, Clara E., dau. of W.T.M. and Estella Francies, b. Dec. 22, 1914, d. Feb. 1, 1915.*
Francies, Mother, Estella C., 1878-1919.
Francies, William T. M., 1876-1964.
Francies, Ada L., 1894-1961.
Burton, Charles O., July 12, 1852 - Jan. 11, 1924.
Burton, his wife, Rosa, May 29, 1859 - April 1, 1919.
Burton, Raymond H., 1894-1947.
Burton, Ruth Alma, 1894-1970.
Fox, Ida May, 1882—.
Twining, Infant, Richard Capler Twining, 1949.
Twining, Hugh B. Twining, 1916-1947.
Twining, Sarah E. Twining, 1877-1936.
Twining, Isaac J. Twining, 1871-1950.
Twining, Roland Twining, 1910-1912.
Twining, Thomas Hollowell, son of Isaac and Sarah E. Twining, d. Dec. 18, 1901, aged 2 mos., and 2 days.*
Burton, Horatio Burton, March 4, 1845 - Jan. 19, 1917.*
Rich, Mother, Mary J. Rich, d. ___ 26, 1912, in the 78th year of her age.
Russell, Matilda J. Russell, Sept. 19, 1882 - March 2, 1944.
Russell, John C. Russell, Sept. 15, 1880 - July 11, 1945.
Nunnally, our baby, Buela Lee, dau. of Rhoda and Emmett Nunnally, b. May 8, 1902, d. April 14, 1903.
Perry Colfield, son of Emmett and Rhoda Nunnally, b. Nov. 3, 1903, d. July 13, 1904. (Verse illegible)
Donovan, Husband, Owen Donovan, husband of Miranda Donovan, d. March 14, 1891, aged 51 years and 7 months.*

Billingsley, Father, Samuel W. Billingsley, d. Dec. 4, 1891, aged 76 years, 9 mos., and 18 days.
Billingsley, Mother, Elizabeth A., wife of Samuel W. Billingsley, d. April 8, 1897, aged 80 years, 4 mos., and 8 days.
Billingsley, Brother, Charles B. Billingsley, b. Aug. 4, 1840, d. Aug. 12, 1914.
Shearman, M. Shearman.
Noyes.
Dobbs, Melvin Stanley, son of William and Benetta Dobbs, illegible.
Dobbs, Mother, Bennetta Knight Dobbs, 1851-1935.
Burton, Father, d. Sept. 11, 1906, aged 79 years and 14 days.*
Burton, Mother, Frances V., wife of William J. Burton, d. Oct. 29, 1917, aged 82 years, 7 mos. and 25 days.*
Gary W. Neal, son, 1952-1961.
James T. Ayres, d. March 13, 1929.
Larch Ayres, d. Sept. 19, 1927.
William E. Neuhauser, Jan. 14, 1887 - June 1, 1958.
Robert, son of Archer and Annie Ayres, March 10, 1904 - July 13, 1905.
George H. Muller, July 15, 1886 - Jan. 19, 1955.
Della A. Muller, July 23, 1888 - Nov. 24, 1964.*
Montgomery, our baby, John Arthur, son of John and Emma Montgomery, b. Sept. 26, 1894, d. July 22, 1895.
Father, William A. Guyton, b. Feb. 26, 1832, d. Jan. 29, 1914.*
Mother, Cecelia, wife of William A. Guyton, b. Aug. 21, 1838, d. April 5, 1901. (verse illegible)
Sister, Susan Beane, third and beloved dau. of Thomas and Polly Bean, b. in Virginia in the year 1843, d. in Greenwood, Sept. 26, 1898.*
Husband, Nathaniel P. Corbin, b. Sept. 22, 1823, d. June 17, 1898.*
Wife, Rachel Frances Evans, wife of Nathaniel P. Corbin, b. Nov. 23, 1816, d. Dec. 30, 1892.*
Mary Lenora Corbin, widow of the late Nathaniel P. Corbin, d. Sept. 1, 1893, aged 26 years.*
Nathaniel P. Corbin, husband of M. Lenora Corbin, d. Oct. 26, 1890, in the 41st year of his age.*
John H. Maxfield, Sept. 25, 1849 - April 16, 1928.
Maxfield, his wife, Georgianna, Dec. 8, 1854 - Dec. 28, 1923.
Johnee Maxfield, b. Sept. 24, 1883, d. _____ 1889.
Isennock, infant dau. of Everett and Velma L. Isennock, April 20, 1933 - May 14, 1933.
Charles H. Russell, 1852-1913.
Gertrude Russell, 1858-1945.
Our nieve, Julia I., dau. of Robert and Mary Fitch, b. Nov. 23, 1885, d. June 22, 1903.*
Husband, Benjamin F. Parlett, b. March 3, 1845, d. Nov. 14, 1914.*
Wife, Mary J. Parlett, wife of B. F. Parlett, b. Oct. 17, 1847 - Nov. 23, 1929.*
Mother, Rebecca, wife of John Fitch, b. June 11, 1823, d. May 1, 1900.*
J. Viola Burton, wife of Oscar J. Burton, d. Feb. 11, 1906, aged 32 years, 2 mos., and 22 days.*
Helen Emily, dau. of Oscar J. and Viola J. Burton, d. May 15, 1904, aged 2 years, 10 mos., and 10 days. (Verse illegible)
Helen R. McComas, b. June 13, 1908, d. May 4, 1971, dau. of Amos P. and Julia Burton McComas.
Ellen N. McComas.
Louisa C., dau. of J. Glenn and Kate E. McComas, b. Jan. 29, 1855, d. June 26, 1909.
Kate E., wife of J. Glenn McComas, d. Nov. 1, 1886, aged 65 years, 2 mos. and 26 days.*
John Glenn McComas, husband of the late Kate E. McComas, b. Aug. 5, 1824, d. Jan. 7, 1907.

Amos P. McCoas (sic) [McComas], March 11, 1870 - April 8, 1949.
Wife, Julia May McComas, wife of Amos P. McComas, b. Aug. 26, 1885, d. Feb. 21, 1909.*
Mother, Florence I. Isennock, 1897-1919.
K. G. E. to my husband, Thomas J. Montgomery, b. April 11, 1840, d. June 28, 1899.*
Mother, Mary C. Montgomery, Aug. 24, 1843 - March 8, 1935.
Bayne.
Billingslea, William C. Billingslea, d. Jan. 14, 1882, aged 68 years, 9 mos., and 2 days.
Wesley T. Billingslea, d. Sept. 26, 1884, aged 35 years, 5 mos., and 28 days.
Children, Mary Ellen Higle, d. Oct. 11, 1850, aged 7 years, 8 mos., and 12 days.
Hannah E. and Amanda Higle, twins, d. Oct. 25, 1854, aged 14 days.
Samuel, Jr., Higle, d. Sept. 7, 1857, aged 1 year, 2 mos., and 4 days.
Rebecca Helen Higle, d. July 14, 1862, aged 9 years, 11 mos., and 27 days, children of Samuel and Belinda Higle.*
Father, Samuel Higle, d. Jan. 16, 1887, in the 74th year of his age.
Mother, Belinda, wife, died July 31, 1886, in the 72nd year of her age.
Katie, dau. of Edwin W., and Alice Shanklin, d. Sept. 3, 1890, aged 4 years, 8 mos., and 9 days.*
May, dau. of Edwin W. and Alice Shanklin, d. Oct. 8, 1903, age 11 years, 2 mos., and 14 days. (verse illegible)
Husband, Charles E. Shanklin, July 11, 1881 - March 27, 1920.
Edwin W. Shanklin, 1860-1945. Mary A., 1863-1938.
Anna Jeanette, wife of Marion Shanklin and dau. of J. W. and M. L. Grover, d. Nov. 3, 1890, aged 27 years, 1 mos., and 19 days.*
Father, Marion F. Shanklin, Feb. 20, 1859 - July 18, 1927.
J. Maurice Shanklin, 1882-1945.
Katherine E. Shanklin, 1882-1952.
Isaiah H. Shanklin, b. Feb. 22, 1820, d. Aug. 30, 1896, age 76 years, 6 mos, and 8 days.
Mother, Sarah Elizabeth, wife of Isaiah H. Shanklin, d. Oct. 7, 1900, aged 68 years.*
Mary E., wife of Benjamin W. Shanklin, b. Dec. 20, 1862, d. Feb. 13, 1921.
Burton, John T., 1859-1900.
Burton, Owen G., 1890-1913.
Burton, May 1883-1883.
Burton, William, 1894-1895.
Louisa Burton, b. July 6, 1883, d. Aug. 15, 1883.
Eliza M. Johnson, Mother, 1833-1902.
William P. Corbin, Father, 1829-1869.
Gorgetta Corbin, 1853-1874.
William H. Corbin, 1865-1868, children of Wm. P. and Eliza M. Corbin.
Our only darling, Dixon W., son of A. B. and E. A. Miles, b. Nov. 12, 1890, d. April 10, 1894, aged 3 years and 5 mos.
Mary Jane Barbour, d. Jan. 11, 1922.
William Barbour, d. Jan. 26, 1920.
Lucretia Barbour, d. March 27, 1919.
Mary Work Barbour, d. Feb. 28, 1896, aged 90 years and 26 days.*
Leonard Dorr who departed this life July 12, 1851, aged 55 years.*
Sarah Door, d. _____ 1850. (verse illegible)
Infant, _____, James M. and Ida V. Billingsley.
Infant, _____, James M. & Ida V. Billingsley, d. Feb. 1, 1889, aged 7 mos.
Leticia Edwards, d. June 27, 1886, aged 80 years.*
Our Mother, Plesent Hedges, b. June 2, 1831, d. May 1, 1889.*
Andrew J. Sims, b. Nov. 3, 1819, d. Nov. 3, 1899.*

Charles Sims, b. May 11, 1861, d. Oct. 24, 1863.*
Mary J. Sims, b. Feb. 9, 1826, d. Feb. 5, 1912.*
Fletcher Bone, d. Sept. 23, 1859, aged 65 years and 11 months.*
Isabella, wife of Fletcher Bone, born in England, died in Baltimore, 1873.
David E. Barbour, d. Aug. 4, 1859, aged 28 years and 23 days.*
Dorothea Mesner, d. March 27, 1857 in the 68th year of her age. A native of Gundelsheim Baden, Germany. Erected by George Mesner of Baltimore.*
Father, J. Mathew Mesner, d. May 16, 1857 in the 73rd year of his age. A native of Gundelsheim Baden, Germany. Erected by George Mesner of Baltimore.*
James Polk, young son of Jacob and Mary Shearman, d. Aug. 8, 1852 in the 11th year of his age.
Jacob Shearman, d. Feb. 10, 1888, aged 91 years and 23 days.*
Mary, wife of Jacob Shearman, d. July 29, 1889, aged 83 years and 6 days.*
Munroe (stone over).
Jemina, wife of R. L. Munroe, d. April 23, 1871 in the 50th year of her age.*
Ann Carman, wife of Caleb Carman, b. Oct. 9, 1822, d. Aug. 22, 1885.*
Husband, Caleb Carman, b. Sept. 8, 1811, d. April 3, 1880.*
Thomas Todd, b. Jan. 19, 1809, d. Jan. 13, 1833, aged 23 years, 11 mos., and 24 days.
Christopher Todd, M.D., b. Feb. 22, A.D. 1763, d. March 30 A.D., 1849 in the 86th year of his age.*
Susanna Todd, wife of Dr. Christopher Todd, d. Sept. 11, 1877, aged 91 years.*
Christopher Todd, b. March 15, 1827, d. Sept. 10, 1835, aged 8 years, 5 mos., and 26 days.
Susan Todd, b. Jan. 11, 1811, d. March 22, 1835, aged 21 years, 2 mos. and 21 days.*
Sarah Todd, b. May 22, 1806, d. Oct. 5, 1831, aged 26 years, 1 mos. and 27 days.*
Frances Todd, b. ? .
Elizabeth Todd, b. Sept. 17, 1816, d. Aug. 10, 1818, aged 1 year, 11 mos., and 21 days.
John Burton, who departed this life Oct. 1, 1857 in the 56th year of his age.
Magdalen, wife of John Burton, Jr., b. March 16, 1803, d. July 1, 1881.
Horatio Burton, d. July 11, 1889, aged 80 years, 1 mos., and 12 days.*
Sarah Jane, wife of Horatio Burton, d. March 9, 1861 in the 72nd year of her age.
Uriah, infant son of Horatio and Sarah Burton, d. Oct. 18, 1861, aged 8 mos., and 14 days.
Oliver Burton, d. 1927.
Harry Burton, d. 1927.
James Burton, d. Jan. 19, 1876, aged 75 years.*
Eleanor, wife of James Burton, d. Dec. 28, ____, aged 51 years.
Mary A. Burton, wife of James Burton, d. April, 1876, aged 65 years.*
Thomas E. Coe, Oct. 10, 1831 - Oct. 10, 1854.
Wm. H. Coe, Sargeant of the 5th Maryland Union Veterans, b. June 30, 1829, d. July 19, 1870.
Henrietta Coe, b. June 10, 1812, d. Dec. 2, 1867.
James Coe, d. Dec. 21, 1879, aged 85 years.
Louisa Scarff, wife of James Coe, b. July 1, 1805, d. Feb. 28, 1895.*
Tacy H. Coe, b. May 9, 1831, d. April 19, 1868.
Howard W. Coe, b. Dec. 11, 1814, d. Jan. 1, 1872.
Charles R. Coe, b. Feb. 15, 1831, d. June 15, 1870.
Father, Samuel Francis, 1817-1861.
Mother, Elizabeth Francis, 1816-1903.
Mary Virginia Francis, 1854-1862.
Amanda Francis, 1847-1864.
Francis Alexander, 1851-1931.
James Francis, 1857-1933.

Harry D. Schunck, 1847-1942.
May E. Schunck, 1874-1945.
Schunck, Father, Harmen.
Conrad Bachman, d. March 31, 1876, aged 54 years.
Annie E. Bachman, d. Dec. 9, 1899, aged 79 years and 6 mos.
Norman, son of Marion F. and Lottie Burton, d. July 22, 1906, aged 4 months.*
Louisa Todd, wife of Owen B. burton, 1825-1904.*
Owen B. Burton, 1812-1900.*
Eleanor, wife of Owen B. Burton, 1820-1856.*
Burton, Owen B., 1853-1883.
Thomas E. Burton, 1844-1852.
John Wesley Burton, 1851-1852, sons of Owen B. and Eleanor Burton.
Flora M. Stevens, 1886-1960.
John L. Stevens, 1883-1908.
Clara E. Burton, Nov. 4, 1859 - May 31, 1943.*
Martha Jane Burton, d. April 27, 1879, aged 23 years, 1 month and 22 days.
Joseph Gwinn Burton, b. March 12, 1807, d. March 5, 1892, aged 84 years, 11 mos. and 23 days.*
Cassandra Burton, wife of Joseph G. Burton, b. July 22, 1820, d. Sept. 29, 1894, aged 74 years, 2 mos. and 7 days.*
Sylvester F., son of J. G. and C. Burton, b. April 24, 1852, d. Aug. 26, 1852.*
John G., son of J. G. and C. Burton, b. June 13, 1849, d. Aug. 25, 1852.
Charles, son of J. G. and C. Burton, b. Feb. 14, 1845, d. Aug. 6, 1852.
Geddis, Andrew, d. Feb. 1870, aged 13 years and 8 mos.
John Geddes, b. May 23, 1799, d. Nov. 19, 1857, aged 58 years, 5 mos., and 27 days.
Mary Ann Arthur, d. Aug. 31, 1899, aged 100 years.
Ellen N., youngest dau. of John and Ann Geddes, b. Oct. 17, 1850, d. Feb. 3, 1863.
Robert Geddis, d. Feb. 24, 1863 in the 24th year of his age.
Margaret Ann Geddis, aged 18 years, 3 mos., and 15 days.
David Geddis, d. Sept. 28, 1861, aged 18 years.
John Geddis, d. Nov. 18, 1873 in the 35th year of his age.

NEW SECTION OF WAUGH CHAPEL CEMETERY

Augustus A. Piper, 1857-1941.
Mamie E. Piper, 1878-1910.
Robert A. Piper, 1895-1935.   Etta M. Piper, 1894-1909.
Mamie M. Piper, 1910-1910.
Charles J. B. Piper, 1905-1959.
Wilson, Clarence E., 1893-1971.
Wilson, Clarence E., Jr., 1916-1923.
Wilson, Edith Pearl, 1896-1919.
Wilson, Sylvia E., 1917-1917.
Andred J. Shearman, 1840-1907.
Wife, Viola N. Corbin, wife of Elmer W. Corbin, b. March 9, 1873, d. March 20, 1910.*
Burton, Clarence E. —
Burton, Caroline L. —
Twele, John M. Maryland S2 U.S. Navy, World War I, Jan. 11, 1895 - June 16, 1955.
Mother, Migen A. Charnock, b. Dec. 19, 1864, d. June 11, 1912.
Blacklock, Josias A., May 12, 1835 - Jan. 26, 1920.
Blacklock, Johanna D., Aug. 23, 1873 - Oct. 22, 1956.
Schofield, Florence Jane Blacklock, 1898-1965.

Billingsley, James McKendee, 1853-1922.
Billingsley, Ida Virginia, 1859-1937.
Billingsley, William Wilson, 1891-1913.
Billingsley, James McKendree, Jr., 1897-1914.
Fantom, Robert W., 1878-1950.
Fantom, Carrie E., 1876-1930.
George H. Shimp, 1863-1949.
Iva N. Shimp, 1869-1920.
William E. Clark, son of George D. and Martle I. Clark, March 18, 1932 - Sept. 20, 1966.
Ruth C., dau. of William E. and Mary A. Clark, d. June 21, 1917, aged 8 years, 7 mos., and 4 days.*
Clark, Mary A., 1865-1937.
Clark, William E., 1861-1931.
Charles E. Clark, Feb. 11, 1890 - June 26, 1966.
Krickham, Carrie E., 1884-1957.
Krickham, Charles E., 1882-1962.
Winneberger, Mother, July 29, 1864 - Oct. 1930.
Winneberger, Father, Nov. 27, 1862 - June 2, 1941.
Winneberger, Son, July 16, 1889 - May 19, 1957.
Winneberger, George E., July 20, 1886 - June 21, 1970.
Rev. Wm. E. Tombaugh, April 11, 1882 - Sept. 11, 1967.
Grace M. Tombaugh, Feb. 26, 1890 - Feb. 15, 1962.
Breidenbaugh, Conrad G., 1846-1932.
Breidenbaugh, Katherine B., his wife, 1855-1928.*
German, H. Grant, 1870-1955.
German, Blanche B., 1880----,
Pearce, Robert C., Sr., 1909-1961.
Pearce, Charles C., 1898-1965.
Pearce, Priscilla A., 1871-1925.
Pearce, John C., 1862-1920.
Pearce, Eleanor, 1903-1958.
Russell, Wife, Louise M., 1894-1964.
Russell, Husband, Frank A., 1887-1965.
Streett, Irene B.
Streett, Abram T., Nov. 3, 1862 - Jan. 3, 1923.
Roberts, Cora May, 1875-1923.
Roberts, Father, Edward R., 1870-1933.
Roberts, Wife, Carolyn M. Krers, 1903-1932.
Leight, Father, John T., 1855-1927.
Leight, Mother, Mary E., 1859-1936.
Leight, Percy J., 1889-1945.
Leight, Edna May 1898----.
Leight, Wife, Sarah M., 1884-1929.
Father, Harold C. Beaver, 1921-1959.
Moores, Otho G. Moores, 1883-1941.
Henrietta Fox, 1874-1968.
Louise Scarff, 1871-1959.
Serick Fox, 1881-1936.
Brother, C. A. Biensack, 1883-1940.
Sanders, Son, W. Wilson, 1917-1933.
Sanders, Father, Harry D., 1888-1938.
Burton, Georgianna, 1860-1934.
Burton, Clifton T., 1863-1934.
Burton, Richard, June 2, 1854 - Oct. 24, 1935.
Burton, Margaret, Feb. 27, 1862 - Feb. 10, 1956.
Burton, Richard E., Feb. 17, 1898 - Aug. 15, 1964.
Schwatka, John M., 1870-1948.

Schwatka, Emma O., 1867-1950.
Pearce, George R., March 10, 1890 - Oct. 19, 1944, Father.
Pearce, Emma K., April 13, 1896 - March 19, 1949, Mother.
Brown, Husband, Frank, Dec. 3, 1882 - Sept. 22, 1954.
Brown, Wife, Martha E., March 10, 1887 - April 23, 1950.
Hardwick, Eleanor E. Hardwick, 1875-1949.
Pearce, John C., 1876-1944.
Pearce, Annie F. Pearce, 1879-1960.
Warfield, Howard R. Warfield, 1894-1967.
Piper, Raymond, 1894—.
Piper, Della O., 1897-1957.
Piper, Laura M., 1871-1954.
Piper, William C., 1861-1939.
Robert Leroy Hyle, Maryland, Sic U.S. Navy, World War II, July 31, 1926 - July 14, 1947.
Stricklin.
George Lance LeBrun, May 10, 1948 - July 23, 1960, "Lanny".
Husband, Hugh Daggs, Oct. 30, 1903 - Sept. 3, 1970.
Smith, Mary M., 1931—.
Smith, Vernon L., 1925-1962.
Unaugst, Dorothy V., 1925-1955.
Leight, George C., 1882-1952.
Leight, Clara L., 1888-1966.
LeBrun, Emma Francies, 1873-1968.
LeBrun, Harry A., 1874-1946.
Miller, Wife, Anna M., April 24, 1874 - Nov. 11, 1947.
Miller, Husband, J. Fred, Aug. 9, 1877 - June 16, 1961.
Piper, Thelma S., Dec. 20, 1905.
Piper, G. Yellott, Jan. 16, 1892 - Jan. 6, 1962.
Known unmarked graves in this section:
Nora A. King, 1961.
Philip King, Sr., 1957.
Philip E. King, 1961.
All graves in Charles E. Burton lot.
Elsie Bailey, 1942.
Anna Houck, 1942.

WORTHINGTON FAMILY CEMETERY

Located on Dogwood Road on "Kahler" property.

Rezin H. Worthington, June 22, 1884, 90 years.
Mary W., wife of Rezin H., b. March 28, 1816, d. Aug. 31, 1854.
Noah W. of Thomas, d. Jan. 9, 1872, 83 years.
Mary O. Fite, relict of Henry Fite, July 25, 1869, 83 years.
Thomas Dye Worthington, July 8, 1823, 34 years old.
Joshua Worthington, Nov. 9, 1804, 14 years.
Marsella, relict of Thomas W., April 27, 1842, 94 years.
Thomas Worthington, March 16, 1821, 82 years old.
Elizabeth Hammond, consort of Thomas Worthington, b. Aug. 17, 1725, d. Oct. 4, 1784, 59 years, 1 mos., 17 days.
Margaret Love Rupp, wife of Walter Ruben Rupp, Nov. 27, 1875 - Aug. 16, 1957.
Walter Ruben Rupp, Sept. 17, 1868 - Feb. 25, 1940.
Celeste Virginia, wife of F. Howard Harvery and dau. of James H. and Annie Worthington Love, Nov. 20, 1870 - Oct. 27, 1924.

Warns, Samuel M., Nov. 2, 1871 - Dec. 9, 1927. Agnes Love Warns, Aug. 4, 1879 - Aug. 29, 1966.
William Williamson, husband of Anne Love Carr, May 20, 1871 - Feb. 14, 1942.
Anne Isabelle Love, wife of William Williamson Carr, Sept. 19, 1872 - Jan. 24, 1958.
Annie Worthington, wife of James H. Love, June 4, 1846 - May 9, 18?_, Mother.
James H. Worthington, husband of Annie Worthington, July 6, 1846 - Nov. 22, 1923, Father.
Anne, consort of John Worthington, Dec. 16, 1820, 54 years.
John Worthington, March 18, 1829, 66 years.
Reuben Worthington, Sept. 18, 1823, 21 years.
Thomas Worthington, Jan. 23, 1834, 49 years.
Noah Worthington of John to his beloved sister, Comfort Worthington, Nov. 28, 1786 - June 25, 1856.
Catherine Althea, wife of J. A. Burgess, June 1, 1865 - Jan. 7, 1912.
Rezin H. W. Love, Feb. 10, 1880 - Feb. 13, 1881.
Nicholas D., son of John and Ann Worthington, d. Jan. 20, 1860, 72 years.
Grenelda C., dau. of Nicholas D. and Matilda Worthington, d. Oct. 7, 1852, 9 mos., 7 days.
Nicholas E. Worthington, son of (balance illegible).
Nicholas J.O.D., son of Nicholas and Matilda Worthington, Jan. 15, 1844, age 4 years, 11 mos., 3 days.
Ann G. Moore, d. April 17, (balance illegible).
Ann Hall Moore, dau. of (balance illegible).
Alfred L. Moore, son of Alfred L. and Ann G. Moore, d. April 28, 1835, 15 mos.
Rachel G. Welsh, June 25, 1828, 17 years, 9 mos.
Husband, Noah H. Worthington, b. March 31, 1835, d. June 1, 1880. Mary A. C. Worthington, wife of Noah, b. Feb. 5, 1835, d. Dec. 16, 1909, children of Noah and Mary A.C. Worthington. Noah d. April 29,1859, age 3 mos., J. Gist d. June 29, 1875, age 19 years. Rezin H., d. July 8, 1875, age 14 mos. Thomas d. April 12, 1876, age 10 years. Rezina d. April 13, 1876, age 4 years. N. Hall d. Aug 11, 1876, age 14 years.
Rezin H. Worthington, J. Mason, Dec. 13, 1839 - March 22, 1872.
Augusta Love Cline, April 1, 1874 - Aug. 13, 1954.
Arthur Leland Cline, Dec. 20, 1857 - March 14, 1930.
Hebb, Henry James 1882-1954. Alma Love, 1885--.
Tall Stone
N. W. of T.
M. O. F.
T. D. W.
J. W.
M. W.
T. W.
E. H.
M. W., 1799.
J. W., April 8, 1802.
J. W., 1802.
A. W.
J. W., 1829.
R. W., 1823.
T. W., 1834.
C. W.
M. W. W.
N. J. O. D. W.
G. C. W.
N. E. W.
N. O. W.
A. G, M.

A. L. M.
A. H. M.
R. G. W.
N. W.
J. W.
R. H. W.
T. W.
R. W.
N.H. W.
Rock wall with iron gate - more stones but damaged and unable to read.
Also on this property is a slave cemetery. Nothing visible but supposedly
large. "Doc" Worthington was always known to have "100" slaves.
Copies by Beverly Griffity in 1969.

COCKEY FAMILY CEMETERY

This cemetery is located at the end of a lane leading from beside the Green Spring Inn on Falls Road, up to the old Stephen Cockey homestead. The inscriptions were copied about 1952 by Mrs. Arthur Armstrong, who has graciously allowed them to be included in this compilation. In a conversation on March 5, 1972, Mrs. Armstrong said there might have been one or two stone not copied.

Thomas Cockey, son of John and Mary Cockey, b. Feb. 5, 1787, departed this life Dec. 30, 1816, aged 29 years, 10 mos., and 25 days.
John Cockey, b. Nov. 5, 1788, d. May 4, 1873. (In 1956 moved to Sater's Baptist Church.)
Mary, beloved wife of John Cockey, b. Aug. 13, 1792, d. Oct. 13, 1846. (In 1956 moved to Sater's Baptist Church.)
Hannah May, dau. of John and Harriet Cockey, b. May 2, 1860, d. 6 Oct. 1861.
Thomas Cockey m. Prudence Gill, his son, John m. Mary Coale. John, the son of John and Mary (Coale) Cockey m. Mary Fishpaw, and their son, John, the 4th, first m. Harriet Parks and second, Emma Hall, The following stones are found to be those of the children of John and Emma Cockey - Mrs. A. M.)
Powell, aged 18 years, d. 28 June 1885.
Clarence Hall, aged 11 years, d. Oct. 9, 1876.
Our little Hattie, aged 5 years, 8 mos., d. 1876.
Our little Sallie, b. Nov. 12, 1876, d. Nov. 7, 1878, dau. of Samuel B. and Laura Cockey.
John F. Cockey, b. July 6, 1851, d. Feb. 21, 1878.
Charles O. Cockey, son of John and Mary Cockey, b. April 6, 1830, d. Nov. 24, 1852. (Charles O. Cockey 1830-1896 (sic) was moved to Sater's Baptist Church, 1956 - Mrs. A. A.)
Elizabeth, widow of Nimrod Skipper, and wife of John H., and dau. of John and Mary Cockey, b. June 27, 1820, d. Dec. 30, 1887.
Harriet, wife of John Cockey, Jr., b. Sept. 3, 1832, d. Oct. 25, 1861, aged 29 years, 1 mo., and 22 days.
Stephen Cockey, 1835-1920. (Note: moved to Sater's Baptist Church in 1956 - Mrs. A. A.)
John Edmund, son of S. J. and Mary A. Reed, b. July 23, 1855, d. Aug. 19, 1856.
Samuel John Reed, Feb. 21, 1827, d. Sept. 26, 1894, and his wife, Mary Ann Parsons, Feb. 4, 1835 - May 22, 1897. (Note: She was the dau. of Edmund Parsons and Mary Ann Cockey, 1816-1837. Mary Ann Cockey was the dau. of John Cockey, 1788-1873, and Mary Fishpaw, 1792-1846 - Mrs. A. A.)
George Joice, Sr., d. Jan. 2, 1856, aged 65 years.

88

Nimrod Skipper, son of John and Sarah Skipper, b. Jan. 2, 1819, d. March 6, 1852.
Samuel Beauregard, son of S. J. and M. A. Reed, b. March 10, 1863, d. June 29, 1864.
Mary Ann, consort of Henry C. Collings, b. Dec. 2, 1842, d. June 2, 1866 in the 24th year of her life, dau. of Nimrod and Elizabeth Skipper.

HUNT FAMILY CEMETERIES
Cockeysville Quad

These inscriptions are found in Ridgely's *Historic Graves*, pp. 123, 124.

This lot is on a farm near Hunt's Meeting House (now Hunt Methodist Church) to the right of the road going to Rockland.

Samuel, son of Job and Margaret Hunt, b. Jan. 1, 1772, d. Feb. 10, 1779.
John Hunt, who departed this life 18th Feb., 1809 in the 62nd year of his age.
Margaret Hunt, d. 26 Feb. 1794, in the 47th year of her age.*
Eliza Hunt was born 11th Aug. and departed this life Jan. 1784.
Samuel Hunt, b. 5th Sept. 1781, departed this life 5th Oct. 1782.
Rachel Anderson, who departed this life 29 April 1817, aged 54 years, 5 mos., and 4 days.
Susan Hunt, consort of J. H. Hunt, departed this life 30 Dec. 1833 in the 45th year of her age.
Elizabeth Chew Haubert, who departed this life 27 Oct. 1846, aged 69 years.
Capt. Lewis Beard, d. 31 Jan. 1853, age 46 years.

This plot is on a farm now rented (c. 1908) by Mr. Fouck, near the Falls Road and near the Brooklandwood farm.

Walter Smith, who departed this life 18 Feb. 1772, aged 33 years, 1 mo., and 15 days.
Elizabeth Bond, who departed this life, 29th Aug. 1806, in the 86th year of her age.
Susannah Hunt, who departed this life, 28th Dec. 1792, in the 49th year of her age.
Phineas Hunt, b. 2 Nov. 1751, d. 6 Feb. 1837, in the 86th year of his age.*
Susannah Hunt, d. 28 Jan. 1847, aged 83 years.
Benedict Hunt, b. 17 April 1783, d. 11 Sept. 1825.
Mother, Prudence Hunt, b. June 1790, d. 2 Aug. 1867.

ST. JOHN'S METHODIST CHURCH

Located on Bellona Avenue, west side, south of Malvern Avenue. Property runs west to Penn-Central Railroad. Cockeysville Quadrant. Church is maintained by Mrs. Ethel Addison, Falls Road. Services now only held about three times per year. There were once many more stones than at present. Copies in October, 1971 by John McGrain.

Father and Mother, Rev. Edwin W. Scott, May 26, 1841 - Nov. 20, 1919.
  Henrietta Scott, Sept. 22, 1835 - March 13, 1880. (E.W.S. & H.S. Foot)
Priscilla Chaney, d. Jan. 30, 1936.
Jennie R. Chaney, d. Nov. 25, 1929.
Scott, A. Louisa, 1873-1956. James T., 1870-1943.

Mother, Priscilla G. Bond, b. March 23, 1828, d. Feb. 25, 1925.
Wm. Walter Scott, 1868-1929. His wife, Henrietta Scott, 1877-1960.
Priscilla, dau. of Matthew and Ellen Yates, b. May 27, 1859, d. Aug. 12, 1926.*
George Yates, husband of Mattie Yates, 1849-1909.
Eliza Jane Chaney, d. March 10, 1906, aged 67 years.
Alice A. Chaney, b. June 18, 1871, d. Sept. 3, 1913.
Roland O. Scott, May 9, 1915 - June 17, 1917.
George A. Scott, Jr., July 15, 1916 - Oct. 9, 1918.
Samuel A., son of J. W. & P. D. Gardmon, June 22, 1895 - July 6, 1897.*
Mother, M. Elizabeth Smith, b. Dec. 1, 1880, d. Aug. 16, 1934.*
Priscilla D. Gardmon, wife of John W. Gardmon, b. Jan. 15, 1863, d. Nov. 2, 1934.*
Scott, Esther E., April 8, 1866 - April 10, 1951. Nathaniel P., d. Oct. 21, 1893.
Father, Geo. A. Scott, June 1, 1892 - Aug. 18, 1916.
George A. Scott, b. Sept. 28, 1857, d. July 20, 1926, husband of Hester L.
 Scott, b. March 17, 1855, d. Jan. 14, 1943.
Some toppled bases.
H. Jerden, d. Feb. 2, 181, aged 34 years.
Sarah J. Phillips, dau. of George and Frances Phillips, 1847-1921.
Anne Youeth Phillips b. Aug. 29, 1876, d. March 17, 1882.*
Sarah Rebecca Yeates, b. May 1, 1870, d. Aug. 30, 1871.* (S.R.Y. - foot)
Aquilla Bond, d. Oct. 23, 1876, in the 26th year of his age.* (A.B. - foot)
Nicholas W. Gross, son of Henry and Sophia Gross, d. June 28, 1876 in the 29th
 year of his age.* (N.W.G. - foot)
Emily Cath. Green, b. Jan. 29th, 1853, d. Aug. 10th, 1882 in her 30th year.*
Ethel E. Green, b. May 14, 1904, d. April 29, 1909.* (E.E.G. - foot)
Matthew, husband of Annie Yates, d. Aug. 7, 1916.
Eliza, wife of John Turner, May 31, 1844 - Sept. 18, 1903.*
Unmarked slab.
Loose - Mother, Father, Daughter.
Lewis Bowen, aged 50 years.* (L.B. - foot)
Turner, John E., 1870-1913. John, Sr., 1844-1923. William F., 1872-1932.
 William A., 1872-1926. Margaret 1876-1937.
Pedestal.
Lucey Meads, wife of James Meads, d. March 26, 1909, age 64.
Harriett Tate, mother of St. Johns (rest sunken)
Marked by wooden posts
White marker - no inscription.
Ann M. Christmas, Nov. 11, 1820, April 4(?), 1917.
Plot with corner markers; no stone.
One loose lithographers stone for 8½ x 11 stationery, apparetnly used as
 marker.

WHITAKER FAMILY LOT
Cockeysville Quad

This cemetery is located on Lincoln Avenue, west of Bellona Avenue and south
of Seminary Avenue in the Lutherville-Riderwood section of Baltimore
County. The information copies by Mr. Evart A. Cornell, Lutherville, Md.

Dennis Whitaker, d. Feb. 1, 1881, aged 83 years.
Eliza Whitaker, d. Oct. 8, 1889.
Unmarked grave for a small child, their daughter.

GOVANE-HOWARD CEMETERY

Located at "Drumquhasle", now known as "Anneslie". These stones are on the property owned at the time of copying by H. F. Birckhead, Govans. This list copies from the inscriptions in filing case of The Maryland Historical Society in October, 1971 by Robert W. Barnes. (Filed as the "Brice-Howard Cemetery") Mr. William Marye, in "Baltimore City Place Names, Part 3", states the cemetery was wrecked by vandals and descendants had the remains removed to public cemeteries. (Maryland Historical Magazine, 58: 227n).

James Govane, d. 1783.
Elizabeth Howard, b. 3 March 1815, d. 17th July 1818. Our Father, James G. Howard, b. 1777; d. 19th Nov., 1819. (N.B. - Family Bible gives date of death as 17th.)
Our Mother, Mary (W.) Howard, b. 19th of Jan. 1779, d. 1st of Nov. 1844.
Mary W. Howard, b. 5th Oct. 1802, d. 5th Jan. 1847. (Bible gives birth date as 3 Oct.)
Anne R., wife of W. Govane Howard, b. 13 March 1799, d. 9 Sept. 1869.
William Govane Howard, b. 19 Jan. 1805, d. 17th Nov. 1848.
William Govane Howard, son of W. Govane Howard, b. 20 Jan. 1840, d. 24 April 1845.
Frances Hillen, dau. of William G. and Anne R. Howard, b. 12 Oct. 1837, d. 24 Dec. 1849.*
Thomas Usher, d. 14th Nov. 1829.
Elizabeth Davies Law, b. 6 Aug. 1846, d. 24 April 1849.
W. G. Law, b. 14 Nov. 1837, d. 19 Nov. 1837.
Nicholas Brice, b. 4 March 1833, d. 28 Aug. 1844.
John Henry Brice, b. 13 May 1803, d. 18 Jan. 1850.

The inscriptions were presented to the Maryland Historical Society by Miss Mildred L. Murdoch, through Dr. J. Hall Pleasants, 3/23/1933.

PROVIDENCE UNITED METHODIST CHURCH
Providence Road and Seminary Avenue

Eleanora, dau. of Isaac and Mary Simms, b. Oct. 25, 1885, d. July 19, 1902.*
Bayne, Wm. Joseph, Oct. 13, 1867 - Oct. 21, 1918. Mary A., April 23, 1870 - Oct. 25, 1954.
Kelso, Annie E., 1882-1892. Ridgely M., 1889-1890. Howard M., 1892-1893.
George A. Kelso, May 13, 1888 - Aug. 25, 1959.
Father, Walter, husband of G. E. Eyre, Oct. 15, 1868 - April 23, 1934.
Mother, Catherine E., wife of W. Eyre, May 29, 1873 - Feb. 18, 1929.
George Hedge, d. Dec. 29, 1898?, aged 33 or (53) years, R.I.P., 3rd Md. Calv., U.S.A.
David Guishard, Jr., d. June 20, 1857, aged 54 years.*
Weathered stone.
Weathered stone.
Isaac Fisher, b. June 17th, 1780, d. April 5th, 1856. (Verse below ground) (I.F. - foot)
Joseph E., son of J. & C. Gorsuch, b. Jan. 1, 1860, d. July 16, 1860. (J.E.G.- foot)
Thomas Grover, d. April 13, 1894 in the 75th year of his age.* Also his wife, Mary J. Grover, b. May 4, 1813, d. March 5, 1895.
Augustus Francis, Sept. 12, 1820 - March 8, 1903. Elizabeth Francis, April 3, 1831 - Aug. 24, 1899.

Several weathered stones.
Father, Wm. W. Corbin, b. Dec. 15, 1789, d. Nov. 11, 1865 in the 76th year of his age. (Footstone - W.W.C.)
Mother, Rebecca, consort of Wm. W. Corbin, b. March 2, 1792, d. June 24th, 1866 in the 75th year of her age. (Footstone - R.C.)
Joshua W. Corbin, Dec. 29, 1829 - Sept. 5, 1873. (Footstone J.W.C.)
Mary E. Corbin, Sept. 23, 1830 - July 23, 1914. (Footstone M.E.C.)
William R. Corbin, April 20, 1870 - March 19, 1932. (Footstone - W.R.C.)
Susanna Corbin Watts, Oct. 20, 1856 - April 19, 1935. (Footstone S.C.W.)
Howard Corbin, Jan. 1, 1854 - March 15, 1937. (Footstone H.C.)
John Torbit, b. Aug. 20, 1818, d. Feb. 20, 1898.*
Elizabeth, wife of John Torbit, and dau. of William and Rebecca Corbin, b. May 28, 1821, d. Sept. 16, 1895.*
Tabitha First (?), consort of Uriah Carter, who departed this life (May ?) 11, 1847, aged 31 years and 19 days.*
Children of ...Torbit, John Torbit, b. 10 Aug. 1846?, d. 31 Aug. 1867. Wm. H. b. 21 (July ?) 1844?, d. 13 Aug. 1845. Huay?, b. 1 June 1850, d. 21 Jan. 1851. Jerome, b. 6 July and d. 12 Nov. 1860. Isaac, b. 24 Aug. 1861, d. 7 May 1863. (8 line verse illegible)
Mary Ann Torbit Francis, Aug. 3, 1848, d. Aug. 5, 1888.
Zaccheus Melvin Francis, Jan. 29, 1875 - Aug. 15, 1894.
Marion Torbit Francis, June 15, 1888 - Sept. 13, 1888.
Infant son of John F. and Ada E. Roberts, March 12, 1905.
Charles Francis, Feb. 11, 1851 - Jan. 6, 1936.
Mary Ann Francis, Aug. 20, 1850 - Feb. 8, 1932.
Peter Torbit, March 2, 1852 - April 25, 1920.*
Corbin, William W., Sept. 2, 1826 - July 23, 1922. Catherine, Dec. 16, 1826- Oct. 31, 1879.
Closest to Providence Road.
Mother, Ellen F. Eyre, March 1, 1877 - May 1, 1961.
Father, Lewis B. Eyre, Aug. 3, 1870 - March 23, 1949.
Father, Thomas Burton, 1889-1958.
Regina A. Walters Brown, Sept. 25, 1916 - March 4, 1921.
Collins, Lewis W., Jan. 21, 1880 - March 7, 1951. Mary L., July 16, 1892 - Oct. 26, 1961.
Donald B., infant son of L. B. and A. E. Wheeler, April 4, 1922.
Melvin E., son of H. B. and S. T. Barton, 1921-1922.
Traband, Mary 1847-1922. Henry 1853-1940.
Edward J. Blakley, Oct. 2, 1899 - Sept. 21, 1927.
Traband, Virginia J., Jan. 19, 1865 - Aug. 27, 1942. William M., Dec. 24, 1859 - May 15, 1934.
George Patterson, 1812-1904.
A. E. Parks, 1849-1939.
C. A. Parks, 1846-1934.
Parks, Father, Wm. H., 1868-1954. Mother, Cora, 1875-1938.
Mother, M. Maud Fowble, April 25, 1868 - May 9, 1930.
Father, Joshua B. Fowble, Sept. 20, 1872 - Aug. 1, 1956.
Mother, Helen F. Myers, Dec. 1, 1902 - March 14, 1972.
Father, William H.Myers, Aug. 10, 1899——
Sarah E. Kellum, departed this life, March 3, 1900, wife of Samuel A. Kellum in her 68th year of age.*
Father, George Bayne, b. Nov. 3, 1815, d. March 2, 1901.*
Edward Traband, son of Henry and Margaret Traband, June 5, 1862 - June 11, 1953.
Margaret, wife of Henry Traband, b. July 23, 1833, d. April 22, 1909.*
Henry Traband, b. March 4, 1829 - Aug. 15, 1915.*
Slade, Abraham, June 27, 1847 - Dec. 12, 1932. His wife, Elizabeth Anne Slade, Aug. 26, 1851 - Dec. 9, 1918.* (Footstones - Mother - Father)

Slade, Nettie E., 1894-1969. Frank D., 1884---.
Andrew J. Sims, husband of Mary E. Sims, 1848-1919.* (Footstone-Father)
Mother, Magdalene Simms, 1865-1947.
Father, Charles E. Simms, 1866-1942.
M. A. Garrison, 1874-1936.
J. E. French, 1879-1948.
G. L. French, 1877-1964.
Simms, John J., 1875-1963. Lillie R., 1882-1969.
Husband, Stewart L. Bayne, 22 years, 3 mos., 10 days.*
Obelisk - Clarence E., husband of Myrtle D. Bayne, June 30, 1892 - Jan. 6, 1919.
Myrtle D. Bayne, wife of Clarence E. Bayne, July 29, 1898 - Sept. 17, 1924.
John T., July 11, 1858 - March 23, 1940. R. Kate, Dec. 20, 1869 - Jan. 3, 1947. Katie B. Baublitz, Jan. 13, 1904 - Jan. 21, 1970.
Bayne, Clarence D., 1885-1957. Laura J., 1887---.
Simms (foot) Bertha V., Aug. 18, 1887---. Isaac F. (foot) Aug. 23, 1885 - Feb. 25, 1932.
Carter (foot) Lydia E., 1888-1923.
Carter (foot) Maurice A., 1876-1947.
Carter (foot) William E., 1911-1923.
Arthur W. Simms, Sept. 16, 1865 - Sept. 21, 1938. Eleanora C. Simms, nee Chenowith, Feb. 15, 1869 - March 30, 1936.
M. Florence Peterson, Nov. 13, 1878 - March 11, 1946.
J. Thomas Peterson, March 25, 1878 - Feb. 22, 1945.
Mother, Laura Jane Carter, Dec. 10, 1841 - Dec. 14, 1925. (Footstone L.J.C.)
Father, Dennis Carter, May 28, 1846 - Dec. 3, 1922.* (Footstone D.C.)
Son, Louis Edward Simms, 1907-1928.
Son, Charles Elmer Simms, 1899-1935.
Dora L., wife of William J. Simms, 1909-1951.
Ruth L., dau. of Dora L. and William Simms, 1931-1940.
Nelson, William W., 1852-1903. Martha M., 1860-1888. 2 markers "N".
Andrew C. Boyd, Sept. 24, 1906 - Sept. 30, 1956.
Herbert S. Guy, Oct. 20, 1893 - Nov. 11, 1950.
Cranston, William H., 1915-1970.
Jesse K. Sims, May 15, 1911 - Dec. 13, 1929.* (Footstone - Son)
Lucy M., dau. of J. J. and L. P. Simms, Oct. 22, 1908 - Jan. 11, 1909. (Footstone - L.M.S.)
Dorfler, March 9, 1841 - Sept. 1, 1924.
Rose A. Dorfler, Feb. 23, 1849 - Nov. 3, 1933.
Torbit, (Masonic Emblem) Mary, 1896---. Wm. Jarrett, 1892-1969.
Tombstone, Baby, illegible - footstone, illegible.
Margaret C. Corbin, Feb. 17, 1880 - Jan. 30, 1958.*
John Corbin, March 14, 1883 - May 9, 1964.
Heubeck, Mattie, 1868-1932. George F., 1863-1933. Elmer E., 1899-1922.
Schrufer, Martha E., Sept. 7, 1902 -. Charles E., Feb. 4, 1897 - Jan. 15, 1961.
Sims, Charles H., 1857-1942. Lydia A., 1857-1943.
Sims, Mattie E., 1886-1970. Eugene E., 1889-1965. Lawrence F., 1891---.
Roberts, John F., Aug. 31, 1867 - March 5, 1954. Ada E., Aug. 30, 1876 - July 31, 1957. (Footstones Father - Mother).
Anna F. Brown, March 16, 1888 - Nov. 27, 1957, Wife and Mother.
Joseph W. Brown, Jan. 1, 1878 - Feb. 13, 1958. Husband and Father.
Luella V., wife of J. James Simms, dau. of Dennis and Laura Sarler, b. Jan. 20, 1876, d. Nov. 22, 1899.*
Dorfler, John C. Dorfler, Jr., July 2, 1896 - March 25, 1897. W. May Dorfler, Jan. 4, 1898 - Oct. 3, 1898.
Winnie M. Dorfler, Nov. 4, 1874 - Aug. 16, 1898.
Mamie E. Dorfler, July 24, 1873 - June 4, 1937.
Robert A. Torbit, Jr., Aug. 1, 1943 - Feb. 21, 1948.

Torbit, Amos N., 1857, Husband 1935. Sarah J., 1861 Wife, 1937. Footstones Father Mother.
Celia R. Torbit, dau. of Amos and Sarah J. Torbit, May 29, 1900 - Jan. 1, 1918.* Footstone C.R.T.
Ballard F. Torbit, Sept. 7, 1854 - March 19, 1918.* Footstone B.F.T.
Clara E. Torbit, Jan. 13, 1869 - Feb. 5, 1923.* Footstone C.E.T.
Laura M., wife of Emory Mansfield, March 6, 1882 - Aug. 10, 1916.* Footstone L.M.M.
Mellor, Father, John Allen Mellor, Aug. 1, 1834 - July 21, 1904.
Mother, Mary Ann Mellor, July 9, 1846 - Feb. 19, 1919.
John Conrad Mellor, Nov. 10, 1869 - Dec. 8, 1944.
Brother, Harry A. Mellor, Sept. 21, 1872 - Sept. 16, 1932.
Father, John R. Corbin, b. Dec. 17, 1850, d. March 18, 1915.*
Mother, Caroline Corbin, b. June 24, 1848, d. March 2, 1910.*
Wilbur E. Roberts, Sr., 1910-1962.
Mother, Ivy Virginia Hudson Roberts, Sept. 2, 1915 - June 26, 1945.
Elmer W. Bayne, Aug. 21, 1901 - March 6, 1972.
Shirley L. Bayne, May 27, 1935 - Nov. 30, 1935.
Guy, Wm. E., 1887-1966.* Gladys V., 1895—.
Guy, James E., March 31, 1884 - Feb. 10, 1940.
Lottie H., July 28, 1892 —.
Edna L. Sargent, June 23, 1889 —.
Edward B. Sargent, Dec. 25, 1881 - Aug. 5, 1956.
Howard M. Treadwell, June 30, 1869 - Feb. 15, 1957. Julia A. Treadwell, June 24, 1875 - June 14, 1943.
James Mary Bessie, Dec. 13, 1892 - Dec. 19, 1958.
Canapp, Father, Earl George, 1892-1949. Mother, Lillie May, 1894-1949.
Heubeck, Husband, Geo. F., 1896-1958. Wife, Laura V., 1897-1961.
Simms, Daniel A. Simms (foot), March 4, 1903 - Feb. 4, 1963.
Shue, Corb B., 1876-1952. Granville S., 1878-1952.
David A. Yates, 1939-1953. Susan M. Yates, 1947-1953.
Guy, James E., May 13, 1860 - April 30, 1930. Laura E., Sept. 5, 1865 - Feb. 16, 1900.
S/Sgt. Grover C. Guy, U.S.A., b. Oct. 13, 1893, d. in the Southwest Pacific area, Dec. 29, 1944, 27 years in the service.
Conrad Neuberger, Feb. 17, 1842 - Feb. 4, 1924.* Footstone Brother.
Father, Isaac G. Blakley, 1865-1944.
Neubeck, Clarence D., 1889-1959. Myrtle I., 1898-1957.

Copied by Mr. & Mrs. Geo. E. Aro., Jr.

TOWSON FAMILY CEMETERY
Towson Quad

Towson Family Cemetery, south side of Shealey Avenue, west of No. 513 Virginia Avenue, Towson. East of York Road and South of Joppa Road. Towson Quad. A photo of Catharine Schmuck stone appears in *Old Towson Town,* by Mary Osborn Odell, Club Courant, November 1939, p. 5f. Mrs. Schmuck was one of 12 children of Ezekiel and Catharine Towson. Ownership of this plot is unknown to county assessment office. See *Historic Cemetery Restored,* concerning the efforts of Mrs. J. Howard Flayhart to restore plot, *Towson Bicentennial 1768-1968,* p. 108. The book cited tombstone of Oliver Schmuck. Shealeys were also buried there.

Empty pedestals.
Stone - no inscription.

Catharine Schmuck, wife of Solomon Schmuck, b. Nov. 30, 1767, d. Dec. 27,
   1834, aged 67 years and 27 days.*
Joseph Yost, departed this life, April 24, 1836, in the 35th year of his age.
   Footstone J.Y.
Footmarker - A.Y.
G. W. Stayler (only a stump)

Copies by J. McGrain, April 6, 1972.

STANSBURY FAMILY CEMETERY
Towson Quad

This cemetery is on the grounds of Pleasant Plains Elementary School, west of
the school itself, between Taylor Avenue and Joppa Road. Today only a few
fragments of stones remain. They are in a lot which has been enclosed and
has a padlocked gate. This almost certainly is the Stansbury family cemetery
referred to on pp. 150-151 of Ridgely, as being on the grounds of Union Hall.
The first four inscriptions, or fragments of inscriptions were copied by
Robert Barnes in April 1972. The remainder are found in Ridgely. Those inscriptions which are followed by the letters T.C. are of stones which have
since been moved to Taylor's Chapel Methodist Church on Hillen Road, on the
grounds of Mount Pleasant Golf Course, Baltimore City.

...ho.., Oct. 14, 1800, d. July 6, 1883.
... resigned...fortified with a...assurance of a ... immortality.
...arted t... on the 11th Decemb..., in the 28th year of his ...
...William? Stansbury, who departed this life, March 7, 1846 in the 50th year
   of his age. (T.C.)
From Ridgely, pp. 150-151.
William Stansbury, b. Jan. 20, 1716, departed this life Nov. 3, 1788, in the
   73rd year of his age.*
Elizabeth Stansbury, wife of William Stansbury, b. July 12, 1721, departed this
   life, Sept. 10, 1799, in the 79th year of her age.*
Jacob Stansbury, b. on March 14, 1755, d. Feb. 22, 1812.* (T.C.)
William Stansbury, who was b. April 4, 1746, departed this life in the 80th
   year of his age.* (T.C.)
Belenda Stansbury, wife of William Stansbury, departed this life April 7, 1830,
   upwards of 80 years old.* (T.C.)
Mary Stansbury, wife of John E. Stansbury, who departed this life, 5th Dec.
   1800 in the 23rd year of her age. (T.C.)
Ann Stansbury, wife of Jn. E. Stansbury, who departed this life the 1st of
   April 1815, in the 32nd year of her age. (T.C.)
Father, John E. Stansbury, who departed this life April 30, 1841, aged 81 years
   and 11 mos.* (T.C.)
Isaac Stansbury, b. July 2, 1752, departed this life Oct. 1792 in the 41st year
   of his age.* (T.C.)
Mary E. Stansbury, Dec. 21, 1846 - June 13, 1887.
William E. Stansbury, son of John E. Stansbury, April 14, 1811 - March 27, 1878.(T.C.
Sarah A. Stansbury, Jan. 15, 1850, aged 4 years, 11 mos.
Sarah Brown, consort of Josiah Brown, and dau. of William Stansbury, who
   departed this life, Aug. 7, 1834, aged 51 years and 6 mos.
Solomon C. Wallace, who departed this life May 7, 1840, in the 52nd year of
   his age.
Mary E. Wallace, b. Aug. 9, 1824, d. Dec. 16, 1829.*
John Wallace, 1832, aged 6 mos., an infant Martha (?).
Benjamin Brady, b. Nov. 29, 1760, departed this life 18 Dec. 1839. He was
for 50 years a pious member of the Methodist Church.* (T.C.)
Samuel Brady (Ridgely gives Beady), b. Oct. 5, 1801, d. 28 Dec. 1871.* (T.C.)

SALEM E. U. B. CHURCH
(Now United Methodist)
Falls Road, Baltimore County, Maryland
- above Beckleysville Road -
Copied April 10, 1971
by Margery Lee Barnes and Robert W. Barnes

Row 1 -

Margaret, wife of David Wilhelm, d. Mar 23, 1905, aged 83 yrs, 8 mos. & 20 days.
David Wilhelm, d. Apr 28, 1888, aged 72 yrs, 7 mos. & 18 days.
Jacob T., son of David and Margaret Wilhelm, d. 10 Jan., 1866, aged 1 yr & 10 mos.
Ada Agnes, beloved dau of Geo. J. & Elsie M. Hare, b. Jan. 21, 1898, d. Aug. 3, 1898, aged 6 mos & 13 days.*
Nancy Marie, dau of John D. and Lulu M. Alban, Jan. 18, 1944 - Jan. 20, 1944.*
ALBAN - Footstones: Lulu M. Nov. 5, 1909 - John D. Oct. 25, 1902 - June 4, 1967.
COX, Mary E., Mar. 16, 1877 - Feb. 9, 1967 - Emory M. Sept. 14, 1869 - Feb. 6, 1937 - Thomas M., Oct. 19, 1899 - April 25, 1906.
HALE, John E., Feb. 28, 1891, - J.F.H., Elva M., July 19, 1902, E.M.H.
CHILCOAT, Effie P., 1887-1956 - G. Aldridge, 1888 -

ROW 2 -

Husband
ARMACOST, John F., husband of Kezia W. Armacost, Mar. 10, 1830 - Sept. 27, 1905
Kezia W., wife of John F. Armacost, Apr. 7, 1830 -
Wife
Illegible
Father and Mother Holtzner, William Holtzner, b. May 16, 1830 - d. July 11, 1906
aged 76 yrs., 1 mo., 25 ds., - Jane Holtzner, b. Sept. 22, 1834 - d. July 1, 1906, aged 71 yrs., 9 mos., 9 days.*
Illegible
Russell E. M., son of J. F. and H. V. Armacost, b. Jan. 21, 1903 - d. May 13, 1904 aged 1 yr., 3 mos., 22 days.*
V. Marie Martin, March 7, 1899 -
Mother
ARMACOST, Joseph F. Armacost, b. Oct. -2, 1871 - d. Apr. 9, 1928, aged 53 yrs., 5 mos., 17 days. Hester V., wife of Joseph F., b. Jan. 22, 1881 - d. Apr. 3, 1910, aged 29 yrs, 2 mos. & 11 days.*
Father
Mother
MARTIN, Edward Martin, b. Feb. 1, 1854 - d. Mar. 27, 1936, aged 82 yrs., 1 mo., and 27 days. - Keziah Martin, b. Feb. 12, 1844, d. Aug. 6, 1917, aged 73 yrs., 5 mos. & 26 days.*
MARTIN, Harvey T., 1876-1947 - Virgie M., 1910 -
MARTIN, B. Edwin, Feb. 23, 1888 - July 4, 1966., Nettie V., Dec. 1, 1888 - Mar. 2, 1959.*
FOWBLE, Gilbert E., July 30, 1901 - Nov. 19, 1962, Ethel G., Sept. 5, 1906.

ROW 3 -

Goldie
Goldie May Rhoten, b. Nov. 6, 1892, d. May 10, 1910, aged 17 yrs., 6 mos. and 4 days., David W. Rhoten, b. Dec. 25, 1862, d. Nov. 21, 1920, Lucy Rhoten, b. Feb. 14, 1867, d. Aug. 4, 1945.

Mattie M., wife of Emory S. Boring, Mar. 20, 1890, Mar. 27, 1912.,
Emory S. Boring, June 15, 1866, Dec. 17, 1931.*
Harmon, Mary E., July 23, 1903, Feb. 6, 1962, William W., Feb. 14, 1894,
Nov. 28, 1966.
Millard F. Stine, June 1, 1902, Apr. 12, 1964.
MARTIN, Russell L., Feb. 8, 1908, Nov. 17, 1965, Mary S., July 24, 1913,
Sept. 10, 1967.

ROW 4 -

Amos B. Armacost, Aug. 3, 1900, July 19, 1967.
John F. Royston, b. Aug. 29, 1886, d. Oct. 31, 1918, aged 32 yrs., 2 mos.
and 2 days.*
Walter E. Royston, b. Oct. 18, 1913 - d. Oct. 23, 1913, aged 5 days.
Our beloved son, Robert Eugene Royston, Nov. 15, 1957, Aug. 13, 1966.
MARTIN, Albert F., Mar. 27, 1881, Dec. 28, 1966, Margie O., July 28, 1883 -
BAUBLITZ, G. Howard, 1878, Dora E., 1878 - 1949, William T., aged 7 yrs.,
D. Elizabeth, aged 14 yrs.
BAUBLITZ, Clarence E., 1902 - 1962, Goldie M., 1898 - 1970, Grayson E.,
1930 -   , Goldie L., 1929 -

ROW 5 -

ASHE, Hattie M., July 25, 1890, Mar. 1, 1945, Harry A., Nov. 23, 1894,
Son, Stanley P., Sept. 12, 1925, Oct. 1, 1926.*
Ruth Baublitz, b. Sept. 14, 1915, d. Sept. 18, 1915.*
Raymond E. Baublitz, b. Oct. 29, 1916, d. Nov. 1, 1916.*
Edith M. Baublitz, b. Oct. 31, 1922, d. Feb. 27, 1923.*
Baublitz, Luther E., 1890 -   , Lillian G., 1897 -

ALMONY-AYRES FAMILY CEMETERY
(Abandoned)

Copied April 10, 1971, by Robert Barnes and R. Wayne White.

This graveyard is in the 7th District of Baltimore County on the South Side of Garrett Road about .9 miles southwest of Old York Road. It stands on a knoll in a clump of trees. Many of the stones are broken and fallen over. The 1877 Atlas of Baltimore County does not show the cemetery, but the house of J. Almony would appear to be near it. The cemetery is not on the Army Engineers quadrangle map, either.

The stones were not copied in any particular order, as they were not in rows.
Mary, wife of Col. James Almony, d. 19 Dec. (1839?), aged 62 (or 69) years, 5 mos., and 13 days.
Broken stone, Col. James Almony, d. Sept. 21, 1833 (or 1855), aged 76 years, (?), and 17 days.
Elizabeth, wife of Benjamin Almany, d. Sept. 19, 1859, aged 55 years, 3 mos., and 6 days.*
Broken stone, ...dau., Benjamin & ....., Almo..., died Feb....
Benjamin Almony, d. June 23, 1834, aged 86 years, 5 mos., 2 (days)....
Sarah, wife of James Almany, d. April 30, 1858, aged 25 years and 4 mos.
Grandison Almony, d. Dec. 8, 1856 in the 11 (?) year of his age.
John Ayres, d. March 10, 1852, aged 68 years.
M.S.A.
T.A., 1836
Thos. Ayres, of Harford County, who departed this life, March 13, 1836, aged 85 years.*
R.A.
In memory....

WHITAKER FAMILY LOT
Cockeysville Quad

This cemetery is located on Lincoln Avenue, west of Bellona Avenue and south of Seminary Avenue in the Lutherville-Riderwood section of Baltimore County. The information copied by Mr. Evart A. Cornell, Lutherville, Maryland.

Dennis Whitaker, d. Feb. 1, 1881, aged 83 years.
Eliza Whitaker, d. Oct. 8, 1889.
Unmarked grave for a small child, their daughter.

HOOK FAMILY CEMTERY

Located on hill west side of Jones Falls Expressway, south of Pimlico Road, in stone-walled plot. Cockeysville Quadrant.

Large central marker - Mary Ann Hook, d. Nov. 24, 1886. Frederick Hook, d. Sept. 1, 1834. H. W. Hook, d. Feb. 28, 1879. Sarah Hook, d. March 27, 1850.
Albert G. Hook, b. Oct. 6, 1835, d. Jan. 4, 1897, aged 60 years, 2 mos. and 28 days.*
Olevia M. Hook, b. April 21, 1831, d. Jan. 10, 1899, aged 67 years, 8 mos. and 19 days.*
Sister, Cordelia Hook, b. Oct. (?), 19, 1828, departed this life Feb. 29, 1876.

Father, Isaac O. Hook, b. Jan. 23, 1801, departed this life Feb. 5, 1875.
T. Tel (Incomplete)
Broken foot marker - W.H.
Copied by J. McGrain, 11/7/70.

ROGERS FAMILY CEMETERY

Near Govans, Baltimore City

The American and Commercial Daily Advertiser, Baltimore of May 7, 1807, contained an obituary of Mrs. Ann Martin. It mentioned that she would be buried in the burial ground of her deceased father, Mr. Charles Rogers, near "Govane's-town" now Govans. W. Hollifield.

DOWDENS CEMETERY

North side of Ridge Road just east of Bel Air Road in extreme Southeast corner of Towson Quad. The driveway is 4310 Ridge Road. This is a Negro cemetery surrounding a very small wooden chapel. There are numerous unmarked burials.

Rev. C. Douton, d. Feb. 5 (broken).*
Flora, wife of Abraham Guddungs, who departed this life Jan. 13, 1855 in the 30th year of her age. (F.G. - foot)
Henry Carroll, aged 24 years, 7 mos., and 8 days. (H.C. - foot)
Louisa Carroll, aged 15 years, 3 mos., and 8 days.
Samuel D. Prescoe, 1868-1946.
Harriet D. Prescoe, 1870----.
Amelia Presco.
Thos. Conway.
Mary Jennings, who departed this life July 22, 1854 in the 47th year of her age.*
Laura Conway.
Mother, 1845-1934.
Father, 1812-1903.
Unmarked.
Mother, 1885-1934.
Mother, Sally Jones, b. 1869, d. Jan. 22, 1938.
H. C.
Cecelia M. Talbott, 1860-1945.
Wesley J. Talbott, d. Feb. 7, 1872, his wife, Elizabeth A. Talbott, b. May 21, 1834, d. April 16, 1918.
Rebecca M. Talbott, 1862-1943.
Johnson, Carrie G., 1875-1957. J. Howard, 1870-1952.
Maggie B. Johnson Pryor, b. Oct. 17, 1900, d. Oct. 8, 1946.
James F. Baker, Sr., May 31, 1900 - May 5, 1972.
James Franklin Baker, Jr., Maryland, Cpl. U.S. Marine Corps, Korea, Nov. 5, 1934 - July 12, 1971.
Kevin Eugene Gray, April 29, 1971, aged 10 years and 5 days.
Lane, Charles R., husband of Mary F. Lane, d. Jan. 19, 1930, aged 45 years.
Lane, Mary F., wife of Charles R. Lane, d. June 26, 1937.
Rev. Alfred Baker, b. March 15, 1852, d. July 24, 1933.*
Fannie A., wife of Alfred Baker, d. May 11, 1920, aged 69 years. (F.A.B. foot)
Eleanora, dau. of Alfred and Fannie Baker, d. Oct. 20, 1909, aged 21 years.

William H., husband of Mary Barnes, d. March 24, 1909, aged 20 years. (W.H.B. - foot)
Father, Richard, husband of Lydia John (sunken-broken). (R.J. - foot).
Henry Warner, 1860----. Harriett S. Warner, 1863-1917. (H.S.W. - foot).
Sarah Wallace, 1880-1968.
Copied by J. McGrain, November 25, 1973.

COCKEY FAMILY CEMETERY

This cemetery is located on Melinda's Prospect in the Worthington Valley. In December 1897, it was owned by Edward A. Cockey. (Copied from *The Progenitors and Descendants of Charles Thomas Cockey*, taken from miscellaneous notes in the possession of Mrs. Ruath C. Cockey Rogers, compiled by her husband, Charles B. Rogers, Feb. 5, 1926, unbound manuscript at M.H.S.)

Cockey, Charles C., b. 1761, d. April 23, 1823.
Cockey, Urath Cockey, wife of Charles, b. 1754, d. Oct. 10, 1824.
Infant child (Cockey ?).

COCKEY FAMILY CEMETERY

This cemetery is located on Melinda, in the Worthington Valley. The property was the home of Mordecai Gist Cockey in November, 1899.

Cockey, Thomas Cockey of Thos., d. Nov. 18, 1813, aged 60.
Cockey, Ruth (Brown) Cockey, wife of Thomas of Thomas, d. May 2, 1816, aged 46.
Cockey, William H. Cockey, son of Thomas and Ruth (dates are obliterated).
Cockey, John Robert Cockey, son of Thomas and Ruth (dates are obliterated).
Cockey, Deborah Powell Cockey, wife of John Robert Cockey (dates are obliterated).
Cockey ?, John Powell (Cockey ?) (dates are obliterated).

COCKEY FAMILY CEMETERY
at Brooklandwood

(Taken from *The Progenitors and Descendants of Charles Thomas Cockey* by Charles B. Rogers, Feb. 5, 1926. Unbound manuscript at M.H.S.) The graveyard was on Brooklandwood Farm on Joppa Road, 1/4 mile west of Falls Road.

Cockey, John Cockey, b. 1683, d. Aug. 5, 1746, aged 63 years.
Cockey, John Cockey, d. 1746.
Cockey, William Cockey, d. 1775, aged 26.
Cockey, William Cockey, died 1756, aged 36.
Cockey, William Cockey, d. 1782, aged 9 years.
Owings, Richard Owings, d. Oct. 12, 1789, age 2 years old.
Baker, Elizabeth Slade Baker, d. Aug. 5, 1780, aged 95, widow Cockey.

The copiest states that Edward A. Cockey was removed to Loudon Park and placed beside the remains of his wife, Urath Cromwell Owings. He died June 1, 1856. Urath and Charles, children of Edward A. Cockey and Alice Councilman are buried at Melinda's Prospect in the Worthington Valley.
Note: This list should be compared with the other list of Cockey tombstone inscriptions at Brooklandwood.

RIDGELY FAMILY CEMETERY
Towson Quad

Located in brick-walled enclosure in southeast corner of Hampton National Historic Site property, immediately north of Baltimore Beltway. Copied by J. McGrain, October 26, 1972.

Louise Roman Humrichouse, wife of John Ridgely, Jr., Nov. 19, 1883 - May 6, 1934.
Howard Ridgely, Jan. 7, 1855 - Sept. 28, 1900.*
Helen Morris Tucker, wife of Howard Ridgely, d. July 4, 1921.* (H.M.R. - foot)
Large mausoleum, a placque, now missing was recorded in Ridgely, *Historic Graves*, p. 148):
Governor Charles Ridgely, b. Dec. 6, 1760, d. July 17, 1829. Priscilla, wife of Gov. Ridgely, d. April 30, 1814. Charles Ridgely, Jr., eldest son of Gov. Ridgely and Priscilla, his wife, b. Aug. 26, 1783, d. July 19, 1819.
Rebecca D. Hanson, wife of Charles W. Hanson and dau. of Governor Ridgely, b. March 5, 1786, d. Sept. 1837.
Charles W. Hanson, d. Dec. 8, 1853 in the 70th year of his age.
Sophia Gough Howard, wife of James Howard and dau. of Governor Ridgely, b. July 3, 1800, d. April 18, 1828.
Priscilla Hill White, wife of Stevenson White and dau. of Governor Ridgely, b. March 17, 1796, d. April 10, 1820.
David Latimer Ridgely, 3rd son of Gov. Ridgely, b. Nov. 19, 1798, d. 1846.
Mary Louisa, widow of David L. Ridgely, b. July 4, 1808, d. Nov. 8, 1863.
Eight children of D. L. and M. L. Ridgely.
John Ridgely of H., son of Gov. Ridgely, b. at Hampton, Jan. 9, 1790, d. at H. July 17, 1867.
Eliza E., wife of John Ridgely of H., b. Feb. 10, 1803, d. Dec. 20, 1867. Three infant children of John and Eliza E. Ridgely.
Mr. & Mrs. Nicholas G. Ridgely, the parents of Mrs. John Ridgely, and John Clemm, son of Daniel and Johanna Ridgely, a young cousin who d. Sept. 26, 1839.
Charles Ridgely of H., son of John & Eliza E. Ridgely, b. March 22, 1838, d. at Rome, Italy on Good Friday, March 29, 1872.
Margaretta S. Ridgely, widow of Charles Ridgely of H, B. Sept. 24, 1824, d. March 31, 1904.
Nancy Davis, d. 1908 aged about 70 years.*
Selena J. Devlin, Oct. 16, 1869 - Feb. 5, 1970. Faithful friend of the Ridgely family for 84 years.
Slab table, Eliza Ridgely, wife of N. G. Ridgely and dau. of M. & E. Eichelberger departed this life the 10th of Feb. 1805, a few hours after the birth of an only daughter, aged 19 years and 2 mos.
John Ridgely, infant son of J. C. & E. R. White, b. March 16, 1852, d. May 7, 1852.* (J.R.W. - foot)
Husband and father, John Campbell, son of Henry and Mary LeRoy White, b. Nov. 20, 1825, d. Feb. 6, 1853.*
Verse.*
Verse.*
Mother, Eliza Ridgely Buckler, b. Oct. 28, 1828, d. March 3, 1894.
Her sons, Henry White, J. Leroy White, William H. Buckler.
Verse.*
Sister, Juliana Elizabeth, eldest dau. of James and Sophia Howard, b. Aug. 25, 1821, d. May 22, 1853.
Note: Ridgely in *Historic Graves*, p. 148, also lists burials of Rev. Charles Ridgely Howard, John Eager Howard, brothers of Mrs. Margaretta Ridgely, her son Charles, and her grandsons, John Stewart and Charles.

ST. JOHN'S CATHOLIC CHURCH
Long Green Pike, Baltimore County, Md.

Historical Marker: "St. John the Evangelist Catholic Church. First Roman Catholic Church in (present) Baltimore County. Founded in 1822. One and one-half mile northeast of Manor Road. Building destroyed by fire, Feb. 25, 1855. Parish relocated to present site. First mass offered Dec. 30, 1855. Baltimore County Historical Society."

Inscriptions copied by Miss Matilda Lacey and Mrs. John Slattery, June, 1972.

Shepperd - footstones: Winfield, infant son of J. W. and Ida M. Shepperd, d. April 4, 1893. Sister, M.L.S., Sister, M.F.S. Monument - 4 sides: Our Father, Josiah Shepperd, d. April 3, 1887, aged 74 years.* Mother, Frances, wife of Josiah Shepperd, d. Feb. 22, 1884, aged 69 years.* Elias Shepperd, 1851-1881. Frances Shepperd, 1853-1924. M. Laura Shepperd, 1855-1945. Footstones: Father, Josiah, Mother, Frances.
Roach, Robert, d. Aug. 23, 1920, age 84 years, native of County Waterford, Ireland. Mary C., d. Aug. 24, 1896, aged 58 years. Native of County Cork, Ireland.
Base, no names
Base, no names
Roach, Edward J., Aug. 21, 1875 - Dec. 7, 1961.
Henkel (Monument). Ferdinand Henkel, b. Sept. 8, 1829, d. Dec. 31, 1865. Magnus Henkel, b. May 4, 1847, d. July 29, 1856. Amalia Henkel, b. March 18, 1844, d. Jan. 8, 1879. Apollonia Henkel, b. Jan. 4, 1804, d. April 14, 1884. Mary L. Schmidt, b. Aug. 27, 1882, d. July 29, 1887.*
Schreiber, Julius, 1856-1941. His wife, Philomana, 1860-1929.
Schreiber, dau. Mary, of Julius and Philomena Schreiber, b. Sept. 5, 1882, d. July 24, 1891. Footstones - P.S./J.S.
Smith, Monument. Charles M., son of James and Catherine Smith, b. April 20, 1878, d. Nov. 16, 1902.* Anna A. Smith, April 7, 1875 - April 21, 1950.
Hanlon, Monument. Erected by their Mother. Ellen, wife of John Hanlon, d. April 23, 1901, aged 83 years. A native of County Cork, Ireland.* John Hanlon, d. Nov. 23, 1899, aged 78 years. A native of County Cork, Ireland.* Daniel, d. Aug. 7, 1864, aged 12 years. John, d. Aug. 25, 1864, aged 13 years, sons of John and Ellen Hanlon.* Their daughters, Sarah Ellen, d. 1864, aged 5 years, Alice d. 1864, 7 years.*
Corcoran, Nora, wife of Daniel Corcoran, d. March 7, 1888, aged 100 years. A native of Mitchelstown, County Cork, Ireland.*
Ohler, Mother, Mary E., wife of James J. Ohler, Sr., d. Jan. 30, 1912, aged 65 years.
Ohler, Father, James J. Ohler, 1833-1922.*
Ohler, Mary, 1883-1954. James J., 1883-1945.
McVeigh, Mother, Katherine McVeigh, b. June 20, 1817, d. May 6, 1911.*
Lynch, John G., d. March 24, 1924, aged 56 years.*
Noonan, Thomas J., d. Feb. 6, 1917, aged 82 years.*
Cochran, Rose K., Nov. 12, 1903 - May 23, 1923.
Cochran, William J., March 14, 1860 - April 24, 1923. Mary J., June 21, 1868 - Oct. 8, 1962.
Cochran, Mary, wife of Daniel Cochran, d. Dec. 27, 1907, aged 90 years.*
Cochran, Daniel Cochran, d. Aug. 29, 1880, aged 60 years.*
Schmidt, John, b. May 1, 1829, d. May 22, 1905. Anna Schmidt, b. June 9, 1835, d. July 5, 1908.
Shanahan, John M., husband of Catharine K. Shanahan, b. in Glankeen Parish of Bourisholeigh Co., Tipperary, Ireland, d. Jan. 20, 1892, aged 66 years.*

Shanahan, Catherine K., wife of John M. Shanahan, b. in Mounkenane County, Tipperary, Ireland, d. May 21, 1892, aged 66 years.*
Lynch, John J. Lynch, d. Sept. 1, 1910, aged 57 years and 5 mos.*
Anora E., wife of John J. Lynch, d. Jan. 2, 1896, aged 44 years, 4 mos. and 27 days.*
McKenna, son, Thomas James, son of Thomas and Anne McKenna, d. Jan. 3, 1944, aged 69 years.*
McKenna, Mother, Anne McGee, wife of Thomas McKenna, a native of Belloran Co., Louth, Ireland, d. Dec. 27, 1908, aged 66 years.* Footstone A.McK.
McKenna, Father, Thomas McKenna, husband of Anne McKenna, a native of White Cross Co., Louth, Ireland, d. Nov. 3, 1902, aged 67 years.* Footstone-T.McK.
McKenna, Dennis McKenna, husband of Margaret McKenna, a native of White Cross County, Louth, Ireland, d. Nov. 19, 1878, aged 78 years.*
McGuire, John J., 1859-1931. Elizabeth A., 1867-1928.
Murphy, Owen Patrick, March 17, 1914 - Dec. 1914. George Stephen, infant, Aug. 2, 1925. Thresa, infant Sept. 5, 1927. Children of J. Golden and Bessie L. Murphy.
Murphy, William L., Maryland Pvt. 339-Inf., 85 Inf. Div., World War II, Feb. 11, 1922 - May 12, 1944, son of J. Golden and Bessie Murphy.
Murphy, J. Golden, 1887-1952. Bessie Leech, 1889-1950.
McCormick, Footstones: Daughter, Margaret Lillian, 1907-1962.
McCormick, Footstones: Son, John Bernard, 1915-1956.
McCormick, Footstones: Mother, Cecelia Nora, 1880-1949.
McCormick, Footstones: Father, Peter James, 1873-1937.
Lynch, Martin B. Lynch, July 22, 1889 - Oct. 24, 1970.
Lynch, Martin J., husband of the late Mary A. Lynch, d. Oct. 31, 1920, aged 62 years.*
Lynch, Mary A. Lynch, wife of Martin J. Lynch, d. Jan. 26, 1901, aged 39 years and 6 mos.
Shanahan, Edward J., son of John J. and Annie J., b. Dec. 1, 1881, d. Feb. 12, 1901.*
Shanahan, Agnes, dau. of John J. and Annie J. Shanahan, d. July 1897, age 7 mos.*
Shanahan, Mother, Annie J., wife of John J. Shanahan, d. Jan. 31, 1897, aged 40 years, 8 mos., 11 days.*
Shanahan, Nellie, infant child of John J. and Annie Shanahan, b. Sept. 2, 1890, d. Jan. 2, 1892 (Verse illegible).
Shanahan, Father, John J., husband of the late Annie J. Shanahan, b. March 1, 1855, d. Nov. 3, 1916.* By his children.
O'Hara, Patrick O'Hara, d. July 30, 188(2), aged 49 years.*
Schmidt, Monument. Christian Schmidt, b. July 18, 1832, d. Nov. 28, 1899.* A native of Germany.*
A. Mary Schmidt, b. Nov. 19, 1839, d. Oct. 14, 1907. A native of Germany.*
Schmidt, Mary K., b. Oct. 22, 1865, d. Feb. 20, 1913. R.I.P.
Hagan, Monument. Hagan, Mary A., wife of D. H. Hagan, d. Oct. 29, 1885, aged 28 years, 8 mos., 22 days.* D. H. Hagan, d. Feb. 13, 1911, aged 52 years.*
Sarah, wife of D. H. Hagan, d. June 14, 1911, 53 years, 1 mos., 2 days.*
Grant, Anna Marie, dau. of James H. & Mary E. Grant, b. June 27, 1896, d. Jan. 15, 1918.*
Grant, John Grant, d. 18 Oct. 1887, aged 75 years. Bridget, d. 5 Aug. 1868, aged 10 years.*
Shanahan, Father & Mother, John T. Shannahan, d. Sept. 22, 1914. Eva, his wife, ...(rest of stone under earth)
McCormick, Alice McCormick, wife of Joseph, d. April 30, 1915, aged 27 years.
McCormick, Joseph, husband of Alice S., 1880-1949.
McCormick, Catherine P., wife of John McCormick, 1879-1969.
McCormick, John McCormick, husband of Catherine, d. Jan. 20, 1917, aged 41 years.
McCormick, Monument stone - no names.
Base only - stone missing.

McCormick, Elizabeth A., wife of John B. McCormick, April 25, 1948 - Oct. 11, 1921. (?)
Shannahan?, (stone turned opposite direction - badly eroded, illegible but appears name could be Shanahan.)
Martin Barry, a native of .....County, Waterford, Ireland who departed this life, Sept. 21, 1832 in the 58th year of his age.
Shanahan, Anna Stasia, wife of Timothy Shanahan, Sr., d. Feb. 6, 1904 in the 72nd year of her age. A native of County Derry, Ireland.*
Shanahan, Bernard V., son of Timothy and Ann Shanahan, d. Feb. 20, 1901, aged 29 years and 15 days.*
Miller, Joseph Stevens R., d. Sept. 1, 1890, aged 12 years and 10 mos.* By his uncles.
McCarroll, Grandfather, John McCarroll, d. Feb. 19, 1885 in the 100th year of his age. A native of County Antrum, Ireland.*
Lynch, Mary M., wife of Charles L. Lynch, 1881-1926. Louis, son of C. L. & M. M. Lynch.* (no dates)
Lynch, Charles L. Lynch, 1882-1950.*
Carroll, Father, Timothy J., 1859-1927. Elizabeth J., 1863---(no date).
Bradley - Monument. John D. Bradley, d. May 1, 1916 in his 83rd year. A native of Ireland. Hannah, wife of John D. Bradley, d. March 2, 1914 in her 68th year. A native of Ireland.* Catherine A., June 26, 1873 - July 26, 1938. Margaret E., 1875-19(6)2. Dennis Leo, Infant son of J. D. and H. Bradley, aged 3 mos., and 17 days. Footstones: Mother, Father and Catherine.
Riley, Thomas Riley, April 13, 1864 - June 12, 1924.*
Riley, Emma A. Riley, April 11, 1878 - June 21, 1956.
Riley, Phillip Eugene Riley, 1910-1970.
Hagan, Monument. James F. Hagan, husband of Annie M. Hagan, b. Feb. 7, 1876, d. April 3, 1916.* Annie M. Hagan, wife of James F. Hagan, b. Aug. 25, 1883, d. Nov. 10, 1940.* Margaret Regina, dau. of J. F. and A. M. Hagan, b. Aug. 16, 1915, d. Dec. 2, 1915.* James J. Hagan, b. Oct. 2, 1916, d. Aug. 12, 1923.
Allender - McIntyre - Monument. Allender, William R., Oct. 13, 1839 - Feb. 12, 1914. His wife, Araminta Holland, Aug. 19, 1854 - April 16, 1885. McIntyre, Edward J., Nov. 14, 1879 - June 24, 1946. His wife, Araminta H. Allender, March 19, 1882 - Nov. 13, 1952. Footstones: Araminta Holland Allender, 1854-1885. William R. Allender, 1839-1914. Edward J. McIntyre, 1879-1946. Araminta H. A. McIntyre, 1882-1952.
McDonnell, Father, Patrick McDonnell, d. June 13, 1863, aged 52 years, a native of County Mayo, Ireland.*
Corrigan, Catherine Mary, dau. of Michael and Margaret Corrigan, d. Aug. 24, 1898, aged 19 years.
Corrigan, Father, Mother, Michael J. Corrigan, aged 30 years (no date).
Margaret M. Corrigan, d. June 1, 1928, aged 72 years.
Bradley - Footstones.
Kelly - Footstones.
Lynch, Margaret, wife of John Lynch, d. Aug. 24, 1895, aged 78 years. A native of County Clare, Ireland.*
Lynch, John Lynch, d. Feb. 20, 1901, aged 92 years. A native of County Clare, Ireland.*
Kelly, Mary, dau. of William J. and Ellen E. Kelly, d. March 21, 1911, aged 26 years.*
Kelly, Margaret, dau. of William and Ellen Kelly, d. June 17, 1904 in the 22nd year of her age.*
Kearney, dau. of Anne C. Kearney, Jan. 9, 1900 - June 12, 1969.
Kearney, Mary Ellen, wife of Frank J. Kearney, d. June 23, 1886 in the 32nd year of her age.*
Kearney, Frank J. Kearney, d. July 30, 1938, aged 82 years.*
Kearney, Catherine A., wife of Frank J. Kearney, d. May 27, 1902, aged 42 years.
Kearney, Mary Elizabeth, wife of Frank J. Kearney, d. June 1, 1919 in the 52nd year of her age.*

Bradley, Dennis L. Bradley, 1874-1959.*
Bradley, Alice Virginia, wife of Dennis L. Bradley (no dates).
Bradley, (Monument), Maria, wife of Daniel Bradley, b. May 17, 18(..), d. May 2(0), 1906.* Daniel Bradley, b. 18(..), d. May 9, 191(7).* May, dau. of Daniel and Mary Bradley, b. Oct. 23, 1883, d. Oct. 20, 188(?). Catherine Tahaney, d. April 8, 189(9), aged 87 years. Jane B., b. Feb. 13, 1901, d. June 23, 1901. Ellen C., b. July (8), 190(2), d. Sept. 1(3), 190(3). Children of Daniel and Maria Bradley.
Shipley, Benjamin R., 1835-1916. Martha A., 1844-1932. J. William, 1876-1939.
Bradley, Father, Daniel Bradley, Sept. 1, 1843 - June 6, 1873.
Bradley, Sister, Catherine, dau. of Daniel and Sarah Bradley, age 14 years. (no dates)*
Bradley, Mother, Sarah Bradley Kearney, Feb. 8, 1840 - June 9, 1907.
Bradley, Mary Emily Bradley, May 26, 1865 - Oct. 12, 1937.
Kelly, Headstone and Footstone - Marian M., 1897-1959. Agnes,1905-1905. Michael P., Annie B., 1873-1936.
Kelly (Monument) William G. Kelly, d. April 11, 1894, aged 71 years, 4 mos., 25 days.* Mother, Mary Ann, wife of William G. Kelly, Feb. 20, 1911, aged 85 years, 10 mos., 25 days.* Katie, dau. of Wm. C. and Mary Kelly, d. Oct. 4, 1862, aged 2 years and 5 mos. Lizzie A., dau. to T. J. and Lizzie Kelly, d. Aug. 5, 1882, aged 5 mos. Footstones: W. G. K. and M. A. K.
Hanlon, Margaret, wife of Michael Hanlon, d. Feb. 16, 1875, aged 15 years.* By her dau., Alice.
O'Donovan, Edward J. O'Donovan, b. Oct. 5, 1874, d. (space).
Jessup (O'Donovan) Letitia Jessup, wife of Edward J. O'Donovan, d. Aug. 2, 1933 in her 60th year.*
McComas, Mary V., wife of Amos P. McComas, b. May 1, 1873, d. Oct. 11, 1900.*
O'Donovan, Edward O'Donovan, d. June 19, 1899 in his 68th year.*
O'Donovan, Ida, wife of Edward O'Donovan, d. Sept. 23, 1883 in her 38th year.* A loving wife and mother.
Quinn, son, James, infant son of Bernard and Emily Quinn, d. Sept. 14, 189(2), aged (3) mos., and 25 days.
Quinn (?) (stone overturned) Footstone: J. Q. (Probably James Quinn).
Quinn, Sarah, wife of James Quinn, d. June 23, 1890, aged 64 years. A native of County Antrim, Ireland.*
Quinn, son, John Joseph, son of James and Sarah Quinn, d. April 15, 1883, aged 25 years, 2 mos., and 14 days. A native of County Antrim, Ireland.*
Wiggington, Margaret C. Wiggington, May 11, 1935 - Oct. 22, 1939.*
Gormley, Ellen Gormley, 1858-1929.*
Marshall, Margaret E. Marshall, Feb. 8, 1919 - July 15, 1962.
Carter, Mary A., Nov. 2, 1891----. John J., Jan. 23, 1888 - March 9, 1960.
Bradley, Patrick Bradley, b. 1836, d. Feb. 8, 1919.*
Thorn-Bradley, Mary A., wife of John H. Thorn, youngest dau. of Dennis and Nancy Bradley, who departed this life, 1 Dec. 1884 in her 36th year.* Also their infant, Mary Alice, 30 Nov. 1884.*
Thorn, Footstone - in front of wife's grave. John H. Thorn, April 2, 1853 - June 26, 1931.
Bradley, Bridget, dau. of Denis and Nancy Bradley, a native of Maghera County, Derry, Ireland who departed this life, June 28, 1861 in the 29th year of her age.*
Bradley, Dennis Bradley, a native of Ireland, d. 25th Jan. 1883 in the 85th year of his age.*
Bradley, Nancy, wife of Dennis Bradley, d. 14 Nov. 1884 in the 77th year of her age.
Kelly, Thomas J. Kelly, husband of Elizabeth B. Kelly, b. July 21, 1848, d. May 10, 1917.* Elizabeth B. Kelly, b. May 8, 1857, d. March 25, 1936. Footstones: Mother and Father.

Kelly, Sarah R., dau. of William and Mary Kelly, d. Sept. 29, 1883, aged 30 years, 9 mos., 2 days.*

Kelly, Mary, wife of Thomas Kelly, d. Oct. 4, 1876, aged 20 years, 11 mos., 5 days.*

Lynch, Mary, dau. of Daniel E. and Mary E. Lynch, d. Aug. 5, 1885, aged 6 mos. and 5 days.*

Lynch, Mary E., wife of Daniel E. Lynch, d. Feb. 6, 1885, aged 26 years, 2 mos., and 14 days.*

McCloskey, Brother, Andrew James, son of John and the late Mary McCloskey, b. July 25, 1852, d. Oct. 20, 1887.*

McCloskey, Brother, John, son of John and the late Mary McCloskey, b. April 7, 1854, d. March 3, 1865.*

McCloskey, John McCloskey, b. Aug. 1, 1820, d. Feb. 27, 1901.*

McCloskey, Mother, Mary, wife of John McCloskey, a native of County Derry, Ireland, d. Feb. 28, 1864, aged 43 years.*

Kearney, Patrick Kearney, a native of County Derry, Ireland, d. Sept. 22, 1882 in the 54th year of his age.*

Kearney, Mary, wife of Patrick Kearney, a native of County Derry, Ireland, d. Oct. 7, 1911 in the 79th year of her age.*

Kearney, Sister, Matilda E. Kearney, b. Dec. 20, 1871, d. Feb. 3, 1917.*

Hyland, James T. Hyland, Feb. 12, 1850 - June 2, 1913. Mary E. Hyland, his wife (no dates).*

Hanlon, John D., April 14, 1886 - July 21, 1960. Martha E., May 8, 1857 (no other date, however excavation has been made for this plot as of June 20, 1972).*

Footstone W.M.E.

Footstones: R.J.S./M.C.S./A.S. - See Shepperd Monument.

Hagan (Monument - 3 sides) William P. Hagan, d. March 25, 1906, aged 73 years, husband of Mary Hagan, a native of Ireland.* Margaret, wife of W. P. Hagan. William T., Francis, George, sons of W.P. and Margaret Hagan.* Sarah, dau. of W. P. and Mary Hagan, d. July 21, 1886, aged 1 mo, and 2 days.*

E..(?) (base only - stone missing)

Shanahan (Monument - 4 sides) Richard Shanahan, b. May 16, 1881, d. May 23, 1881. Margaret Shanahan, b. Sept. 13, 1883, d. July 15, 1884. Margaret C. Shanahan, b. May 19, 1858, d. Apr. 30, 1893. Richard J. Shanahan, b. July 18, 1850, d. Oct. 8, 1899. Annie Shanahan, b. March 11, 1885, d. Feb. 14, 1886. Agnes M. Shanahan, b. March 30, 1893, d. Dec. 12, 1893.

Shanahan, James J., 1848-1903 (footstone)

Burke, Catherine D., wife of Richard Burke, a native of the County Tipperary, Ireland, d. Jan. 10, 1890, aged 104 years.* By J. C. Shanahan & wife.

Cain, son, William J., b. Jan. 25, 1905, d. March 8, 1956.*

Cain, Mother, Margaret Anna, wife of Charles H. Cain, b. Aug. 11, 1869, d. July 25, 1932.

Cain, Father, Charles H. Cain, b. Sept. 21, 1861, d. Feb. 4, 1917.*

Carroll (Monument) Father, James Carroll, native of the County Wexford, Ireland, b. Sept. 20, 1820, d. July 23, 1898. Mother, Bridget, wife of James Carroll, native of the County Wexford, Ireland, d. Oct. 26, 1856 in the 28th year of her age. Rosetta Carroll, native of the County Armaugh, Ireland, b. Aug. 15, 1820, d. Sept. 10, 1879. Footstone: B.C.

Hays (Carroll) John Hays, father of Bridget Carroll, a native of Co. Wexford, Ireland, d. Dec. 15, 1856 in the 61st year of his age.* Erected by his son.

Neipert, Elizabeth, d. Sept. 1, 1878, aged 58 years, native of Ireland, County of Wexford.

Doyle, Catharine, wife of Peter Doyle, d. Aug. 14, 1882, aged 57 years, a native of Co. Wexford, Ireland.*

Doyle, James T., son of Peter and Catherine Doyle, d. June 8, 1887, aged 15 years. Peter Doyle, d. July 28, 1891 in the 68th year of his age.*
Skelton (Monument) Catherine, wife of John Skelton, b. Oct. 16, 1815, d. Feb. 12, 1891, a native of County Wexford, Ireland.* John Skelton, b. Sept. 10, 1819, d. Nov. 21, 1884, a native of Co. Wexford, Ireland.* Maggie, d. Dec. 1859, aged 2 years. Michael, d. Feb. 1861, aged 6 years. Children of J. & C. Skelton.*
McCarthy, Sister, Mary E. McCarthy, b. Feb. 1, 1864, d. Dec. 30, 1881.*
Nagle-McCarthy, Patrick Nagle, 1829-1881. Bridget Nagle, 1830-1888. Owen McCarthy, 1823-1888. Mary McCarthy, 1825-1903. Ellen E. Nagle, 1857-1928.* Owen McCarthy, Sr., 1799-1874. John Nagle, 1864-1878. Mary Nagle, 1870-1878. Eugene Nagle, 1874-1888. Ellen Nagle, 1834-1909.
Kelly, (D. Kelly plot) Alice, wife of Darby Kelly, d. May 20, 188(7 or 2), aged 59 years, a native of County Derry, Ireland.* Footstone: A.K.
Kelly (D. Kelly plot) Darby Kelly, d. March 7, 1888, aged 64 years, a native of County Waterford, Ireland. (Verse covered) Footstone: D.K.
Vereker (D. Kelly plot) James D. Vereker, b. in Co. Kilkenny, Ireland and d. on Oct. 8, 1929, age 64 years.* Footstone: J.V.
Vereker (D. Kelly plot) Alice Vereker, b. in Baltimore County, Maryland and d. on Jan. 12, 1941, aged 76 years.* Footstone: A.V.
Martin, Mother, Bridget Martin, d. Dec. 25, 1908, aged 76 years. Thomas F. Martin, d. Dec. 26, 1893, aged 22 years. Jos. M. Martin, d. Oct. 17, 1885, aged 1 year and 3 mos. Footstones: B.M., T.F.M., J.M.M.
Martin, Father, Patrick Martin, d. May 13, 1897, aged 80 years. John J. Martin, d. April 16, 1891, aged 30 years. Jos. J. Martin, d. Dec. 7, 1896, aged 27 years. Footstones: P.M., J.J.M., J.J.M.
Corcoran, Willie M., d. Sept. 27, 1882, aged 6 yrs. & 8 mos.* Maggie, d. July 18, 1875, aged 10 mos. Children of Denis and Mary Corcoran.*
Smith, Adolphine K. Smith, d. Feb. 13, 1934.
Smith, J. Holmes Smith, M.D., b. March 30, 1857, d. June 21, 1919.*
Smith, Adele Maude, wife of Dr. J. Holmes Smith, d. Nov. 2, 1890. Footstones: A.M.S., J.H.S.
King, David King, b. June 1, 1800, d. Jan. 18, 1871. Eliza M, wife of David King, b. April 9, 1813, d. July 23, 1857.* James Blair King, son of David and Eliza M. King, d. Sept. 5, 1857, aged 3 mos., and 5 days.* David King, Jr., son of David and Eliza M. King, d. May 21, 1865, aged 10 years, 6 mos., and 2 days.* Footstones: J.B.K., E.M.K., D.K.
Ryan, Margaret, wife of Denis Ryan, a native of the parish, Holy Cross, County Tipperary, Ireland, d. Nov. 1, 1877, aged 75 years.*
Hays, Dennis Hays, native of County Tipperary, Parish of Holy Cross, Ireland, d. Dec. 22, 1858 in the 15th year of his age.* Footstone: D.H.
Bell, Mary Shepperd Bell, wife of William H. Bell, 1881-1957.
Lynch, Michael H. Lynch, husband of Ella L. Lynch, d. Jan. 26, 1906 in the 62nd year of his age.* Willie, d. Sept. 19, 1889, aged 1 yr. and 1 mos. Francis T., d. Sept. 21, 1889, aged 10 mos. Ella, d. March 8, 1893, aged 6 mos. Children of M. H. & E. L. Lynch.* Lynch footstones: Mother, Frances and Father, William.
Lynch, Sister, Mary R., dau. of Michael H. & Ella L. Lynch, b. Dec. 3, 1892, d. Oct. 20, 1918.
Kearney, Bridget Kearney, b. in the County Tyrone, Ireland, d. Oct. 16, 1893, aged 62 years.* Footstone: B.K.
Burns, Alice, wife of Peter Burns, d. March 31, 1886 in the 65th year of her age.* Footstone: A.B.
Burns, stone missing - probably Peter Burns. Footstone: P.B.
Burns, John T., son of Peter and Alice Burns, b. Jan. 22, 1852, d. Sept. 24, 1875, aged 23 years, 8 mos., and 2 days.* Footstone: J.T.B.
Noonan, Patrick Noonan, d. Sept. 25, 1876, aged 65 years.*

Noonan, Mary, wife of Patrick Noonan, d. June 3, 1891, aged 75 years.* Footstone: P.N., M.N.
Noonan, James C. Noonan, d. Oct. 12, 1896, aged 45 years.* Footstone: J.C.N.
Noonan, Mary, wife of Peter Noonan, d. Jan. 1874 in the 23rd year of her age.* Their two beloved daughters. Footstones: T.N., M.N.
Noonan, Peter Noonan, d. May 16, 1910, aged 64 years.*
Tahaney, John Tahaney, 1861-1915.* Mary Ann, wife of John Tahaney, 1864-1946.* Francis Joseph Tahaney, 1898-1918.*
McGilligan, Hugh McGilligan, a native of County Derry, Ireland, who departed this life, 15th of Nov. 1866, aged 84 years.
McGilligan, Mary, wife of Hugh McGilligan, who departed this life 25th of March, 1879, aged 93 years.*
McGilligan, Margaret, wife of Patrick M. McGilligan, who departed this life, 3rd of May 1885, aged 53 years.*
McGilligan, Patrick McGilligan, d. Jan. 17, 1897, aged 72 years. A native of County Derry, Ireland.*
McGilligan, Margaret, dau. of Patrick and Margaret McGilligan, Sept. 22, 1865 - Jan. 12, 1941.*
Lagan, Andrew Lagan, d. May 8, 1892, aged 75 years.*
Lagan, Mother, Annie Lagan, wife of Andrew Lagan, d. June 15, 1906, aged 75 years.*
Lagan, James P. Lagan, d. Dec. 2, 1892, aged 29 years.*
Lagan, Andrew J. Lagan, b. June 18, 1870, d. Oct. 18, 1959.*
Lagan, Ellen M., wife of Andrew J. Lagan, d. June 24, 1934, aged 65 years.*
Miller, Margaret T. Miller, wife of Frank Miller, d. Sept. 8, 1911, aged 31 or 34 years.*
Shanahan, Elizabeth F., dau. of the late John J.& Annie J. Shanahan, b. April 12, 1892, d. Nov. 2, 1918.* Mary E., 1925-1927.
Rinehart, Henry F. Rinehart, Dec. 28, 1924 - Mar. 23, 1942.*
Doyle, Sarah J. Doyle, b. Jan. 26, 1861, d. Mar. 12, 1928. Mary C. Doyle, b. Aug. 4, 1869, d. June 30, 1927.* Footstones: S.J.D., M.C.D.
Shepperd, Elias Shepperd, d. Nov. 3, 1893 aged 75 years, 2 mos. and 24 days.* Samuel Shepperd, 1868-1906. John S., son of Elias and Catherine Shepperd, d. Feb. 22, 1897, aged 25 years.* Catherine E. Shepperd, wife of Elias Shepperd, d. April 16, 1913, aged 68 years. Footstones: Father & Mother.
Shepperd, Children, J. Bernard Shepperd, 1875-1876. S. Genevieve Shepperd, 1881-1883.
Shepperd, Brother, John S. Shepperd, 1872-1897.
O'Neil, in memory of Patrick O'Neil.
O'Neil, Mary O'Neil, wife of Michael O'Neil.*
Michaels, Jane Michaels, b. in Dublin, Ireland.*
O'Neil, Sarah O'Neil, wife of Henry O'Neil, b. in Dublin, Ireland.*
O'Neil, Henry O'Neil, husband of the late Sarah O'Neil, d. Feb. 12, 1908.*
Gugerty, Patrick Gugerty, d. May 17, 1888, aged 59 years.* Mary, wife of Patrick Gugerty, d. Dec. 16, 1864, aged 33 years.* Peter Gugerty, brother of Patrick Gugerty, d. Aug. 17, 1856, aged 21 years.* Catherine, wife of Patrick Gugerty, d. May 13, 1878, aged 47 years.*
Kearny, Patrick, Walter, Sallie, Charles, Francis, children of John J. and Mary E. Kearney.
Shanahan, Anna L. Shanahan, 1874-1930.
Shanahan, J.L.S.
Callahan, Charles J., Sr., 1862-1918. Mary M., 1872-1934. Charles J., Jr., 1901-1961. Edward, 1917-1918.
McClaskey, John McClaskey, a native of Co. Derry, Ireland, d. June 28, 1858 in the 22nd year of his age.*
McClaskey, Daniel, a native of the Parish Comber, Clady. Co., Londerry, Ireland, d. May 1, 1873 in the 76th year of his age.* Erected by his son, Michael.

McCluskey, Father, Michael McCluskey, a native of County Derry, Ireland.
(rest below ground) Footstone: M.McC.
Shepperd, Mary Shepperd, 1801-1878.
Pearce, Sarah Pearce, 1808-1889.
Shepperd, Brother,Samuel Shepperd, 1868-1906.
Shepperd, James Shepperd, 1803-1866.
Shepperd, Edith Mary, dau. og J. W. & M. C. Shepperd, d. March 11, 1879, aged 7 mos. and 11 days. Footstone: E.M.S.
Allison, Arthur, d. Nov. 24, 1863 in the 20th year of his age. Isabel Allison, d. April 22, 1888 in the 33rd year of her age. Children of James and Rose Allison.
A.P.D. (Small stone)
Shanahan, Denis J. Shanahan, Sept. 24, 1854 - Oct. 19, 1923.*
Shanahan, John I. Shanahan, b. Dec. 17, 1879, d. May 20, 1917.* Footstone: J.I.S.
Shanahan, Annie E. Shanahan, wife of Denis J. Shanhan, Sept. 25, 1867 - June 26, 1941. John J., son of John J. and Rose Kelly Shanahan, June 28, 1926 - March 11, 1927. Husband, Patrick J. Shanahan, d. May 28, 1910, aged 58 years.*
Crilley, Footstones: Henry 1863-1935. Rose A., 1865-1928. Edith M., 1899-1932. Harry J., 1897-1950.
Hickey, Husband, John Hickey, a native of the Parish Nobber, Co. Meath, Ireland, who departed this life, 6th of May, 1867 in the 55th year of his age.
Hinder (Vandervalk) Hinder Footstones: Mary H. Vandervalk, May 10, 1902 - September 30, 1962. Anne M., Jan. 24, 1872 - Nov. 20, 1944. George D., Oct. 9, 1870 - Jan. 25, 1945.
Boarman, Robert Boarman, d. March 24, 1886, aged 83 years.* Elizabeth A., his wife, d. June 16, 1896, aged 81 years.* Nannie T. Boarman, 1850-1930. Charles Walter, d. May 21, 1889, aged 34 years.* Joseph E., d. May 24, 1861, aged 20 years.* Sons of R. & E. A. Boarman. Sarah, d. May 9, 1864, aged 9 years.* Elizabeth C., d. March 25, 1873, aged 20 years.* Daughters of R. and E. A. Boarman.
White, Patrick, husband of Mary A. White, d. Dec. 18, 1892, aged 78 years. A native of New Ross Co. Wexford, Ireland.*
White, Mary A., wife of Patrick White, d. June 26, 1904, aged 78 years. A native of New Ross, Co. Wexford,Ireland.* Footstones: P.W. & M.A.W.
Lacey, Margaret T. Lacey, Oct. 23, 1862 - Jan. 27, 1923.*
Hinder, Frederick Hinder, 1824-1899. Catherine Hinder, 1849-1936.* J. Harry Hinder, 1875-1903. Sister M. Victoria S.N.D., 1882-1905. J. Fielding Hinder, 1869-1900.* Footstones: Sr.M.V., F.H.,J.F.H.
Hinder, Mary K. Hinder, b. April 20, 1893, d. April 1, 1909. Loretta G. Hinder, b. March 4, 1897, d. May 31, 1914.* Footstones: M.K.H., L.C.H.
Merney, Ann Carroll, wife of Michael Merney, a native of the County Wexford, Ireland, d. Aug. 24, 1873, aged 61 years. Footstone: A.C.M.
Hennessy, Richard, son of William and Ann Hennessy, d. Oct. 31, 1881, aged 19 years.
Hennessy, William Thomas, son of William and Annie Hennessy, b. Nov. 21, 1864, d. Jan. 23, 1865.
Base only - Footstone: M.D.
Kearney (Smith)(Hoffman). Francis A., son of Francis B. and Bridget Kearney, b. July 12, 1866, d. Nov. 13, 1911.* Emma V. Smith, wife of Francis A. Kearney, b. Feb. 13, 1867, d. April 12, 1952.* Bridget, wife of Francis B. Kearney, d. Jan. 4, 1870, aged 33 years and 5 mos. A native of County Derry, Ireland.* Helen Hoffman, dau. of Francis & Bridget Kearney, b. April 29, 1868, d. Sept. 9, 1897.* Footstones: H.H., F.B.K., B.K., F.A.K., E.V.S.K.
McCarthy (Kelly) Footstones: Ruth McVesely, 1902-1968. Charles, 1872-1946. Annie E. Kelly, 1869-1943.

Leegh, George Clinton, son of William H. and Margaret Leegh, d. April 8, 1892. Age 10.
Sullivan (Colgan), Irvin J., husband of Emily Colgan, Nov. 9, 1888 - Jan. 12,
   1926. Footstone: I.J.S.*
Riley, Henry Riley, Feb. 15, 1873 - Dec. 12, 1925, wife, Laura, (on back of
   stone)*.
Lynch, Martin T. 1876-1934, wife, Laura V., R.I.P.
Frederick, wife of Clara R., wife of Henry J. Frederick, b. Sept. 30, 1968, d.
   (rest underground).
Bradley, Charles J., infant son of John and Elizabeth Bradley, age 3 mos.
Quinlin, Chas. H. Quinlin, d. April 14, 1888. Age 56.
Quinlin, Mary E., wife of Charles H. Quinlin, d. May 9, 1884. Age 51.
Quinlin, Leonard G. Quinlin, d. March 13, 1875. Age 75.
Quinlin, mother, Ann Quinlin, b. Aug. 31, 1796, d. March 14, 1881, Age 84.
Ryan, William Ryan, d. April 11, 1867*, County Tipperary (illegible) . Age 53.
Carr, (P. Kelly Plot), Ellen, wife of Thomas Carr, d. Jan. 31, 1872. Age 90.
Kelly, (P. Kelly Plot), Annie J., dau. of Peter and Ann Kelly, d. May 3, 1884. Age 24.
   Footstone: A.K.*
Kelly, (P. Kelly Plot) Base only - Footstone: P.K.
Kelly, (P. Kelly Plot), Ann, wife of Peter Kelley, d. April 9, 1902. Age 76.
   A.K.*
Scarff, John E. Scarff 1896-1966.
Scarff, John Scarff, d. Oct. 31, 1868. Age 50.
Slade, Elizabeth, wife of Edward, d. Jan. 25, 1868. Age 80.
Slade, Edward Slade, b. April 3, 1796, d. Aug. 6, 1879.
Hanlen, Sarah Jane, wife of James Hanlen, d. Aug. 6, 1880. Age 28.
Davidson, Jones Davidson, d. March 3, 1891. Age 68. Martha Clotilda, dau. of J. and
   E.B. Davidson (remainder underground)
Davidson, Sarah E.B., wife of Jones Davidson, d. April 21, 1913. Age 87. Orissa E.,
   dau. of J. and S.E.B. Davidson, d. May 6, 1865. Age 7.
Bullock, Solomon, d. May 7, 1861. Age 71.
Bullock, Abigal A.E., wife of Solomon Bullock, d. Dec 19, 1865. Age 65.
   Footstone: A.A.E.B.
Frederick, Clara R., wife of Henry J. Frederick, b. Sept. 31, 1869, d.*
   (underground).
Bradley, Charles J., infant son of John and Elizabeth Bradley, aged 3 mos.
Jenkins, (Obelisk) Oswald Jenkins, wife Sarah, dau. Ann. (side) Mary, dau. of
   Oswald and Sarah Jenkins, d. Aug. 17, 1894. Theresa J., dau. of the late
   Oswald and Sarah Jenkins, d. Oct. 3, 1909. (side) Ellen, eldest dau. of the
   late O. and S. Jenkins, d. Jan. 17, 1885. (side) I. W. Jenkins, wife
Henrietta, children Jesse Jenkins, Ellen Herbert.
Herbert, Joseph, son of Joseph and Eleanor, Herbert, d. June 16, 1887.*
McQuillan, Mary Ann, wife of William McQuillan, d. Oct. 20, 1871.* Age 26 of County Down.
Dornan, Mary Jane, dau. of William and Rose Dornan, d. Dec. 20, 1873, Age 15.
Cummings, Robert, husband of Catharine Cummings, b. 1824, d. Jan 1871.
   Of County Antrim.
Fitzsimons, Philip, d. April 10, 1871. Age 54 of County Cavan.
Fitzsimmons, in memory of Bridget Fitzsimmons, d. Jan. 5, 1853. Age 76 of County Kilkenny
   (Base only) Footstone: P.F.
Fitzsimmons, Bridget, wife of Patrick Fitzsimmons, d. March 14, 1884
The Jenkins Family Plot - enclosed within a wall of stone. Plaque: Michael
C. Jenkins, wife Charity Ann Wheeler and thirty-four of their descendants,
Michael C. Jenkins, b. Dec. 2, 1736 in St. Marys County. On Oct. 4, 1770 he
acquired 288 acres in "Long Green Valley" a part of "Gunpowder Manor",

property of the sixth Lord Baltimore. He d. at Long Green, Jan. 1802.
This tablet erected 1954 by Michael Oswald Jenkins of the Fifth Generation.
Annie M. Jenkins, b. June 4, 1843, d. Oct. 9, 1902.*
Richard Hillen, son of George Jenkins, Nov. 23, 1850 - Dec. 31, 1929.
Mary J., wife of Richard Hillen Jenkins, dau.of Ignatius and Anne Marie Jenkins, b. Sept. 3, 1855, d. Nov. 14, 1949.*
Ann Ellen Barroll, dau. of Mark W. and Ann M. Jenkins, and wife of James W. Barroll, b. Oct. 19, 1833, d. Feb. 4, 1905.
Rebecca H. Jenkins, b. July 21, 1838, d. May 4, 1883.*
Maria Woodland, d. April 5, 1900, faithful nurse in the families of Mark and John W. Jenkins. Age 85.
Lydia M. Jenkins, wife of George M. Jenkins, dau. of David Armour, wife Maria Moore, b. in Missouri, Nov. 16, 1822, d. in Baltimore, Md., Aug. 29, 1912.
George Jenkins, d. Dec. 30, 1882, age 72. William H. Saxton, Jr., d. March 31, 1882, aged 6 yrs. and 7 mos. George Jenkins Saxton, d. June 15, 1883, aged 4 yrs. and 11 mos.
George and Lycurgus, infant sons of George and Lydia Jenkins.
Ignatius, son of Michael C. and Charity Jenkins, b. 1776, d. 1819.
Michael C. Jenkins, son of William Jenkins and Mary Courtney, b. 1736, St. Mary's Co., d. at Long Green, 1802.
Charity, wife of Michael C. Jenkins and dau. of Thomas Wheeler, d. 1820.*
Ann, dau. of mich'l C. and Charity Jenkins, and wife of Charles Hopkins, b. 1772, d. 1836.*
Mark W. Jenkins, d. July 13, 1871. Age 67.
Ann M., wife of Mark W. Jenkins, d. March 26, 1891. Age 82.
Wm. Armour Jenkins, Jr., husband of Mary Katherine Jenkins, son of Wm. Armour and Louisa W. Jenkins, b. March 2, 1889, d. Feb. 15, 1941.*
Eugene Jenkins, d. 1912.
Arthur, son of John W. and Alice Shaw Jenkins, d. Nov. 21, 1882, aged 16 yrs.*
Talbot Winchester Jenkins, b. May 18, 1854, d. Jan. 8, 1922. Wife, Matilda Banks Jenkins, b. April 10, 1861, d. Oct. 19, 1932.
Wm. Armour Jenkins, husband of Louisa W. Jenkins and son of George and Lydia M. Jenkins, b. March 19, 1859, d. Nov. 9, 1937.*
Louisa W. Jenkins, wife of Wm. Armour Jenkins, daughter of Mark and Ellen Wilcox, b. Dec. 7, 1858, d. Sept. 22, 1932.*
Addie Webb Jenkins, wife of William Jenkins, b. Jan. 10, 1836, d. Sept. 30, 1881.* At Bloomsburg, St. Mary's Co.
William Jenkins, b. Dec. 23, 1835, d. April 27, 1912, son of Mark W. and Ann M. Jenkins, husband of Adelaide Webb Jenkins and Confederate Veteran of the Civil War.*
Laura Augusta, wife of Josias Jenkins, b. March 16, 1836, d. Sept. 12, 1904.
Josias Jenkins, son of Josias and Elizabeth A. Jenkins, b. July 22, 1823, d. Jan. 14, 1861.*
Mich'l F. Jenkins, son of Josias and Elizabeth A. Jenkins, b. July 22, 1823, d. Jan. 14, 1861.*
Josias Jenkins, son of Michael C. and Charity Jenkins, b. March 17, 1781, d. April 20, 1823.*
Elizabeth A. Jenkins, wife of Josias Jenkins, b. Nov. 18, 1787, d. June 7, 1859.*
John Hillen Jenkins, d. March 31, 1852, aged 15 years, R.I.P.*
Elizabeth A., wife of John Hillen Jenkins, d. July 20, 1891. Age 74.
Harry W., 1915-1916, son of Susan W. and Frank B. Jenkins.
Elizabeth Jenkins, June 1, 1867, Oct. 26, 1946.
Minnie J. George, 1855-1931.
Josias J. George, 1853-1929.*
Mary, eldest dau. of Philip T. and Ellen (E) George, b. Feb. 20, 1818, d. June 20, 1856.*

111

William Edmondson, eldest son of Josias J. and Minnie J. George, b. Aug. 17, 1883, d. Sept. 27, 1887.*
Favour, Father. Margaret, wife of John B. Favour, d. April 7, 1887. Age 77.
Amoss, sister Theresa C., wife of O. C. Amoss, d. Sept. 10, 1866. Age 28. Baby Oliver C., d. Sept. 19, 1866, aged 15 mos.*
Ramsey, Helen Ramsey, d. Jan. 20, 1870 (underground).
Favour, Bennie S., son of J. C. and Jennie Favour... (underground) Footstone: B.S.F.
McDermott (broken), Sept. 14,..., age 14 years. Erected by his affectionate father. Mary Dermott, d. Sept. 25, 1930. Age 86.
Lunday (obelisk), James Lunday, Sr., d. Nov. 15, 1895.* Sarah Jane, dau. of James and Mary Lunday and wife of John J. Bradley, d. Oct. 20, 1894. Age 54. Mary E. Lunday, Aug. 12, 1815 - Oct. 2, 1907. Footstone: Father.*
Cummings, James B. Cummings, son of Cathering and the late Robert Cummings, b. May 14, 1862, d. Jan. 16, 1890.*
Cummings, Cummings (on base). John H., d. March 26, 1900. Margaret, d. July 24, 1889. Katherine M., d. June 21, 1938. Margaret J., d. Dec. 24, 1943. Rose H., d. Sept. 12, 1964.
Klapaska, John A. Klapaska, husband of Barbara R. Klapaska, b. in Russia 1871, d. Jan. 13, 1922.*
Klapaska (Sims), Mom, Barbara Klapaska Sims, March 14, 1878 - Dec. 16, 1959.
Klapaska, Raymond Klapaska, son of Barbara and John Klapaska, b. June 7, 1897, d. Feb. 5, 1938.
Sparks, Joe Morrison Sparks, husband of Pauline P. Sparks and son of Francis Morrison and Remare Sparks, b. Oct. 12, 1872, d. Aug. 2, 1961. Pauline Pleasants Sparks, wife of Joe Morrison Sparks and dau. of Brooke and Elizabeth Jenkins Pleasants, b. June 29, 1871, d. Aug. 8, 1961.*
Pleasants, Lizette Armour Pleasants, dau. of Brooke and Elizabeth Pleasants, b. May 3, 1875, d. April 3, 1966.*
Fleury, B. Augustine Fleury, son of Paul A. and Corinne Fleury, b. Jan. 22, 1881, d. April 4, 1955.*
Jenkins (Pleasants), Elizabeth Jenkins, wife of Brooke Pleasants and dau. of George and Lydia M. Jenkins, b. Jan. 29, 1840, d. Nov. 6, 1930.*
Pleasants, Brooke Pleasants, son of Thomas Snowden Pleasants, wife Elizabeth Brooke, b.Goochland Co., Va., Feb. 17, 1829, d. in Baltimore, Md., Aug. 4, 1901. Enlisted June 15, 1861 at Memphis, Tenn. as Private in Co. E 6th Battalion 7th Tenn. Cavalry C.S.A. Capt J. S. White. Afterwards transferred to Co. K 7th Miss. Cavalry C.S.A. Was surrendered with others at Citronelle, Ala. by Lieut. Gen. Richard Taylor C.S.A. to Major Genl. Ganby U.S.A. May 4, 1865 Paroled at Grenada, Miss., May 19, 1865.*
(small stone) T.Q. - M.A.Q.
Smith, son, Edward J. Smith, May 13, 1905 - Sept. 15, 1923.
Smith, Father, Edward R.I., Jan. 19, 1870 - Feb. 13, 1948. Mother, Catherine L., Dec. 15, 1876 - March 30, 1949.
Smith, dau., Catherine A. Smith, Jan. 11, 1897 - Dec. 28, 1962.
Lynch, Agnes. Agnes Loretta Lynch, 1897-1928.*
Lynch, George J. Lynch, Oct. 23, 1896 - Sept. 30, 1939.*
Lynch, Elizabeth M. 1900-   . John E. 1887-1955. Edward 1889-   .
Cochran, John D. and Helen M., 1921, infant children of Wm. J. and M. Grace Cochran.
Cochran, son, Chas. F. Cochran, son of Wm. J. and M. Grace Cochran, Feb. 12, 1914 - Feb. 16, 1935.*
Cochran, William J., June 26, 1890 - May 15, 1968. Mary Grace, Oct. 18, 1894 - July 22, 1971.

Cochran, Charles B., April 15, 1892 - Oct. 17, 1968.*
Davies, Alfred H., 1869-1956. Carrie B., 1871-1947.
Webster, William H. Webster III, Jan. 25, 1946 - Dec. 4, 1965.
Hinder, Frederick C., 1893-1962. Helen Kelly, 1891-1968.
Bartlett, Lydia Troy Bartlett, wife of Richard T. Bartlett, b. Aug. 6, 1895, d. March 7, 1969.*
Bartlett, Richard Turner Bartlett, husband of Lydia Troy Bartlett, b. Sept. 2, 1889, d. July 12, 1962.*
Troy, Anne Pleasant Troy, wife of William Beatty Troy, b. July 21, 1868, d. Dec. 23, 1943.*
Troy, William Beatty Troy, son of Alexander J. and Maria S. Troy, b. Sept. 18, 1860, d. April 11, 1933. Footstone: Troy.*
Lancaster. Our beloved babies, Eddie, d. July 1876, aged 8 mos. Johnnie, d. June 25, 1890, aged 8 mos. Sons of John O. and Maggie Lancaster. Footstones: E.L. and J. L.*
Lancaster, John O. Lancaster, husband of Margaret Lancaster, d. Nov. 9, 1897.* Footstone: J.O.C.*
Lancaster, Margaret, wife of John O. Lancaster, d. Nov. 1, 1914. Footstone: M.L.*
Kelly, Susie L. Kelly, dau. of the late Michael and Matilda Kelly, b. March 19, 1855, d. Jan. 30, 1921.*
Traynor, Traynor, Patrick F., 1859-1936, wife Matilda F. 1859-1939.
Dannenman, Mary A., Nov. 22, 1869 - Aug. 21, 1955. John H., Aug. 19, 1870 - Feb. 18, 1943.
Smith (Dannenmann), dau., Ida. E. Dannenmann Smith, June 28, 1909.
Cunningham. Footstone: Melvin C., 1903-1946.*
Carroll, Michael Carroll, b. June 20, 1854, d. Aug. 11, 1920. Footstone: M.C.*
Maynes, Patrick Maynes, b. Sept. 29, 1840, d. Aug. 1, 1916. Footstone: P.M.*
Allender, John W., son of Mont and Mollie J. Allender, d. March 8, 1915. Footstone: J.W.A.*
Brinker, Augustus C. Brinker, Oct. 1, 1852 - June 27, 1909. Footstone: A.C.B.
Kelly. Footstones: Sarah E. 1870-1951. Joseph M. 1866-1951. Mary A. 1890-1967. Margaret L. 1894-1907. Sarah E. 1905-1905.*
Wilson, Marie Nathalie, dau. of Henry and Armida C. Wilson, b. Dec. 4, 1890, d. June 23, 1906.*
Kelly, Francis W., son of William J. and Ellen E. Kelly, April 4, 1889 - Jan. 6, 1930.* Footstone: F.W.K.
Kelly (stone overturned). Footstone: E.E.K.
Kelly, William J. Kelly, husband of Ellen E. Kelly, d. Nov. 11, 1912.* Footstone: W.J.K.
Carroll (Allen), Patrick J., husband of Catherine A. Carroll, b. March 12, 1812, d. May 4, 1891. Catherine Allen, wife of Patrick J. Carroll, b. Nov. 29, 1838, d. Nov. 1, 1906. Footstone: Carroll.* (small stone) In memory of our little darling Papa and Mama.
Lacey, Susie Loretta, wife of Nicholas Lacey, b. March 9, 1883, d. May 12, 1911, infant son, Nicholas Lacey, b. Jan. 2, 1866, d....*
Leech, mother, Margaret, wife of William H. Leech, d. Aug. 23, 1910. Father, Wm. H. Leech, d. April 7, 1915. (side) Uncle George Leech, brother of Wm. H. Leech, d. Aug. 29, 1931. Footstones: Father-Mother.*

Shanahan, sister, Sarah A., dau. of Timothy and the late Ann Shanahan, d. Dec. 20, 1915. Age 54.
Shanahan, sister, Mary Teresa, dau. of Timothy and the late Ann Shanahan, d. Jan. 11, 1907. Age 47.
Bradley, Francis, infant son of A. J. and M. E. Bradley, d. Jan. 2, 1908.
Mary E., wife of Andrew J. Bradley, b. Jan. 26, 1874, d. Jan. 8, 1908.
Andrew J. Bradley, d. April 29, 1912. Age 41.
Engle. Footstones: Mother, Ellen E., Sept. 19, 1881 - July 23, 1908. Father, Howard J., Dec. 25, 1876 - Oct. 4, 1947. Ann E., Dec. 18, 1909 - Jan. 6, 1969.
Dalton, Joseph P., 1871-1928. His wife, Margaret F. 1872-1940. Margaret R. 1914-1929.*
Jenkins, Requiescat, Michael Oswald Jenkins, S. Sgt. 12th Air Force U.S. Army, Aug. 22, 1913 - Feb. 3, 1944. Son of Michael Oswald and Isabel Sloan Jenkins.*
Jenkins, Jenkins, Michael Oswald, Oct. 11, 1880 - Oct. 5, 1966....?...*
Hagan (Meyers). Rose Ann Mary, dau. of W.P. and Mary Hagan, wife of L.A. Meyers, d. June 6, 1906. Age 23.
Rahll. Footstones: John Joseph, 1883-1968. Matilda A., 1881-1951.
Rahll, Mary A., wife of George Rahll, b. June 3, 1847, d. Jan. 20, 1921.*
Rahll, George Rahll, d. June 12, 1891. Age 49, a native of Italy.
Quigley, Michael Quigley, d. July 21, 1854. Age 29 of County Tipperary.
Quigley. Erected by Daniel Quigley, mother, Bridget Quigley, d. Sept. 15, 1852. Age 76 of County Tipperary.
Hanley, mother, Elizabeth, wife of Daniel T. Hanley, d. March 1, 1904. Age 87. Footstone: E.H.*
Hanley, father, Daniel T. Hanley, d. Aug. 14, 1894. Age 79 of County Tipperary.
Hanley, John J. Hanleyn... (no dates).
Ady, Nettie M., dau. of Francis and Caroline Ady, d. Dec. 22, 1899. Age 37.
Ady, Benjamin W. Ady, d. Jan. 6, 1904. Age 54.
Ady, Francis H., son of Benjamin W. and Annie E. Ady, d. Sept. 30, 1906. Age 26.
Bradley, 1840-Dennis K.-1923-1852-Catherine-1920. 1871-James-1900.
Bradley. Footstone: Mary Ellen Bradley, 1877-1954.
Daugherty, father, Richard Dougherty, husband of Mary A. Dougherty, b. Oct. 3, 1847, d. Sept. 6, 1928.*
Dougherty, mother, Mary A., wife of Richard Dougherty, Aug. 5, 1859 - Jan. 6, 1920.*
Roach, husband, William J., 1880-1964. Wife, Elizabeth A., 1885-1963.
Kearney, 1860-Michael J.-1903. 1862-Margaret C.-1911. 1892-Rose R.-1961. 1888-E. Mary-1963.
Donahue, Thomas Donahue, d. Nov. 24, 1891. Age 95 of County Derry. Mary, wife of Thomas Donahue, d. Aug. 30, 1894.* Age 90 of County Derry.
Shipley, father, Joshua Shipley, 1838-1917. Mother, Honora Shipley, 1850-1937. J. Francis Shipley, 1875-1892.
Shipley, father, Eugene (G.), 1877-1950. Mother, Mary A., 1876-1928.*
Shipley, infant children of Eugene (G.) and Mary A. Shipley.
Stine, George Stine, b. May 30, 1843, d. Jan. 17, 1905. His son, John Lawrence, b. April 21, 1870, d. May 6, 1924. Footstone: J.L.S.*
Kennedy, mother, Annie F., wife of P.J. Kennedy, d. Jan. 7, 1907. Age 80 of Queen Co., Ireland.
Kennedy (metal marker). Ad...e Kennedy, Sept. 25, 1950.
Rahll, John J., son of Michael and Mary Rahll (underground).
Rahll, Michael E., Nov. 3, 1871 - Dec. 20, 1946. Mary F., his wife, May 13, 1881 - March 20, 1929.*

Jenkins, Annita, infant dau. of R. Hillen and Mollie Jenkins, b. Feb. 3, 1885, d. July 18, 1885.*
Jenkins, M. Frances, dau. of R. Hillen and M.J. Jenkins, b. Nov. 18, 1894, d. Sept. 11, 1895. R.I.P.*
Smith (Jenkins). Her husband, Marshall A. Smith, Aug. 9, 1889 - Jan. 19, 1969, wife, Mary Armor Jenkins, May 1, 1890 - Dec. 19, 1966.
Jenkins, Mark Willcox Jenkins, 1894- , Eugenia Tunis Jenkins, 1903-1968.
Kelly, Mary Matilda, infant dau. of Andrew P. and Mamie Kelly, d. Aug. 26, 1904, aged 4 mos. Andrew P. Kelly, 1867-1963. Mary L. Kelly, 1878-1941. (side) Mary Matilda, wife of Michael Kelly, b. Aug. 30, 1828, d. April 8, 1900. Michael Kelly, b. June 4, 1820, d. Aug. 4, 1895. (On base of monument - White House Farm/Fallston). Footstones: M.M.K., M.K., M.M.K., M.L.K.*
Kearney, John Kearney, d. Aug. 28, 1877, age 41 of County Derry. Bridget, wife of John Kearney, d. Nov. 29, 1893, age 61 of County Roscommon.
Livingston, John G., Sept. 21, 1870 - July 6, 1940. Katie E., Oct. 28, 1969 - Sept. 5, 1921. Footstone: Edward J., March 16, 1892 - Jan. 1, 1957.*
Crilley, Joseph Alfred, son of L. and C.A. Crilley, d. ... 17, 1898 (underground).*
Crilley, Estella Marie, dau. of J. (I) and C. (A.) Crilley, d. Aug. 10, 1896. Age 3.
Smith, John J., 1867-1907. Mary R., 1867-1953.
Hagan, mother, Regenia M. Hagan, d. Nov. 19, 1917. Age 76. Father, James F. Hagan, d. July 10, 1907. Age 66.
Crilley, 1831-Henry, Sr.,-1908. 1835-Mary-1901. 1873-James-1922. 1870-Emma F.-1952.
Muller, John Herman, d. 1908, Josephine Hoen, d. 1930. Mary Hoen, d. 1941.
Goldsborough, Marion E. Goldsborough, b. Jan. 23, 1852, d. April 18, 1913.*
Miller, Peter Miller, Sr., 1829-1911. His wife, Elizabeth A. 1834-1927. Footstones: P.M., Sr. - E.M. - John H. Miller, 1864-1945. Peter J. Miller, 1872-1949.*
Billingslea. Footstone: Albert A. 1905-1955.*
White (Jenkins), Jacob Paul White, husband of Frances L. Jenkins, b. Jan. 25, 1844, d. Aug. 18, 1912.*
White (Jenkins), Frances L. White, wife of Jacob P. White, dau. of George and Lydia M. Jenkins, b. Dec. 26, 1852, d. Jan. 30, 1935.*
Jenkins (Casey), Jenkins Ann, 1889- , wife of George Jenkins, dau. of Andrew H. and Mary Quayle Casey. George, 1883-1963, husband of Anne C. Jenkins, son of R. Hillen and Mary J. Jenkins.
Lynch, William Francis, d. Sept. 19, 1902. Marie d. May 6, 1906. Children of John and Teressa Lynch.*
Lynch, F. Teresa, 1868-1942. John, 1861-1946.
Lynch, Julia, wife of Dennis Lynch, d. Oct. 27, 1911. Age 85.
Lynch, Dennis Lynch, husband of Julia Lynch, d. Jan. 21, 1894. Age 70.
Smith, father, James Smith, d. Dec. 28, 1893 . Age 90. Mary A. Smith.
Boarman (Ady), Martha Ady, wife of Francis B. Boarman, d. Nov. 7, 1910. Age 65.
Boarman, Francis Ady, d. Jan. 24, 1876, aged 7 mos. Robert d. Oct. 20, 1877, aged 1 mo. Children of Francis B. and Martha Ady Boarman. Footstones: F.A.B., R.B.*
Gibbons, Sarah Gibbons, wife of Peter A. Gibbons, Dec. 5, 1819 (?), May 24, 1933 (?). (side) Peter A. Gibbons, d. April 12, 1887. Age 39. (side) Sarah A. Gibbons, Feb. 4, 1876 - Nov. 16, 1962. Footstones: S.A.G., P.A.G.*

Glen, M. Elizabeth, dau. of John and Mary Glen, b. Jan. 5, 1917, d. Jan. 9, 1920.*
Lynch, Thomas H. Lynch, husband of Mary A. Lynch, d. Feb. 18, 1901 , Age 63 of County Clare.Footstone: T.H.L.*
Lynch, mother, Mary A. Lynch, wife of Thomas H. Lynch, d. Feb. 16, 1919. Age 81 of County Cork. (base only). Footstone: H.S.L.
Lilly, Helen Jenkins Lilly, 1851-1929.
Lay (Lilly), Lay Richard Edward, 1875-1932. His wife Marie Joseph Lilly, 1877-1956.
Lilly, George Cromwell Lilly, 1888-1933.
Riley, Riley Patrick, 1825-1910. Alice, wife, 1836-1910.*
Riley, Margaret A. Riley, Sept. 29, 1870 - April 17, 1924. R.I.P.
Riley, Frank, 1868-1931. Annie B., 1877-1959.
William, Mary William, 1863-1942.
Gates-Baker, Frances B. Gates, 1897-   . Gertrude C. Baker, 1881-   .
Footstones: F.B.G. - G.C.B.
Nagle, Frances P., 1920-   . Eleanor G., 1913-1960.
Smith, Ida L., wife of J. Frank Smith, b. Aug. 19, 1892, d. Oct. 22, 1918.*
Kelly, father, John M. Kelly, 1856-1907.
Kelly, mother, Sarah E., 1858-1933.
Kelly, Laura J. Kelly (no dates).
Kelly, Alice M., dau. of Michael and Sallie Kelly, b. Oct. 29, 1888, d. Oct. 2, 1902.*
Poteet, Mary C., wife of James H. Poteet, 1878-1943.
Poteet, Lillian Irene, dau. of James H. and Mary C. Poteet, Oct. 16, 1920 - June 12, 1923.*
Poteet, James Howard, son of James H. and Mary C. Poteet, d. Aug. 24, 1901, aged 1 mo. and 7 days.*
Cochran. Footstones: Catherine V., b. Aug. 13, 1872, d. Sept. 5, 1957. Anthony, b. Jan. 6, 1871, d. April 3, 1942.
Cochran, Joseph L., son of Anthony and Kate Cochran, d. Aug. 1, 1897, aged 10 mos. Footstone: J.L.C.*
Cochran, William, son of William and Hannah E. Cochran, b. Sept. 24, 1896, d. May 21, 1897. (side) Murris Cochran, d. April 3, 1916. (side) Bridget and Alice, children of Morris and Bridget Cochran. (side) Bridget, wife of Morris Cochran, d. March 9, 1895. Age 62. B.C., W.C., M.C., M.C.*
Bode, mother-father, Anna Barbara, wife, 1824-1908. Conrad Bode, 1822-1900 (verse illegible).
Bode, father, Nicholas Bode, 1863-1911 (verse illegible).
Kennedy, Mary C. Kennedy, d. Jan. 9, 1919. Age 50.
Kennedy, mother, Catherine N., wife of Joseph Kennedy, b. in Queens County, Ireland, d. April 11, 1910.* Footstone: C.N.K.*
Kennedy, father, Joseph Kennedy, d. May 13, 1898. Age 60.
DeBaugh, father, Augustus DeBaugh, d. Jan. 31, 1916. Age 86. Mother, Eva E. wife of Augustus DeBaugh, d. Feb. 21, 1903. Age 73. Albert J., d. Dec. 5, 1907, aged 5 mos. Eva A., d. Aug. 9, 1911, aged 9 mos. Children of Frederick T. and Emma T. DeBaugh. Footstones: A.DeB.-E.E.DeB.*
Smith, Elizabeth Ann Smith, dau. of the late, James and Mary Ann Smith, d. Jan. 23, 1910. Age 66.William Smith, son of the late James and Mary Ann Smith, d. Feb. 22, 1908. Age 55.
Roach, John A., Dec. 21, 1859 - Nov. 29, 1937. Margaret M., Aug. 13, 1872 - March 1, 1921.
Lancaster, Elizabeth, 1905-1919. (This is a footstone and could go with Roach above). Foostones: Lancaster, John B., 1879-1942. Elizabeth J., 1879-1954.
Buchanan, Marie, dau. of William and Agnes Buchanan, d. July 21, 1900, aged 6 mos.

Roach, IHS, Edward Roach, d. Dec. 31, 1904.Age 60,loving memory of Mary C., wife of Edward Roach, d. Feb. 2, 1917.* Age 72.
Cochran (monument-4 sides), John Maurice, b. Oct. 23, 1834, d. Aug. 13, 1898. Eugene Leo, b. Oct. 14, 1897, d. March 2, 1898. James Walton, b. April 10, 1899, d. Sept. 30, 1901 (side). Children of William and Hannah Cochran.*
Shanahan, father, Timothy J. Shanahan, d. Oct. 29, 1914. Age 53.
Shanahan, mother, Margaret J., wife of Timothy J. Shanahan, b. March 22, 1866, d. July 17, 1955.*
Bode. Footstones: Paul P., Nov. 19, 1857 – July 4, 1935. Annie M., Aug. 15, 1858 – Feb. 17, 1939. Joseph P., July 20, 1895 – Sept. 20, 1964. Babies (no names) – Headstone-BODE.
Colgan, Leon Clarke, son of Edward J. and Irene L. Colgan, d. May 8, 1901, aged 6 yrs. and (8) mos. Only lent.
Colgan, A. Walter, son of Edward and Irene Colgan, 1888-1920.
Colgan. Headstone: Colgan.
Lagan, Michael Lagan, d. Jan. 27, 190(3). Age 49.
Lagan, Jennie L., wife of Michael Lagan, d. April 5, 1909. Age 47.
Martin. Headstone: Martin. Footstones: Charles B., 1876-1949. Mary Melrose, 1919-1919.
Cooney, John, Sept. 23, 1862 – April 21, 1925. His wife, Nora Agnes...?.*
Nash, Katie E. Nash, wife of John J. Nash, b. March 5, 1863, d. June 24, 1927. Footstone: K.E.N.*
Healy-Cummings. Headstone: Healy. Footstones: Ellen M., 1860-1937. Robert J. Cummings, 1893-1931. Thomas J., 1853-1902.
Steadman. Headstone: Steadman. Footstone: John V.-Mary E.-S. Jane. Austin, baby, infant dau. of John (E.), Mary E. (Austin), 1897.
Knowles, John M. Knowles, d. Nov. 2, 1896. Age 80 native of Manchester, England.
Donahue, wife, Annie Donahue, d. Nov. 21, 1896, age 28 of County Galway.
Donahue, mother, Anne G., 1880-1943. Father, Michael J., 1867-1951.
Bopp, Mary Donahue Bopp, 1902-1941. R.I.P.
Groves, Willie, William Kennedy, son of William and Katharine Groves, d. Jan. 26, 1909. Age 23.
Bradley, father, Dennis A. Bradley, d. March 3, 1911. Age 71.
Bradley, mother, Ann J., wife of Dennis A. Bradley, d. Jan. 28, 1912. Age 66.
Footstone: D.A.B. and A.J.B.*
Bradley (Hines), Susan A. Hines, wife of Bernard Bradley, July 31, 1914.*
Elwood, Sally Dalton Elwood, 1859-1913. Footstones: Dalton and Viola S., 1860-1934.
Healy, wife, Ellen L., 1894-1933. Husband, Thomas J., 1884-1962.
Rahll, Roberta K., 1889-   . Robert J., 1877-1963.
Shanahan, Joseph (D.), son of Thomas and Mary Shanahan, d. July 19, 1899, aged two mos. and 26 days. Footstone: J.D.S.*
Gugerty, Alice M., 1870-1954. Peter J., 1867-1931.
Gugerty, Willie Albert, son of Peter J. and Alice M. Guerty, d. Jan. 12, 1901, aged 5 yrs. and 6 mos.*
Gugerty, Annie Marie, dau. of Peter J. and Alice M. Gugerty, d. May 12, 1897, aged 2 mos. and 2 days.*
Shanahan (McBride), Michael A. Shanahan, d. Oct. 1, 1935. Age 67. Mother, Mary Shanahan, b. 1828, d. Feb. 14, 1912. (side) Father, John C. Shanahan, b. 1826, d. Aug. 13, 1907. (side) Catherine McBride, b. Feb. 23, 1856, d. Aug. 9, 1937. Footstones: C.M.B., M.A.S., M.S., J.C.S.*
McCloskey, William McCloskey, 1860-1929. Footstone: W. McC.
McCloskey, Margaret McCloskey, 1858-1943. Footstone: M.McC.
Kearney, Bridget Kearney, 1854-1938. Footstone: B.K.
Proctor, Mariana Proctor, d. May 16, 1886. Age 55.
Clifford, Samuel Clifford, d. Nov. 15, 1899. Age 78.

Kelly, husband, John Kelly, husband of Catharine Kelly, 1839-1919. R.I.P.
Kelly, Catharine Kelly, 1854-1929.*
Grant, sister, Mary A. Grant, 1854-1920. R.I.P.
Horan, mother, Mary A., wife of Patrick T. Horan, d. Aug. 30, 1904. Age 51. Thomas, son of P.T. and M.A. Horan, d. July 25, 1890, aged 4 mos. and 20 days. (side) Patrick, husband of Mary A. Horan, d. Dec. 16, 1918. Michael Horan, d. Feb. 10, 1920. (side) Sarah, d. Dec. 1, 1892, aged 4 mos. Patrick, d. Nov. 6, 1895, aged 4 yrs., John, d. Nov. 16, 1895, aged 9 yrs. Children of P.T. and M.A. Horan.*
Doyle, Andrew Doyle, Sept. 7, 1852 - Dec. 3, 1909. Mary Elizabeth, his wife, Feb. 22, 1858 - May 4, 1900.
Doyle, Michael Doyle, b. Feb. 16, 1862, d. Sept. 28, 1890. (side) Mary A. Doyle, d. April 21, 1928. Bridget A. Doyle, d. Aug. 30, 1930. (side) Michael Doyle, Feb. 18, 1823 - Aug. 24, 1867. His wife, Mary Doyle, Jan. 6, 1832 - Aug. 28, 1893. (On part of headstone: Michael Doyle - a native of the ....?). Footstone: Michael Doyle - M.D.*
Stein, Catherine, dau. of John and . M. Stein, d. April 5, 1892. Age 36.
Stein, John P. Stein, d. April 1, 1931, age 13. Margaret A. Stein, d. June 1, 1937. Age 79.
Dalton, Catharine L., dau. of John B. and Catharine Dalton, d. Oct. 21, 1890. Age 38. (side) In memory of John B. Dalton, d. May 20, 1898. Age 83 of County Roscommon. Sister - Mother.*
Alexander (metal market), William J. Alexander, 1895-1970.
Dalton, James, son of William (J.) and Annie Dalton, d. Oct. 21, 189(0) or (8) aged..days.*
Dalton. Footstones: Dalton, William J., 1863-1936. Annie L., 1866-1941.
Dalton, Guy S. Dalton, Sept. 22, 1893 - Sept. 26, 1953. Footstone: John A. Dalton, Oct. 7, 1898 - Aug. 2, 1963.
Blair, Henrietta, wife of Charles Blair, d. March 8, 1889. Age 65.
Tilghman, Ellen Tilghman, d. Dec. 15, 1887. Age 80.   E.T.*
Austine, John C., d. Jan. 28, 1933. Mary E., d. March 19, 1948.
Cochran, Mary Margaret, Jan. 19, 1929 - March 9, 1932. Footstone: Charles C. Cochran, Jr., Jan. 1, 1954 - Jan. 2, 1954.
Cochran, Raymond, 1898- . Julia, 1898- .
Reamy, T. Judson, 1922-1927. Agnes T., 1886-1959. J. Joseph, 1928. Julian A., 1881-1967.
Cochran, William, d. April 17, 1926. Hannah E., wife, March 11, 1945.*
Isennock, infant son of Clyde A. and Clare E. Isennock, May 1926.
Carroll, William J., Jan. 6, 1855 - Aug. 24, 1930. His wife, M. Virginia (no other inscription).
Swift, Mary A. Swift, d. April 6, 1931.
Alexander, John J., July 17, 1860 - Aug. 15, 1930. His wife, Ella G., Feb. 12, 1870 - April 24, 1936. Footstones: Father - Mother.
Hanley, Catherine, Sept. 26, 1864 - Dec. 29, 1848. Daniel T., Jan. 5, 1856 - July 20, 1934.
Hagan, Ella Hagen, 1871-1935.
Warschek, E. G. Natz Warschek, 1863-1934. Footstone: E.G.N.W.*
Tomlin, Joseph Tomlin, Oct. 7, 1857 - May 25, 1935.
Carroll, James H. Carroll, March 30, 1850 - July 9, 1935. Emma J. Carroll, Aug. 23, 1859 - Aug. 24, 1939.
Shanahan, Joanna A., Jan. 1, 1857 - Feb. 11, 1945.
Burke, Richard M., 1858-1930. Mary J., 1860-1934.
Lynch, infant, dau. Joseph P., 1899-1942.
Kelley, son, James H., 1884-1969. Mother, Mary, 1849-1935. Father, John, 1855-1949. Dau., Bessie, 1886-1928.
Davis. Footstone: Brother, William, 1876-1927. (Davis)
Sullivan, father, Robert H., Aug. 27, 1956. Mother, Annie L., April 19, 1930.*

Sullivan, Sara R. Clarence J., Dec. 19, 1962.
Grant, Mary Ann, dau. of John and Mary Grant, Jan. 24, 1924 - March 2, 1926.*
Grant. Footstones: John W., 1888-1956. Lily May, 1888-1942.
Bugholtz, Alma Hoen Bugholtz, July 23, 1856 - April 4, 1928.*
Kirkwood, Anna Hoen Kirkwood, April 8, 1862 - Aug. 21, 1948.
Kearney, J. Kearsley Kearney, Nov. 25, 1889 - Nov. 18, 1950.
Kearney, Agnes B. Kearney, Oct. 11, 1887 - April 16, 1952.
Shanahan, John J., 1892- . Rose K., 1897-1971.
Shanahan, Dennis C., 1904-1968. Evelyn M., 1913- .
Hanlon, George Leo Hanlon, Maryland, CBM U.S. Navy, World Wars I and II, April 22, 1901 - Oct. 18, 1960.
Hanlon, George J., d. Feb. 16, 1931. John P., Jr., d. May 14, 1932.
Allender, Family of Nicholas Allender. Footstone: Joseph M. Allender, 1884-1969.*
Riley, Archer, 1870-1942. Jessie, 1873-1937.
Thomas, Minna Muller, Thomas, d. May 8, 1929. Requiescat Sub Coelis. Clarissimis.
Thomas, Albert Louis Thomas, Nov. 17, 1886 - March 8, 1949.
Allender, Martha J., 1851-19.. Montraville J., 1851-1937.
Harrison. Footstone: Katherine J. Harrison, d. May 3, 1963.
Skelton. Footstone: Catherine A. Skelton, d. Oct. 10, 1952.
Skelton. Footstone: Thomas P. Skelton, d. Feb. 18, 1945.
Haller. Footstone: Catherine J. Haller, d. March 6, 1934.
Bradley. Headstone: Bradley. Footstones: John J., Jr., 1908-1930. Lillian K., 1885-1944. John J., 1877-1942.
Smith. Headstone: Smith. Footstones: Joseph Charles, 1905-1966. William John, 1877-1951. Mary Agnes, nee Hayes, 1883-1929.
Ward. Headstone: Ward. Footstones: Jessie Ann, 1906-1934. Letta A., 1883-1947. Robert D., 1870-1944. Owen T., 1860-1932. J. Lewis, 1865-1930.
Roach, J. Edward Roach, 1895-1944.
Gibbons. (Headstone). Footstones: Eva B. Gibbons, July 11, 1886 - Feb. 26, 1951. Peter A. Gibbons, Feb. 6, 1878 - June 27, 1951. Richard P. Gibbons, Sept. 15, 1920 - Sept. 23, 1964.
Weakley. (Headstone). Footstones: Ethel, Nov. 21, 1934- . Carl, July 2, 1936.
Lynch. Headstone: Lynch. Footstones: J. Leo, 1919-1936. Joseph W., 1916-1936. Estelle M., 1887-1937.
Dentry, Henrietta Dentry, Nov. 7, 1867 - May 21, 1960.
Dentry, Charles G. Dentry, Nov. 21, 1863 - Dec. 10, 1934.
Dentry, Robert H. Dentry, Aug. 3, 1866 - May 12, 1949.
Dentry, Dr. C. Gordon Dentry, Dec. 13, 1894 - Sept. 1, 1953.
Colgan, A. Bruce Colgan, April 9, 1919 - July 7, 1960.
Colgan, Louis P. Colgan, b. Jan. 30, 1884, d. March 26, 1932. Footstone: Father.
Kelly. (Headstone). Footstones: Bessie A., 1888-1950. William J., 1885-1955.*
McKenna, Anna R., wife of Arthur McKenna, 1852-1932.*
Scarff. (Headstone). Footstones: John E. Scarff, father, 1861-1933. Agnes Scarff Heckrotte, 1894-1966.
Sullivan, W. Sullivan, wife, Rose, Oct. 1, 1934.
Jenkins (Herbert), Henry Hillen Jenkins, son of J. Hillen Jenkins and Rebecca Harbert, b. June 17, 1888, d. Jan. 15, 1963.*
Jenkins (Shaw). J. Hillen Jenkins, son of John Wilcox Jenkins and Alice Shaw, b. Sept. 2, 1855, d. Aug. 27, 1934.*
Jenkins (Harbert). Rebecca Harbert, wife of John Hillen Jenkins, b. Sept. 2, 1860, d. June 15, 1936.*
Allender, mother, Mary L. Allender, 1890-1937.

Minnick. (Headstone). Footstone: Sarah A., 1858-1930. Mother.
Kennedy, Margaret E. Kennedy, Feb. 6, ..?-April 5, 1969.
Tahaney, Hugh P., 1896-1932 (Tahaney).
Smith. (Headstone). Footstones: Sarah S. Finney, 1887-1946. Dennis J.,
1883-1947. George L., 1882-1961. (Behind stone). Footstones: Edward J.,
1894-1938. Helen M., d. 1942. James T., 1874-1966.
Hoffman, Mary V., 1920-1935.
Burke, Rose A. Burke, March 3, 1892 - July 15, 1953.
Maroney, Peter J. Maroney, Dec. 8, 1872 - Jan. 19, 1938.
Infants, 1913-1914 (Riley?).
Riley. (Headstone). Footstones: Mary Ellen, 1883-1952. James H., 1860-1937.
E. Grace, 1881-1911.
Shipley, Clara M. Shipley, Jan. 25, 1903 - Nov. 12, 1938.
Worrell, Esther L., Nov. 23, 1909 - Jan. 21, 1970.
Worrell, Anita Louise Worrell, 1939-1939.
Hanlon. (Headstone). Footstones: Margaret Dalton, 1856-1947. James, 1838-
1933. Alice Kathryn, 1892-1957. George Leo, 1890-1960. (Behind) William H.,
1910-1964. Mary Hanlon, 1883-1945. William A., 1877-1942.
Schmidt. Footstone: Edgar John, Nov. 6, 1882 - Oct. 16, 1930.
Bode, Raymond Bode, 1897-1947. Footstone: Bode and Schmidt.
Shipley. (Headstone). Footstones: Benjamin F., 1882-1935. Nettie B.,
1883-1965.
Holland, E. Jennie, 1866-1951. Carville W., 1859-1937.
Holland, Bernard C., 1888-1957.
Kelly, Loretta M., 1886-1939. Martin J., 1894-1969. John J., 1892- .
Riley, J. Joseph, d. March 11, 1937.*
Paschek, Stephen Paschek, d. Aug. 20, 1942 ,age 52, native of Galacia.
Lilly (Browne), Lilly, Mary Helen Scott Browne, Dec. 2, 1883 - Oct. 14, 1951.
Austin Jenkins, Dec. 24, 1883 - Jan. 23, 1962.
Blake (Smith). Blake, Archer F., 1883-1944. Mary C., 1898- . Mary L.
Smith, 1932- .
Lancaster (Hanlon). (Headstone). Lancaster. Footstones: William H., 1910-
1964. Mary Hanlon, 1883-1945. William A., 1877-1942.
Colgan, Edward J., Colgan, Jr., 1879-1942.
Bradley (Neumann). (Headstone). Bradley. Footstones: Mary Neumann, 1873-
1927. Hugh Bradley, Oct. 24, 1899 - April 17, 1964. Hugh F. Bradley, M.D.,
1866-1940.
Colgan. (Headstone). Footstones: Ann J., 1873-1948. John C., 1872-1946.
Roland B., 1906-1963.
Aiken, C. Gerard, Jr., 1916-1968. Winifred A., 1911- .
Cain, Mary C., 1898-1953. Frances D., 1894-....
Cain, Reta Agnes Cain, infant dau. of Francis and Mary Cain, b. April 22, 1940,
d. May 5, 1940.
Childress. (Headstone). Footstones: Elizabeth C., 1880-1954. Reuben V.,
1874-1939.
Plock, Anne C. Plock, wife of William E. Plock, b. Aug. 4, 1879, d. Sept. 23,
1955. William H. Plock, husband of Anna C. Plock, b. Sept. 5, 1883, d.
July 7, 1912. *
Thom, Agnes D. Thom, Oct. 18, 1882 - Feb. 15, 1969.
Jones, Jones, C. Leo, Oct. 23, 1893 - July 8, 1962. Sarah E., Aug. 13, 1898 -
April 14, 1940. Footstones: Mother, rest in peace. Clarence Leo Jones,
Maryland P.F.C., Btry A 310 Fld Arty, World War I, Oct. 23, 1893 - July 8,
1962.*
Rahll, Wilson Francis, 1875-1953. Clara Mary, 1883-1941. Footstone: Mother.
Cochran, Howard L., 1887-1957. Catherine M., 1885-1953.
Cochran, John, 1865-1945. Frances Elizabeth, 1864-1946.

Hinder. Headstone: Hinder. Footstones: Clara T., April 27, 1890 - June 15, 1945. Francis J., Feb. 18, 1887 - May 19, 1972.
Livingston, George J. Livingston, July 16, 1906 - Jan. 6, 1951.
Shanahan, 1926-John-1947. 1888-Bernard-1968. 1899-Anna J.-1966.
Shanahan, Mary A., 1881-1959. Timothy J., 1884-1968.
Pulsford, Henry J., 1880-1955. Clara A., 1888-1964.
Hagan, Joseph G., 1883-1941. Letitia A., 1886- .
Allen, Gertrude H., 1891-1967.
Colgan (Ady), Colgan, Stanley M., 1876-1954. Laura Ady, 1883-1955.
Ltyle, Sterling F., 1902-1956. Violet K., ...
Lane, Margaret, 1883-1954. Harry, 1886- .
Lynch, John D., 1900-1953. Mary Terry, 1899-19...
McGraw, Thomas F. McGraw, Sept. 17, 1882 - Jan. 27, 1956.
Kearney, brother, Joseph J., 1894-1963. Sister, Katherine, 1896-1964.
Kearney, husband, Frank (I.), 1891-1958.
Cochran, Teresa K., dau. of George W. & Alice A. Cochran, Oct. 19, 1965 - June 26, 1966.
Lynch (Hanlon). Headstone: Lynch. Footstone: Ethel Hanlon, 1898-1969. Walter M., 1895-1952.
Smith. Headstone. Footstone: Son, James Francis, 1923-1958. Father, Warren Kemp, 1896-1953. Mother, Anna Regina, 1907-1945.
Stiertz, Frank S. Stiertz, Jr., Maryland, 2d Lieut., AAF Pursuit Sq. World War II, Sept. 17, 1919 - March 15, 1942.
Riley, W. Francis, June 30, 1876 - Oct. 12, 1945. J. Bernard, Sept. 5, 1921 - May 28, 1955. Rhoda M., March 29, 1890- .
Hart, wife, Mary E., 1885-1949.
Turner. Headstone: Footstones: Katherine T., July 21, 1881 - Nov. 27, 1967. Thomas E., Feb. 4, 1879 - Sept. 16, 1927. Barbara, dau. of John L. & Margaret Turner, Feb. 12, 1848 - Feb. 14, 1848.
Bradley, Joseph P. Bradley, 1874-1949.
McCarty, Agatha S., 1870-1968. Frank P., 1865-1946.
Shipley, Joseph G., 1874-1960. Mary C., 1868-1963.
Donahue, Martin Joseph, March 18, 1904 - April 22, 1947. Rosa Anna, April 25, 1904 - Aug. 12, 1948.
Stengel, father, Harry C., July 24, 1893 - April 30, 1947. Mother, K. Inez, June 9, 1899- .
Shipley, Frederick L., 1879-1947. Genevieve C., 1888- .
Lynch. Headstone: Lynch. Footstones: Paul F., 1891-1947.
Holden. Headstone: Footstones: Matthew L., 1886-1947. Marion E., 1879-1963.
Weaver, Thomas J., 1866-1948. Margaret L., 1884-1967.
Holden, sister, Marion A., May 5, 1919 - . Brother, Matthew L., May 24, 1921 - Dec. 25, 1968.
George, Edith Simms George, 1893-1969.
George, A. Ellicott George, 1889-1967.
Love, Sarah George Love, Oct. 28, 1886 - July 3, 1958.
Preston, Kenneth F. Preston, 1918-1955.
Bacon, Thomas P., 1895-1958.
Cochran, Maurice N., 1907-1954.
Lilly, Edward Jenkins Lilly, 1880-1954.
Batchelor, Charles J., Sr., May 30, 1891 - Feb. 1, 1970. Leonora G., Aug. 1, 1903 - .
Batchelor, Charles Jerome Batchelor, Jr., 1939-1953.*
Bradley, Frank Mark, 1882-1960. Clara Gibson, 1888-1946.
Dalton, W. Fred, 1896-1950. Helen L., 1898-1969.
McGuire, James A., 1898-1953. Agnes S., 1890- .
Mitchell, Mary M., 1886-1965. William T., 1879-1959.

Gardner. Headstone. Footstones: Mary Ellen, 1907-1970. Laurence Eugene, 1904-1948. Joseph F., 1892-1950.
Smith. Headstone. Footstone: Wilhelmina T., 1916-1955.
Smith, F. Mitchell Smith, 1890-1949.
Grant, James W., May 24, 1898 - June 20, 1957. Louise T., Jan. 10, 1905 - .
Wertzer. Headstone: Footstones: Son, Bernard F. Wertzer, 1931-1958. Mother, Katharine S. Wertzer, 1893-1966. Father, Bernard F. Wertzer, 1892-1963.
Smith, Milford, Jan. 7, 1888 - April 10, 1951. Caroline K., Sept. 27, 1892 - .
Dalton, 1901-F. Carl-1951. 1904-Lida E.- . Dau., 1949-Mary Lida-1949.
Caine, Charles A., 1901-1950. A. Juanita, 1903- .
Winkler, Susan Marie, Oct. 23, 1890 - . Adam Henry, Aug. 27, 1889 - Sept. 30, 1950.
Powers.
Kelly, Michael R., 1865-1954. Frank P., 1860-1949.
Murphy, Daniel P., Aug. 7, 1888 - Jan. 7, 1964. Rose A., June 17, 1888 - Oct. 14, 1969.
Eisenhardt, Charles Joseph, Nov. 26, 1890 - Sept. 4, 1955. Helen M., Sept. 5, 1894 - Dec. 13, 1969.
Carroll, John J., 1894-1953. Ellen C., 1893-1965.
King, Charles E. King, 1891-1951.
King, Eugenia B. King, 1895-1953.
Dohony, Margaret C. Donohy, 1884-1970.*
Dohony, Thomas F. Dohony, 1885-1950.*
Bradley, Hugh D., 1888-1951.
Rehberger (Martin), Rehberger, George Edward, M.D., 5th Md. Vol., Spanish American War, Lt. Col. Med. Corps., World War I, b. Nov. 25, 1880, d. Sept. 28, 1971. Lena Martin, wife and mother, b. Sept. 10, 1890, d. June 17, 1951.*
Reier. Headstone: Footstones: William Henry, Jr., 1911-1951. Julia A., 1883-1957. William H., 1876-1971.
Vereker. Headstone. Footstones: James N. Vereker, Md. Pvt. 182 Station Hosp., World War II, March 17, 1901 - June 10, 1952. Brother, Frank N. Vereker, Md., PFC. Co. B 313 Regt. 79 Div., World War I, June 20, 1891 - Dec. 27, 1968. Wife, Sue Keenan Vereker, 1893-1968. Brother, Paul Leenan, 1889-1957.
Conti, Joan E., dau. of Angelo and Mary K. Conti, June 19, 1951 - Sept. 21, 1958.
Alexander, Robert, 1899-1969. Margaret T., 1894- .
Lingan, Anne P. Lingan, 1879-1967.
Weaver, Alphonse J. Weaver, Jan. 18, 1916 - June 19, 1958.
Ohler, Frank J., 1888-1958. Mary C., 1890- .*
Lancaster, George F., 1882-1965. Irene E., 1886-1957.
Cochran, Susan C., 1910-1960.
Shea, Danny Shea of Merryland Farm, 1897-1959.
Cochran, Edward L., 1916-1959.
Muller, Dr. J. Herman, 1884-1958. Victoria L., 1887- .
Toy (Colgan), Virginia P. Toy, nee Colgan, b. March 11, 1909 - Oct. 1, 1958.
Riley, Joseph F. Riley, Jr., July 27, 1953 - July 6, 1958.*
Hanley, father, Christian Leo, Dec. 26, 1886 - Dec. 27, 1957. Mother, Anne W., April 22, 1891 - Nov. 11, 1968.
Shanahan, W. Bruce Shanahan, Dec. 19, 1934 - Nov. 15, 1970.
Lewis, God bless our baby, Thomas Joseph Lewis, Feb. 8, 1957 - Dec. 22, 1957.
Miller, William L., M.D., 1886-1959. Anna M., 1885-1971.
Glenn. Headstone: Footstone: Wife, Lillian Hedges, Dec. 7, 1929 - Sept. 15, 1956.
Murphy, 1891-1957. Joseph Wharton Murphy.*
Dalton, Eugene E., 1910-1957.
Ensor, Carvel L., July 18, 1879 - June 27, 1958. Blanche M., Sept. 3, 1884.
Martin, Timothy B., 1902-1961. Mary F., 1902-1968.
Koegel, William A., 1900-1962. Anne E., 1907- .

Hinder, M. Rebecca, July 9, 1872 - Jan. 30, 1969. Mary V., Aug. 23, 1884 - April 6, 1965.
Bittner, Brian K. Bittner, son of Joseph and Lotus Bittner, Feb. 3, 1960 - Feb. 3, 1960.
Bevard, Katherine D. Bevard, 1891-1963. Wife of Listen B. Bevard.
Jelliman, Jennie M. Jelliman, June 3, 1900 - July 17, 1963.
Jelliman, Douglas H. Jelliman, Feb. 25, 1893 - April 3, 1966.
Cochran, G. Wilbur, March 3, 1900 - Feb. 10, 1964. M. Thelma, Sept. 5, 1901 - .
Schulte, Joseph G., Feb. 22, 1894 - . Regina U., March 6, 1902 - Dec. 9, 1964.
Hanlon, J. Maurice, 1894-1965. Mary T., 1895- .
Hartman, father, John M., Feb. 5, 1918- . Mother, Theresa M., Jan. 12, 1920 -. Son, John Wm., April 11, 1948 - July 1, 1965.
Hartman, mother, Clara C., Jan. 31, 1897- .
Lynch, Alice M. Lynch, Jan. 1, 1890 - Feb. 28, 1962.
McNancy, husband, Joseph T., 1886-1969. Wife, Marie A., 1886-1962.
Vining, Ralph E., 1889-1961.
Bachman, John S. Bachman, Jr., 1949-1959.
Mueller, Michael J., 1898- . Charlotte M., 1893-1959.
Carman, Leonard J., 1888-1959. Clara C., 1889-1969.*
Cochran, Anne M., 1901-1959.
Mueller, Paul M. Mueller, Jan. 16, 1954 - Aug. 5, 1961.*
Eichelberger, Irene E., Nov. 23, 1905 - Dec. 22, 1961.*
Robinson, Joseph N., 1896-1963. Marguerite Y., 1906- .
Livingston, Joseph J., May 7, 1913 - Jan. 1, 1965. Dolores S., July 5, 1913 - .
Chandler (Livingston), Ann E. Chandler, nee Livingston, 1935-1965.
Cochran, F. Edward, Oct. 10, 1893 - Jan. 26, 1966. Sarah A., Sept. 23, 1904 - Jan. 17, 1972.
Connor, Raymond C., Dec. 7, 1888 - Feb. 4, 1968. Arabella A., June 3, 1900 - May 3, 1968.
Cochran, Mary B. Cochran, April 15, 1893 - Jan. 23, 1965.
Ohler, husband, Milton J., 1911-1965. Wife, Caroline M., 1923- .
Hagan, James T. Hagan, Nov. 20, 1913 - April 15, 1965.
McQuaid, Wilfred T., 1905- . Gladys M., 1909-1969.
Meise, husband, John, 1918-1963. Footstone: John Erhard Meise, Md., T. Sgt. H 2 Det UK Base, World War II, Feb. 11, 1918 - Feb. 8, 1963.
Lauf, father, Christian, 1890-1962.
Bayer, Joseph John, Jan. 21, 1889 - Jan. 7, 1963.
Dilworth, David Burgan, 1923- . Mildred Bryne, 1919-1966.
Vogler (Shanahan), wife, Julia A. Vogler, 1902- . Shanahan.
Vogler, husband, Herman E. Vogler, 1885-1963.
Bees, John F., Sr., Jan. 26, 1908 - May 14, 1965. Mary M., Dec. 8, 1909 - .
Kelly, John T., 1887-1966. Emily M., 1888-1971.
Shanahan, husband, Robert E., 1901- . Margaret M., 1901-1964.
Betlejewski, father, Albert F., 1905- . Mother, Anna A., 1908-1966.
McGuire, Charles L., 1891-1966. Margaret T., 1892- .
Cochran, Mary B., 1902- . Leo A., 1900-1966.*
Schafer, father, William H., 1901-1967. Mother, Caroline N., 1903-1970.
Miller, Henry J., 1890-1968. Mary M., 1894- .
Carter, Michael J. Carter, Jan. 5, 1947 - Oct. 24, 1971.
Dalton, Frank, 1901-1968. Margaret, 1905- .
Jones, David C., 1884-1968.
Durkin, mother, Anna E., 1935-1968.

Quesenberry, Lonnie R., Sept. 8, 1896 - May 5, 1971. Martha E., March 1, 1896 - .
Lilly, Ruth Douthit Lilly, 1914-1971.
Lauf.
Studz, Edward, 1902-1967.
Boxman, William Earl, April 22, 1917 - Sept. 12, 1967.
Kelly, Charles A., Aug. 15, 1912 - Aug. 28, 1968. F. Louise, Aug. 15, 1915 -
Kelly, Howard A., Oct. 6, 1914 - June 12, 1967.
Dalton, Regina Ann Dalton, Feb. 27, 1945 - May 16, 1967.
Shanahan, John F., 1905-1967. Kathryn I., 1909- .
Dalton, John T., Jan. 6, 1896 - March 9, 1967. Gladys E., Dec. 13, 1905 -

Ball, Walter N., 1915- . Catherine E., 1914-1966.
Kyle (eichelberger), Dorothy L. Kyle, nee Eichelberger, Oct. 13, 1944 - Aug. 15, 1966.
Kelly, J. Clark Kelly, 1899-1968.
Cochran, H. Stirling, 1921-1968. Michael K., 1943-1967. Cochran.
Ahl, Geraldine T. Ahl, 1948-1969.*
Clark, Martin J., Oct. 3, 1906 - Aug. 27, 1969. Ruby A., Sept. 6, 1913 -

Danenmann, John L., 1895-1970. Elizabeth C., 1897- .
Scheper, Anthony J. Scheper, Md. SP 4 U.S. Army, Vietnam, Oct. 7, 1950 - July 10, 1970.
Lancaster, Ralph L., 1920-1970. Patricia A., 1932- .
Colgan, George C., Sr., July 23, 1901 - June 5, 1971. Grace C., Feb. 13, 1910 - .

GRACE UNITED METHODIST CHURCH

Falls Road and Ridge Road, Northwest corner, Cockeysville Quad. Minister J. Kemper. Church erected 1890, improved 1952, per cornerstone inscription. Shown in 1877 Hopkins atlas plate of District 8 as Ridge M.E. Meeting House. Copied by J. McGrain, July-August 1972.
W.F., 13-0.
E.M., 13-1.
D.B.
XX, Moore (monument).
Mother, Margaret L., 1882-1967.
Father, Daniel B., 1882-1929.
Son, William H., 1907-1948.
A (corner marking).
Seward, Thomas Jane (one row closer to road) (vast space).
Margaret A., dau. of Thos. G. and Hannah Tracey, d. Feb. 3, 1869, aged 3 mos. and 17 days.*
Abraham Parks, d. Aug. 6, 1838. (A.P. - hd).* Age 21.
Michel Russell, d. Nov. 28, 1877.* Age 65
Geo. Myars, Nov. 2, 1799 - Jan. 10, 1858, buried (G.M. - hd).*
Ruth N., wife of George Myers, d. Sept. 16, 1889. (R.N.M. - ft).* Age 78
W.F., 2-0 (corner markers).
a. (east). P. Elizabeth Green, d. Feb. 22, 1884. Age 75. William Stewart, d. Dec 4 1887.*
b. (south). P. Samuel H. Perry, Aug. 28, 1862 - Oct. 22, 1863. Joseph S., Perry, Aug. 22, 1861 - Jan. 25, 1867.
c. (west). P. Simeon H. Perry, Sept. 1, 1809 - March 20, 1898. Emeline M. Perry, June 30, 1828 - March 27, 1909.

d. (north). P. Mariana Perry, June 6, 1872 - Nov. 29, 1874. Rachel E. Perry, May 3, 1867 - Dec. 1, 1868. (E.M.P., S.H.P., on individual markers).
(blank pedistal).
Son, Samuel Elsworth DeVeas, who was killed in a seaplane accident, Aug. 5 at San Diego, Cal., Feb. 23, 1897 - Aug. 5, 1919. Son of Franklin E. and Maggie F. DeVeas.*
Franklin E. DeVeas, 1869-1950. Maggie F. DeVeas, 1879-1960. (F.E.D. - corner markers).
Baublitz, Leona M., Jan. 29, 1891. Benjamin H., Dec. 11, 1888 - Feb. 17, 1958.
Jeremiah Baublitts, Sept. 24, 1837 - Aug. 10, 1928 (long space).
Sproul, Nelson, 1858-1937. Sarah E., 1867-1946 (Metal marker: Golden Rule Council, JR. OUAM/6) (N.S., S.E.S. - foots).
William C. Sproul, Jan. 9, 1852 - Oct. 25, 1882. (W.C.S. - ft).
Sproul, Rebecca, 1870-1937. Rosa, 1872-1943.
Mary Jane, wife of Jeremiah Baublitts, March 20, 1844 - June 15, 1909. (M.J.B. - ft).*
Gill (monument).
Charles B., 1906-1923.
L. Edward, 1873-1942.
Ida V., 1877-1961.
Zepp, John W., June 11, 1872 - Jan. 18, 1947. Margaret E., June 4, 1874 - March 19, 1956.
Larkins, William H., Dec. 29, 1841 - May 13, 1910. Wife, Sarah A., April 6, 1848 - Oct. 15, 1908. (S.A.L., W.H.L. - heads).*
Baby
Baby, Larkins.
Edith, Emma, dau. of John H. and Harriet O. Shad, d. March 28, 1858, aged 6 yrs. and 18 days. (E.E.S. - head).
William, Nelson, son of John H. and Harriet O. Shad, d. Dec. 28, 1857, aged 3 yrs. and 6 mos. and 12 days. (W.N.S. - hd).
Mother, Elizabeth M., wife of Thomas D. Tawney, d. Jan. 29, 1896. (E.M.T. - ft).* Age 71.
Father, Thomas D. Tawney, d. Jan. 30, 1902. (T.D.T. - foot).* Age 79.
(Willow symbol). Margaret Irena, dau. of T.D. and E.M. Tawney, d. Feb. 12, 1862, aged 2 mos. and 7 days.*
Ann Rebecca Tawney, Sept. 2, 1847 - Jan. 1, 1836.(?)(A.R.T. - ft).
(finger pointing down). Louisa J., dau. of John and Catharine Long, Aug. 28, 1851 - June 8, 1853.*
W (?) Wallis, son of ..Sharp(?), d. Sept. 1, 1852, aged 2 yrs., 5 mos. and 17 days. (illegible verse-3 lines; illegible inscription and finger symbol on rear). (W.W.S. - ft).*
(to rear of No. 17) (Broken stone, buried in two parts): "Aged 51 years and 6 months".
McCaslin (monument).
Pearl P., June 22, 1886 - June 25, 1968.
Charles Kerr, Feb. 22, 1886 - Sept. 23, 1935 (with McCaslin monument).
Long (monument).
Minnie M., 1864-1950.
John S., 1855-1944.
Arthur L., 1903-1908.
John R., 1897-1901.
Levinia E. Seipp, d. April 8, 1885.* Age 23.
Conrad Seipp, d. Feb. 22, 1884. (C.S. - hd).* Age 66.
Elizabeth Seipp, d. Jan. 11, 1873. (E.S. - hd).* Age 49.
(Willow symbol). Hesakiah Mallonee, July 11, 1789 - July 19, 1853. (H.M. - hd).
John R. Gent, March 13, 1810 - Oct. 6, 1891. (J.R.G. - hd).*

Mother, Ann C. Gent, July 11, 1807 - Jan. 15, 1903. (A.C.G. - hd).*
a. Long.
b. Long, Henry, 1840-1925. Hester, 1843-1934.
George C., son of Henry and Hester Long, Jan. 20, 1872 - May 5, 1874, aged 2 yrs., 3 mos. and 15 days. (G.C.L. - foot).*
a. Long.
b. Long, Howard W., Sept. 17, 1887. Lauri I., May 2, 1892 - July 30, 1964. (Willow symbol). Samuel G., son of Henry and Hester Long, Oct. 4, 1852 - July 2, 1853. (S.G.L. - hd).*
Catherine, dau. of Henry and Elizabeth Long, b. Sept. 1, 1851 (rest sunken). (C.L. - hd).*
William H., son of Henry and Elizabeth Long, July 26, 1843 - Nov. 22, 1851. (W.H.L. - hd).*
(fragment; same design as No. 22, with headstone marked M.L.).
Henry S. Hipsley, d. July 19, 1866. (H.S.H. - hd).* Age 47.
Martha E. Hipsley, d. March 25, 1888. (M.E.H. - hd).* Age 71.
Mary E. Hipsley, Sept. 18, 1845 - July 26, 1925. (M.E.H. - hd).*
John Wisner, Sept. 13, 1820 - May 29, 1903. (J.W. - hd).*
(clasped hands symbol). Sarah, wife of George W. Dearholt, d. Nov. 4, 1892. (S.D. - hd).* Age 62.
George W. Dearholt, Nov. 10, 1830 - April 5, 1878. (G.W.D. - hd).*
Hoffman, John M., Aug. 21, 1882 - July 2, 1957. Mary M., April 21, 1887 - Jan. 22, 1935.
George H., son of J.G. and A.C. Young, Sept. 23, 1918 - March 23, 1932. (G.H.Y. - hd).*
Anna Young, Feb. 27, 1884 - Aug. 13, 1925.
Hanna Kirkpatrick, d. Jan. 14, 1863.
John T. Tawney, Aug. 18, 1866 - Nov. 23, 1929.*
Mary B., wife of John T. Tawney, d. Dec. 2, 1910. (M.B.T. - hd).* Age 34.
Talbert (monument, both sides) (to east of No. 7):
Margaret Talbert Ensor, Oct. 6, 1914 - Jan. 17, 1940.
Wilbur B., March 18, 1927 - Jan. 26, 1942.
Charles M., June 16, 1929 - Jan. 26, 1942.
Lawrence F., Oct. 3, 1912 - Sept. 27, 1918.
Gladys E., Nov. 16, 1909 - March 16, 1910 (to west of No. 7):
Elizabeth L., Oct. 21, 1884 - March 16, 1961.
Robert L., Nov. 19, 1882 - May 13, 1969.
Minnie V., Nov. 22, 1919.
C. Albert, Oct. 21, 1908 - July 1, 1968 (end of Talbert monument - No. 7).
Gladys E., dau. of Robert and Elizabeth Talbert, Nov. 16, 1909 - March 16, 1910. (Note: this is same name as No. 12).
Childs (monument - both sides) (to east of No. 18):
Bertha A. Rauschenbach, 1886-1934.
William C., 1861-1935.
Mary L., 1857-1933.
Kate V., dau. of John R. and Ann C. Gent, April 4, 1850 - Jan. 7, 1866. (K.V.G. - hd).*
Martha E., dau. of John R. and Ann C. Gent, Sept. 4, 1836 - Dec. 16, 1866. (M.E.G. - hd).*
Christie A., dau. of John R. and Ann C. Gent, Nov. 4, 1839 - May 14, 1870. (C.A.G. - hd).*
Andrew Klinedinst, d. Dec. 27, 1872. (A.K. - hd).* Age 52.
Isabel, wife of Andrew Klinedinst, b. ..., d. ... 25, 18.., (I.K. - hd).
Hoffman.
Charles T., 1886-1961.
Annie M., 1887-1937.

Troyer, Albert M., Nov. 18, 1900. Irene E., Jan. 6, 1901. Doris E., Oct. 25, 1919 - Dec. 15, 1924.
Forwood, Elizabeth K., Jan. 28, 1889. Charles W., May 13, 1867 - June 25, 1956.
(off pedistal). John H., infant son of Cornelius and Christiana Leaf, d. March 8, 1874, aged 1 mo. and 9 days.*
(hand-clasp symbol). Cornelius Leaf, April 29, 1851 - Nov. 12, 1891, Marble Lodge No. 123 I.O.O.F. and Hebron Lodge No. 74, K. of P. (C.L. - foot).*
(hand-clasp symbol). Christiana Leaf, May 1, 1853 - March 16, 1925. (C.L. -hd).*
Aunt Mary M. Tracey, Aug. 3, 1812 - Nov. 22, 1891. (M.M.T. - hd).
Father John Leaf, Feb. 2, 1804 - Oct. 22, 1895.
Mother Ann, wife of John Leaf, April 3, 1810 - Nov. 1, 1892. (A.L. - hd).
Rachel Price, d. Aug. 26, 1890. (R.P. - hd).* Age 72.
Father, mother, William Price, March 6, 1827 - Nov. 8, 1908. Lucinia, wife of William Price, May 31, 1840 - Jan. 5, 1907. (L.P., W.P. - heads).*
Mordecai, son of .. and .. Price. Thomas M., ... Price.*
Mary Dehoff, Dec. 29, 1792 - July 18, 1876. (M.D. - hd).*
Louis A. Dehoff, Oct. 10, 1798 - Dec. 24, 1873.
Joseph D. Parrish, grand son of Lewis A. and Mary Dehoff. d. Aug 12, 1871.
Jesse Dehoff, June 29, 1830 - Oct. 17, 1856. (J.D. - hd).*
Lewis T., son of Nehemiah and Mary A. Parrish, Feb. 1, 1857 - Nov. 3, 1860. (L.T.P. - hd).*
Mary Ann, wife of Nehemiah Parrish, Sept. 11, 1832 - Dec. 25, 1865. (M.A.P. - hd).*
Sarah A., wife of Ignatius Creager, Sept. 26, 1823 - Jan. 1, 1862. (S.A.C. - hd).*
(top broken). Christian (sic) Lewis Dehoff, Dec. 16, 1827 - May 29, 1854. (C.L.D. - ft).*
McCaslin, Thomas R., 1863-1939. Annie E., 1860-1933.
Hannah, Ruff, d. ..., aged 73(?) years. (H.R. - hd).
.. ..., March 22, 1846, aged 10 years, 2 mos, 2 days.*
(rough stone).
Son, Charles P. Crue, Dec. 8, 1931 - Dec. 8, 1964.
Joshua Cain, March 10, 1834 - Aug. 24, 1895. Martha E. Cain, July 31, 1840 - Nov. 27, 1916.*
Perla J., dau. of Joshua and Martha E. Cain, d. Sept. 15, 1872, aged 16 mos. and 3 days.*
John W. F. Cain, son of Joshua and Martha E. Cain, Feb. 28, 1859 - April 6, 1860, aged 13 mos. and 6 days.*
Larmore (monument - both sides).
John H., Jr., 1892-19...
Mildred V., 1898-1937.
Larmore, Richard E., 1890-1965. Margaret E., 1893-1965.
George W. Simmons, 1868-1959 by his children.
Susan R. Simmons, 1871-1928 by her children.
Jones, Wm. Henry Jones, Jan. 17, 1877 - Nov. 6, 1896. Son of Nicholas and Mary Jones. (W.H.J. - hd).*
Julia S., dau. of Nicholas and Mary M. Jones, April 13, 1870 - Oct. 4, 1891. Meads (signature). (J.S.J. - ft).
Laura V., dau. of Nicholas and Mary M. Jones, d. Feb. 9, 1881. Age 23.
(clasped-hands symbol). Nicholas Jones, d. Nov. 24, 1885. Age 56.
(clasped-hands). Mary M. Jones, Jan. 26, 1835 - March 11, 1926.
N. Cornelius, son of Nicholas and Mary M. Jones, d. May 8, 1887. Age 15.

Charles W. Myers, Jan. 1, 1845 - Dec. 20, 1804 (sic).*
Etta C., wife of Charles Myers, Oct. 20, 1845 - Jan. 22, 1890. (E.C.M. - ft).*

Arthur G., son of Charles and Ellie C. Myers, d. July 21, 1880, aged 1 yr., 6 mos. and 1 day. (A.G.M. - ft).*
Charles E. Leaf, 1905-1918.
Aquilla M. Leaf, 1875-1942.
Josephine, dau. of Henry and Johanna Leaf, Aug. 20, 1870 - April 29, 1889. (J.L. - ft).*
(finger pointing up). Henry Leaf, April 21, 1815 - July 8, 1900. (H.L. - ft).*
(finger pointing up). Johanna, wife of Henry Leaf, d. June 11, 1887. (J.L. - ft).*
Mary E. Leaf, dau. of Henry and Joanna Leaf, Dec. 22, 1861 - Aug. 11, 1883.*
Joshua Calvin, son of Joseph and Emelia Leaf, d. Sept. 6, 1861. (J.C.L. - ft).*
Sarah Tipton, Oct. 1, 1791 - July 23, 1880.*
Bertha J., wife of Benj. Forwood, d. March 14, 1904. (B.J.F.).*
Benjamin L. Forwood, Aug. 8, 1869 - June 18, 1937.
Leonard Forwood, son of Cora and Benjamin Forwood, Feb. 5, 1912 - May 14, 1928. L.F.).*
Cora J. Forwood, Aug. 26, 1889 - Jan. 8, 1950.
George W. Dobson, husband of Hannah S. Dobson, June 6, 1840 - June 8, 1905. (G.W.D.).*
Hannah S. Dobson, wife of George W. Dobson, Sept. 5, 1839 - May 5, 1918. (H.S.D.).*
William M., son of Wm. J. and L.B. McCaslin, May 19, 1892 - Nov. 25, 1918. (W.M.McC).*
William J., husband of Lillie B. McCaslin, Aug. 16, 1860 - Sept. 20, 1935. (W.J.McC). *
Lillie B., wife of Wm. J. McCaslin, Jan. 8, 1863 - Oct. 12, 1938. (L.B.McC).* (space with R.E.L. corner markers).
Ely Hinkle (rest sunken). (E.H.H. - ft).*
(finger point). Mary Jane Harris, Dec. 5, 1847 - May 13, 1852. (rest sunken). (M.J.H.).*
(stone fallen). William Harris, d. Sept. 26, 1890. (W.H. - ft).*
Harris, Louisa A. Harris, April 1819, June 1918. (L.A.H. - ft).*
Joshua Jones, d. July 11, 1853. (J.J.).*
Susan Jones, d. March 10, 1872. (S.J.).*
Susan E. Jones, d. Jan. 17, 1878 (rest of inscription obstructed). (S.E.J.).*
William M., husband of Eliza Frantz, d. (rest sunken). (W.M.F.).*
Bessie A., only dau. of W.M. and Eliza Frantz, Dec. 29, 1874 - Dec. 19, 1876.*
Eliza Frantz, Aug. 8, 1828 - Jan. 22, 1892.*
Crue, Mildred J., 1906-   . Charles E., 1900-1951. Infant, 1924.
Son, Charles P. Crue, Dec. 8, 1931 - Dec. 8, 1964.
Sereta Irene, dau. of Leonard W. and Ruby I. Wade, Dec. 15, 1946 - March 1, 1947.
Father, Nicholas Tracey, d. Nov. 24, 1855.*
Mother, Elizabeth Tracey, Dec. 13, 1810 - March 18, 1893.*
Sister, Mary, wife of Chas. W. Shipley and dau. of Nicholas and Elizabeth Tracey, Oct. 13, 1840 - Feb. 19, 1891.
Lee J. Smith, June 4, 1864 - May 12, 1961.
Roberta DeVas Burnwell, April 12, 1902 - Nov. 26, 1960.
Harr.
William E. Harr, May 9, 1894 - Aug. 7, 1959.
Gover, Walter W., Feb. 25, 1890 - June 1, 1960. Virgie V., June 4, 1895.
Havens, C. LaRue, Sept. 20, 1897 - Feb. 15, 1967. Adeline E., Aug. 16, 1906 -.
McCaslin, Stella M., 1893-1956. Ridgeway A., 1894-   .
Frank, John L., 1896-1968. Isabell M., 1897-   .

Brewer.
Marie M. Brewer, nee Ravner, Aug. 15, 1905 - June 2, 1943.
Donald Watson Brewer, April 4, 1903 - Feb. 23, 1966.
Albert M. Jones, March 31, 1867 - Aug. 6, 1947 (A.M.J.).
Jones, Harvey Geist, husband of Anna K. Jones, April 24, 1895 - Feb. 28, 1941. At rest. (H.C.J. - ft).
Jones, Joshua H. Jones, d. Sept. 29, 1892.* (J.H.J.). Age 21.
Wn. Harvey Jones, husband of Rachel B. Jones, b. Feb. 6, 1834 - Nov. 7, 1853. (Wm.H.J.).*
Mother, R.B. Jones, 1840 - 1924.
(uprooted). Wm. Francis Jones, July 28, 1865 - Dec. 11, 1865, aged 4 mos. and 14 days. (Wm.F.J.).
Aquila F., son of W.H. and R.M. Jones, aged 11 mos. and 2 days.*
Isabel, dau. of Geo. T. and Ann B. Joice, Sept. 17, 1854 - Feb. 3, 1853 (?). (I.J.)*
Sarah E., dau. of Geo. T. and Ann B. Joice, Feb. 4, 1849 - Oct. 14, 1854. (S.E.G.).*
(Lamb symbol). Valverde A., son of George and Annie Joice, d. Oct. 28, 1862 (rest sunken).
(Lamb). Frank, son of George and Annie Joice, d. Sept. 4, 1863, aged 5 years and 10 mos.
George T. Joice, May 29, 1822 - Aug. 16, 1873. (G.J.).*
Leaf (both sides).
Margaret E., 1881-1959.
Joshua H., 1868-1955.
Larmore, Margaret E., 1860-1935. John H., 1844-1921.
Foster, Milton H., 1873-1939. Betty C., 1874-1947.
Pearl C., child of J.C. and A.F. Parks, Dec. 2, 1880 - Feb. 14, 1883.*
Dad).
Mother). (No corresponding monument).
Father).
Charles M. Myer, 1854-1932, wife, Mary L. Myer, 1854-1927. C.M.M., M.L.M. - foots.
Hoffman.
Ida B., Nov. 27, 1898 - July 28, 1949.
Oscar G., May 4, 1896 - May 13, 1970.
Charles G., May 19, 1903 - June 1, 1964.
Mollie E., Feb. 17, 1870 - July 23, 1956.
George C., July 10, 1865 - Aug. 2, 1946.
Carver, Conrad J., 1875-1966. Margaret May, 1882-1935. (Father, Mother).
William Dorsey, son of Conrad J. and Mary M. Carver, Nov. 10, 1902 - June 13, 1904.*
Wm. Roland L. Carver, Nov. 3, 1868 - May 11, 1925. Mary Carver, Oct. 3, 1871 - April 20, 1944. (M.C. - W.R.L.C.).
Kelly, Ann Elizabeth, wife of Eli Kelly, Dec. 30, 1837 - March 22, 1913. (A.E.K.).*
Kelley, Eli Kelley, Jan. 6, 1833 - July 30, 1902.*
a. (south). Sarah Jones, d. Jan. 25, 1892. (S.J.).* Age 84.
b. (east). Holy Bible.
c. (north). Aquilla Jones, d. March 31, 1893.* Age 81.
Aquila H., son of J.D. and N.R. Childs, Nov. 29, 1869 - Aug. 22, 1870.*
Father, John Skipper, Oct. 17, 1798 - Oct. 9, 1875. "I know that my Redemmer liveth."*
(enormous willow and scene). Sarah, wife of John Skipper, May 11, 1799 - Oct. 6, 1854.*
Susannah, dau. of John and Sallie Skipper, d. July 8, 1860, aged 11 mos. and 2 days.
Gent, Edward P., 1880-1961. Ada F., 1891-   .

Mary C., wife of Edward P. Gent, July 15, 1887 - May 30, 1912.*
Charles Edward, son of Chars. and Louisa Myer, April 19, 1885 - May 2, 1888.*
a. (front-east). Tawney, Mary C., wife of Thomas E. Tawney, Dec. 22, 1812 - April 10, 1900. Here ... . Noble life .. ... Mother. A devoted wife.
b. (south-left). Earnest C., son of T.E. and M.C. Tawney, Sept. 2, 1880 - Sept. 7, 1880. Suffer the little children. To come unto me.
c. (north-right). Thomas E. Tawney, June 11, 1845 - Nov. 25, 1911.*
(willow scene). Erected to the memory of Elizabeth Tipton, Aug. 5, 1797 - Sept. 6, 1856. (E.T. - ft).*
(willow). Stephen Tipton, d. Nov. 9, 1861. Age 75. (S.T. - ft).*
Brother, S. Jefferson Tipton, d. May 14, 1897. Age 72.
Belt, 1817-Thomas-1893. 1818-Catherine J.-1890. 1858-Ellen Matilda-1922. 1862-Caroline C.1932.
Garling, Sophia A., Feb. 2, 1869 - May 1, 1932. Frank, Jan. 29, 1863 - July 21, 1936.
Mother, Eliza C. Worden, 1805 - May 14, 1875. (E.C.W.).*
James Worden, Nov. 14, 1814 - Feb. 24, 1904. (J.W.).*
Mother, Mary Brown, d. March 20, 1864. Age 52.
Sarah, dau. of Wm. and Priscilla Carver, aged 3 years and 1 day.*
Florence, dau. of Wm. and Priscilla Carver, d. Jan. 24, 1866, aged 2 years and 11 mos. and 29 days.*
Charles Edwin, son of Wm. and Priscilla S. Carver, d. July 21, 1879, aged 4 mos. and 28 days. (fallen).*
a. (east). Carver.
b. (left-south). Priscilla Stevenson Carver, wife of William Carver, April 3, 1836 - March 26, 1909.*
c. (north-right). William Carver, Nov. 16, 1835 - May 3, 1918. (P.S.C.) (W.C.).*
Mary Ann Minnick, Sept. 4, 1833 - June 27, 1920.
William Carver, son of Milton H. and Bettie C. Foster, March 9, 1896 - July 18, 1897, aged 1 year and 4 mos. and 9 days (illegible).*
Father, Nathan Carver, 1797 - Oct. 30, 1845 (N.C.).
Mary W., wife of Arthur G. Stump, Feb. 25, 1883 - June 1, 1917. (M.W.S.).*
Long, Charles H., July 29, 1856 - April 21, 1945. His wife, Margaret Ann, Dec. 28, 1857 - Sept. 26, 1930. (C.H.L. - M.A.L.).
George Edward, son of Charles and Annie Long, Dec. 10, 1888 - Dec. 5, 1895.* (fallen - unmoveable).
a. (east). George Albert, son of Geo. and Martha Thomas, d. April 15, 1862. Ruth Ann, dau. of Geo. and Martha Thomas, d. April 27, 1862.
b. (west). George Thomas, 1821-1859. Martha Thomas, 1824-1905.
George Albert, son of Geo. and Martha Thomas, d. April 15, 1862, aged 10 years, 6 mos. and 26 days. (G.A.T.) (Note: same as a).*
Ruth Ann, dau. of Geo. and Martha Thomas, d. April 27, 1862, aged 11 years, 10 mos. and 15 days. (R.A.T.).*
Ruth A. Gorry, Jan. 6, 1805 - Dec. 9, 1878. (R.A.G.).*
(willow scene). Thomas Cox, Jan. 8, 1809 - (sunken) March 16, 185...
Cover, N. Jefferson, May 17, 1882 - Oct. 5, 1958. Mabel, Sept. 28, 1888.
William Musgrave, d. Oct. 18, 1862. Age 56.
Elizabeth, dau. of John and Susannah Cox, March 11, 1804 - March 17, 1898. At rest. (E.S.).*
Father and mother, John Cox, Feb. 11, 1769 - May 13, 1858. Susannah, wife of John Cox, Jan. 4, 1785 - March 27, 1867. (J.C. - S.C.).
Phebe Cox, Oct. 8, 1807 - Sept. 8, 1875. (P.C.)*. Age 67.
(loose). Arthur Cox, son of Uriah and Mary Cox, March 16, 1857 - March 9, 1858. (A.C. - ft).*
George Frederick, son of Uriah and Mary Cox, July 27, 1845 - May 27, 1852. (G.F.C.).
Charles Thomas, son of Uriah and Mary Cox, April 4, 1848 - May 7, 1852.

John Edward, son of Uriah and Mary Cox, April 25, 1850 - Feb. 24, 1852. (J.E.C.)
Mary, wife of Uriah Cox, April 8, 1820 - May 7, 1879. (M.C.).*
Uriah Cox, May 15, 1813 - Dec. 24, 1891. Rest in peace. (U.C.).*
John Tracey, d. Jan. 27, 1874. Age 81.
Sarah Ann, wife of John Tracey (sic), d. Dec. 26, 1858.
Marion A., 1902. Maude O. 1908-1948. Larmore.
G. A. Whiteford (flat marker).
Harr.
Ella M., 1887-19 .
G. Edgar, 1889-1938. Father, F. G. Gover,
Mother, Mary A. Gover, Feb. 5, 1817 - July 22, 1894./Dec. 8, 1813 - Dec. 29, 1892
Raver, Joshua J., 1863-1948. Emma D., 1868-1950.
Emma V., dau. of Joshua J. and Emma Raver, Dec. 7, 1900 - Nov. 6, 1902. Charles
  L., son of Joshua J. and Emma Raver, March 19, 1896 - July 22, 1897.*
Harr, J. George, 1860-1924. John I., 1887-1906. Kate D., 1861-1925. Mildred
  M., 1906-1906 (on back: Harr).
Swem.
Son, Edwin B., 1897.
Dau., Margaret Swem Lutz, 1884-1910.
Dau., Emma E., 1883-   .
Mother, Elizabeth, 1859-1951.
Father, Ely K., 1854-1944.
George W. Dearholt, Jan. 28, 1863 - Oct. 26, 1930. (G.W.D.).*
Annie J. Dearholt, wife of George W. Dearholt, Feb. 12, 1864 - Dec. 15, 1915.
  (A.J.D.).*
Baby, Ella Lenora Tawney, Aug. 1, 1900 - Oct. 5, 1900, aged 2 mos. and 4 days.*
Melvin Webster, son of J.L. and A.L. Tawney, April 10, 1914 - Nov. 23, 1914.*
John L. Tawney, June 25, 1851 - Nov. 25, 1920. At rest.
Annie L. Tawney, Aug. 30, 1870 - Sept. 29, 1944. At rest.
L. Elwood Gent, son of Arnold G. and Sadie V. Gent, Oct. 24, 1904 - June 19,
  1921. (L.E.G.).*
Emma Keene, wife of Samuel W. Gent, Aug. 13, 1858 - May 6, 1918, aged 60 years.
Samuel U. (?) Gent, July 24, 1847 - Aug. 18, 1922.
Gent, Julian Sonders, 1822-1869. Thelma M. Hartman, 1902-   .
Gent, brother-Clarence M., 1875-1951. Sister-Myra Ann, 1893-1952.
Raymond A., son of O.W. and Hannah R. Gent, d. Jan. 19, 1894, aged 10 years, 9
  mos. and 16 days. (R.A.G.).
Hannah R., wife of O.W. Gent, d. Jan. 9, 1902, aged 49 years, 7 mos. and 25 days.
Gent, Orrick W., Nov. 25, 1844 - Jan. 25, 1933.*
Neuberger, Charles L., Aug. 24, 1888 - July 7, 1957. Estella I., April 27, 1898.
Frank Shaw, 1885-1958.
Trimble (both sides).
Father, Albert H., 1884-1953.
Mother, Zula E., 1884-1967.
Son, Norman L., 1913-1947.
Gent (both sides).
Allan C. Gent, Oct. 1, 1888 - July 4, 1967.
Annie Dearholt Gent, Feb. 26, 1887 - May 8, 1958.
Evelyn Rosalie, dau. of Allan C. and Annie V. Gent, Sept. 8, 1928 - Nov. 15,
  1929.
Dearholt. Effie J., April 10, 1897 - April 13, 1960. Rev. Moreland E., Aug.
  19, 1893 - Dec. 24, 1951.
John Gartling, June 14, 1856 - June 16, 1941. Wife, Mary E. Gartling, Aug. 30,
  1858 - March 5, 1921. At rest. (.J.G. - M.E.G.).
George Daniel Gartling, April 27, 1894 - May 2, 1961.
Ann Irene Gartling, Jan. 15, 1904 _____.
Simmons, Eleanor, 1886-1958. -blank-.
John H. Klimper, March 22, 1848 - Dec. 30, 1920.

Baby (Baublitz), Oct. 19, 1935.
Baublitz, Carrie B., Nov. 20, 1899. Howard F., Aug. 11, 1884 - Dec. 1965.
Alice Baublitz, Feb. 23, 1889 - May 18, 1929.
BAUM, John W., 1854-1938. Georgianna, 1860-1939. Hoffman.
Harr, Herbert F. Harr, March 30, 1896 - June 5, 1949. Ethel M. Harr, Oct. 29, 1907.
Gartling, William F., 1895-1947. Elizabeth B., 1903-1954. 1929-Charles S.- 1929.
Long.
Mother, Rosella W. Long, 1870-1949.
Ida May, Jan. 29, 1887 - Feb. 7, 1937.
Father, John F. Long, 1864-1952.
Myers, Father, Thomas M., 1880-1944. Mother, Edith V., 1883-1954.
J. Homer Gover, Dec. 16, 1893 - March 15, 1943.
Lloyd, 1st Sgt. Newton J.W., Maryland State Police, 1913-1969. Requiescat in Pace.
Lloyd, C. Virginia, 1913-1962. Requiescat in Pace.
Lloyd, at rest, Maude E.V., 1885-1967.
Charles H. N., 1885-1956.
Charlotte Elaine, dau. of C. Fred and Catherine E. Lloyd, Aug. 2, 1945 - Sept. 1, 1945.
Newton J.W., Jr., son of C. Virginia, Newton J.W. Lloyd, June 2, 1935 - Jan. 31, 1939. Budded on earth to bloom in heaven.
G.C. Alan, infant son of C.H.N. and M.E. Lloyd, Oct. 14, 1922 - Jan. 4, 1923.*
George E. Swem, Aug. 30, 1892 - March 1, 1970.
Blanche A. Swem, 1892-1923.
Gill, Harry E., 1886-1968. Sarah F., 1890-1966.
Wust, Mary E., July 20, 1882 - Feb. 26, 1952. John L., July 31, 1876 - June 21, 1948.
a. (east). Father, John Leonard Wust, April 24, 1812 - Feb. 25, 1896.*
b. (south-left). John Paul Wust, 1877-1891.
c. (rear). W., mother, Anna Barbara Wust, Oct. 8, 1816 - Oct. 3, 1894.*
Wust, Jacob, 1840-1927. Barbara, 1851-1938. (J.W. (B.W.).
Samuel J. Gover, 1849-1935, wife Louisa A., 1835-1925. (L.A.G., S.J.G.).
Adolphine A. Klimper, March 22, 1815 - July 21, 1905. (A.A.K.).*
John H. Klimper, Oct. 14, 1805 - Jan. 28, 1892. (JHK).*
Long, father, Wm. Royden, Aug. 24, 1895 - July 17, 1951. Mother, Marian C., Sept. 1, 1895 - Jan. 9, 1967. (space).
Childs.
James W., Jr., Sept. 16, 1907 - Feb. 10, 1939.
Long, Robert E., Sept. 18, 1880 - March 17, 1958. Hattie Halbert, Nov. 18, 1877 - June 2, 1964.
Florence A. Shaw, 1890-   .
Lark. Toy, 1917-19 . -blank-.
(burial - no stone yet).
Williams, Francis R., 1904-   . E. Marie, 1907-   .
Eric William Gent, July 11, 1971 - July 18, 1971.
Klob, Valentin (monument).
Helena M. Valentin, 1873-1936.
R. John Klob, 1875-1935.
Jeannie Klob, 1881-1932.
Tawney (monument - both sides).
John Thomas Tawney, May 7, 1932 - Nov. 27, 1932.
Alma L. Kelley, Sept. 7, 1895 - Dec. 17, 1934. (A.L.K.).
William F. Kelley, Aug. 17, 1890 - Feb. 27, 1971.

Lark, George W. Lark, 1884-1940. Virginia C. Lark, 1884-1951.
Storm, 1885-William H. Storm-1963. 1888-Emma E. Long, wife-1942. 1926-Earle R. Storm-1941.
Little, James W., 1869-1942. Lillian M., 1877-1967.
Long, John R., 1902-1966. Dorothy A., 1915-   .
Son, Harry R. Gill, 1941-1969.
(new burial - no stone).
Taylor, Harry W., 1891-1963. Grace A., 1891-1956.
Alma W. Taylor, April 9, 1889 - Dec. 25, 1962.
Peter Sarvino, 1892-1940.
Crabson, Harry M., 1889-1968. Bertha E., 1895-1950.
(new burial).
Gartling (monument).
William, 1866-1950.
Mary K., 1881-1964.
Long, Charles H., 1887-1958. Elsie E., 1889-1969.
Nellie M. Gover, Oct. 18, 1889 - Jan. 27, 1952.
Mother, Carrie C. Wieland, 1892-1964.
Forwood (monument - both sides).
Wife, Lillian Elizabeth, Nov. 16, 1916 - Oct. 1, 1955.
Fishpaw, Harry M., 1897-   . Nieta M., 1899-   .
Powers, Harvey M, May 31, 1894 - Dec. 2, 1968. -blank-.
Shaneybrook (monument).
John Conrad, April 28, 1925 - March 9, 1954.
Tawney, Carver L, 1894-   . Ethel G., 1902-1954.
Charles Henry Simmons, 1887-1957.
Raymond B. Beebe, April 9, 1907 - Sept. 3, 1958.
Raver (monument - both sides).
Lester Dearholt Raver, Jan. 29, 1941 - Feb. 23, 1959.
Good, Ellis M., 1914-   . Gretta L., 1915-1964.
Emma E. Hall, Nov. 23, 1873 - Aug. 4, 1967.
Tawney, Pearl A., March 25, 1895. Charles W., April 23, 1893 - Aug. 30, 1968.
Sproul, Calvin L., Sr., March 20, 1906 - Nov. 25, 1968. Florence C., Jan. 5, 1916 -   .
Gill, Raymond L., 1892-   . Beulah P., 1898-1968.
J. Claude Jackson, 1889-1966. Annie E., wife, 1893-   .
Young, Dabney H., 1897-1957. Della, 1900-   . Walter D., 1922-   .
Ruth Fleming Reppert, Aug. 28, 1920 - Sept. 18, 1968.*
Christine Reppert, Jan. 8, 1952 - June 14, 1958.
Sewell, James F., Dec. 27, 1908 - May 18, 1964. Blanche K., July 5, 1901 - Feb. 4, 1968.
Burl Dean Wade, Sept. 6, 1957 - March 12, 1965, son of Leonard and Ruby Wade.
Harman, Robert F., 1901-1968. Mabel M., 1905-   .
Evelyn V. Jackson, 1927-1964.
McCabe, Curtis G., Aug. 11, 1903 - Aug. 16, 1967. Helen G., Dec. 20, 1905 -   .
Whitaker, Casper A., Aug. 8, 1880 - Nov. 16, 1963. Mary A., May 12, 1880 - Feb. 18, 1963.
DeVeas, William A., 1909-1966. Mildred M., 1909-   .
Raver, J. Clifton, Dec. 24, 1892 - Dec. 13, 1964. Nellie J., Feb. 11, 1892 -   .
Jones, husband, Walter W., 1914-1966. Wife, Henriette, 1916-   .
Harr, G. Herbert, May 21, 1928 - Nov. 29, 1966. Beatrice M., May 11, 1928 - Nov. 29, 1966.

GITTINGS FAMILY CEMETERY

Located on De Ford (formerly Gittings) property, off of Long Green Pike north of Long Green Road. Copies Nov. 12, 1973 by Matilda Lacey and Robert Barnes.

James Gittings, April 22, 1790 - Feb. 22, 1829.*
Elizabeth Gittings, consort of James Gittings, she was b. ...1742(?),...1818.
Richard Gittings, b. ...
Mary Gittings...
George Gittings, d. Feb. 2, 1802 (?), in the 32nd year of his age.
John... Ringgold, 1799 - Aug. 4, 1812 (?).
James Gittings, son of Richard and Polly Gittings, b. June 25, 1791.
James Gittings, Sept. 25, 1768 - March 9, 1819.
Mrs. Harriet Gittings, d. Oct. 22, 1828. Age 45 years and 11 (?) days. *
James C. Gittings, d. Aug. 12, 1839, in the 42nd year of his age.
Rebecca Nicols Gittings, wife of James C. Gittings, b. Feb. 11, 1804 - May 13, 1844.*
W. R. S. Gittings, 1830-1897.

FORK CHRISTIAN CEMETERY

John F. Beck, 1898-1948.
G. Marshall Hooper, March 4, 1898 - Sept. 19, 1960.
Temple (Obelisk), Susie A., wife of John B. Temple, d. Nov. 2, 1900. Rena T., dau. of J.B. and S.A. Temple, d. July 13, 1900, aged 1 year and 5 days, f/s Rena and mother.*
John W., son of George K. and Rebecca A. Pearce, d. Dec. 18, 1886, aged 1 year and 15 days.
Alice A., dau. of George K. and Rebecca A. Pearce, d. Nov. 22, 1892, aged 5 years and 6 days.
Rebecca A., wife of George K. Pearce, d. April 28, 1924, aged 82 years and 11 mos.
George K. Pearce, d. May 21, 1900, aged 66 years, 5 mos. and 20 days.
Sisson, Georgia V. Sisson, June 29, 1871 - Dec. 29, 1919.
"Willie", William T., son of Charles C. and Georgia V. Sisson, d. April 18, 1898, aged 10 mos.
L.H. Sisson, July 26, 1833 - July 19, 1918.
Ida May, dau. of Parker and Katie Pearce, 1904-1905.
Pearce, Katie May, 1885-1948, wife of Parker M. Pearce.
Pearce, Parker M. Pearce, 1879-1954.
Hooper, Christopher C. Hooper, June 15, 1857 - March 30, 1901. Mary E. Hooper, wife, Oct. 3, 1855 - July 9, 1924.
Bessie L. Hooper, 1888-1962.
William J. Francis, June 29, 1853 - Dec. 29, 1932, wife, Ida May, Dec. 12, 1864 - April 12, 1929.
Elsie A. Pearce, Webster D. Pearce, 1902-1938.
Sophia Rufenacht, Jan. 13, 1873 - Nov. 4, 1929.
Herman Rufenacht, Oct. 20, 1870 - Nov. 20, 1940.

Sisson, George J., 1872-1949. Lillian, 1874-1950.
Temple (Obelisk), Elma S. Temple, March 8, 1872 - July 9, 1955. N. Edward Temple, Dec. 22, 1857 - Feb. 21, 1932.
Jackson, Ella L., 1891- . Charles R., 1921-1960.
Mary Ellen, wife of N. E. Temple, d. Jan. 21, 1915.*
Charles R. Jackson, Maryland PFC WW II 889 Ord Ham Co., Feb. 6, 1921 - Oct. 21, 1960.
Hall, Lottie J. Wiker, 1875-1943.
Mother, Charlotte J., wife of Charles H. Wiker, d. Aug. 18, 1901.*
Father, Charles H. Wiker, Oct. 28, 1948 - March 19, 1928.
Edith A., dau. of George N. and Amsey E. Orem, d. March 3, 1909, aged 1 mo.
Orem, George N., 1873-1953. Amsey E., 1884- .
Robert H. Robertson, 1860-1934.
Betty M. Robertson, 1877-1950.
Edward A. Robertson, 1827-1908.
Janette A. Robertson, 1835-1909.
Temple, Bateman T., 1878-1941. Katie M., 1884- .
Dorothy Leola, dau. of Bateman and Katie Temple, Aug. 10, 1915 - April 22, 1916.
Roland Bateman, son of Bateman and Katie Temple, Nov. 13, 1908 - Nov. 21, 1908.
Nora Leona, dau. of J. Lester and Mamie B. Smith, d. Dec. 21, 1915, aged 1 year and 7 days.
William Royston, son of J. Lester and Mamie B. Smith, April 26, 1915 - Sept. 1, 1918.
Smith (Obelisk), J. Lester Smith, May 2, 1874 - May 21, 1955, wife, Mamie B., Oct. 13, 1890 - Aug. 6, 1940. Nora, wife of J. Lester Smith, April 21, 1874 - Nov. 7, 1909. Samuel M. Smith, Nov. 5, 1853 - Feb. 15, 1915. Frances, wife of S. N. Smith, b. July 22, 1843.
Bessie W. Dilworth, Jan. 5, 1822 - Nov. 17, 1912. T. F. Smith, March 27, 1868 - Feb. 15, 1916.
J. Lester Smith, May 2, 1874 - May 21, 1955.
Mamie B. Smith, Oct. 13, 1890 Aug. 6, 1940.
Fiefield S., son of Fiefield and Harriet M. Chatterton, d. May 8, 1903.*
(Obelisk), Albert M. League, husband of Sallie P. Magness League, April 23, 1853 - Aug. 15, 1911. Sallie P. Magness, wife of Albert M. League, Oct. 24, 1863 - June 14, 1936. Emery Leroy, only son of Norman E. and Etta League Jackson, April 27, 1910 - Aug. 24, 1910. Walter Clifton, only son of Albert M. and Sallie P. Magness League, April 27, 1887 - Oct. 24, 1887, f/s SML. John McMullen Jackson (dates in ground), Helen Ruth Jackson, 1919-1924. (E.L.J. - W.C.L.).
Sisson, L. H. Sisson, May 15, 1875 - Oct. 12, 1936. Rosetta M. Sisson, July 12, 1880 - March 16, 1953. Genevieve Sisson, Oct. 18, 1915 - April 20, 1918.
Margie M., dau. of Louis H. and Rosie Sisson, d. Nov. 30, 1913.*
George T., son of Tilton and Florence Beares, July 5, 1926 - Aug. 24, 1931.
Earl Samuel, son of Florence and Tilton Beares, Jan. 23, 1929 - Dec. 18, 1945.
Lloyd S., husband of Mildred M. Enderson, Oct. 2, 1907 - Sept. 3, 1932.
Pearce, Alfred W., 1905-1953. Dennis B., 1875-1961. Blanche A., 1882- .
Charles Bevard, March 14, 1841 - July 10, 1885.
Julia Carlin, dau. of Benj. E. and Mary W. Zulauf, Jan. 27, 1919 - Sept. 30, 1918.
Helen Walther, 1892-1950.
Mother, Annie L., wife of Franz Walther, Oct. 11, 1865 - July 7, 1936.
Father, Franz A. Walther, d. July 11, 1911.*
Reynolds, Shelton H. Reynolds, March 17, 1857 - Aug. 23, 1923. Willie A. Reynolds, wife, Nov. 6, 1859 - Feb. 16, 1949.
Ernest S. Marshall, Feb. 15, 1905 - Feb. 29, 1920.
Marshall, Addie M., 1879-1936. Thomas E., 1879-1939.

Marshall, Annie T., Jan. 24, 1848 - Sept. 25, 1928. P. Beverly, April 7, 1846 - April 17, 1926.
Mabel Marshall Coe, 1885-1946.
Ida May, wife of Shelton W. Reynolds, April 26, 1894 - June 25, 1924.
Cloman (Obelisk), Earle W., April 6, 1917 - July 30, 1917. G. Mildred, July 24, 1912 - March 9, 1919.
Temple, Beulah, July 20, 1914 - March 30, 1916. Ellen L., Feb. 26, 1916 - April 20, 1916.
League, C.W. League, June 9, 1842 - Oct. 7, 1924, wife, Belle Magness, Aug. 24, 1861 -   .
Annie M. Shanklin, June 8, 1863 - June 7, 1929.
Franklin, Erma V., Dec. 28, 1916 - Oct. 13, 1932, 15 years.
Gloria M., dau. of J. Raymond and Yvonne Orem, Sept. 5, 1950 - Feb. 4, 1954.
J. Raymond Orem, 1910-1954.
Our Mother, Mamie Norman, d. Jan. 20, 1950, aged 27 years.
J. Harold Horsman, 1903-1959.
Orem, Harold E., 1913-   . Rosie J., 1923-1963.
Elliott, L. Elmer, Nov. 8, 1902 - July 5, 1943.
Baby son of Lehman and Gertrude Clayton, b. and d. 1937.
Mother, Annie Lee Marchman, 1892-1950.
Rufenacht, Carl E., March 20, 1894 - March 7, 1964.
Arthur M. Sisson, May 5, 1880 - Jan. 31, 1959.
Lee A. Sisson, Nov. 4, 1907 - Aug. 10, 1964.
Donald R. McCluskey, 1952-1958.
John E. Baublitz, Maryland PFC TRP C 2 Cavalry World War I, Nov. 11, 1894 - June 15, 1951.
John M., husband of Emma F. Baublitz, Nov. 7, 1871 - Feb. 29, 1924.
Infant children, Emma F. Baublitz - Russell Wagner.

FORK METHODIST CHURCH CEMETERY

Fork M.E. Church established in 1773. One acre of ground given by James J. Baker near the "Forks of the Gunpowder" for Fork's Meeting House. Now known as Fork United Methodist Church. Copies by Matilda C. Lacey and Daisy Watkins in October 1971.

Day, Amanda Jane, July 20, 1825 - Jan. 12, 1826.
Day, Presbury, Nov. 1824 - Dec. 1827.
Day, Adaline, d. Oct. 1, 1856, aged 1 year, 10 mos. and 99 (?) days.
Riddle, Wilbur Hicks, March 30, 1859 - July 5, 1935. M. Augusta Payne, Oct. 31, 1851 - March 30, 1937. Charles Joseph, May 20, 1894 - April 13, 1896.
Gorsuch, James F. H. "Doctor of Medicine", Aug. 1846 - Sept. 1932. Annie P. Riddle, wife of Dr. J. F. H., Nov. 1855 - July 1894. Helen V., April 1, 1885 - Feb. 1929. J. Fletcher H., Jr., (Attorney at Law), Sept. 1899 - Dec. 1938 "Interred in Druid Ridge."
Charity , Aug. 5, 1799 - April 26, 1847.*
Day, Ishmael, March 20, 1792 - Dec. 27, 1872.*
Day, Ann E, wife of Ishmael Day, March 11, 1805 - Dec. 6, 1868.*
Riddle, Charles Joseph, March 22, 1823 - Dec. 21, 1898. Husband of Louisa Day, Feb. 28, 1830 - Feb. 13, 1914.*
Phillips, Cecelia, wife of J. William Phillips and dau. of Samuel and Charity Day, May 28, 1840 - April 25, 1911.*

Harrison, F. George, Feb. 14, 1861 - July 13, 1954.
Mobray Crewe. John W., 1844-1888. Georgia, 1861-1947. Joseph, 1873-1933.
Wilson, George Washington, d. Jan. 16, 1851. Aged 11 years, 5 mos. and 18 days.*
Herron, Mary Elizabeth, dau. of L. D. and Sally P. Herron, Feb. 1. 1865 - June 26, 1865.*
Hall, Eliza, wife of Edward C. Hall, d. April 10, 1869 (verse illegible).*
Hall, Edward C., d. Feb. 19, 1859.*
Hall, Lee, 1855-1855 (?) (cannot truly determine dates).
Hall, Richard C. Hall, Sept. 23, 1826 - Aug. 5, 1849.
Hall, Fred W., Nov. 9, 1813 - Nov. 13, 1841.
Hall, Sam M., Dec. 1811 - Aug. 29, 1835.
Hall, Blanch H., d. Sept. 25, 1855.*
Hall, Robert Lyon, Dec. 12, 1781 - March 24, 1847.
Clayton, George E., 1883-1952. Eva M., 1882-1939.
Clayton. Footstone: John E., 1881-1957.
Clayton, Beulah Leona, dau. of J. E. and Lillian Clayton, d. Sept. 21, 1913. Aged 4 mos. and 21 days.*
Flowers.
Ray, Lorraine A., 1931-1938.
Blakistone, Herbert H., 1840-1916. His wife, Emma McCubbin, 1852-1905.
McCubbin, Martha, 1827-1899.
Ray, Harry C., 1889-1944.
Ray, Dorothy W., 1892-1965.
Magness, Susan Ida, dau. of Joseph and Julia I. Magness, May 7, 1800 - May 18, 1867 (verse illegible).
Magness, Mary Lucretia, d. Aug. 27, 1818, aged 4 years, 6 mos. and 25 days (verse illegible).
Treadwell, Stephenson Treadwell, Jan. 19, 1777 - Dec. 11, 1863.
Treadwell, Nellie, dau. Stephen Treadwell, d. April 2, 1877.*
Treadwell, John W., Feb. 21, 1812 - Oct. 5, 1877.
Treadwell, Mary A. Treadwell, wife of John W. Treadwell, d. Jan. 17, 1865.*
Hitchock, Daniel W., 1878-1955. Mary E., 1884-1932.
Blakeley, Richard, 1854-   . Mary E., 1860-1929.
Francis, Charles, May 13, 1780 - Oct. 20, 1855.*
Francis, Charles H., son of (illegible), Jan. 7, 1860 - Aug. 27, 1861.
Blakeley, husband, John Blakeley, d. Feb. 8, 1911.*
Blakeley, wife, Elizabeth, d. Sept. 15, 1911.*
Dodson, baby, John M. Dodson.
Proctor, Frances M., Nov. 3, 1831 - July 19, 1858. Dau. of Robert and Mary Proctor.
Coleman, Pleasance, July 17, 1831 - Nov. 29, 1863. Wife of William Gorsuch.
Proctor. Our sister Amanda Proctor, March 12, 1838 - June 25, 1882.*
Proctor. Our father, Robert S., Jan. 3, 1793 - Jan. 22, 1883.*
Proctor. Our mother, Mary, June 17, 1798 - June 5, 1887.*
Proctor. Our sister, Rebecca J., Feb. 23, 1825 - Feb. 25, 1903.*
Proctor, Caroline, Feb. 1, 1827 - March 15, 1904.*
Richardson, Elizabeth, 1823-1923, wife of J. T. Richardson.
Richardson, J. Thomas, 1825-1855, husband of E. T. Richardson.
Kuban.
Day, Luther L., Nov. 2, 1828 - Jan. 30, 1905. He giveth his beloved sleep.
Day, Elizabeth F., Dec. 10, 1829 - Aug. 5, 1862, wife of Luther Day.*
Clayton, Howard C., son of Wells and Mary E. Clayton, April 15, 1849 - Dec. 24, 1858.
Clayton, Wells Clayton, consort of Mary D. Clayton and son of Joseph and Sarah Clayton, Jan. 9, 1822 - Dec. 8, 1857.*
Clayton, Joseph Clayton, March 1778 - Feb. 8, 1852.*
Clayton, Sarah, d. Oct. 31, 1868.*

Clayton, husband, Issac F. Clayton, d. March 24, 1916.*
Pearce. Mother Esther Ann Smith, wife of George R. Pearce, d. July 28, 1915.*
Pearce, Charles B., son of George B. and A. Pearce, d. Aug. 1, 1898, aged 17 mos. (verse illegible).
Francis (double stone). Isaac Francis, Aug. 3, 1821 - Jan. 20, 1900. Maria Francis, Sept. 22, 1823 - Feb. 5, 1904.
Bayne, Sarah P., wife of F. M. Bayne, Jan. 31, 1851 - Jan. 28, 1883 (verse illegible).
Groves, Marion, son of J. and M. Groves, Jan. 28, 1888 - Aug. 8, 1888.*
Groves, Martha Ellen, wife of John H. Groves, May 20, 1857 - March 1, 1888 (verse illegible).
Willingham, Mary C. Willingham, Oct. 5, 1882 - Feb. 14, 1962.
Blakeley, Mary, Jan. 5, 1855 - Nov. 15, 1929. Amoss, Aug. 1, 1859 - Feb. 24, 1924.
Bond, wife, Althea Ellen, wife of William H. Bond, Oct. 8, 1878 - May 29, 1941.*
Bond, husband, William H., Dec. 13, 1871 - Sept. 18, 1921.*
Bond, William R., d. Oct. 9, 1882, aged 51 years, 8 mos. and 19 days (balance illegible).*
Bond, J. Nicholas Bond, d. Jan. 4, 1886.*
Bond, John Bond, Feb. 12, 1812 - Feb. 9, 1872.
Bond, Catherine M., wife of John Bond, d. May 5, 1905.*
Beares, Susan Beares (illegible).
Wells, John Wells, d. March 30, 1803.*
Bond, Webster D. Bond, husband of Martha J. Bond, d. May 25, 1908.*
Bond, Martha E., dau. of Webster D. and Martha J. Bond, d. Dec. 21, 1909.*
Bond, Ella, dau. of Calvin and Hannah Bond, d. Sept. 23, 1918.*
Meyers, Baldwin W. Meyers, Nov. 28, 1834 - Dec. 16, 1886.*
Meyers, Mary D. Meyers, Oct. 19, 1850 - Aug. 6, 1881 (verse difficult to read).*
Schuman, Louis, 1862-1937. Elizabeth B., 1857-1937.
Bond, David F. Bond, d. March 20, 1910.*
Smith, M. J., 1878-1935.
Bond, Calvin A., son of David F. and Mary J. Bond, d. Jan. 12, 1919.*
Pearce, J. Pearce, son of David F. and Mary J. Bond, d. Aug. 31, 1911. Aged 8 years.*
Dahler (double stone), George Dahler, d. Jan. 20, 1908 (balance illegible).*
Dohler, William George, son of George and Amanda Dohler, d. July 24, 1904.*
Dohler, Sarah E., dau. of George and Amanda Dohler, d. June 21, 1867.*
Turner. Sister. Helen Virginia, dau. of William and Alice Lancaster Turner, Jan. 15, 1894 - Sept. 11, 1914.*
Lancaster, husband. E. Hudson Lancaster, Sept. 29, 1852 - March 28, 1908.*
Lancaster. Martha A., wife of E. H. Lancaster, d. Dec. 1, 1895 (verse illegible).*
Lancaster, ...
Dilworth, Randolph R., son of Geo. and Sarah Dilworth, d. Aug. 30, 1890.*
Dilworth, George Dilworth, 1835-1915. Sarah Ann, wife of George Dilworth, d. April 2, 1931.*
Booker, Hannah, wife of Joseph Booker, d. Sept. 6, 1852.*
Booker, Elizabeth, dau. of Joseph and Hannah Booker, d. Aug. 12, 1852.
Foard, Robert Foard, Oct. 3, 1874 - Feb. 17, 1881. Louisa Ann, wife of Robert Foard, Sept. 13, 1818 - Dec. 2, 1865. Mary C., Thomas O., William E., James L., Uriah B., children of R. and L. A. Foard.
Holland, (illegible).
Clayton, Elizabeth Clayton, d. Jan. 11, 1887 (illegible).*
Clayton, Rebecca, wife of Elijah Clayton, d. Aug. 14, 1893.*
Clayton, Garrett, son of Elijah and Rebecca Clayton, Oct. 24, 1850 - June 1, 1855 (verse illegible).
Illegible.

Wisnom, Zellor, dau. of A. and T. Wisnom, d. March 13, 1882, aged 17 mos. and 23 days (verse illegible).
Wisnom, Emily Jane, dau. of A. and T. Wisnom, d. Aug. 1, 1887, aged 17 mos. and 15 days.*
Wisnom, father, Alexander Wisnom, d. Nov. 24, 1890.*
Wisnom, mother, Temperance R., wife of Alexander H. W., d. Aug. 2, 1917.*
Parker, dau. Ida May Parker, dau. of Alex and T. Wisnom, d. April 2, 1903 (verse illegible).*
Parker, James Parker, 1871-1951.
Watkins, infant son of Burton and Helen Watkins, d. May 7, 1918.
Watkins, Isaiah Slade, son of John Watkins, 1831-1904.
Watkins, Anne M., wife of Isaiah Watkins, b. Nov. 24, 1857 (illegible).*
Watkins, George W., ..., April 3, 1851 - Sept. 18, 1855.
Watkins, Eliza Rebecca, dau. of Horatio Burton, 1844-1966 (?).
Blair, Stephen H., son of Alice and ... Blair, d. Jan. 1, 1865, aged 2 years.
McClure, James McClure, March 10, 1798 - Jan. 30, 1839.*
Baldwin, Mary Baldwin, .. (illegible) (native stone-amateur carving).
Francis, father, William Francis, d. Nov. 17, 1852 (illegible).*
Francis, Elizabeth R. Francis, d. Feb. 17, 1878.*
Meyer, sister, Christiana Meyer, Nov. 11, 1810 - July 8, 1843. Brother, Louis Meyer, Feb. 13, 1844 - July 8, 1844.
Meyer, father, Henry Meyer, Dec. 16, 1800 - Feb. 19, 1878.*
Meyer, mother, Christiana Meyer, Dec. 11, 1808 - May 20, 1877.
Meyer, husband, John L. Meyer, 1878-1962, wife Agnes, 1887-....
Meyer (double stone), father, Henry R. F. Meyer, Oct. 19, 1822 - Nov. 2, 1888. Anne Catherine, Dec. 18, 1838 - Dec. 30, 1906.*
Bawell, Hannah H. F., wife of Daniel Bawell, d. Aug. 31, 1889.*
Clayton (double stone), father, Josiah N. Clayton, June 17, 1812 - March 13, 1893. Mother, Amelia M., wife of Josiah Clayton, March 22, 1816 - Sept. 19, 1881.*
Doyle, James Doyle, Feb. 24, 1834 - Jan. 27, 1882.*
Clayton, Agnes E., March 10, 1881 - June 8, 1932. Wilbur, Sr., Feb. 11, 1870 - Nov. 9, 1949.
Pearce, mother, Sophia Pearce, Nov. 17, 1820 - Jan. 8, 1872.*
Dampman, husband, William Dampman, Jan. 20, 1812 - Sept. 22, 1876.
Dampman, mother, Catherine, wife of William Dampman, 1815 - Aug. 25, 1905.*
Dampman, Catherine Rebecca, dau. of W. and C. Dampman, Aug. 3, 1854 - Dec. 12, 1860. Aged 6 years, 4 mos. and 9 days.
Dampman, husband, Albert H. Dampman, d. March 2, 1866.*
Proctor, Wilbur Proctor, 1860-1943.
Francis, brother, Charles S. Francis, son of William and Elizabeth R. Francis, May 10, 1817 - March 29, 1885 (verse illegible).
Allender, July 30, 1880. Lizzie only child of Mont. and Mollie Allender (verse illegible).*
Carter, Joshua Carter, d. March 7, 1862.*
Holland, sister, Mary A. Holland, dau. of Robert and Mary Proctor, d. July 19, 1868.*
George, George, George E., d. Aug. 19, 1887.*
Dahler (double stone), father, Andrew Dahler, d. Sept. 3, 1906. Mother, Margaret George, wife of Andrew Dahler, d. April 19, 1907.*
Proctor, Mary Ellen, dau. of Joshua and Frances Proctor, d. March 9, 1869.*
Carter, Joshua Carter, d. March 7, 1862.*
Hale, Sarah J. W. Hale, 1823-1907. Annie Day Hale, 1857-1884. Helen A. Bisselle, 1855-1914. Cordella W. Hale, 1865-1917. Footstones: A.D.H.-C.W.H. - H.A.B.
Smith, Joseph A. Smith, Feb. 22, 1810 - Oct. 10, 1878.*
Smith, infant son of Annie A. and the late Joseph A. Smith.

Frick, Conrad Frick, June 21, 1848 - Sept. 28, 1880.*
Frick, Henry Edwin, son of Conrad and Mary E. Frick, d. Aug. 4, 1873. Aged 11 mos. Footstones: H.E.F.-M.O.F.
G.H.A.
H.A.
Arthur, Mary E., wife of George H. Arthur, d. Oct. 1, 1873. George H., d. Oct. 18, 1881. Aged 11 days. Lillie, d. Jan. 14, 1893. Aged 4 years and 29 days. May d. 1892. Aged 2 years.*
Magness, Julia Ann, wife of Stephen P. Magness, Nov. 9, 1837 - April 5, 1868. Annie Florence, dau. of S. P. and the late Julia A. Magness, Dec. 8, 1865 - April 14, 1868.*
Treadwell, Susan, wife of Wm. S. Treadwell, May 26, 1803 - June 16, 1877.
Treadwell, William S. Treadwell, Dec. 21, 1810 - Aug. 17, 1888 (verse illegible).
Treadwell, Elizabeth M. Mordew, wife of Wm. S. Treadwell, April 17, 1840 - April 24, 1917.*
Stone down.
Guyton, Rebecca Guyton, d. Feb. 15, 1882.*
Guyton, Henry Guyton, d. Nov. 14, 1877.*
Franciscus, Frances Franciscus, d. Feb. 10, 1876.*
Guyton, Samuel Guyton, d. Oct. 20, 1873.*
Guyton, Elizabeth, wife of Samuel Guyton, d. March 18, 1883.*
Clayton, John W. Clayton, Jan. 8, 1798 - Jan. 26, 1872.
Clayton, Ann, wife of John W. Clayton, Jan. 12, 1803 - Feb. 22, 1872.
Wright, Caleb Wright, husband of Annie R. Wright, Aug. 1, 1855 - Feb. 12, 1889 (verse illegible).
Wright, mother, Ruth A. McCubbin, 1860-1902. Children, Henrietta King, Sophia Duvall, Helen Amoss, Edith R. Graff, 1879-1906.
Raynard, Florence Raynard, b. June 28, 1885 (rest underground).
Gorsuch, Sarah E., dau. of Wm. and Caroline M. Gorsuch, Aug. 11, 1893. William Gorsuch, d. Nov. 1870. Caroline M., wife of Wm. Gorsuch, d. March 27, 1900.*
Gorsuch, Hattie, wife of ... Gorsuch, Aug. 28, 1815 - Oct. 16, 1880 (verse illegible).
Gorsuch, Benjamin Wilson Gorsuch, Dec. 24, 1844 - Jan. 8, 1928.*
Gorsuch, Emma F., wife of B. W. Gorsuch, 1851-1902.*
Proctor, Maud G., dau. of John C. and Mary Proctor, b. Oct. 18, 1872. Aged 1 year and 11 mos.
Grummer, Feb. 11, 1885. Nathaniel Grummer, aged 23 years.
Cassaday, Sarah E. Cassaday, May 7, 1853 - Nov. 3, 1927. Clayton J. Franklin, son of J. G. and S. E. Clayton, b. Nov. 10. Blakeley, 1880 - Dec. 16, 1915. Joseph Blakeley, June 14, 1858 - Aug. 14, 1895.
Clayton, E. Clayton.
Mast, Malinda J. Mast, 1857-1929.*
Beares, John Beares, d. May 30, 1884 (verse illegible).*
Beares, Sarah R., wife of John Beares, d. Sept. 9, 1888. Footstones: SRB-JB.*
Watkins, John Watkins, Feb. 26, 1803 - May 25, 1878. Minerva Slade Watkins, Aug. 3, 1811 - Sept. 3, 1818.
Watkins, William Paret, son of Samuel and G. Blanch Watkins, May 12, 1898 - Sept. 3, 1898.*
Watkins, Emma B., dau. of J. B. and Clara I. Watkins, Feb. 17, 1876 - April 27, 1879.*
Watkins, John Beale Watkins, 1838-1905. Footstone: J.B.W.
Watkins, Clare A. Watkins, 1846-1923. Footstone: C.A.W.
Watkins, Samuel, July 10, 1870 - Jan. 22, 1947. C. Blanche Bagley, June 16, 1876 - July 11, 1955.
Carman, Elijah Carman, Jan. 13, 1802 - Nov. 7, 1859. Lucretia, wife of Elijah Carman, May 22, 1798 - Feb. 13, 1872. Ellingsworth Carroll, son of Elijah

and Lucretia Carman, Sept. 29, 1837 - Aug. 7, 1905. Esther Ann, dau. of Elijah and Lucretia Carman, Jan. 1, 1831 - Oct. 10, 1911. Lucretia Eleanor, dau. of Elijah and Lucretia Carman, Aug. 10, 1832 - March 15, 1859. Martha Elizabeth, wife of F. F. Brognard, dau. of E. and L. Carman, March 11, 1829 - June 6, 1870. Mary Emily, dau. of E. and L. Carman, Nov. 6, 1834 - June 5, 1928.
Brognard, Mary S., June 15, 1852 - July 22, 1852. Frank G., Aug. 17, 1853 - Sept. 9, 1921, children of F. F. and Martha E. Brognard.
Carman, Annie B. Carman, Nov. 19, 1877 - Jan. 11, 1921, dau. of Caleb C. and Annie E. Carman.
Carman, Charles Clinton, son of Caleb C. and Annie E. Carman, June 26, 1870 - June 13, 1910.
Carman, Caleb C. Carman, d. March 8, 1917.*
Carman, Annie Eliza, wife of Caleb C. Carman and dau. of Thomas and Mary Foard, d. May 12, 1885.*
Carman, Caleb E., son of C. C. and A. E. Carman, d. March 22, 1883. Aged 5 days.
Carman, Thomas Elijah, d. Sept. 19, 1881. Aged 13 weeks. Emma Bulah, d. Sept. 20, 1881. Aged 1 year, 3 mos. and 27 days, children of C. C. and A. E. Carman.
Carman, Mary Lancaster, dau. of C. C. and Annie E. Carman, Feb. 15, 1876 - July 3, 1876.
Carman, Benjamin F. Carman, son of C. C. and Annie E. Carman, July 25, 1867 - July 17, 1808 (??).
Carman, Lily Carman, dau. of C. C. and Annie E. Carman, July 21, 1866 - Aug. 10, 1866.
Appel, John H., Dec. 30, 1863 - Jan. 30, 1926. Emma, wife, Aug. 15, 1867 - Jan. 30, 1919.
Appel, John H. Appel, 1892-1959. Bertha Appel, 1895-   .
Appel, infant, dau. of John H. and Bertha Appel, d. April 3, 1920.*
Montgomery, George R., 1867-1943. Wm. B. Campbell, 1905-1929. Florence M., 1873-1964.
Campbell, Stanley G., 1900-1947.
Beares. Footstones: Son, William D., 1872-1950. Son, G. Thomas, 1882-1940. Mother, Sarah E., 1849-1926. Father, George H. 1849-1929.
Sample, baby, Lillian Marie.
Sauers, father, Joseph B., 1906-1940. Grandfather, W. Howard, 1881-1947.
Sauers, Mary Catherine Fischer, wife of Howard Sauer, d. Nov. 10, 1818.*
Sauers, William, infant son of W. H. and M. C. Sauers, b. and d. on Nov. 4, 1918.
Nolan, Joseph E., 1884-1933. Agnes E., 1886-   .
Ries, George F., Jan. 30, 1887 - March 27, 1968. Husband of Agnes E. (Nolan) Ries.
Dahler, Flora A., 1887-   . J. Henry, 1872-1957.*
Sample, H. F., March 31, 1868 - Feb. 27, 1936. Florence M., wife, d. Oct. 17, 1918.*
Sample, George, baby, son of H. F. and F. M. Sample, d. Sept. 22, 1918. Aged 1 month, only sleeping.
Boyd, Earl Ewing, March 10, 1953 - April 19, 1953.
Needer, Francis J., 1877-1943. Annie B., 1879-1930. Their sons, Francis M.W., 1916-1917. Walter P., 1924-1939. George, 1902-1963.
Kirkolian, Arthur, 1892-1949.
Grayson, Jesse R., 1884-   . Martha V., 1884-1964.
Pearce, Ernest C., 1895-1970. Bertha M., 1900-   .
Pearce, Erma Louise, dau. of Ernest and Bertha Pearce. Edith Estella, March 1, 1923 - March 3, 1923.
Pearce, Albert Leroy, infant son of Ernest and Bertha Pearce, b. and d. June 11, 1919.*
Wisnom. Headstone: Footstones: Clayton Wisnom, 1870-1941. Margaret Wisnom, 1867-1934.

Holland, George H., 1892-1966. Pearl C., 1899- .
Holland, George Arthur, Aug. 7, 1924 - Nov. 20, 1969.
Collins, Thomas L., Maryland Sgt. 9301 Tech. S.U.C. Unit, World War II, July 7, 1926 - Jan. 9, 1971.
Byer, Mary Ida, mother, 1913-1965.
Ford, Giles F., Petty Officer 3rd Class, July 30, 1948 - July 17, 1969.
Berl, Annie K., 1908-1967. Marion F., 1910- .
Pickens, Erma M., 1918- . George W., 1916-1969.
Hagy, husband, Jacob T., 1881-1965. Wife, Lena B., 1894- .
Hagy, Hubert H., son of J. T. and L. B. Hagy, Oct. 25, 1919 - April 14, 1922.
Dilworth, father, Francis, 1852-1920. Mother, Jane W., 1850-1925.
Wisnom, Mildred Alverta, dau. of Wilmer and Laura M. Wisnom, d. Feb. 21, 1908. Aged 8 mos. and 25 days.*
Baublitz, Charles, 1873-1946.
Mulligan, Sarah Frances, wife of George Mulligan, Nov. 11, 1871 - March 16, 1916.
Clayton, Arthur R., 1871-1944. Lilly, 1872-1936.
Clayton, A. Raymond, March 20, 1905 - March 14, 1953. Clayton, Edward L., 1911-1937.
Byer, John G., 1880-1958. Rosa L., 1882- .
Byer, Edward Carl, Oct. 10, 1907 - Nov. 10, 1968.
Foard, Percy Foard, June 12, 1894 - Aug. 21, 1965. Lola Brown, May 18, 1896 - .
Carter, David I., 1861-1944. Margaret V., 1862-1944.
Everett, Robert Gordon, 1884-1960.
Dilworth, Julius D., husband of Emma I., Nov. 20, 1930 - Feb. 21, 1864 (??).*
Isennock, Maurice E., Dec. 14, 1894 - Feb. 28, 1971. Sarah E., Sept. 7, 1908 - .
?
?
Arthur, John Arthur and his wife, M. Elizabeth. Dau., Florence Arthur James, 1885. Son, Clarence E., 1880-1957 and wife, Lucy G. Arthur, 1875-1956. Jessie F., wife of Clarence E. Arthur, Feb. 10, 1878 - Sept. 12, 1907.
Footstones: M.E. Arthur 1857-1952. John Arthur 1849-1926.*
Roberts, Elizabeth, 1888-1930.
Roberts, Melvin, son of H. H. and Elizabeth Roberts, May 20, 1918 - Oct. 17, 1918.*
Roberts, Roy Henry, son of H. H. and Elizabeth Roberts, Jan. 3, 1913 - May 4, 1915.*
Russell. Footstones: Harry W. Russell, 1882-1958. Florence M. Russell, 1881-1933. Lillian C. Russell, 1902-1962.
Bowers, Joseph M., 1890-1960, husband. Clara F., 1891-1952, wife.
Allbright, Edna, 1909-1950, wife.
Phipps. Footstones: Clifton P. Phipps, Sept. 14, 1919 - June 13, 1954. E. Rosalie, Feb. 3, 1926 - .
Loy-Rhodes, John E., 1900- . Hilda M., 1899- . Virginia, 1881-1969. John H., 1895-1971.
Barrett, William E., 1929- . Estelle M., 1934-1965.
Treadwell, Edward B. Treadwell, Jan. 11, 1861 - Jan. 1, 1925. Footstones: E.B.T. and I.M.T.
Jeffers, Evans, father-Ogden S., 1840-1921. Mother, Sarah E., 1849-1937. Martha R., 1876-1940. William W., 1856-1934.
Mast, Annie Mast, wife of Samuel C. Mast, March 12, 1887 - July 10, 1912. Samuel Porter, July 2, 1912 - July 3, 1913. Queenie Nan, July 2, 1912 - July 30 1912. Twin children of Samuel and Annie Mast.
Dilworth. Footstones: George E. Dilworth, 1863-1947. Martha J. Dilworth, 1862-1944.

Clayton, Ross D. Clayton, Dec. 23, 1909 - Aug. 9, 1964. Hazel R. Clayton, March 23, 1910 - .
Kyle, Francis Allen, July 3, 1958 - Jan. 27, 1959.
Kyle. Headstone: Footstones: Earl C. Kyle, Maryland, P.F.C., 486 Bomb Cr. A.A.F., World War II, Jan. 2, 1919 - June 26, 1964. Lee Jackson Kyle, 1884-1959. Kate I. Kyle, 1894- .
Kyle, W. Armour, March 24, 1917 - Nov. 9, 1968.
Moorefield, James H., 1882-1949.
Dunkes, father, Albert M. Dunkes, Aug. 7, 1900 - April 4, 1957.
Wright. Footstones: Frank E., 1800-1958. Margaret R. .....
Flowers, Harry E. Flowers, 1901-1966. Gladys E., 1908- .
Beyer, Herman Beyer, Sept. 12, 1895 - Jan. 14, 1966. Rose R. Beyer, Aug. 21, 1891 - June 23, 1967.
Mobray. Footstones: Walter C., 1880-1926. Sarah G., 1878- .
Clayton: Footstones: Father, Harry M., 1886-1926. Mother, Sadie Eck, 1890-1952. Son, Alvin M., 1920-1927.
Clayton, Mary Elizabeth, dau. of H. M. and S. A. Clayton, April 15, 1914 - Sept. 5, 1914.*
Foard, Leonard Foard, 1859-1919. Wife, M. Lillie Foard, d. May 9, 1939. J. Stanley Foard, 1893-1965. Wife, Mary L. Foard, d. .....
Willig, Herman H., 1886-1967. Tressie L., 1890- . Footstone: Willig, Martin, 1828-1921.
Willig, baby infant dau. of Herman H., and Tressie L., b. and d. Dec. 27, 1911.*
Woodhouse. Footstone: James W., 1917-1936.
Nafzinger, Moses E., Nov. 1, 1857 - Dec. 13, 1939. Emma C., March 29, 1866 - April 2, 1950.
Breidenbaugh. Footstones: Christian P., 1888-1952. Lillie - March 1889 - .
Breidenbaugh, John C., Dec. 22, 1882 - March 29, 1958. Ida E., Jan. 8, 1886 - .
Tombaugh (2 small stones), E. C., 1946-1946. W. L., 1943-1943.
Schweikart, Voelker M., 1892-1952.
Schweikart, Harry, 1885-1960.
Schweikart, Elizabeth, 1861-1951.
Schweikart, Martin, 1855-1940.
Russell. Footstones: Wade H., 1890-1971. Mabel, 1887-1967.
Isennock. Footstones: George Price, Jan. 1, 1877 - Dec. 18, 1867. Georgia Ella, Jan. 24, 1885 - April 8, 1965.
Fox, Alice A. DeGruchy, 1882-1963. George, 1876-1967.
Johnson, Augustus C., 1877-1960. Annie M., 1877-1961.
Mohrig, Charles R., April 19, 1839 - Sept. 22, 1920. Father, Eliza A., Jan. 4, 1854 - Feb. 14, 1923. Mother.
Johnson, George H. Johnson, 1879-1914, son.*
Foard, Albert T., 1853-1906. Laura C., 1853-1935.
Foard, Ida, wife of Walter P. Reckord, 1884-1925.
Carter.
Grover. Footstones: Charles W., 1867-1941. Marian E., 1874-1935.
Snyder, Jessie G., . William I., 1848-1962.
Popp, Adam W., Jr., 1907- . Julia E., 1912- .
Kolb, George A., July 8, 1880 - Feb. 26, 1965. Daisy A., July 3, 1884 - Dec. 24, 1961.
Clayton, Jesse A., 1878-1948. Anna F., 1882-1963.
Haile, George M. Haile, 1850-1920. Emma Foard, wife of George M. Haile, 1855-1913.*
Foard, Sylvester Foard, d. March 4, 1893. Aged 6 years, 5 mos. and 13 days.
Sally Deets, d. Feb. 28, 1893. Aged 5 years, and 2 days. Children of George M. and Emma Foard Haile.
Mast, J. G. Mast, 1877-1948. Lillie May, wife of J. G. Mast, 1879-1920. Drucilla, dau. of J. G. and L. M. Mast, 1903-1919.

Mast, Millard G., d. Jan. 2, 1911. Aged 2 years, 10 mos. and 23 days (verse illegible).
Kyle, Clara, wife of James Kyle, May 9, 1896 - Aug. 22, 1938. James Kyle, 1889-1970.
Murray. Footstones: Father, Irven W., 1882-1961. Mother, Louisa M., 1884-1956. Son, William, 1919-1942.
Lancaster, mother, Emma May, 1872-1947.
Carter, John B., Maryland P.F.C. U.S. Army, World War I, April 21, 1888 - June 13, 1960.
Snavely. Footstones: Louise Chase, May 3, 1888 - May 11, 1963. Ada Rittenhouse, Sept. 23, 1884 - Oct. 29, 1948. Guy Everett, Oct. 26, 1881. Emma Rohrer, Dec. 18, 1859 - May 17, 1937. Charles G., Feb. 21, 1860 - July 24, 1953.
Bennett. Footstones: Thomas F., Sept. 18, 1870 - March 9, 1962. Anna Mary, May 8, 1879 - Jan. 4, 1957.
Offutt. Footstones: Wife, Marie W., 1910- . Husband, Lowell H., 1903-1957.
Watkins. Footstones: John Watkins, 1880-1967. Lillian T., 1876-1970. Harry G. Watkins, 1873-1958.
Dilworth. Footstones: Francis L., 1902-1966. Inez U., 1903- .
Pearce, Thomas Pearce, Aug. 27, 1848 - Oct. 30, 1928. Georgeanna Pearce, June 21, 1859 - Dec. 21, 1932.*
Burton, William Burton, 1827-1902. Susanna H. Burton, 1846-1918. Charles Gorsuch, 1848-1911.
Hinks, Margaret J., March 14, 1866 - Jan. 21, 1916.
Keefer, Mary E., 1937-1938.
Bowen, mother, Jane Elizabeth, wife of Benjamin F. Bowen, d. Feb. 13, 1905 (verse illegible).*
Hofferbert. Footstones: Husband, John, 1872-1941. Wife, Lena, 1877-1964. Husband, John Randall, 1902-1954.
Eisner, John Edward, July 29, 1890 - March 2, 1971. Helen C., Jan. 23, 1894 - .
Daylor, Adam G., 1886-1960. Mary B., 1891-1956.
Altevogt, Elizabeth, 1888-1954.
Clayton, Jim, May 25, 1927 - July 27, 1961.
Chenoweth, Margaret A., 1879-1940.
Burton. Footstones: C. Walter, 1883-1936. Mary Foard.....
Jordan. Footstones: Father, John H., 1881-1949. Mother, Marie K., 1884-1941.
Jordan, John W., 1915-1969. Florence E., 1916-....
Wells, Paris M., 1872-1947. P.F.C.A. Curtis Wells, Dec. 3, 1925 - Feb. 7, 1945.*
Duncan, Richard, son of Dewey C. and Willie E. Duncan, June 13, 1943.
Marken, Ora C., Aug. 6, 1892 - Aug. 21, 1944. Mary A., Aug. 22, 1885 - Dec. 15, 1953.
Marken, Jack G., Sr., March 29, 1914 - . Lillian E., Nov. 16, 1915 - July 31, 1968.
Pannill, William C., 1895-1956. Lillian M., 1894- .
Zulauf. Footstones: Benjamin F., 1886-1966. Mary A., 1889-1960.
Eckhart, Clarence E., Nov. 8, 1902. Elizabeth L., Aug. 9, 1904 - Aug. 3, 1970.
Lancaster, Frank X., Maryland P.F.C. BTEVC Coast Arty, World War II, Sept. 18, 1908 - March 9, 1911.
Clayton, Elmer L., 1900-1953. Footstones: Baby son of Elmer and Ethel Clayton, b. and d. May 6, 1942. Baby son of Elmer and Ethel Clayton, b. and d. Aug. 27, 1929. Baby son of Lehman and Gertrude Clayton, b. and d. 1935.
Wilgis, Van E., 1860-1924. Elizabeth B., 1868-1927.*
Hall, Preston R., Jan. 1, 1900 - Feb. 1, 1965. Mary M. nee Wilgis, Sept. 18, 1905 - .

Wilgis, William Stewart Albert, son of Van E. and Elizabeth O. Wilgis, d. March 20, 1903. Aged 16 mos.*
Cranston. Footstones: Father W. Laurence, Dec. 1, 1868 - Nov. 11, 1962. Mother, Mollie C., Oct. 17, 1869 - Oct. 12, 1951.
Mumma. Footstones: Elmer L., 1907-1957. M. Virginia, 1907-1949.
Dunty, James Harvey, June 29, 1891 - May 8, 1949. Della G. DeGruchy, Dec. 16, 1887 - March 3, 1949.
Appel, Ross Clarence Appel, Aug. 23, 1904 - Oct. 9, 1969.
Cornthwaite, wife, Virginia D., 1862-1933. Husband, Howard J., 1855-....
Dilworth, William Dilworth, 1845-1901. Emma E. Dilworth, 1851-1929.*
DeGruchy, David J. R., 1856-1939. Came to America from Jersey C.I. England 1873. His wife, Mary Grace Blakeley, 1858-1938. D.J.R.De.G. - M.G.B.De.G.
Butler, Recardy Lee, wife of Benjamin B. Butler, Oct. 28, 1845 - Jan. 19, 1882.*
Butler, Benjamin F., d. May 14, 1901.*
Orem, husband and wife Isaac Orem, Aug. 31, 1851 - Oct. 28, 1937. Susan, his wife, Jan. 8, 1848 - Nov. 3, 1917.*
Eck, Phillip A., Aug. 3, 1867 - Aug. 5, 1911. Hannah A., wife of Phillip A. and dau. of George and Amanda Dahler, Feb. 25, 1866 - Oct. 24, 1910.*
Eck, John T., 1877-   . Mary E., 1873-
Stocksdale, Anna Belle, Feb. 18, 1852 - Feb. 25, 1934. Albert J., May 30, 1845 - Aug. 23, 1921. Leonard A., April 4, 1881 - Aug. 25, 1932.
Blackeley, Lewis, husband of Ann E. Blakeley, d. 1913-   .*
Blakeley, Ann E. Blakeley, wife of Lewis.
Lancaster, C. Leonard, 1875-1965.
Clayton, Robert L., 1863-1940. Sena M., 1882-1970. Footstones: William L. Clayton, Aug. 19, 1894 - Sept. 11, 1945.*
Lancaster, William, son of Charles and Emma Lancaster, d. May 3, 1903.
Lancaster, Ethel, dau. of Charles and Emma Lancaster, d. Sept. 1902.
Lancaster, Ralph N., son of Charles and Emma Lancaster. Leonard E., son of Charles and Emma Lancaster.
Sipes, R. Norman, 1910-1955.
Hoffman, William C., Oct. 26, 1876 - Feb. 4, 1942. Annie L., July 22, 1883 -

Isennock. Footstones: Infant son, Hudson, April 28, 1943. Father, George W., 1878-1951. Mother, Mamie M., 1883-1960.
Isennock, Annie M., 1894-1962. Raymond H., 1895-1953.
Unmarked.
Reter. Footstones: George, 1867-1942. Anna A., 1876-1931.
Montgomery, George W., husband of Mary E. Montgomery, Feb. 22, 1844 - June 25, 1960. Mary E. Montgomery, wife of George W. Montgomery, June 6, 1845 - March 23, 1923.*
Fischer, Frederick F., Dec. 7, 1862 - Dec. 26, 1944. Clairissa C., Sept. 16, 1867 - Aug. 2, 1942.
Hoelzer, Leonard, Aug. 27, 1823 - March 12, 1900. Mary B., June 22, 1829 - Sept. 15, 1910.*
Lancaster, Mary Alice, wife of William Turner, d. March 14, 1901.*
Lancaster, William Turner, d. April 29, 1914.*
Scott, husband, Arthur M. Scott, 1905-1942.
Scott, wife, Susie R., 1876-1950. Husband, William A., 1875-1946.
James, Morris W., Dec. 29, 1872 - Oct. 25, 1945. Etta F., Aug. 19, 1876 - Aug. 28, 1959.
Clark, I. Wallace, Aug. 24, 1879 - Dec. 17, 196_ -   . Mary J., Nov. 17, 1878 - .....
Mancuso, mother, Patrina, 1887-1970.
Dawes, Mary in the 85th year of her age, July 28, 1839.
Unmarked.

DeMoss, Henry L., Jr., 1911-1955. Elizabeth M., 1903-1969.
DeMoss, Harry L., Sr., 1890-1969. Bernadine A., 1886-....
DeMoss, Joseph J., infant son of Harry L. and Bernadine A. DeMoss, March 23, 1909 - Aug. 19, 1910.*
DeMoss, Edgar, Feb. 11, 1878 - Jan. 16, 1954. Laura A., Oct. 18, 1874 - April 28, 1952.
DeMoss, Charles J., infant son of Edgar and Laura DeMoss, March 20, 1906 - July 27, 1906.*
Robertson, George P., 1878-1938. Father.
Simone, Louis, Maryland CPL 3 Field Arty 6 Division, Feb. 8, 1896 - June 24, 1945.
Hale, Capt. Henry Hale, b. Oct. 11, 1754, d. (could not read balance).
Ely, William A., July 3, 1859 - March 7, 1930. (illegible).
DeMoss, Joel G. DeMoss, Aug. 1, 1816 - March 1, 1914. Ann B., wife of Joel G. DeMoss, 18..-1915.
Clayton, Amos W., May 22, 1872 - Nov. 29, 1905.*
Foard, Thomas, Aug. 26, 1846 - Feb. 28, 1914.*
?
Foard, Raymond G., Feb. 8, 1893 - Dec. 29, 1949.
Schultz, mother, Mary E., 1874-1934. Father, Lewis W., 1875- .
Smith, A. Leroy, 1903-1951.
Smith, Bruce M., 1876-1948. Sena M., 1875-1959.
Foard, Thomas, March 22, 1789 - Oct. 21, 1863.
Foard, June 16, 1795 - April 9, 1869.
Beaumont, Elias, d. Sept. 8, 1904.*
Beaumont, Martha M., wife of Elias Beaumont, d. July 28, 1895.*
Williams, George C., 1881-1956. Lydia S., 1880-1957.
Hagy, David N., Maryland SS GT 336 Tac. FT1PSAAF Vietnam, Oct. 27, 1948 - March 7, 1971.
Clayton, John B. M., husband of Sarah A. Clayton, Sept. 17, 1833 - May 2, 1901.*
Clayton, Sarah A., wife of John B. Clayton, March 1835 - Feb. 1898.*
Daylor, George W., 1859-1925. Annie E., 1868-1933.
Domhardt, Anna M., March 15, 1837 - Sept. 26, 1896.*
Heinbuch, son, Chas. C., 1906-1926. Father, Wm. A. Heinbuch, 1873-1934.
Foard, Sylvester, March 11, 1817 - Feb. 26, 1877.*
Foard, Ann, wife of Sylvester, Aug. 22, 1825 - July 17, 1896.*
Foard, Eliza J., March 15, 1851 - Aug. 4, 1852.
Foard, Mary A., May 28, 1852 - June 29, 1853.
Foard, Mary Minerva Foard, Oct. 26, 1860 - Feb. 1, 1937. William Foard, b. Dec. 7, 1876. Andrew W. Foard, Sept. 6, 1854 - Dec. 28, 1854. Mary L. Foard, Jan. 1, 1823 - July 26, 1889.*
Hall. Footstones: John, 1842-1905. Sarah, 1851-1937. James, 1869-1936. Annie R., 1879-1895.
Isennock, William H., Aug. 11, 1869 - Oct. 18, 1928. Wife, Martha E., April 9, 1871 - Sept. 29, 1960.
Blair, Vinton B., 1882-1956. Edith Hall, 1887-1957.
Wright, Johnnie, son of John T. and Susan M. Wright, May 30, 1860 - June 21, 1893. Footstone: J.W.*
Tucker, John E., 1873-1937. Marie L., 1875-1947. Footstone: John G. Tucker, 1907, son, 1907.
Detamore, Robert L., 1885-1950. Carrie W., 1873-1930.
Wright, Joshua L. Wright, Sept. 4, 1801 - March 28, 1877. Mary Wright, Oct. 21, 1814 - March 19, 1894.*
Wright, Mamie, dau. of W. O. B. and Martha J. Wright, Aug. 22, 1878 - July 11, 1870.

Blair, Bessie M. Hall, wife of Harry E. Blair, Aug. 30, 1884 - Oct. 27, 1908.
Baby, Feb. 28 - March 4, ...*
Clayton (double stone), father, J. W. B. Clayton, d. March 9, 1925. Mother,
Mary E. Hilton, wife of J. W. B. Clayton, d. Nov. 1, 1904 illegible.
Clayton, Howard E., 1866-1944. Lillian B., 1872-1950. Footstone: J.W.B.
Clayton.
Clayton, infants, Grace Clayton, 1893. Grason Clayton, 1894.
McCarren, mother, Mrs. Sarah McCarren, March 2, 1815 - Feb. 18, 1889 (verse
illegible).
(Obelisk) Smith, Florence S. Zapp, 1865-1943. Rosa M. Smith, Feb. 28, 1894 -
Feb. 17, 1897. Ira V. Smith, April 6, 1907 - May 3, 1967. Sarah I. Smith,
March 8, 1876 - June 13, 1932. Ira M. Smith, April 17, 1872 - Sept. 30,
1949. David R. Smith, May 16, 1842 - Aug. 1, 1905. Rosenna Smith, b. April
6, 1838. SMITH (on base of obelisk - brass marker (F)(T)(T) I.O.O.F.22.
Footstones: Mother - Father - Wife.
Foard. Footstones: Father, Franklin T., 1866-1931. Mother, Emma McC., 1868-
1960.
Foard, infant dau. of F. T. and E. E. Foard, Oct. 11, 1903. (Two small foot-
stones:) B.E.F. - E.F.
Foard (obelisk). Carrie R., wife of John B. Foard, July 30, 1873 - June 20,
1894. FOARD (at base of obelisk). Footstone: C.R.F.
Riddle, John Riddle, d. May 27, 1853. Footstone: J.R.*Age 65.
Riddle, Sarah, wife of John Riddle, d. Aug. 3, 1877. Footstone: S.R.* Age 89.
Riddle, Martha J. Riddle, Feb. 11, 1841 - April 18, 1853. Footstone: M.R.
Foard, Benjamin F. Foard, May 26, 1830 - Nov. 16, 1892. Eleanor Foard, Dec.
10, 1833 - May 21, 1913. illegible.*
Wilson, John C. Wilson, 1848-1930. Annie E. Wilson, 1857-1938. (Wilson on big
stone).
Wright (large stone WRIGHT). Footstones: Berlin F. Wright, 1883-1958. Mary
E. Wright, 1854-1912. Eleanor Wright, 1877-1934.
Monnin, Frank W., 1893-1956. Norah W., 1895-   .
Carter, Thomas S., 1908-1969.
Dilworth, Mabel C., 1888-   . Raymond, 1888-1946.
Maynard, Lillian D., 1920-1956. R. Leslie, 1919-(Interred in St. Stephens
Cemetery).
Willick, John A., 1871-1956. Emma, 1877-1957.
Baublitz, husband, William J., 1900-1946. Wife, Bertha M., 1884-1948.
Cole, Irby C., Sr., March 5, 1901 - March 5, 1954.
Knicely, Perry H. Knicely, Sept. 10, 1941 - May 6, 1954.
Clayton, Clayton, Marnice E., 1905-   . Carl S., 1902-1955.
Clayton, Carl L. Clayton, 1937-1955.
(Metal marker) Harry Flowers.
(Metal marker) James L. Keefer, 1882-1955.
(Metal marker) Mary C. Keefer, 1874-1959.
Ball, Randolph E. Ball, 1941-1958.
Isennock, William R., Oct. 20, 1883 - May 29, 1959. Neva L., Jan. 29, 1898
-
DeFields, Jay W., 1888-1963. Cecilia E., 1892-1958.
Bond, 1889 Edna Bond, 1971 (Marker by: McComas Funeral Home).
Pearce, David A. Pearce, 1893-1957. Violet H. Pearce, 1895-   .
Carter, husband, Dennis W., 1872-1957. Wife, L. Grace, 1875-1955.
Hoyt, son, Jesse Hoyt, 1916-1960.
Guyton, Carl E. Guyton, 1888-1949.
Amoss, Judith E. Amoss, Feb. 23, 1944 - Feb. 28, 1944.
Beares, father, Samuel T., 1878-1946. Mother, Mary E., 1882-1954.
Shackelford, Edward H. McClean, 1947-1967.
Carter, father, Howard C., 1870-1938. Mother, Ida J., 1873-1940. George H.,
1900-1936.

Holland, husband, Winifield N., 1897-1942. Wife, Anna E., 1897-1949.
Ulrich, sister, Susan Dilworth Ulrich, 1868-1936.
Bradford, Georgeanna Eliz., wife of George W. Bradford, 1871-1944.
Bradford, George W. Bradford, 1881-1948.
Watkins, Charles S. Watkins, 1870-1961.
Watkins, Burton W., 1883-1946. Helen B., 1898-1961.
Lane. Footstones: Robert, 1865-1947. Sarah C., 1863-1945.
Hipley, father, Adolph, 1890-   . Mother, Martha P., 1898-1963.*
Hilferty, Edward F., 1908-1964.
Hilferty, Warren J. E. Hilferty, 1946.
Flowers, father, Adolphus H., 1879-1950.
Flowers, mother, Eleanor R. Flowers, 1899-1948.
Flowers, husband, James M., 1910-1962.
Flowers, Leonard L. Flowers, May 19, 1922 - April 11, 1970.
Lang, Elmer Leroy, Jr., 1930-1966. Father, Elmer Lang, Sr., June 27, 1905 -
   April 2, 1958. Ella B., 1870-1949. Pearl I., 1900-1944.
Ewing, sister, Mary E. Ewing, June 10, 1936 - Sept. 1, 1955.
Sample, father, Harry F., April 19, 1902 - Dec. 9, 1956. Mother, Lillian M.,
   Oct. 18, 1912 - Sept. 1, 1952.
Fischer, Mabel I. Fischer, 1894-1970.
Mast, Elmer S., June 5, 1892 - Oct. 31, 1970. Margaret C., June 22, 1896 -
   Oct. 18, 1966.
Clayton, baby, George Keith, Aug. 2, 1960 - Aug. 5, 1960.
Bond, William H., Aug. 26, 1885 - May 16, 1956. Edna M., April 6, 1889 -   .
Bond, Herbert B., Dec. 30, 1903 - May 23, 1964.
Rembold, Leonard S., 1893-1954.
Pearce, Charles E., 1924-1950. Catherine V., 1928-   .
Barnhardt, Albert F., 1901-1952.
Plack, Henry E., 1871-1956. Sarah E., 1880-1953.
Bradford, Rachel R. Bradford, 1850-1935.
Wade, father, Wm. L. Demedius Wade, Oct. 19, 1888 - Jan. 3, 1936.
(Illegible). Old stone with name inked on.
Cole, Adolphus H., 1879-1950. Sarah E., 1880-1961. James M., 1910-1962.
Crue.
(Metal Marker McComas undertaker), 1913. Pauline Chisholm, 1971.
Roberts, baby, Mildred D. Roberts, d. Aug. 29, 1943. Aged 10 days. Asleep.
Bond, Daniel W., 1894-1958. Marie A., 1899-1958.
Bond, Boyd Merritt Bond, Maryland Pvt. 117 Inf., World War II, Sept. 12, 1921 -
   Oct. 2, 1944.
Braggs, 1906-1951.
Sample, Hyland A., April 7, 1904 - March 3, 1966. Bessie M., b. Sept. 18, 1908.
Gunnarsson, William Gunnarsson, Maryland PFC Co. A 8 BG 6 Inf. 34 B D E, July
   9, 1941 - Dec. 31, 1969.
Shanklin. Footstones: Herbert B., Dec. 30, 1943 - May 23, 1964.
Rembold, Leonard S., 1893-1954.
Smith, Ira B., 1909-1959. L. Hazel, 1907-1966.
Alexander, Sarah C. Alexander, 1902-1934.
Alford, son, Robert T., 1923-   . Mother, Hattie V., 1892-1971. Dau., Dorothy
   V., 1921-1934. Footstone: Dorothy V. Alford, 1921-1934.
Cole, Georgia Christine, dau. of Milton and Golda Cole, Dec. 24, 1934 - Feb.
   15, 1938.*
Bowen, son and brother, Kevin M. Bowen, April 8, 1955 - April 9, 1955.
Ball, Frank L. Ball, July 23, 1896 - Nov. 3, 1955.
Weichert, father, George E., 1864-1939. Mother, Ida A., 1869-1948.
Stickel, son, Thomas F. Stickel, Nov. 17, 1938 - May 8, 1942.*
Cole, wife and mother, Florence Elizabeth Cole, May 23, 1913 - Feb. 15, 1963.
Bowen, Blanche E., 1862-1954. John H., 1867-1956.
Bandelier, Fred J., 1883-1956. Mary F., 1892-1955.
Beares, Kile, baby Beares Kile, July 2, 1942.

GORSUCH FAMILY CEMETERY

Located on grounds of "Charlesborough", south of Cherry Hill Road and east of Fork Road. Copied October 23, 1973 by Robert W. Barnes.

Joseph Gorsuch, d. March 4, 1822 in the 32nd year of his age.
Little Willie, William H., son of Thomas and Hannah Gorsuch, d. Sept. 13, 1812 (?). Aged 2 years, 2 mos. and 10 days.
Son, Charles W., son of Thomas and Hannah Gorsuch, d. Sept. 21, 1833. Aged 4 years, 4 mos. and 2 days.
Hannah J., wife of Thomas Gorsuch, d. Aug. 15, 1861 in the 54th year of his age.
Thomas Gorsuch, d. Dec....
Boy, Howard Miles Gorsuch...(stone underground).
Babes, Annie J. Gorsuch. Aged 16 days. Maggie E. Gorsuch...(stone underground).
Infant, Charles L., son of Joseph and Margaret E. Gibson, d. Sept. 9, 1861. Aged 7 mos. and 10 days.
Lafay[ette?]... so[n of?]... Charles and El..., d. S...
This cemetery is quite overgrown and there were many fragments of stones that could not be read.

JOHNSON FAMILY CEMETERY

On grounds of "Fork Forest", built 1818; west of Harford Road, about 1 mile north of Fork. Copied November 12, 1973, by   Matilda Lacey and Robert Barnes.
Joseph G. Johnson, Dec. 26, 1789 - March 8, 1846.*
--- Johnson, March 11 (or May), 1841.*
Matthew Johnson, d. March 5, 1813 (or 1815 or 1843 or 1845).*
James Johnson, July 26, 1788 - July 23, 1869. Aged 81 years.

ST. JOHN'S EPISCOPAL CHURCH

The church and cemetery are located within the triangular boundaries of the intersecting roads of Bradshaw Rd., Jerusalem Rd., and Route #1 (Belair Rd.) in the 11th District. The grounds hold both the old church and the larger, newer church.

Because it is triangular in shape, we divided the cemetery into three sections. All readings were taken using the old church as a divider. With the Belair Rd. entrance to the old church as a starting point, the area to the left shall be known as Section 1; the area immediately to the right and continuing on to a STAR marker shall be known as Section 2; the area to the right of the STAR marker and continuing on to the "point" shall be known as Section 3.

There are still many vacant spaces in which burials are still made and many of the rows are not in a straight line. Therefore, some stones listed in a certain row may actually be found by a visual scan of the area either to the front or back of said row. Many old family plots take up several rows and these are recorded as a whole plot. Again, a look around will soon locate all the stones in the plots which are bounded by markers or low walls.

Row 1 in all cases is the row along the Belair Road edge of the cemetery and counts away from the old church.

The State Roads sign post reads, "The old church here standing was built by Edward Day at his own expense and consecrated in 1817 to replace St. John's at Joppa Town which, built in 1725, lay in ruins."

The stone in the walk at the entrance to the old church reads "Dedicated to the glory of God and in memory of all who worshipped in the old church, Mother's Day, May 14, 1944. The initial offering for the Walk Fund came through the efforts of Mrs. May E. Moore.

John G. Howard, d. Dec. 1844, also Ellen, dau. of Dr. John C. and Marianne Howard. Aged 7 years.
Marianne, wife of Dr. John C. Howard, d. Nov. 17, 1864. Requiescat in pace. A.A.D.
F.A.C.
Thomas M. Dietz, Maryland Sgt. Co. 8 26 Inf. Div. Vietnam DSM-OLC-AM-PH, Sept. 18, 1947 - March 18, 1969.
Miller, George H., 1885-1965. Lillian N., 1903- .
Randerson, wife, Audrey, 1904- . Husband, Albert, 1889-1969.
Stephen W. Falls, d. May 19, 1871. Aged 72 years.
Henrietta I. Howard, wife of Stephen W. Falls. Aged 70 years.
Mary Ann Sadler, d. Sept. 2, 1873 in the 79th year of her age.
Frances M., relict of Robert S. Wilson, d. May 4, 1863.* Age 67 years.
S. Haven Wilson, April 24, 1838 - March 26, 1914.
Jacob H. Munnikhuysen, 1802-1892.
Charlotte E., wife of Jacob H. Munnikhuysen and dau. of Col. John Beale and Margaret Howard, d. May 6, 1891.* Age 86 years.
Mary O., dau. of Jacob H. and Charlotte E. Munnikhuysen, d. Sept. 25, 1884.*
James C. Munnikhuysen, 1843-1917.
Lydia E., dau. of James C. and Annie R. Munnikhuysen, d. March 16, 1886. Aged 6 mos. and 18 days.*
White, James F., M.D., July 7, 1900 - June 24, 1959.
George Dilworth, d. March 8, 1875. Aged 87 years.
Susan Dilworth, d. Jan. 8, 1862. Aged 70 years.
Mollie V., wife of Thomas Blair, d. April 19, 1862.* Age 25.
Thomas O. Blair, Jan. 14, 1849 - April 10, 1929. Rest in peace.
Annie E. Blair, March 1, 1857 - July 21, 1946. Rest in peace.
Oliver B. Blair, Sept. 2, 1879 - June 8, 1942. Rest in peace.
Ann, wife of Oliver Blair, d. April 15, 1894.* Age 72.
Oliver Blair, d. May 21, 1891.* Age 77.
Herman T., son of Thomas O. and Annie E. Blair, 1893-1967.
Blair, Robert Blair, Nov. 15, 1855 - Nov. 30, 1918.
Emma A., wife of Robert Blair, Aug. 25, 1851 - Nov. 20, 1885.*
Abraham Whisler, d. March 16, 18??.* In his 77th year.
Mary, wife of Abraham Whisler, d. Oct. 28, 1857.* In her 92nd year.
Samuel Whisler, d. Jan. 13, 1863.* Age 55.
Father, August Sauer, d. May 31, 1911. Age 60. Mother, Margaret E., wife of August Sauer, d. Sept. 10, 1904.* Age 53.
Charles A., son of August and Margaret Sauer, d. July 29, 1889. Aged 9 mos. and ? days.
Francis Dilworth, Feb. 2, 1814 - Feb. 4, 1901. Hanna Dilworth, Jan. 12, 1821 - June 28, 1901. Both born in Ireland.

Mother, Elizabeth Sweitzer, July 19, 1815 - Dec. 30, 1878.*
Ella Miller Hogan, May 16, 1909 - Sept. 14, 1967.
Mother, Mary Ross, 1885-1960.

Note: The next four are under a large monument to DILWORTH.

Hogan, 1881. John M., 1940.
Estella, 1872-1932.
James R., 1861-1936.
Chester R., 1905-1937.
Robert S. Wilson, d. Jan. 10, 1816.* Age 56.
August E. Wahaus, Maryland Pvt. Med. Dec. 146 Infantry, World War I, June 19, 1887 - Feb. 13, 1957.
Edward C. Dietz, Aug. 12, 1882 - Jan. 3, 1962.
Sarah Levering Dietz, Sept. 27, 1879 - May 28, 1941.
Cecil Hopkins Bagley, M.D., son of Dr. Charles and Ella V. McCauley Bagley, Aug. 17, 1893 - April 15, 1961.
Virginia Jackson Mattingly, dau. of Howard W. and Ella M. G. Jackson, June 14, 1899.
Mattingly, Donald E., July 29, 1898. Nellie Ruth, May 14, 1898 - April 28, 1959.
John H. Miller, Jr., Oct. 2, 1942 - May 20, 1943.
Stone at the rear of the old church reads "To Elizabeth, daughter of Edward Day and wife of John B. Bayloys, died Aug. 1825. A tribute of affection by her daughter Caroline."
Action, sister, Virginia E. Dwyer, Sept. 24, 1913 - Aug. 5, 1967.
Hannah A. Grover, April 13, 1831 - Nov. 12, 1922. Brother, R. Lee Grover, Sept. 27, 1867 - Sept. 24, 1919.
Grafton Grover, Jan. 30, 1821 - June 7, 1897.*
Lizzie E., dau. of Grafton and H. A. Grover, Feb. 9, 1852 - March 11, 1876.*
Ann Chapman Wright, 1871-1951.
Catherine E., wife of Jonathan J. Chapman, d. April 22, 1881.* 39 years old.
Jonathan J. Chapman, Sept. 16, 1818 - Dec. 22, 1878.
Lydia Fletcher, d. Nov. 28, 1853.* Age 53.
Benjamin Ringgold, d. March 29, 1863.* Age 66.
Margaret West Gittings, July 29, 1828 - Oct. 14, 1878.
Lillian West Gittings, wife of Dr. D. S. Gittings, Sept. 26, 1798 - Jan. 16, 1847.
Dr. David S. Gittings, Aug. 17, 1797 - March 12, 1887.
Varina Stanton, wife of David S. Gittings, Jr., Dec. 12, 1830 - Nov. 17, 1904.
David S. Gittings, March 20, 1835 - March 22, 1890.
Jemima Richardson, d. Jan. 21, 1981.* Age about 90.
Thomas Armstrong, Nov. 19, 1834 - Feb. 4, 1905.
Martha Jane Armstrong, July 28, 1836 - Feb. 4, 1881.*
Mary Garrett, March 4, 1797 - March 26, 1881.
Jesse Garrett, Oct. 25, 1796 - April 8, 1828.
Harry W. Chambers, March 6, 1810 - Sept. 1, 1886.
Sarah J. Smith, April 24, 1832 - Oct. 25, 1857.*
Our father, John E. Bull, d. Jan. 1, 1889.* Age 43.
Otho Lee, infant son of John E. and Marian Bull, Oct. 18, 1878 - April 10, 1879.
Priscilla G., wife of Upton Reid, d. Dec. 27, 1876.* Age 84.
Upton Reid, d. July 17, 1861.* Age 81.
Moore, mother, Anna W., 1867-1944. Father, James J., 1853-1929.
Our brother, John F. Moore, June 7, 1837 - April 30, 1916.*
Our brother, Wesley A. Moore, Sept. 30, 1843 - May 27, 1872. Christopher C. Moore, April 26, 1862 - Oct. 14, 1869.*
Our sister, Mary E. Moore, Oct. 24, 1860 - March 20, 1879.*
Our mother, Mary A., wife of Alexander Moore, d. Feb. 6, 1892.* Age 70.

Our father, Alexander Moore, d. April 26, 1891.* Age 81.
John Y. Day, Feb. 6, 1803 - March 19, 1879.*
Ann Marice, wife of John Y. Day, Oct. 18, 1801 - Jan. 4, 1875.*
Mrs. Elizabeth Hughes, d. Aug. 6, 1871, in the 99th year of her age.
Mrs. Elizabeth M. Hingkley, d. Sept. 1, 1855. Aged 58 years.
M. Topham, son of T. Johnston and Mary Cornelia Evans, Aug. 1, 1850 - Oct. 2, 1856. Aged 6 years, 2 mos. and 22 days.
(child's grave - unreadable). Aged 5 years and 21 days.
Charles Grupy, d. Oct. 29, 1845. Adolphus, his brother, June 17, 1830 - Nov. 1832.*
Elizabeth B. Grupy, d. Oct. 2, 1850.* Age 52.
Jacque Grupy, d. Aug. 16, 1855.*
Fletcher Grupy, July 23, 1853. Aged 8 mos. and 23 days.
George W. Grupy, July 10, 1853. Aged 8 mos. and 10 days.
Francis Grupy, Dec. 15, 1750 - Sept. 26, 1843.*
Daniel R. Smith, d. July 27, 1894.* Age 75.
Jennie Adele Topping, April 13, 1864 - Sept. 10, 1911.
Barbara Ann Baltz, 1967.
James F. Cloman, Feb. 18, 1843 - Oct. 4, 1926. A. Moore, wife of J. F. Cloman, Feb. 27, 1845 - Feb. 18, 1916. C. Edward Cloman, May 26, 1878 - Dec. 31, 1940.
Baby, Wilberta, son of J. F. and A. A. Cloman, June 17, 1882 - Aug. 13, 1883.
Large center stone reads CAIN surrounded by 6 smaller stones as follows: Charles B., 1881-1955. Joy E., 1890-1956. Dau., Cora May, 1885-1934. Wife, Julia, 1847-1934. Husband, Daniel H., 1837-1897. Dau., Florence A., 1830-1937.
Laurence T. Shoul, Maryland Pvt. Co. D 11 Ammo. Tn., World War I, July 24, 1893 - Dec. 1, 1970.
Robert A., son of M. J. and I. F. Tyson, Jan. 25, 1880 - Feb. 20, 1892.*
Isaac F., husband of Martha J. Tyson, March 23, 1844 - Nov. 2, 1904.*
Alice A., wife of Hutson Wood and dau. of E. J. and M. A. Tyson, Nov. 1, 1852 - May 11, 1889.
Edwin E. Tyson, June 19, 1857 - Oct. 31, 1886.*
Oscar H., son of Edward and Agnes Tyson, Sept. 21, 1881 - Feb. 28, 1884.*
Edwin E., son of Edward and Agnes Tyson, Nov. 16, 1886 - Aug. 23, 1887.*
Martha A. Tyson, d. Nov. 20, 1881.* Age 54.
Elijah J. Tyson, d. Dec. 16, 1871.* Age 54.
Alice J. Janes, 1895-1936.
Susan R., wife of W. J. Dilworth, Nov. 6, 1850 - Aug. 26, 1909.*
Wm. J. Dilworth, Dec. 4, 1843 - July 22, 1915.*
Phineas P. Pyle, Feb. 23, 1821 - Feb. 27, 1889.
Elizabeth Pyle, Dec. 23, 1829 - Feb. 18, 1889.
(Center stone reads BARRETT surrounded by):
Son, James E., 1899-1906. Mother, Alberta, 1874-1945. Father, Andrew J., 1867-1946. Son, Frank E., 1903-1963.
(Center stone reads BUCKINGHAM surrounded by the following):
Arthur G., 1893-1965. Harvey S., 1868-1941. Margaret A., 1892-   . Mary E., 1867-1947. Leila K., 1891-1909.
Mother, Margaret, wife of Anthony Dilworth, d. Aug. 26, 1881.* Age 69.
Father, Anthony Dilworth, d. April 9, 1894.* Age 90.
Henry Sugar Hammon, Dec. 3, 1855 - Jan. 17, 1859.
William D. Hammon, Dec. 23, 1850 - June 24, 1856.
Amanda Hammon, March 31, 1819 - Dec. 2, 1880.*
Dominick Hammon, May 5, 1818 - Feb. 19, 1886.*
Burton, Charles E., 1856-1934. Medora J., 1863-1944.
Cornelia, dau. of Henry and Jane Scarff, d. Oct. 14, 1889.* Age 26.
Alice, dau. of Henry and Jane Scarff, d. Oct. 30, 1881.* Age 24.
Henry Scarff, 1824-1895. Jane Scarff, 1837-1923.

Elizabeth A., wife of John P. Dillworth, d. Jan. 11, 1886.* Age 47.
Martha K., wife of H. Smith and dau. of P. P. and E. H. Pyle, 1858 - Feb. 16, 1889.
Joseph, husband of Agnes Nichols, Oct. 30, 1828 - April 28, 1903, wife, Agnes, March 5, 1829 - March 8, 1917.
Eddie and Mammie Freeman (no dates).
Ira Freeman, d. July 2, 1878. Aged 49 years.
Augusta M. Freeman, d. June 9, 1893. Aged 65 years.
Frances M. W. Hutton, April 19, 1846 - Nov. 11, 1901. Philena M. Hutton, cremated, Jan. 17, 1944.
Gilpin O. Hutton, Oct. 3, 1847 - July 27, 1914.
George Allen Hutton, Nov. 5, 1881 - Sept. 2, 1958.
Mother, Maria Kirk Holland, 1850-1913. Dau., 1889. Cora Olive, 1890.
Father, Charles Oliver Holland, 1843-1927.
Agnes Kirk Holland, wife of Dr. John D. Fiske, 1884-1960.
Dau., Jane Esther Holland, 1877-1960.
Mary Elizabeth Winston, 1850-1917. Jesu Merci.
Dr. E. W. Altvater (no dates).
Cassandra, wife of Dr. E. W. Altvater, d. Dec. 1, 1886. Aged 17 years.
To our little boy, George Barney Altvater, d. July 7, 1881. Aged 1 year and 15 days.*
(Consists of 8 staggered stones in one plot):
Mary Janette Rumsey, 1861-1953. Mary Rumsey, 1790-1877. Mary J. Bullus, 1821-1901. Frances Eunice Evans, wife of John Bealle Howard Rumsey, 1834-1929. John Bealle Howard Rumsey, 1823-1917. Josephine Etting Rumsey, 1866-1949. Hugh Evans Rumsey, 1867-1948. John Howard Rumsey, 1870-1961.
John Dilworth, Aug. 1, 1818 - Oct. 18, 1891.
Elizabeth, wife of John Dilworth, Nov. 26, 1813 - Sept. 15, 1838.
George W. Dilworth, d. Dec. 9, 1896. Aged 56 years.
Sarah A. Cranston, wife of Alex R. Cranston, Sept. 22, 1825 - March 29, 1900.*
Mary E. Cranston, Dec. 29, 1845 - Jan. 1, 1923.
(Consists of 5 stones placed around a League monument in one plot):
George W. League, d. Dec. 9, 1897. Ida J. Gunn, dau. of C. W. and E. A. League, Nov. 30, 1855 - July 28, 1900. Lelia E. League, Oct. 26, 1864 - March 25, 1922. C. LeRoy Gunn, May 9, 1891 - Sept. 10, 1956. Elizabeth A., wife of George W. League, only dau. of Thomas Gorsuch, d. Dec. 20, 1891.* Age 60.
Jennie M. Bell, June 27, 1967 - Sept. 20, 1951.
Sarah E. Dutton, wife of Edward J. Bell, Nov. 30, 1825 - Oct. 23, 1896.
Mary A. Bell, 1860-1927.
Annie Bell, Aug. 10, 1861 - June 10, 1947.
(One plot of 12 stones surrounding a GORSUCH monument):
Florence A. Gorsuch, 1876-1883. Edward C. Gorsuch, 1873-1932. Walter G. Odell, 1879-1961. Frank M. Gorsuch, 1865-1962. Joseph H. Gorsuch, July 23, 1836 - Dec. 27, 1905. Margaret E. Gorsuch, Nov. 28, 1839 - Sept. 6, 1907. Thomas Bosley Gorsuch, April 23, 1834 - April 27, 1914. Amelia Elizabeth Berrien, wife of Thomas Bosley Gorsuch, April 27, 1856 - April 1, 1911. Carrie B. Gorsuch, 1888-1954. Augusta O. Gorsuch, 1868-1930. Thomas H. Gorsuch, 1863-1950. Joseph C. Gorsuch, 1871-1951.
H. Fred Bragg, Sept. 7, 1900 - Sept. 29, 1954.
Mary Sterett Kirkland, dau. of Elizabeth Blanchard and Samuel Noyes Kirkland, March 11, 1936 - Oct. 21, 1938.
Charlotte E. Gittings, wife of James E. Lindsay, 1842-1933.
James Early Lindsay, M.D., Sept. 22, 1836 - Feb. 7, 1882.
(One stone):
James Murray, Aug. 20, 1827 - June 4, 1886. Patrick Murray, Aug. 15, 1835 - July 4, 1874. McGrigor Murray, Jan. 5, 1826 - Sept. 25, 1856.
Cabel Yelverton Peyton, Oct. 21, 1878 - July 28, 1950.

Susan Larmour Peyton, May 20, 1879 - Dec. 28, 1938.
Cabel Yelverton Peyton, Jr., Oct. 15, 1905 - Aug. 4, 1925.
Rev. John Worrall Larmour, 1842-1924. Priest of the parish, 1884-1916.
Mary Griswold Larmour, 1848-1920.
Louise C., wife of Kinsbury Larmour, M.D., Aug. 28, 1870 - Dec. 24, 1894.*
Edward W., son of E. W. and C. Altvater, d. Feb. 6, 1891. Aged 15 years.
Blanch May, dau. of R. J. and E. F. Dilworth, d. July 28, 1890. Aged 10 weeks.
Ethel E., dau. of R. J. and E. F. Dilworth, d. Feb. 22, 1865(?). Aged 12 weeks.
Robert James Dilworth, Dec. 23, 1842 - Nov. 14, 1921. His wife, Emily Frances Burgan, Jan. 10, 1853 - Jan. 31, 1916.
Florence M. Braden, Aug. 21, 1856 - Nov. 26, 1910.
(12 staggered stones, no particular order, in one plot surrounding a large central monument bearing the names TAYLOR-CATOR-BROWN):
Wm. Nelson Brown, 1874-1959. Mary Benerable Brown, 1905-1913. M. Adele Taylor, 1884-1900. Joseph E. Cator, 1812-1898. Robert, Eliz. and Joseph Taylor, infants. Robert and Esther Taylor, infants. Elizabeth Dove, wife of Joseph Cator, 1818-1856. Mary Jane Cator, wife of Benj. F. Taylor, 1845-1926. Harry L. Cator, 1862-1890. Benj. W. Cator, 1843-1911. Joseph LeCompte Taylor, 1877-1953. Benjamin E. Taylor, 1840-1919.
Charlotte Bullus Day, 1835-1922.
Edward Anderson Harris, d. Jan. 4, 1909. Aged 92 years.
Agnes Howard, consort of Edward Howard, d. Dec. 27, 1815. Aged 71 years.
Charlotte Howard, consort of Edward A. Howard, d. Dec. 29, 1809. Aged 32 years.
Edward A. Howard, d. Sept. 29, 1854, in the 79th year of his age.
John Beale Howard, d. Dec. 25, 1855, in his 66th year.
Henry C. Rumsey, d. Oct. 18, 1834, in the 67th year of his life.
Thomas Adler, d. April 9, 1801. Aged 39 years.
Sybill Holland, d. Nov. 16, 1862, in the 91st year of her age.
Charles H. Thompson, April 2, 1826 - Oct. 26, 1904.
Margaret A., wife of Charles H. Thompson, d. Dec. 28, 1892, in her 61st year.
Minervol, dau. of C. H. and M. A. Thompson, May 8, 1853 - Sept. 19, 1870.
To our brother, Albert L., son of C. H. and M. A. Thompson, d. Feb. 1, 1890.* Age 24.
(3 stones below "NUMBERS" headstone):
Son, William, 1867-1890. Mother, Katherine L., 1837-1895. Father, Benjamin F., 1827-1910.
Alfred A. Chapman, Jan. 11, 1860 - Aug. 9, 1916.
Charlotte J. Chatterton, wife of Alfred A. Chapman, 1861-1943.
Allen Dirck Keyser, 1891-1958.
Lelia Moselly Keyser, 1899-1944.
Newberry Allen Smith Keyser, M.D., 1860-1922, his wife, Blanche Rumsey, 1864-1956.
Julia Oldham, wife of Thomas Kowalski, May 30, 1823 - Dec. 18, 1891.*
Dr. Wm. Fell, d. Jan. 16, 1801. Aged 36 years and 6 mos.
Latitia Day, d. March 10, 1814. Aged 50 years.
Rebecca Young Day, d. Aug. 1, 1815. Aged 21 years.
M. Edward Day, d. May 23, 1779.* Age 50.
John Young Day, d. Oct. 9, 1805.* Age 35.
Edward A. Day, Sept. 3, 1796 - Nov. 19, 1823.
Agnes Ann, dau. of Wm. and Charlotte Orso Day, Nov. 17, 1831 - Dec. 7, 1845.*
Charlotte Orso, wife of William Day, Aug. 4, 1798 - Nov. 19, 1870.
Wm. Young Day, March 1, 1798 - Aug. 31, 1879.
(Hard to classify as a single row - some stones are head to head and staggered.) An upright thin slab next to the TAYLOR monument bears a double inscription which at this writing is almost entirely gone. We copied the inscription from "Historic Graves of Maryland and Washington" by Helen W. Ridgley, which reads as follows:
Stephen Onion - Iron Master, born Feb. 10, 1694 at Brewood in Staffordshire in England - dpd this life Aug. 26, 1754. His body here interred. Elizabeth

Russell Onion, born July 12, 1734, departed this life June 10, 1742. Her body here interred. How great God's Pow'r is none can tell. Nor think how large His grace. Not man below nor sai'ts that dwell on High before His face.
(A small group of stones by the side road of the new church read as follows):
Andrew Gibson, d. Sept. 1, 1904.* Age 79 years.
Susanna F., wife of Andrew Gibson, d. Sept. 21, 1896.* Age 62 years.
Grandfather, Edward Day, Aug. 17, 1759 - Sept. 10, 1842.*
Raymond Webster McDorman, Dec. 1, 1901 - Aug. 7, 1969.
(One tall center monument in a plot at the side of the new church reads):
R. M. Chatterton, June 17, 1842 - Aug. 15, 1897. Joseph Chatterton, June 1, 1828 - Jan. 8, 1899. Simms Chatterton, Jan. 16, 1868 - March 5, 1888. Hugh Chatterton, Jan. 16, 1868 - Aug. 6, 1888. J. H. Chatterton, Feb. 1, 1857 - Aug. 21, 1901. Charles B. Chapman, Jan. 15, 1864 - Dec. 27, 1936. Frances H. Chapman, Jan. 2, 1865 - April 23, 1953.
(Seven stones in one plot as follows):
Alfred Chapman, 1894-1896. Mariana Chapman, 1918-1918. Catherine Chapman, wife of Verton T. Fitzell, 1896-1937. Charles A. Resh, 1887-1947. May J. Altvater, wife of Walter J. Chapman, 1872-1937. Walter J. Chapman, 1873-1961. Charlotte Gladden, 1891-(none).
Edwin A. Thompson, 1864-1942.
Anne E. Thompson, 1868-1945.
Robert H. Chapman, 1871-1948. Josephine W. Chatterton, wife of Robert H. Chapman, 1872-1948.
H. J. Moore, Howard J., 1858-1921.
Edna L. Schubert, 1865-1944.
Mary G. Crampton, wife of Edward P. Brown, 1869-1915.
Abraham S. Baldwin, M.D., July 4, 1826 - Jan. 9, 1907. Martha E. Baldwin, April 16, 1841 - Feb. 20, 1924. Clarence E. Baldwin, Sept. 2, 1869 - Sept. 5, 1941.
Dilworth, Lehman L., 1877-1944. Mary M., 1874-1957.
(Begin this row at the rear of the new church).
Charles Henry Rumsey, Nov. 23, 1862 - Feb. 13, 1951.
Merryman, Marvin, 1877-1956.
Mary Virginia Merryman, Aug. 13, 1857 - June 6, 1925.
Lillian Merryman, 1884-1970.
Walter, Clarence L., 1901-1957.
Jones, Paul, 1908-1919. Olive, 1887-1919.
Jones, George F., 1861-1934. Sarah E., 1869-1955.
Ida B. Jordan, wife of C. A. Chatterton, d. Dec. 24, 1907. Aged 34 years.
John C. Wiker, 1881-1930.
Edna L. Wiker, 1883-1965.
C. Augustus Moore, 1849-1918. Mary E., wife, 1858-1941.
Charles E., Mary L., Harry W., John B. Arthur, children of C. A. and M. E. Moore.
(Four stones staggered near edge of cemetery along Jerusalem Road read):
Francis Kinloch Read, Sept. 5, 1895 - Dec. 21, 1963.
Fischer, Edna Irene, 1894-1965. Adolph E., 1891-1962.
Karen Lee Sterling, 1949-1965.
Charles McKnight, Col. U.S. Army, Sept. 16, 1891 - Oct. 9, 1969.

ST. PAUL'S LUTHERAN CHURCH CEMETERY

Church organized in 1850 in home of Mr. Klausmeier on Jericho Road. Cornerstone of church laid in 1850. In early years only German services were held - English used exclusively since 1938.

Campbell, Charles W., 1912-1956. Thelma C., 1920.
Busler, Howard W. Busler, March 16, 1919.
Campbell, Charles W. Campbell, June 26, 1940 -
Kinney. Brother and son, Michael E. Kinney, Nov. 6, 1946 - May 2, 1970.
Hinz, Albert, Aug. 2, 1898 -   . Freida, June 17, 1914 — June 13, 1970.
Colgan, infant dau. of L. P. and M. M. Colgan, Jan. 1, 1918 - Jan.
(Stones with hole in for railing with name Klausmeier at Colgan and Gilbert Klausmeier stones):
Klausmeier, George Klausmeier, April 5, 1855 - Jan. 25, 1934. Anna M. Klausmeier, Sept. 5, 1856 - Nov. 18, 1931. Footstones: Father - Mother.
Klausmeier, Frederick H., Dec. 23, 1885 - May 2, 1905. Footstone: Son.
Clausmeier, father, John H. Clausmeier, Feb. 14, 1822 - Dec. 31, 1903. Mother, A. M. Elenore Clausmeier, March 21, 1820 - Nov. 28, 1895.*
Klausmeier, Hierachet in Gott, J. Gilbert Klausmeier Gestorben, Aug. 15, 1888. Alter 31 Jabr 3 Mo. and 15 tage. Dien Lauf hoh ich yollendet. Und sag Eirchgirte nacht. Mein Botder su gepproset. Den er haeswhl germachr.
Wirsing, Hier ruhit in Gott, C. Wilhelm Wirsing, Geb: in Steinbach K. Preussen. Den April 4, 1826. Gest: den Juli 4, 1866: o ## John 21:10 (verse illegible).
Regle Hierinhit, Eva M. Regel, Geb., d:11 Jan. 1811. Gest. d: Marz 14, 1885. Sehg sind die Todlen die in dem Herrensterben.
Germeyer, Maria Germeyer Geboren. Den. Nov. 6, 1803. Gestorben, Den Marz 16, 1884. Alter 80 Jahre 4 monat stud...(illegible).
Herold, Zum Andenkerian, Rosine. Galtin now, George Herold. Gest. den 21 Sept. 10, 1883, im alter ven, 66 yahrn 10 Monian, und 21 Tager Ver..?..
Wirsing, Hier ruh, Pauline F. Tochtervon, w. of M. Wirsing. Geb. den. Sept. 29, 1857. Gest. den. 28 April 7, 1883. Bas Klud ven weiser Sude, Zag mir mein. Herland an Doss ich auf Zion's Waide, num Rosenbreicher Karn.
Schneider, Unser ibener Gethe of Vater, Ferdinand Schneider. Geb. den. May 15, 1827. Gest. den. April 12, 1883. Ruhe sanf in dienar Gruff, Bis dich Jesus wiedu raft.
Schneider, Hier ruher, Anna Maria, Gallincam, Frederich J. Schneider, Geb. 2a Euslbriella Wurlingberg. Dec. Dec. 29, 1811. Gest. den Janri 1, 1878. Tiltor: 63 Ja June 5 mo. 23 tagi (verse illegible).
Hanf, Martin L., 1832-1876.
Schneider, Wlater Oscar, son of Theodore and Anna Schneider, Dec. 31, 1895 - July 28, 1919. At rest.
Maier, Adam G., 1859-1942. Pauline, 1862-1946.
Lang. Lang, Christian Lang, Sept. 26, (nothing recorded). Augusta C. Lang, June 6, 1846 - Dec. 1, 1914.*
Dietz, John Dietz, Nov. 19, 1846 - Nov. 13, 1914. Katherine Dietz, March 16, 1851 - Dec. 26, 1928.*
Sweitzer, Arthur Harrison, son of George and Louise Sweitzer, Oct. 2, 1890 - Feb. 10, 1894. Footstone: A.H.S.*
Wirsing, Martha Wirsing, March 24, 1890 - April 2, 1890. Annie M., Sept. 16, 1887 - Oct. 31, 1888.
Snyder, Willie, son of B. and E. Elizabeth Snyder, Dec. 4, 1876 - July 25, 1887.*
Schneider, Hier ruhet, Clara L. Gefuhia Tochler and B. and L. Schneider. Geb. d. Dec. 4, 1885. Gest d. June 28, 1887. Dein vergessen evir nich.
Dietz, Hier ruhet in Gott. Katherine Eva Tochter von John and Kath. Dietz. Geb. Nov. 1877. Gest. d. Dec. 1, 1880.
Wirsing, dau., Wilhelmina S. F. Wirsing, 1892-1900.
Schneider, Alfred Godfred, Oct. 18, 1899 - July 16, 1900. Irene Marion, b. April 19, 1902. Children of Theodore and Anna Schneider.
Pilhofer, Hier Ruher, Johann Pilhofer. Geb. den Juni 10, 1861. Gest. d. Feby 19, 1874. Alter 12 Jabre 8 mo. and 9 tage.
Riley, William Raymond Riley, Aug. 18, 1959 - Aug. 29, 1964.*

Nussle, Hier Ruht, Jacob Nussle. Geb. den. Sept. 30, 1857. Gest. den June 2, 1922. Seine Geliebte Gattin, Augusta. Geb. den Sept. 7, 1869. Gest. den Marz 22, 1925. Footstones: JN-AN.
Unkart, George, 1874-1950. Catherine 1882-19...
Unkart, Unkart, William E., son of George and Katherina Unkart, May 13, 1902 - Jan. 15, 1903.
Erbe, Henry G., husband of Louisa A. Erbe, June 3, 1884 - Jan. 16, 1924.
Seitz, Hier ruht, Peter Seitz. Geb. n. Holenstadh Baiern den April 1786. Gest. den April 5, 1870. Alter 84 Jahre 5 tage.
Schneider, Matilda L. Schneider, June 2, 1868 - June 8, 1869.
Unkart, William Unkart, 1852-1929. His wife, Elizabeth, 1851-1922 (at bottom UNKART). Footstones: Father - Mother.
Byer, Byer, John, 1857-1943. His wife, Augusta, 1856-1926.
Snyder, Snyder, Isaac E., 1854-1944. Elizabeth, 1859-1939.
Base - no stone.
Ostheim, Henrietta Veronika, dau. of Henry and Mary Ostheim, May 11, 1855 - Jan. 19, 1862. Aged 6 years, 8 mos. and 28 days.*
Ostheim, Charles W. Henry, son of Henry and Mary Ostheim, Nov. 10, 1860 - March 11, 1862. Aged 1 year, 4 mos. and 1 day.*
Ostheim, Mary Elizabeth, dau. of Henry and Mary Ostheim, July 18, 1853 - Feb. 6, 1862. Aged 8 years, 6 mos. and 19 days. Footstones: H.V.O. - C.W.H.O. - M.E.O.*
Snyder, John F. Snyder, 1884-1925.
Steinmetz, Christena, wife of John Steinmetz, 1836-1864.
Sneider, Louis A. Sneider, July 17, 1862 - Oct. 21, 1864. George Sneider, April 18, 1861 - Dec. 26, 1861.
Wise, mother, Elizabeth Wise, d. July 24, 1861. Aged 38 years.
Pilhofer, Hier ruh't, Conrad Pilhofer. Geb. den Marz 4, 1858. Gest. d. Sept. 9, 1860. Alter 2 Jahre 6 Mo. and 5 tage. Lass binder und Erwachsendein Sich Himel ewig freun.
Schulte, mother, Theresa C., wife of Rev. Paul Schulte, 1859-1930.
Schulte, dau., Eleanor Marie, dau. of Rev. Paul and Theresa Schulte, 1904-1918.*
Schulte, Rev. Paul Schulte, 1852-1905.
Wirsing, Hier ruhet in Gott. Eva Margaretha Ehe frau von Wilhelm Wirsing, Feb. 9 - Sept. 1807. Gest Marz 9, 1832.
Byer, 1891. Edw. H., 1892. 1893. Henry., 1894.
Snyder, father to my husband, Bernard J. Snyder, d. Nov. 8, 1899.*
Snyder, mother, Elizabeth Snyder, Jan. 27, 1875 - March 7, 1931. Footstones: B.J.S. E.S.*
Sweitzer, Jesus Mercy, George Sweitzer, April 25, 1845 - Dec. 15, 1909. His wife, Louise H., May 16, 1865 - April 11, 1926. SWEITZER (at bottom). Henry George Sweitzer, son of George and Louise Sweitzer, Oct. 26, 1864 - Nov. 14, 1946. Karl Klemmich, Dec. 25, 1880 - March 4, 1917. Footstones: G.S. - L.H.S. - K.K.
Lentz, Adam Lentz, Dec. 25, 1831 - Jan. 24, 1911.
Ernst, mother, Christiana, wife of John Ernst, May 10, 1824. - June 9, 1904.
Pilhofer, Mutter, Hier Ruhet in Gott. Margaretha Pilhofer. Geb. den Nov. 9, 1820. Gest. den. 26 OKT 1911. Alter 90 Jahr monot 1 und 16 tage. Wir huben hier Keine Blevbende Statte, Ober d. Tuknftige sughin Wir.
Pilhofer, Vatter, Hier Ruhat in Gott. Johann Pilhofer. Geb. den. Nov. 22, 1817. Gest. den. Feb. 15, 1901. Alter 83 Jahr 2 Monat und 22 tage. Seigetreubis in den Tod. So will ich Dir Die Krone. Des Liben Geben.
Snyder, father, Frederick Snyder, d. Oct. 22, 1800. Aged 85 years and 18 days (verse illegible). Footstone: F.S.
Ernst, father, John Ernst, March 7, 1814 - April 29, 1900. Footstone: J.E.
Pistor (or Pister), Charles, son of Wendel and Philipina Pistor, Aug. 30, 1871 - July 27, 1899.

Unkart, Eliza M. Unkart, July 21, 1811 - April 18, 1898. Footstone: E.M.U.*
Unkart, George Unkart, Aug. 8, 1808 - Aug. 8, 1894.*
Lang, mother, Barbara Lang, Nov. 29, 1822 - Jan. 15, 1894. Footstone: B.L.*
Lang, father, Frederick Lang, Feb. 16, 1822 - Jan. 12, 1894. Footstone: F.L.*
Dietz, Hier Ruhet in Gott, Philipp Dietz. Geb. den Sept. 14, 1819. Gest. den Sept. 19, 1892. Alter 73 Jahre, Selig und died Todlen die in dem Herren stuben.
Sporlader, Hier Ruhet in Gott, Louisa Sporlader, Frau von Louis Sporlader. Geboren, Nov. 1, 1810. Gestorben Oct. 5, 1889. Footstone: L.S.
Millitzer, mother, Anna M. Millitzer, May 18, 1821 - March 14, 1907. Father, Ernest Millitzer, May 1, 1820 - Nov. 16, 1906.*
Hipley, father, Joseph Hipley, July 15, 1868 - Oct. 30, 1918. Mother, Augusta, wife of Joseph Hipley, March 11, 1862 - Sept. 26, 1937.
York, father, Albert A. York, May 7, 1889 - May 19, 1919. Aged 30 years.
York, J. Walter York, 1898-1920. Asleep in Jesus.
York, York, Ferdinand A., 1851-1941. Caroline G., 1859-1943.
Schwandtner, Margurieta Schwandtner, Feb. 22, 1872 - June 10, 1932. H. Schwandtner, Sr., 1859-1943.
York, father, William R. York, Dec. 25, 1879 - July 21, 1933. Rest in peace.
Dietz, brothers, Dietz, Frederick H., 1886-1931. C. H. Henry, 1881-1943.*
Dietz, Dietz, father, John H., 1873-1933. Mother, Mary A., 1878-1952.
Unkart, Unkart, Louise K., Oct. 29, 1877 - Aug. 17, 1946. Thomas, Feb. 1, 1877 - Dec. 4, 1950.
Unkart, Unkart, Fred C., 1879-1969. Anna A., 1886-1969.
Schwantner, Herman, 1890-.... Elizabeth, 1888-1961.
Nussle, Nussle, Johanna D., 1884-1950. John J., 1882-1969.
Meads, Meads, Clinton W., 1905-19.. Margaret M., 1909-1953.
Cawdry, Robert Max Cawdry, April 22, 1955.
Unkart, Sept. 25, 1934 - April 17, 1953. William Unkart.
DeWitt, Edward C. DeWitt, Oct. 17, 1912 - Feb. 3, 1963.

SALEM METHODIST CHURCH

The church is located on the Franklinville Road, between Upper Falls and Franklinville, close to where the road intersects with Bradshaw Road.
Land for Salem Church was given by William M. McCubbin. The original lot of 1 acre was part of Belt's Prosperity. The church building was erected in 1847. The church is no longer used since the erection of the new church. The old building is soon to be demolished.
(Notes by Miss Matilda Lacey who copied the cemetery in November 1971.)
The church is shown as "Salem M.E. Ch." on the plat of the 11th Dist. in the 1877 Atlas. Neither church nor cemetery is shown on the White Marsh Quad Map. (Notes by R. Barnes).

McCubbin, Mary, wife of James McCubbin, Feb. 3, 1772 - April 30, 1850.*
McCubbin, son of George and Sarah I. McCubbin, Sept. 8, 1810 - Jan. 28, 1850.
McCubbin, Amanda, wife of J. Oliver McCubbin, d. July 26, 1868.* Age 23 years.
McCubbin, John H., son of George H. and Sarah McCubbin, Feb. 27, 1842 - Aug. 29, 1871.
McCubbin, Sarah A., wife of George H. McCubbin, April 1, 1810 - July 3, 1872. Footstone: S.A.McC.
McCubbin, George W. McCubbin, Sept. 8, 1850 - Aug. 13, 1881. Footstone: G.W.McC.

McCubbin, Leander, son of Leander and Hannah McCubbin, Feb. 19, 1850 - July 28, 1851. Aged 17 mos. and 9 days.
.... Minna, dau. of .. (illegible).
Frazier, Penelope, consort of Sam'l Frazier, d. Dec. 2, 1848.*
DeMoss, Sarah W., wife of J. DeMoss, d. Dec. 24, 1852, in the 48th year of her age.
McCauley, Martha Ann, consort of William McCauley, d. Oct. 15, 1852.* 21 years old.
Mayes, Daisy J., April 25, 1875 - Sept. 24, 1949.
Mayes, Wilbert F., April 3, 1873 - July 1, 1932.
Dixon, Susan R., consort of James Dixon, d. March 26, 1852.* 27 years old.
Dixon, James H. Dixon, d. June 14, 1850, in the 32nd year of his age.
Armor, McCubbin. Footstones: Charles G. Armor, 1849-1929. Susan McCubbin Armor, 1854-1921. Helen E. McCubbin, 1851-1925.
Kershaw, Ann Mary Rebecca, wife of Henry Kershaw, Feb. 21, 1831 - July 25, 1857.* Footstones (in back of next three stones): T.F.F. - H.C.E. - C.S.E. - N.McC. - S.M.
Tovell, Samuel, Sept. 24, 1858 - Dec. 4, 1939.
Tovell, Reuben, July 19, 1822 - July 23, 1903.*
Tovell, Laura U. Tovell, March 28, 1840 - Dec. 2, 1928. At rest.
Tovell, Sarah Ann, dau. of Caleb and Mary Tovell, d. Aug. 19, 1851.
DeMoss, Hannah R., wife of John DeMoss and dau. of Nathan and the late Elizabeth Howard, July 6, 1824 - March 7, 1876.
DeMoss, Laura J., dau. of John J. and Hannah R. DeMoss, Dec. 13, 1856 - July 18, 1883.
Forsyth, Mary J., widow of the late Thomas E. Forsythe, d. Jan. 25, 1888.* Age 56.
Forsythe, Thomas F. Forsythe, d. Dec. 18, 1868. Aged 12 years.
Ely, Harriet C. Ely, wife of John S. Ely, d. Aug. 1, 1865. Charles J., infant son of John S. and Harriett C. Ely, d. Sept. 22. 1865. Aged 2 mos.
McCubbin, Nicholas McCubbin, June 1, 1805 - April 28, 1878.*
Kelley--Collins, Amos O. Kelley, 1804-1890. Thomas B. Collins, 1865-1889.
Deiter, John W. (no dates) Emily J. (no dates). March 5, Treadwell, Clarissa, d. Dec. 8, 1908. Age 66. Stephen S. Treadwell,/ 1920*
McCubbin, William, d. Jan. 6, 1882. Mary A. McCubbin, d. June 1, 1878.* Age 76.
McCubbin, Mahala, wife of Lloyd R. McCubbin, d. Feb. 5, 1877.* Age 72.
Sheffield, Mary A., consort of John P. Sheffield, d. Oct. 25, 1862.* 18 years old.
Wilson, Olivia A. Wilson, d. April 10, 1902. Aged 54 years and 6 days.
Wilson, William A. Wilson, d. Sept. 27, 1905. Aged 55 years and 17 days.
Campbell, father, John G. Campbell, Jan. 19, 1842 - April 5, 1897. Mother, Mary E., wife of John G. Campbell, June 1, 1850 - March ?6, 1914. Ida Belle, June 27, 186- - June 12, 187-. Mary J., Aug. 8, 1871 - May 12, 1896, dau. of J. G. and M. C. Campbell, their infant son, b. and d. March 15, 1883.
Hurtt, mother, Eliza Hurtt, Jan. 31, 1814 - March 8, 1903.
Hurtt, my husband, ..., July 4, 1809 - Jan. 19, 1851.
Harvey, Sidney B., April 29, 1930 - Feb. 26, 1958.
Lavoie, son, Ernest, Jr., Jr., March 5, 1923 - Nov. 12, 1963.
Lavoie, wife, Alice I., Jan. 6, 1900 - Dec. 9, 1966. Husband, Ernest, Sept. 19, 1886 - July 21, 1962.
Litchfield, A., Sept. 27, 1808 - July 30, 1865.
Hammond. (Footstones): J. Dominick, May 23, 1872 - Oct. 12, 1945. Joshua, June 25, 1841 - Sept. 5, 1926. Augusta, June 10, 1847 - Jan. 17, 1940.
Kyle, husband, Orville Kyle, Feb. 25, 1887 - Sept. 21, 1917.*
McCubbin, Owen McCubbin, Feb. 12, 1846 - Feb. 19, 1881.*
McCubbin, Fannier, 1851-1905.
Earp, Lydia A., wife of James Earp, June 22, 1822 - June 22, 1902.
Earp, James, Balto., Ball'y, Md. L. A.
Earp, Sadie W., wife of Charles M. Earp, Oct. 15, 1839 - Jan. 28, 1891.

Parker, Martha E., wife of John W. Parker, Nov. 26, 1853 - Jan. 4, 1937. John
W. Parker, Feb. 14, 1843 - Dec. 5, 1913. Martin, husband of Martha E.
Pfeiffer, d. Sept. 17, 1884. Aged 43 years.
Cardwell. Footstones: Baby Mary Jane, 1919-   . Son, Loring Nelson, 1923-
1962. Mother, Mary Ann, 1888-1940. Father, Marion Lawrence, 1885-1963.
(4 marble cornerposts with letter "C").*
Collins, Charles H., 1868-1950. Mary A., 1873-1959. (metal marker - I.O.O.F.
22).
Corbin. (Footstones): Margaret E. (no dates). Elias, July 8, 1937.*
Brandt. (Footstones): John W., 1876-1918. Ella M., 1876-1962.
Bell, Harry B., June 25, 1883 - Oct. 4, 1945. William U., 1851-1901.
Bell, mother, Catherine D. Bell, 1883-1933. Ida Frances, 1863-1936.
Davidson, David, 1879-1959. Bessie E., 1879-1955.
Deal, Ella H., d. Aug. 13, 1941.
DeMoss, Adella M. DeMoss, Jan. 27, 1874 - March 8, 1898.*
Norwood, Harry M., 1869-1945. Lillian M., 1874-1951. James L. 1840-1913.
Harriet F., 1832-1911.
Mucaulay. (Footstones): William E., 1907-1940. Bruce G., 1881-1943.
(I.O.O.F. Marker) Bruce G., Jr., 1911-1960.
Jones. (Footstones): Edith, 1879-1962. Samuel G., 1877-1927.
Burton, Rumsey T., husband of Amelia Burton, Sept. 7, 1856 - March 12, 1900.
Amelia, wife of Rumsey T. Burton, Nov. 16, 1859 - Jan. 13, 1901. Cora A.,
dau. of R. F. and A. Burton, Dec. 21, 1885 - June 5, 1907.*
Barton, son, Hollis R., son of Charles F. and Annie R. Barton, July 27, 1878 -
June 10, 1908.
Barton, Charles Ira, son of Charles F. and Annie R. Barton, Feb. 19, 1881 - Dec.
15, 1891.*
Harrison, wife, Susie G. Harrison, 1895-1921.
Guyton. (Footstones): William W., 1851-1901. Ida Frances, 1863-1936. Marry
Anne, 1815-1904. Underwood, 1816-1890.
Skillman, Franklin D., Aug. 10, 1850 - Feb. 27, 1912. Martha E., 1857-1935.
Footstones: F.D.S. M.E.S.*
Burton, mother, Annie R. Wells, wife of Charles F. Burton, May 30, 1860 - Aug.
17, 1914. Father, Charles F. Burton, May 5, 1853 - June 16, 1926.*
Bell, Bertha S., 1878-1957. William W., 1878-   . (Footstones): Edward U.,
1859-... Belle E., 1857-1929. Annie E., 1851-1928. Jarrett E. Staniford,
Feb. 6, 1847 - Oct. 21, 1908.
Bell, Wendell O., 1920-1968.
Ely. (Footstone): M. Carrie, 1868-1956. I. Augusta, 1863-1928.
Knight. (Footstones): Angeline Knight, 1867-1951. Leonard Knight, 1860-1918.
(metal I.O.O.F marker). Arthur L. Knight, 1895-1918.
Hook. (Footstones): Minnie M. Hook, 1872-1948. Wm. H. Hook, 1862 -1909.
Thompson. (Footstone): John C., 1862-1921. Ida K., 1870-1954.
Burton. (Footstones): Josephine L., 1857-1926. James H., 1863-1942.
Bell, Nelson, June 15, 1842 - April 16, 1913.
Bell, Ellen C., wife of Nelson Bell, Jan. 24, 1888 - Feb. 26, 1907.
Brevard, Mattie A. Brevard, June 30, 1821 - July 16, 1888.*
Brevard, John Brevard, June 8, 1844 - June 23, 1891.
Brevard, Laura E. Brevard, Sept. 17, 18.?. - Nov. 27, 1920.
Baxter, father, John W. Baxter, Sept. 20, 1828 - Dec. 18, 1897.
Hoover, son, Gordon S. Hoover, May 22, 1919 - April 25, 1939.
Hoover, Mabel U. Hoover, Nov. 7, 1921 - Nov. 8, 1921.
Hoover, Charles E., Feb. 18, 1885 - Nov. 11, 1925. Edith M., his wife, Jan. 8,
1885 - Aug. 19, 1953. (Footstones): E.M.H. C.E.H.
Elliott, sister, Irene O. Elliott, 1905-1923.
Nichols. (Footstones): Thomas S., 1866-1940. Ella B., 1868-1924.
Waldram. (Footstones): Jennie, 1855-1944. George, 1863-1952.

Jones (Footstones:) Lizzie S., b. Dec. 21, 1874, d. April 18, 1925.
John J., b. Aug. 26, 1871, d. Nov 20, 1940. Carrie L., b. April 1, 1885 - Jan. 4, 1938.
Ferguson, Joseph M., b. July 5, 1859, d. April 21, 1925. His Wife, Sophia S., b. May 7, 1862, d. Feb. 18, 1921.
DeMoss, Harry G., 1862 - 1922.
Belt, Walter E., Sr., 1880 - 1958. Bertha M., 1884 - . Margaret U., 1907 - 1926.
Burton, Ella Lorraine, b. Nov 17, 1923, d. April 1, 1925. Footstone: Baby.
Bachtel (Footstones:). Wife, Lula B. Hammond, b. March 21, 1888, d. May 21, 1970. Husband, E. Clinton Hammond, b. Oct. 17, 1877, d. Sept. 9, 1967. Samuel Bachtel, b. May 8, 1854, d. July 3, 1924.
Ayres (Footstones:) Charles L., 1910 - 1968. Annie M., 1890 - . Charles M., 1888- 1955. Son, Vernon E., 1920 - 1933.
Huber (Footstones:) John A. Huber, b. Jan. 4, 1879, d. Jan. 25, 1960. Sadye E. Huber, b. April 16, 1883, d. Dec 13, 1956.
Barton, Ethel S., b. Feb. 10, 1887 - . William R., b. Aug. 12, 1883, d. Sept. 4, 1964.

SURNAME INDEX

ADLER	154	BARNES	68,100	BITTNER	123
ADY	75, 114	BARR	76	BLACK	41,48
AHL	124	BARRETT	49,52,142,152	BLACKLOCK	84
AIKEN	120	BARROLL	111	BLAIR	17,118,139
AIREY	56	BARRON	56		146,147,150
ALBAN	96	BARRY	6,46,60,104	BLAKE	120
ALDER	1	BARTLESON	37	BLAKELEY	137,138,145
ALEXANDER	118,122,148	BARTLETT	113	BLAKISTONE	137
ALFORD	148	BARTON	92,160,161	BLAKLEY	92,94
ALBRIGHT	142	BASSLER	24,25,48	BLANSHARD	72,73
ALLEN	75,113,121	BATCHELOR	121	BOARMAN	109,115
ALENDER	104,113,119	BATES	65	BODE	8,116,117,120
	139	BAUBLITTS	125	BOISLINIERE	50
ALLISON	109	BAUBLITZ	93,97,125	BOND	27,52,69,89
ALMONY	98		132,136,142		90,136,147,148
ALTEVOGT	144		147	BONE	83
ALTVATER	153,154,155	BAXTER	160	BOOKER	138
AMES	48	BAWELL	139	BOOTH	39
AMOS	140	BAYER	123	BOOZE	77
AMOSS	112,147	BAYLOYS	151	BOPP	117
ANDERSON	40,47,50,89	BAYNE	32,82,91,92	BORING	97
ANGEL	40		93,94,138	BOSLEY	38,40,43,44,
ANZEL	40	BAYSMAN	14		45,52,67
APPEL	141,145	BEACH	35	BOSWELL	14
ARCHER	78	BEALE	28	BOWEN	21,27,90,144
AREACOST	96,97	BEAMER	76		148
ARMOR	159	BEAN	81	BOWERS	74,142
ARMOUR	111	BEARD	89	BOXLEY	42
ARMSTRONG	40,151	BEARDSLEY	34	BOXMAN	124
ARNOLD	22	BEARES	135,138,140	BOYCE	40,45
ARTHUR	84,140,142		141,147,148	BOYD	93,141
ASHE	97	BEAUMONT	146	BRADFORD	148
ASHTON	6,41,42	BEAVER	85	BRADLEY	104,105,110,112
ATKINS	74	BEEBE	133		114,117,119,120
AULD	13	BEES	123		121,122
AUSTIN	117	BECK	55,134	BRADON	154
AUSTINE	118	BELL	21,23,24,25	BRADY	16,56,57,95
AYRES	34,81,98,161		26,34,107,153	BRAGG	153
BACHMAN	84,123		160	BRAGGS	148
BACHTEL	161	BELVIN	56	BRANDT	160
BACON	34,121	BELT	130,161	BRANNOCK	25
BAGLEY	32,33,140,151	BELTZ	2	BRAY	38
BAHN	57	BENNETT	13,28,35,144	BREIDENAUGH	76
BAILEY	5,86	BENSON	37,42	BREIDENBAUGH	77,85,143
BAKER	8,56,99,100,116	BERL	142	BRENNAN	54,59
BALDWIN	139,155	BERNARD	54	BREVARD	160
BALL	124,147,148	BERRY	38,47	BREWER	26,129
BALTZ	152	BETLEJEWSKI	123	BRICE	91
BANAHAN	57	BEVARD	123,135	BRINKER	113
BANDELIER	148	BEYER	143	BROACH	34
BANGE	9	BICKFORD	43	BROGNARD	140
BANKS	111	BIENSACK	85	BROOKE	112
BANNISTER	37	BIGLEY	26	BROOKS	10,31,69
BARCLAY	42	BILLINGSLEA	78,82,115	BROWN	10,17,18,24,26
BARKHAM	36	BILLINGSLEY	78,81,85		54,55,86,92,93
BARBOUR	82,83	BINDER	48		95,130,154,155
BARKER	41	BIRCKHEAD	91	BRYAN	1,8,27
BARNHART	12,74,75,148	BISSELLE	139	BRYNE	60

BRYON	17	CASEY	37,115	COFIELD	34,49
BUBERT	34	CASLIN	49,51	COLBERT	63
BUCHANAN	42,116	CASSADY	140	COLE	44,45,64
BUCK	6,43	CATOR	154		147,148
BUCKINGHAM	152	CAVANEY	54	COLEIN	14
BUCKLER	101	CAWDRY	158	COLEMAN	137
BUCKLEY	40	CHALK	16,17,18,38	COLGAN	110,117,119,120
BUCKNELL	68	CHAMBERS	51,55,151		121,122,124,156
BUCHOLTZ	119	CHANDLER	123	COLLINGS	89
BULL	151	CHANEY	89,90	COLLINS	58,92,142
BULLOCK	110	CHAPMAN	151,154,155		159,160
BURGAN	154	CHARNOCK	84	CONCANNON	59
BURGESS	87	CHASE	144	CONNELL	57
BURK	62	CHATTERTON	154,155	CONNOR	54,59,60,123
BURKE	106,118,120	CHELL	39	CONRAD	133
BURNHAM	12,15,16,17,19	CHENOWETH	20,21,24,25	CONTI	122
	21,25,26,27		34,93,144	CONWAY	59,99
BURNS	27,31,32,49	CHENWORTH	79	COOK	7,8,14
	60,107	CHERBONNIER	50	COONEY	117
BURNWELL	128	CHEW	89	CORCORAN	102,117
BURTON	46,76,77,79	CHILCOAT	30,49	CORBIN	81,82,84,92
	80,81,82,83	CHILDRESS	120		93,94,160
	84,85,92,144	CHILDS	126,129,132	CORNTHWAITE	145
	152,160,161	CHIPMAN	36	CORRIGAN	104
BUSLER	156	CHISHOLM	148	COSTA	55
BUSSEY	53,55	CHRISTMAS	90	COSTELLO	61
BUTLER	28,38,48,145	CLARK	39,40,54,55	COTTER	57
BYER	142,157		69,85	COUNCILMAN	100
BYRD	26		124,145	COUNSEL	79
BYRNE	61	CLARKE	26	COURTNEY	111
BYRNES	58	CLAYTON	136,137,138	COVEHEY	52,55
CAIN	106,120,127,152		139,140,142	COWLEY	47
CAINE	122		143,144,145	COWLING	22,23
CALLAHAN	108		146,147,148	COX	9, 20,96,130
CALLENDER	19	CLEMENTS	27,48		131
CALVERT	48	CLIFFORD	117	CRABSON	133
CAMPBELL	43,55,57,87	CLIFTON	52	CRAMPTON	155
	141,156,159	CHATTERTON	135	CRANSTON	93,145,153
CANAPP	94	CHILCOAT	3,96	CREAGER	127
CANAVAN	50	CLINE	16,28,87	CREAMER	80
CANOVA	49,50	CLOMAN	136,152	CRILLEY	109,115
CARDWELL	160	CLUSMAN	24	CRISS	26
CARMAN	83,123,140,141	COALE	37,88	CROCHAN	61,62,63
CARNEY	55,57	COCHRAN	102,116,118	CROMWELL	100
CARR	55,87,110		120,121,122	CROSS	20,32,40
CARRICK	43		123,124	CROUT	32
CARROLL	47,99,104,106	COCKEY	13,14,16,20	CROWTHER	38,39,43,46
	113,118,122		28,29,32,40		47
CARTER	92,93,105,123		42,43,44,46	CRUE	25,27,28,42
	139,142,143,144		47,53,88,100		43,127,128,148
	147	COCKRAN	39,40,112	CUMMINGS	61,110,112,117
CARVER	129,130		113,117	CUNNINGHAM	113
CARY	55	COE	46,77,93,136	CURRAN	75
CASE	43	COFFEY	33	CURRENS	76

CURRIER	3	DIXON	159	EICHLER	34,38
CURSEY	73	DOBBS	81	EICHOLTZ	75
CURTIS	9	DOBSON	27,122	EICUS	31
DAGGS	86	DODSON	137	EISENHARDT	122
DAHLER	141,145	DOHLER	138,139	EISNER	144
DALTON	51,114,118	DOHONY	122	ELLARD	28
	121,122,123,124	DOLL	33	ELLIOTT	14,136,160
DAMPMAN	139	DOLLING	55	ELWOOD	59,61,117
DANCE	78	DOMHARDT	146	EILWOOD	81
DANENMANN	124	DONAHUE	114,117,121	ELY	146,159,160
DANIELS	85	DONOVAN	25,80	EMERSON	47
DANNANMAN	113	DONNELLY	53,59	EMORY	26, 74
DARE	34	DOOLING	59	ENDERSON	135
DAUGHERTY	114	DOOR	82	ENGLE	7,23,114
DAUGHTON	57	DORAN	55	ENSOR	9,28,51 ,67
DAVENPORT	64	DORFLER	93		122,126
DAVIDSON	110,160	DORNAN	110	EPPLEY	31
DAVIES	91,113	DORNIN	37	ERBE	157
DAVIS	7,47,101,118	DOSS	3	ERLER	11
DAWES	145	DOTTY	26	ERNST	157
DAWSON	33	DOUGLAS	48	EUBANK	14
DAY	27,136,137,151	DOUTON	99	EVANS	39,40,79,81,152
	152,154,155	DOWDEN	99	EVERETT	142
DAYHOFF	76	DOWNEY	33	EWEN	15
DAYLER	144	DOXZEN(E)	14,28	EWING	148
DAYLOR	146	DOYLE	51,74,106,107	EYRE	91,92
DEAL	35, 40,160		108,118,139	FAGER	7
DEARHOLT	126,131	DRIVER	62	FALES	73
DeBAUGH	116	DUER	46	FALLS	150
DeFIELDS	147	DUERING	31,32	FANTOM	85
DEDAL	27	DUGGAN	62	FARLEY	51,57,62
DeGRUCHY	145	DUKE	57	FAUNTLEROY	38
DeHOFF	127	DUNCAN	44 ,45,144	FAUST	79
DEITER	159	DUNKES	143	FAVOUR	112
DEITZ	34	DUNLAP	34	FAY	37
DeLUCIA	48	DUNLOP	40	FEWHELY	63
DEMENT	55	DUNTY	145	FEENEY	56,57
DEMEAD	11	DURHAM	9	FELL	154
DeMOSS	146,159,160,161	DURKIN	58,123	FENDLAY	50
DENT	51	DUTTON	153	FERGUSON	69,70,161
DENTRY	119	DUVALL	140	FIELD	27
DETAMORE	146	DWYER	151	FINNEY	120
DeVEAS	125,133	EAGAN	56	FISCHER	145,148,155
DEVESE	23	EARP	159	FISHER	23,34,91
DEVLIN	101	EASTER	43	FISHPAW	14,15,23,75
DeWITT	158	EBAUGH	2		88,133
DEY	23	ECCLESTON	53	FISHPAUGH	23,24
DIETZ	150,151,156,158	ECK	145	FISKE	153
DILWORTH	123,135,138	ECKERD	21,27	FITCH	81
	142,145,147,150	ECKHART	40,144	FITE	85
	131,152,153,154	EDWARDS	27,37,82	FITZELL	155
	155	EGAN	51	FITZGERALD	56,58,59,61
DISNEY	26	EHLERS	79	FITZPATRICK	58
DITSCHLER	50	EHRET	41	FITZSIMMONS	110
DITZEL	25,27	EICHELBERGER	101,123	FLANNIGAN	50
DIVERS	72		124	FLEMKE	10

FLETCHER	151	GENT	31,46,125,126	GRUPY	152
FLEURY	112		129,130,131,132	GRUMMER	140
FLOWERS	19,143	GEORGE	111,112,121	GUDDUNGS	99
	147,148	GERMAN	25,75,79,85	GUGERTY	106,117
FLYNN	54,60	GERMEYER	156	GUISHARD	91
FOARD	77,138,141	GIBBONS	59,63,116,119	GUNKEL	47
	142,143,146,147	GIBSON	155	GUNN	153
FOGLE	49	GILBERT	28	GUNNARSSON	148
FOOTE	63,64	GILES	28	GUY	93,94
FORD	52	GILL	26,57,86,125	GUYTON	52,75,81,140
FORIEN	55		132,133		147,160
FORNWALT	72,73	GITTINGS	41,42,134	HACKEL	78
FORSYTH(E)	159		151,153	HACKETT	8
FORWOOD	21,127,128,133	GIVEN	30	HACKLER	3
FOSTER	12,130	GLADDEN	155	HAGAN	103,104,106,114
FOUCK	89	GLADFELTER	57		115,118,121,123
FOWBLE	41,92,96	GLASS	40	HAGERTY	60
FOX	8,76,79,80	GLEASON	63	HAGY	142,146
	85,143	GLEN	116,122	HAILE	9,143
FRANCIES	80	GOLDBERG	37	HALBERT	36,73,132
FRANCIS	72,74,77,83	GOLDSBOROUGH	115	HALE	96,139,146
	91,92,134,137	GOOD	133	HALL	28,41,57,88
	138,139	GOODMAN	24		133,137,144,146
FRANCISCUS	140	GOODWIN	14,47	HALLER	119
FRANK	128	GORDON	55	HALLIGAN	56,57,58
FRANKENFIELD	36	GORMLEY	105	HALLIWELL	41
FRANKLIN	37,38,136	GORRY	130	HAMPTON	38
FRANTZ	39,128	GORSUCH	29,67,68,69	HAMILTON	26
FRASER	37		72,73,91	HAMMON	152
FRAZIER	64,159		136,140,149,153	HAMMOND	77,86,159,161
FREDERICK	110	GOSLIN	47	HAMP	78
FREELAND	32	GOUGH	52,101	HANF	156
FRENCH	93	GOVANE	91	HANLEN	110
FREEMAN	153	GOVER	128,131,132,133	HANLEY	56,61,114
FRICK	140	GRAEFE	7		118,122
FRIED	8	GRAFF	140	HANLON	102,105,106
FROCK	14,18,19,20	GRAFTON	9,35		119,120,123
FROESHER	45	GRAHAM	54	HANLY	59
FULLER	57	GRANT	103,118,119,122	HANNA	39
FUNKHAUSER	56	GRAU	72	HANNIBAL	7,8
GAGLIANO	52	GRAY	28,99	HANSON	101
GALLOWAY	38,40,44	GRAYSON	141	HARDING	35
	45,69	GREAGER	15	HARDWICK	86
GALLUP	10	GREASER	32,33	HARE	15,21,27,28
GANBY	112	GREB	16	HARLOW	61
GARDMON	90	GREELEY	20	HARMAN	14,15,22,26
GARDNER	122	GREEN	24,44,45,80		133
GARLING	130		90,124	HARMON	96
GARRETT	151	GREENWELL	30	HARR	128,131,132,133
GARRISON	93	GRICE	16,17	HARRINGTON	34,55
GARTLING	131,132,133	GRIFFIN	39	HARRIS	19,45,56
GARTON	8	GRIFFITH	30,31,40,45		128,154
GATES	116	GRIMM	51	HARRISON	34,74,119
GATHWRIGHT	47	GROGG	2		137,160
GEORGE	139	GROSS	90	HARRYMAN	11,68,69
GEDDES	84	GROVER	77,79,91	HART	121
GEDDIS	84		143,151	HARTMAN	38,123,131
GEMMILL	27	GROVES	117,138		

HARVERY	86	HOLDEN	121	JESSUP		105
HARVEY	159	HOLIDAY	23	JOHN		48
HATTEN	34	HOLLAND	80,104,120,138	JOHNSON		6,64,74,82
HAUBERT	89		139,142,148,153			99,143,149
HAUPTMAN	49		134	JOICE		88,129
HAVENS	128	HOLLENSHADE	36	JONES		14,18,21,23,27
HAVILAND	32,52	HOLMES	46,58			45,99,120,123
HAYES	119	HOLTZNER	96			127,128,129,133
HAYS	106,107	HOOD	68			155,160,161
HEALY	117	HOOK	98,99,160	JORDAN		144,155
HEATH	3	HOOPER	134	JUSTICE		24,27
HEEB	87	HOOVER	160	JUSTUS		17,18
HEDGE	91	HOPKINS	5,71,111	KANE		51,55,59,60
HEDGES	82,122	HORAN	62,118	KARNS		23
HEDRICK	14	HORN	9	KEARNEY		1,104,106,107
HEINBUCH	146	HORNER	37			109,114,115
HENDRICKSON	45	HORSMAN	136			117,119,121
HENKEL	102	HORST	73	KEARNS		58,55
HENNESSY	109	HOTTES	40	KEARNY		108
HENRY	2,47	HOUCK	86	KEATING		60,61,62
HERBERT	110	HOWARD	91,101,150,154	KEEFER		144,147
HERMINAU	25	HOYT	73,147	KEIFFER		24
HEROLD	156	HUBER	161	KELLEHER		56
HERRINGTON	35	HUBERT	69	KELLEY		20,34,35,46
HERRON	137	HUDSON	94			60,118,129,132,159
HERTZLER	71	HUGHES	63,152	KELLER		24,26
HESS	39	HUMRICHOUSE	101	KELLUM		92
HESSIAN	60	HUNT	72,73,89	KELLY		35,46,50,53,58
HETRICK	78	HURTT	159			62,104,105,106
HEUBECK	93,94	HUTCHESON	38			107,109,110,113
HICKEY	109	HUTCHINS	46			115,116,118,119
HICKS	55	HUTCHISON	17			120,122,123,124
HIGGINS	63	HUTTON	153			129
HIGLE	82	HYATT	40	KELSEY		9
HILBINGER	39,41	HYLAND	52,106	KELSO		91
HILFERTY	148	HYLE	86	KEMP		42
HILGERMAN	35	INCE	22,28	KEMPER		124
HILKER	1	INSENNOCK	9,75,81,82	KENNEDY		28,53,54,60
HINDER	109,113,121,123		118,142,143			114,116,120
HINES	60,61,62		145,146,147	KENNEL		70,71
HINKLE	1,128	ISLAUB	25	KENNEY		21,33,39
HINKLEY	152	ISON	28			49,52,53
HINKS	144	JACOBS	28,75	KENNY		56
HINZ	156	JACKSON	34,47,64,133	KEOUGH		53,57
HIPLEY	148,158		135,151	KERCHNER		28
HIPPLE	24	JAMES	12,94,145,152	KERR		125
HIPSLEY	126	JAMISON	48	KERSHAW		159
HISLEY	26	JARRETT	23	KEYS		43
HITCHCOCK	137	JEFFERSON	130,142	KEYSER		29,154
HOELZER	145	JELLIMAN	123	KILKENNY		56
HOEN	115	JENKINS	8,110,111,112	KILLMURRAY		55
HOFFERBERT	144		114,115,119,120	KILROY		56
HOFFMAN	1,2,40,51,54	JENNINGS	99	KING		9,10,86,107
	63,109,120,126	JERDEN	90			122,140
	129,145	JESSOP	5,6,38,41	KINNEY		156
HOGAN	151		42,45,46,47	KIRKLAND		153

167

KIRKOLIAN	141	LAY	116	LYNCH	102,103,104,106	
KIRKPATRICK	126	LEACH	50		107,110,112,115	
KIRKWOOD	119	LEAF	16,127,128,129		116,118,119,121	
KLAPP	72	LEAGUE	135,136,153		123	
KLAPSKA	112	LEAMAN	74	LYON	22	
KLAUSMEIER	155,156	LeBRUN	46,86	LYONS	23	
KLEIN	8,75	LEE	9	LYTLE	121	
KLEMMICH	157	LEECH	50,113	MacKENZIE	78	
KLIMPER	131,132	LEEGH	110	MacNICHOLAS	54	
KLINEDINST	126	LeFAIVRE	23	MAGEE	52	
KLING	59	LEICHT	85, 86	MAGLIDT	14, 25	
KLOB	132	LEMMON	68	MAGNESS	135,137,140	
KLOSS	55	LENIHAN	62	MAGUIRE	50	
KLUSMER	24	LENAGHAN	55	MAIER	156	
KNAPP	41	LENARD	53	MALEHORN	43	
KNICELY	147	LENTZ	157	MALLONEE	125	
KNIEL	8	LEROY	10	MALONE	39,61	
KNIGHT	160	LEUTNER	76	MAMA	31	
KNOWLES	117	LEUTZ	36	MANCUSO	145	
KNOX	77	LEVERING	28	MANION	59	
KOEGEL	122	LEWIS	122	MANNION	60	
KOHLER	10	LIDDLE	76	MANSFIELD	94	
KOHLHOFF	58	LILLY	116,120,121,124	MARBLE	48	
KOLB	143	LINDEMAN	49	MARCHMAN	136	
KONE	36,38	LINDLEY	68	MARICE	152	
KOWALSKI	154	LINDSAY	56,59,60,153	MARK	40	
KRICKHAM	85	LINDSEY	74	MARKEN	144	
KROUT	39	LINGAN	182	MARKS	63	
KUPISCH	57	LINS	8	MARKLAND	55	
KURTZ	35,36	LINTZ	7	MARONEY	120	
KYLE	124,143,144,159	LINX	8	MARSH	10,11,26,51	
LACEY	109,113	LIPS	79	MARSHALL	6,9,48,64	
LAGAN	108,117	LISSAUER	65		105,135,136	
LAKE	26	LITCHFIELD	28,159	MARTIN	15,57,60,96	
LANAHAN	34	LITTLE	133		97,99,107,117	
LANCASTER	113,116,120	LIVINGSTON	54,115		132	
	122,124,138		121,123	MAST	70,71,75,140	
	144,145	LLOYD	132		142,143,144,148	
LANE	20,22,28,99	LOATS	30	MATTHEWS	4,26,29	
	121,148	LOFTUS	41,47,62	MATTINGLY	151	
LANG	148,156,158	LOGAN	50,60	MATTISON	17	
LAMAR	50	LONG	125,126,130	MAX	57	
LARK	132,133		132,133	MAXFIELD	81	
LARKINS	125	LOOMIS	76	MAYES	31,159	
LARKS	64	LOOSE	90	MAYNARD	147	
LARMORE	127,129	LOVE	37,38,46,86	MAYNES	113	
LARMOUR	154		87,121	MAYS	31,34	
LASIETT	27	LOY	142	McABEE	2	
LAUF	123,124	LUBEY	76	McALLEER	61	
LAUGHLIN	12	LUCAS	33	McBRIDE	48,117	
LAURITZEN	47	LUNDAY	112	McCABE	135	
LAUTENBACH	41	LUNDY	59	McGAFFREY	28	
LAUZON	63	LUNGER	75	McCANN	14	
LAVIN	58	LUPO	52	McCARREN	147	
LAVOIE	159	LUTZ	22,131	McCARROLL	104	
LAW	91	LUX	29,42	McCARTHY	121	
LAWRENCE	56	LYNCH	12,37,46 52	McCASLIN	125,127,128	

McCAULEY	159	MERRYMAN	3,4,5,8,13	NASH	117	
McCAY	48		17,34,37,41	NAUGHTON	61	
McCLASKEY	108		42,43,44,45	NAYLOR	34	
McCLOSKEY	106,117		49,67,68,155	NEAL	74,81	
McCLESKEY	41	MESNER	83	NEEDER	141	
McCLURE	139	MEUHAUSER	70	NEIFERT	106	
McCLUSKEY	109,136	MEYER	16,139	NELSON	36,93	
McCOMAS	81,82,105	MEYERS	43,75,114,138	NESTOR	60	
McCONNALL	63	MICHAEL	2	NEUBECK	94	
McCORMICK	13,15,103,104	MICHAELS	108	NEUBERGER	94,131	
McCUBBIN	137,140,158,159	MILLER	10,26,32,49	NEUHAUSER	71,78,81	
McCULLOUGH	27		70,71,86,104	NEUMANN	120	
McDERMOTT	55,59,112		108,115,122,123	NEVIN	55	
McDEVITT	55		150,151	NEWBERRY	37	
McDONNELL	54,57,63,104	MILLITZER	158	NEWSOM	28,29	
McDONOUGH	50,56	MINNICK	37,38,120,130	NICHOLS	153,160	
McDORMAN	155	MINTON	34	NIEBERDING	51	
McDOWELL	34	MITCHELL	14,121	NIEMCZYK	50	
McEVON	57	MOBRAY	137,143	NISBET	65	
McGANN	62	MOHRIG	143	NOLAN	141	
McGARTHY	49	MONAGHAN	61,62	NOONAN	102,107,108	
McGILLIGAN	108	MONAHAN	60	NOPPENBERGER	50,51,52,55	
McGINNIS	53	MONCURE	14		56,57,58,59	
McGLANNAN	55	MONNIN	147	NORMAN	102,107,108	
McGOWAN	58	MONTGOMERY	81,82,141,145	NORWOOD	160	
McGRAW	52,121	MOORE	51,52,57,87	NOYES	81	
McGREARY	46		111,124,150,151	NUNNALLY	77,80	
McGUIRE	103,121,123		152,155	NUSSEAR	42	
McIHINNEY	55	MOOREFIELD	143	NUSSLE	157,158	
McINTURFF	75	MOORES	46,47,85	O'BANNON	75	
McINTYRE	104	MORGAN	49,73	OBER	28	
McKANN	26	MORRIS	34,68	O'BRIEN	56	
McKELVEY	74	MORRISON	40,46,57	O'CONNOR	51,52,62	
McKENNA	103,119	MORTLAND	30	O'DONOVAN	105	
McKEON	62	MOTT	33	OFFUTT	40,42,144	
McKITTRICK	56	MUELLER	123	O'HARA	54,58,61	
McKNIGHT	57,155	MUCAULEY	160		82,103	
McLAUGHLIN	63	MULCAHEY	53	OHLER	102,122,123	
McMAHON	26,27	MULLENBERG	74	OLDHAM	154	
McNANCY	123	MULLER	81,115,122	OLER	17	
McNEAVE	23	MULLIGAN	142	O'NEIL	108	
McNEYE	62	MUMMA	73,74,75,80	ONION	154,155	
McNICHOLAS	57,58		145	OREM	135,136,145	
McQUAID	123	MUNGOVAN	38	ORMOND	51	
McQUILLAN	110	MUNNIKHUYSEN	150	ORSO	154	
McVEIGH	102	MUNROE	77,83	OSBORNE	32	
McVESELY	109	MURPHY	55,103,122	OSTHEIM	157	
MEADS	70,90,156	MURRAY	49,53,56,61	OSWALD	10	
MEDARY	69		144,153	OWEN	65	
MEINSCHEIN	63	MUSGRAVE	130	OWENS	9,61	
MEISE	123	MUSGROVE	18,26,33	OWINGS	44,65,100	
MELLOR	93	MUZZY	75	PALAGANO	41	
MELVIN	59	MYER	129,130	PANNILL	144	
MEREDITH	62	MYERS	33,93,124	PARADISI	49	
MERGENHARDT	74		127,128,132	PARKER	139,160	
MERNEY	109	NAFZINGER	70,71,143	PARKS	18,19,22,23	
MERRICK	26	NAGLE	107,116		30,32,33,35	

PARKS	44,45,88,92	QUINLIN	110	ROACH	102,114,116
	124,129	QUINN	54,61,105		117,119
PARLETT	44,79,81	RAFFERTY	48,50,52,63	ROBERTS	51,78,85,92
PARRISH	127	RAHILL	114		93,94,142,148
PARSONS	8,18,88	RAHLL	114,117,120	ROBERTSON	9,135,146
PASCHEK	120	RAMSEY	112	ROBINSON	22,123
PATTERSON	63,92	RANDOLPH	64	RODGERS	59
PAUL	54	RANDERSON	150	ROEBUCK	64
PAYNE	136	RAPP	33	ROGERS	99
PEARCE	24,28,78,85	RAUSCHENBACH	126	ROHRER	144
	86,109,134,135	RAVER	131,133	ROSE	12
	138,139,141,144	RAVNER	129	ROSS	47,151
	147,148	RAY	137	ROTHENHOEFER	60
PEDONE	27	RAYNARD	140	ROWLES	28
PEERCE	69,70	READ	155	ROYSTON	4,27
PEIRSOL	47	REAMY	118	RUBY	18
PERRY	2,72,124,125	REBER	33	RUDD	50
PERSON	52	REED	76,88,89	RUDIGER	9
PETERS	34,52	REUSE	78	RUFENACHT	134,136
PETERSON	93	REDD	38	RUFF	127
PEYTON	153,154	REGAN	51,52,54	RUHL	8,34
PFEIFFER	160	REGEL	156	RUMSEY	153,154,155
PHELAN	56	REHBERGER	122	RUPP	86
PHILLIPS	31,72,73	REID	151	RUSSELL	28,31,48,80
	90,136	REIER	122		81,85,124
PHIPPS	142	REILLY	50,51,54,57		142,143
PICKENS	142	REINHARD	72	RYAN	7,107,110
PIERSOL	9	REINHARDT	72	SADLER	7,41,150
PILHOFER	156,157	REITZ	47	SAMPLE	141,148
PINDELL	38,43	REMBOLD	148	SANDERS	50,85
PIPER	84,86	RENNOUS	13,16	SARGENT	94
PISTOR	157	REPPERT	133	SARLER	93
PLACK	148	RESH	155	SARVINO	133
PLAT	68	RETER	8,145	SATER	12,13,29
PLEASANTS	112	REYNOLDS	135.136	SAUER	150
PLOCK	120	RHODES	142	SAUERS	141
POCOCK	9,21	RHOTEN	96	SAVERD	55
POE	32,47	RICH	80	SAXTON	111
POPP	143	RICHARDS	87	SCALLY	49, 53,61
POTEET	47,65,66,116	RICHARDSON	9, 35,137	SCARFF	83,85,110
POWERS	54,55,58,122		151		119,152
	133	RICKETTS	43	SCHAEFER	34
PREBLE	56,57	RIDER	12,15 ,18	SCHAFER	123
PRESCOE	99	RIDDLE	136,147	SCHARIO	58
PRESTON	121	RIDGELY	5,13,65,66	SCHENK	38
PRICE	12,14,15,16		101	SCHEPER	124
	18,32,44,50	RIEFNER	74	SCHMIDT	74,102,103,120
	53,127	RIES	141	SCHMUCK	94,95
PRIGEL	76	RILEY	28,46,104,110	SCHNEIDER	156,157
PRIMUS	58		116,119,120,121	SCHNIDER	70
PROCTOR	47,117,137		122,156	SCHOFIELD	84
	139,140	RINEHART	108	SCHRUFER	93
PRYOR	99	RINGGOLD	151	SCHREIBER	102
PULSFORD	121	RIPPEON	36	SCHUBERT	155
PYLE	152,153	RITTENHOUSE	144	SCHULTE	123,157
QUESENBERRY	124	RITTER	25 ,70	SCHULTZ	146
QUIGLEY	114			SCHUMAN	138

SCHUNCK	84	SKIPPER	8,13,21,48		STRICKLIN	86
SCHURMAN	9		76,88,89,129		STROH	31
SCHWATKA	85,86	SLADE	8,73,92,93,110		STROMBERG	51
SCHWANTNER	158	SMITH	1,9,10,21,22		ST RS	40
SCHWEIKERT	143		23,25,26,27,28		STUDZ	124
SCIPP	18		37,42,60,61,63		STUMP	130
SCOTT	15,29,38,89		64,69,72,73,66		SULLIVAN	15,55,110
	90,145		89,90,102,107			116,119
SEEBURGER	59		109,112,113,115		SUMRELL	25
SEIPP	125		116,119,120,121		SURRATT	26
SEITZ	157		122,128,135,138		SWANN	64
SEWARD	124		139,146,147,148		SWEAM	2
SEWELL	133		151,152		SWEENY	2
SHACKELFORD	147	SNAVELY	144		SWEITZER	151,156,157
SHAD	125	SNYDER	48,49,51,143		SWEM	16,20,22
SHADE	16,60		156,157			131,132
SHANAHAN	102,103,104	SOMMERVILLE	52		SWIFT	118
	106,108,109,114	SOTH	10		SWOPE	47
	117,118,119,121	SOUTHARD	76		TAHANEY	105,108,120
	122,123,124	SPARKS	51		TALBERT	126
SHANEYBROOK	52,133	SPENCER	32		TALBOTT	66,99
SHANK	39	SPERA	48,60		TALBBOTT	11,26,39,40
SHANKLIN	80,82,136	SPERTZEL	7			42,65
	148	SPICER	34,50		TANDENUR	7
SHARP (?)	125	SPORLADER	158		TARBERT	78,79,80
SHAW	119,131,132	SPROUL	125,133		TATE	90
SHEA	49,50,54,62	STAINES	21,25,28,38		TAWNEY	125,126,130
SHEALEY	94	STAMBAUGH	10			131,132,133
SHEARMAN	79,83,84	STANDIFORD	27,77,160		TAYLOR	27,44,65,74
SHERLER	35,36	STANLEY	34			112,133,154
SHEFFIELD	159	STANTON	62,63,151		TEMPLE	134,135,136
SHELLEY	8,9	STANSBURY	41,67,95		THACKER	35,36
SHEPPERD102,106,108,109		STATON	33		THOM	120
SHERMAN	81	STAYLER	95		THOMAS	31,37,54,75
SHERMER	10	STEADMAN	117			119,130
SHERRER	54	STEIN	20,118		THOMPSON	7,28,44,154
SHERTZER	74	STEINMETZ	157			155,160
SHIELDS	28	STELTZ	49		THORN	105
SHIMP	85	STENGEL	121		THUMA	36
SHIPLEY	36,114,120	STERLING	155		TILGHMAN	28,42,118
	121,128	STERRETT	61		TILLERY	34
SHOCK	16,22,24,25	STEVENS	84		TIPTON	128,130
	26,27,28	STEWART	47,124		TODD	66,68,83
SHOUL	49,152	STICKEL	148		TOMBAUGH	85,143
SHUE	94	STIERTZ	121		TOMLIN	118
SIBLEY	28	STINCHCOMB	47		TONGUE	47
SIMONE	146	STINE	97,114		TOOLAN	62
SIMMONS	127,131,133	STINHAGEN	18		TOOMEY	61
SIMMS	80,93	STOCKSDALE	145		TOPPING	152
SIMS	76,82,83,91	STOREY	48		TORBIT	92,93,94
	93,94,112	STORM	133		TOVELL	159
SIPE	27	STOVER	79		TOWSON	13,94
SIPES	9,145	STRAHAN	40		TOY	122
SISSON	134,135,136	STRAN	27		TRABAND	92
SKELTON	107,119	STRAYER	74,75		TRACEY	31,56,57,124
SKILLMAN	160	STREETT	85			127,128,131

TRAYNOR	113	WATKINS	73,139,140	WISNOM	139,141,142
TREADWELL	94,137,140		144,148	WITAKER	90
	142,159	WATSON	62	WITHERS	17
TRENT	8	WATTS	27,92	WITMER	47
TRIMBLE	131	WAYSON	51	WOLF	21
TRIPLETT	25	WEAKLEY	119	WOLLET	12
TROY	113	WEAVER	121,122	WOOD	8,46,152
TROYER	7,127	WEBER	22	WOODALL	39
TRUMAN	21	WEBSTER	44,47,113	WOODEN	18,19
TUCHTON	74	WEICHERT	148	WOODHOUSE	143
TUCKER	64,101,146	WEISSMAN	34	WOODLAND	111
TULLY	49,61	WELCH	67	WOOLF	78
TURNBAUCH	9	WELLS	138,144	WORDEN	130
TURNER	90,121,138	WELSH	50,54,60,61,87	WORRELL	120
TURNEY	34	WENZEL	18	WORTHINGTON	38,43,86,87
TWELE	84	WEHNSDORFER	18	WRIGHT	44,64,140,143
TWINING	80	WERTZER	122		146,147,151
TYRIE	37,40,52	WEST	23	WUST	132
TYSON	73,152	WETHERELL	33	WYATT	56
UHLER	20,36	WHEATLEY	25	WYNN	59
ULRICH	148	WHEELER	8,9,30,92	YAGEL	25
UNAUGST	86		110,111	YATES	90,94
UNKART	157,158	WHISLER	150	YEATES	90
USHER	91	WHITAKER	98,133	YELIOTT	43
VALENTIN	132	WHITE	52,101,109,112	YINGLING	37,38
VANderVALK	109		115,150	YODER	71,74
VAN HORN	52	WHITEFORD	131	YORK	158
VAN PRADELLES	44	WICKER	135	YOST	95
VAUGHN	28	WIELAND	133	YOUNG	26,126,133
VEREKER	107,132	WIGGINGTON	105	ZAPF	147
VINING	123	WIGHT	38,40	ZEALOR	78
VOOLER	123	WIKER	155	ZEPP	125
VOGT	34	WILCOX	111	ZINK	22,23,26,39
WADE	29,128,133,148	WILDNER	23		40,43
WADSWORTH	24	WILGIS	144,145	ZINKHAN	7,8
WAGNER	34	WILHELM	96	ZOOK	70
WAHAUS	151	WILLIAM	118	ZSENYUCH	49
WAINWRIGHT	30	WILLIAMS	26,50,132,146	ZULAUF	135,144
WALDENBERGER	56	WILLIAMSON	87		
WALDHAM	160	WILLINGHAM	138		
WALKER	13,29,48,49	WILLIANGHAN	77		
WALLACE	95,100	WILLICK	147		
WALSH	59	WILLIG	143		
WALTER	49,155	WILLIS	11		
WALTERS	70,92	WINDER	64		
WALTHER	135	WILSON	15,21,64,84		
WALTON	75		113,137,147,150		
WALTZ	70		151,159		
WARD	5,58,149	WIMSETT	18,19		
WARFEL	71	WINNEBERGER	85		
WARFIELD	86	WINKLER	122		
WARNER	31,100	WINSLOW	48		
WARNS	87	WIRSING	156,157		
WARREN	53	WISE	157		
WARSCHEK	118	WINSTON	153		
WATERS	43,57	WISNER	126		

www.ingramcontent.com/pod-product-compliance
Lightning Source LLC
Chambersburg PA
CBHW050810160426
43192CB00010B/1712